FINANCING AMERICAN PROSPERITY

A SYMPOSIUM OF ECONOMISTS

FINANCING
AMERICAN PROSPERITY

A SYMPOSIUM OF
ECONOMISTS

Contributors

Benjamin M. Anderson   Alvin H. Hansen
John Maurice Clark   Sumner H. Slichter
Howard S. Ellis   John H. Williams

Editors

Paul T. Homan   Fritz Machlup

New York
THE TWENTIETH CENTURY FUND
1945

COPYRIGHT 1945 BY THE TWENTIETH CENTURY FUND, INC.

First published October 1945
Second printing January 1946
Third printing December 1946
Fourth printing January 1949

MANUFACTURED IN THE UNITED STATES OF AMERICA
BY E. L. HILDRETH & COMPANY, BRATTLEBORO, VERMONT

FOREWORD

Both public policy and economic theory are focused, as never before, on financial and fiscal problems. There is hardly any subject in policy or theory on which opinions differ more widely. This is unfortunate because the daily welfare of every man, woman and child is dependent — more than most of them know — on what the government does, or does not do, about taxes, borrowing and spending, and on the financial policies of private agencies. Because the subject is so transcendently important and because the experts differ so widely about it, the Fund commissioned six leading economists, with special knowledge and experience in the field, to give their views. This volume is the result.

The Fund chose the participants to represent the whole spectrum of responsible economic opinion. The Fund asked each one to formulate the postwar fiscal and financial policies he favors and to justify them by fact and theory. No one of them read the contribution of any other before publication, so this is a symposium rather than a debate. But one of the editors has, in the final chapter, summarized objectively the views of the contributors so as to highlight their points both of difference and agreement.

The Fund offers this volume to the public in the hope that it may contribute to the solution of the grave postwar problems we now face. To each of the distinguished participants and editors goes the Fund's appreciation for his part in this interesting and stimulating venture.

EVANS CLARK, *Executive Director*
The Twentieth Century Fund

330 WEST 42D STREET
NEW YORK 18, NEW YORK
AUGUST 1945

CONTENTS

Contents

Chapter 1

INTRODUCTION

Paul T. Homan[1]

For some years now that the war is over the United States will be engaged in getting rid of the distortions in its economic organization and activities, and in its relations with the outside world, which were introduced through the mobilization of its productive resources for war. The nation will have to readjust its affairs to the requirements of a peacetime economy. The policies to be determined will, however, reach far beyond the process of liquidating the economic consequences of the war. Far-reaching and long-lasting decisions will have to be made concerning the ways and means of establishing and maintaining a healthy operation of the economic system upon lines that will secure and improve the physical well-being and satisfy the conscience and the aspirations of the population at large.

The ends of public policy are varied, nor are they defined by all in similar terms. Concerning one broad objective of economic policy, there is a large measure of agreement in the United States: maintaining productive output at a high level and providing steady employment at ample remuneration. To this end the government of the United States is deeply committed. In the years just ahead, fundamental economic legislation will be debated on grounds that are plausibly related to this goal. Its attainment is necessary for the attainment of other, noneconomic improvements in civilized life.

The objective — prosperity with ample employment opportunities — may be pursued by a government of narrower or of broader powers, according to circumstances. Nor is there necessarily only a single way to pursue it. Any nation is likely to use means as far as possible consistent with its own historical tradition of social organization. And it may well be content with something less than perfection in the result,

1. Professor of Economics, Cornell University; Managing Editor, *The American Economic Review*.

lest in striving for perfection in this one direction it give up more than it wishes in others.

The Role of Government in Economic Life

The American government, through most of its history, has concerned itself but little with any such goal. Indeed, in most Western countries it has, on the whole, been a dogma of public policy that the government need intervene but slightly to provide livelihood for the people and to improve their economic well-being. Not merely public men and economists but the people at large have believed that prosperity was best served by allowing individuals to pursue their private interests, subject to certain measures to provide public services, to restrain the private exercise of monopolistic powers and to maintain a sound currency.

The merits of this economic program have often been called into question by persons who have foreseen an inevitable tendency toward private monopoly, an increasing gulf between the poor and the rich and, in the more cataclysmic versions, a state of instability and recurrent depression leading to an absolute decline in the well-being of the mass of the people. Actual experience has not verified the more extreme prophecies of calamity. Indeed, a strong case can be made for the economic program which has been pursued, if one looks at the rapid development of our resources and a widely distributed improvement in the economic position of the people at large. Nevertheless, it has not been possible to ignore the waves of business depression which have brought loss of employment in their train; nor the persistence of conditions which, even in more prosperous times, left many persons unemployed and many others in chronic and precarious poverty; nor the concentration in private hands of very great power over the livelihoods of others.

These matters have been the concern of economists and statesmen for a long time. Economists have for years given searching examination to ways and means of minimizing the instability of economic activity, particularly through the exercise of central control over banking operations. In the sphere of national policy, however, action had gone little beyond an effort to maintain a competitive structure of industry and to improve the monetary and banking systems.

The Growing Agenda of Government

The deep and prolonged depression which began with the financial collapse of 1929 called into question not merely the adequacy of existing means of combating depression but indeed the basic conceptions which underlay them. The demand arose in many quarters for much stronger measures of government action to salvage particular groups from immediate financial disaster, to provide emergency employment and to devise the means for preventing such trains of economic disaster in the future. The measures actually adopted were of a miscellaneous and often inconsistent character. They were the product of diverse political pressures and they were concerned more with emergency aid to ill-affected groups than with permanently maintaining high levels of employment.

They had, however, a lasting political effect. The federal government has become increasingly committed to a policy, which future administrations will find it difficult to reverse, of initiating active and direct measures to maintain the national income at a high level and to encourage, if not to assure, employment to those able and willing to work. The permanence of this political purpose, and of a collateral emphasis upon the more equitable distribution of income, seems assured, since it appeals not merely to millions who wish to escape from the precariousness of their livelihoods, but also to almost all persons of intelligence and good will who see no reason why poverty should periodically stalk the land when we have such magnificent resources of materials, equipment, technical knowledge and human enterprise. The existence of the political purpose has not yet brought forth any generally acceptable program of action. It has, however, presented a challenge to the intellectual ingenuity and inventiveness of economists, and has stimulated the most extensive and concentrated analysis which has ever been given to any problem of economic policy.

The Problems of the Postwar Economy

The war blotted the problem from sight — for the time being. Unemployment disappeared. But the specter remains. Now many millions of men and women from the armed forces will need to be absorbed into peacetime jobs. Millions engaged in war production will need to be transferred to other occupations. The vast government demand for war equipment will be withdrawn from the markets. Comprehensive readjustments will have to be made throughout all spheres of domestic and international industry and trade. Can all this be accomplished in a manner rapidly to restore the means of livelihood to those dependent upon the new peacetime economy?

No one can doubt that the process of readjustment to peace will entail severe trials. But an even more serious question arises. Can the means be found to ensure that, at some later period, there will not develop another deep depression such as overtook us a decade after the last war? And, looking into a more distant future, are the means at hand to keep people fully employed in a world which, it may be hoped, will remain at peace? These are the portentous questions which provide the setting to the essays in the present volume.

How to achieve the immediate economic end — without sacrificing the essential freedom of American economic and political institutions — is a question to which the best thought of American economists is devoted. There are no quick and easy answers. The measures which will be proposed for treatment of the problem are, however, being brought to focus. The exact character of the arguments to which they will give rise is crystallizing.

A List of Questions

The contributors to this volume were presented with the following list of questions:

1. *During the transition period* immediately ahead:
    a. What general economic circumstances may be expected, e.g., business collapse; boom and inflation; or a mixed situation with successive phases?
    b. To what degree are private enterprise and investment likely to be adequate to care for rapid reconversion and re-employment?
    c. What special government financial measures are required in order to avoid the dangers of business collapse and unemployment on the one hand, and an inflationary rise in the price level on the other? How should the flow of liquid savings accumulated during the war be controlled? What, if any, financial aid should be extended to facilitate reconversion and re-employment?
2. *Beyond the immediate transition period,* what "compensatory role" should government finance play in smoothing out *cyclical fluctuations?* What adjustments from one phase of the cycle to another should be made in tax rates and structure, central bank and Treasury policy, government spending for relief and public works, social security policy, debt retirement policy and other aspects of government financial management?

3. *From a longer-run standpoint* than that of cyclical fluctuation, is there reason to believe that government financial policy must "compensate" for a persistent tendency for the volume of monetary savings to exceed the supply of investment opportunities? What role should federal expenditures play in the long-run maintenance of business stability and a high level of employment in the postwar period? How should such expenditures be financed?

4. What forms of postwar taxation should be adopted in order to ensure the maintenance of an optimum rate of activity and expansion on the part of private enterprise? Can a flexible taxation and borrowing policy be designed to ensure continuity of spending and investing so as to maintain full employment and production?

5. What special types of financial control, such as controls over commercial bank credit, consumer credit, real-estate credit, and the flow of funds into investment, are needed in order to ensure stable domestic prosperity in the postwar world?

6. Can government fiscal and financial measures *alone* ensure the maintenance of relatively full production and employment both in the short run and in the long run? If not, what other conditions need to be established:

a. In the field of international financial arrangements, such as stabilization of foreign exchange relationships, control of capital movements, the use of gold in settlement of international balances, commercial policy, etc.?

b. In the field of nonfinancial domestic policies, for establishing the collateral conditions within which the proposed financial policies can be most effective?

The Task of the Contributors

The contributors were asked not to regard the questions as an outline for their essays, but simply as an indication of the general purpose which the volume was intended to serve. Using the questions as a point of departure, they were requested to present, according to any pattern which suited them, their views concerning practical ways and means by which public policy could aid in maintaining full and stable employment for the working population and thereby security of livelihood and a high level of economic well-being. The questions have furnished certain common guidelines, that run through all the essays. They have not, however, prevented any contributor from making whatever emphasis is best suited to his experience and convenience, nor debarred him from restating the questions in his own way if he has felt that their wording has prejudiced the argument which he has wished to present.

The questions do not provide a basis for an argument in favor of a broad substitution of public for private enterprise as the means to full and stable employment. This is not to prejudge the merits of that argument. The purpose of the book was narrower: to throw light upon issues which are, or in the very near future will be, matters for immediate policy decisions. The problem will be how to make the existing type of economic system work well, not what sort of system to adopt in its place.

The term "financing" in the title of the volume is less limiting than might at first appear. It does not imply that a prosperous economy necessarily calls for "financing" in the narrow sense of raising and allocation of funds by the fiscal and monetary agencies of the government — or by anybody else. Nor does it imply that it is "financial" policy upon which prosperity in America chiefly depends. The use of the term "financing" is by no means incompatible with a conclusion that, under circumstances favorable to private economic activities, sustained prosperity could be "self-financing."

Analysis of the effects of financial policies, that is, of measures in the fields of money, banking, taxation, fiscal policy and international finance is not possible without direct reference to the broader pattern of economic arrangements within which financial influences are designed to produce their effects. Consequently, the essays will be found to touch upon matters of economic policy on a broad front. This is especially the case with respect to the problem of monopoly and the extent to which the government should foster the competitive structure of business since this is, in conjunction with financial questions, the most fundamental economic problem with which public policy has to be concerned.

The Achievement of the Symposium

In view of the complexity of the issues with which the contributors have to deal, the essays are extremely brief. The limitations of space force the authors to assert what they would wish to demonstrate and to omit many reservations and qualifications. But brevity has this offsetting merit: it sets out problems and proposals in stark relief. Economic issues are complex, the analysis of them involved, but in the end, in a democratic community, they have to be stated in sufficiently bald terms for the electorate and legislators to comprehend.

On this score, the present volume is in some sense ground-breaking. The matters discussed are the subject of an extensive technical and controversial literature. Some parts of this literature have been reduced to popular form, even to cocksure recipe. But nowhere else has the emergent thought of economists upon the problems of policy been reduced to such blunt statements in such brief form. The form of presentation is not "popular." Technicalities remain. The reading is not easy. But the broad outlines of the problems and of the proposed measures for dealing with them stand out in a form comprehensible to the careful and intelligent reader.

The volume also demonstrates how imperative it is that economists, combining the virtues of academic discipline and acquaintance with the world of affairs, become partners with statesmen. The problems presented are ones upon which the Congress of the United States will have to commit itself in the years just ahead — by constructive legislation or by evasion, for good or for ill. They present questions upon which statesmen must have the advice of technically competent guides, lest they fumble blindly and ignorantly with the destinies of the people. Skeptics say that legislators have to deal with matters upon which they are necessarily inexpert, that the advice of economists to them is divided and contradictory, and that they are swayed by the interests and prejudices of constituents who cannot possibly know where the public interest lies. We live, of necessity, in the contrary faith that democratic government is not an imbecile. Novel problems are necessarily marked by tentative and exploratory thought. Early legislation to meet them will undoubtedly be imperfect. But one must not offhand deny that, in combination, our most competent technical thinkers and our most intelligent and disinterested statesmen can, with tolerable results, cope with the problems that beset us.

Differences in Assumptions, Objectives and Practical Judgment

Economists who attempt to give answers to questions of future policy designed to cope with future developments must necessarily start from some set of reasonable assumptions. It is very cumbersome to warn the reader at each point of the analysis that a "reasonable assumption" is not meant to be a "prediction." For example, in order to discuss postwar demand and postwar employment in quantitative terms, an assumption about the end of the war and the termination of government war expenditures was needed. Most contributors chose 1947 as the first normal postwar year. But in making this assumption they did not intend to predict the exact length of the war. Thus, when the contributors speak of "1947," this should not be taken literally but merely as an abbreviation for a longer expression such as, "the first year without government war expenditures."

Economic analysis of the ways and means of achieving and maintaining "full employment" cannot be limited to that goal alone. The goal itself can only be considered within a particular social system, and people (including economists) differ among themselves as to the kind of system they believe to be desirable. But even where there is substantial agreement on the kind of economic and social system desired, reasonable people differ in their interpretation of the effects of the operation of various economic forces within the system. Their judgments as to policy are affected accordingly.

In their academic studies economists are free to analyze the influence of economic forces under abstract, or ideal, conditions of their own creation. But when they propose measures for achieving prosperity and security in the real world, they must reckon with practical and political realities.

These reflections may explain some of the differences of opinion among the contributors to this volume. The differences, whatever their reasons may be, deserve serious consideration, for they represent the thinking of men of outstanding professional competence. But it is the agreements and not the differences among the contributors which should concern us most. The areas of agreement and the parallel courses of thought probably forecast a crystallization of professional economic opinion on the central problems of postwar economic policy.

Chapter 2

THE ROAD BACK TO FULL EMPLOYMENT

Benjamin M. Anderson[1]

I. POSTWAR EMPLOYMENT FOR TEN MILLION MORE THAN IN 1939?

How can we expect in the postwar years to give employment to 55 or 56 million people, when we employed few more than 45 million in 1939?

There are those who see in this an almost insurmountable problem, which calls for heroic efforts on the part of government to create new "purchasing power" through governmental borrowing from the banks, heroic programs of public works expenditures, make-work policies on the part of business enterprises, taxation schemes to force investment, and vast monetary and credit schemes to force a big export trade.

I see in it merely the problem of relaxing the restraints and inhibitions which government itself in recent years has placed upon capital, business enterprise, and labor, which prevent their getting together on mutually advantageous terms, producing goods and services, the sale of which will give them the income which makes them good customers for other producers.

Who will employ the 10 million workers? The answer is that in part they will give employment to one another, each buying part of the products that the others produce, and that for the rest, they will receive employment from those already employed, and in part give employment to those already employed.

The Record of Employment and Unemployment

In the days when the making of jobs was not looked upon as a federal government function, the problem solved itself amazingly well. The following table, which I have taken from the *Economic Record* of the National Industrial Conference Board of March 20, 1940 (page

1. Professor of Economics, University of California, Los Angeles; Consulting Economist, Capital Research Company, Los Angeles.

78) gives the record of employment and unemployment in the United States for the years 1900 to 1939 inclusive.

TOTAL UNEMPLOYMENT IN THE LABOR FORCE
(*In Thousands*)

	Total Labor Force	Employment	Unem-ployment	Unemployment as Per Cent of Labor Force
Annual average				
1900	29,025	27,378	1,647	5.7
1901	29,959	28,238	1,721	5.7
1902	30,905	30,405	500	1.6
1903	31,842	30,319	1,523	4.8
1904	32,605	31,175	1,430	4.4
1905	33,653	33,032	621	1.8
1906	34,647	34,790	— 143[a]	...
1907	35,631	34,875	756	2.1
1908	36,580	34,284	2,296	6.3
1909	37,454	36,735	719	1.9
1910	38,133	37,580	553	1.5
1911	38,668	37,097	1,571	4.1
1912	39,089	38,169	920	2.4
1913	39,500	38,482	1,018	2.6
1914	39,789	37,575	2,214	5.6
1915	40,083	37,728	2,355	5.9
1916	40,314	40,127	187	0.5
1917	40,752	42,685	—1,933[a]	...
1918	41,088	44,187	—3,099[a]	...
1919	41,159	42,029	— 870[a]	...
1920	41,897	41,339	558	1.3
1921	42,445	37,691	4,754	11.2
1922	42,966	40,049	2,917	6.8
1923	43,760	43,011	749	1.7
1924	44,549	42,515	2,034	4.6
1925	45,009	44,192	817	1.8

(*Continued on next page*)

a. Such negative unemployment arises statistically from the fact that persons are drawn into the labor force during periods of increased labor demand who are not reckoned as members of the labor force. This is particularly true in agriculture. The increases in employment in agriculture in May, June, and September 1929, are largely, if not entirely, responsible for the negative unemployment in these months.

	Total Labor Force	Employment	Unem- ployment	Unemployment as Per Cent of Labor Force
1926	45,962	45,498	464	1.0
1927	46,939	45,319	1,620	3.5
1928	47,914	46,057	1,857	3.9
1929	48,354	47,925	429	0.9
1930	49,025	45,216	3,809	7.8
1931	49,664	41,551	8,113	16.3
1932	50,182	37,704	12,478	24.9
1933	50,830	38,086	12,744	25.1
1934	51,402	41,002	10,400	20.2
1935	51,879	42,357	9,522	18.4
1936	52,382	44,783	7,599	14.5
1937	53,011	46,639	6,372	12.0
1938	53,699	43,600	10,099	18.8
1939	54,393	45,314	9,080	16.7

We were often dissatisfied in the old days with the way in which our economic machine worked. Following the unnecessary money panic of 1907, for example, we had in 1908 an unemployment of 2,296,000 people, which was 6.3 per cent of the working force. To be sure this dropped to 719,000 the following year which was only 1.9 per cent of the working force, but we recognized that there were defects in the system which permitted the heavy unemployment of 1908, and we worked hard on financial studies which culminated in the Federal Reserve Act of 1913, designed to make future money panics impossible.

What Is Full Employment?

We had no good statistical records in those days of the volume of unemployment. The problem was not forced upon us often enough. That one or two per cent of the population should be unemployed we regarded as a matter of course, when allowance is made for seasonal unemployment, for sickness, and for men shifting from one job to another, and for that rather considerable part of the population which was unwilling to work all the time and which preferred roving around. But an unemployment which rose to 6.3 per cent disturbed us.

When in 1921 the annual average of unemployment reached 4,754,-

000 or 11.2 per cent of the working population, in the crash that followed the wholly unsound postwar boom of 1919–1920, we were gravely concerned. But we still did not regard it as the function of the federal government to make work or to create purchasing power for the purpose of relieving the unemployment. We left the people free to work things out.[2] The people worked things out quickly. The unemployment figure dropped in 1922 to 2,917,000 or 6.8 per cent, and to 749,000 in 1923, or 1.7 per cent of the working force.

Viewed in the perspective of the years 1931–1939, the record for 1900–1923 is amazingly good. The worst year, 1921, is better than the best year of the 1931–1939 period, namely, 1937. And 1937 was followed by a collapse, whereas 1921 was followed by radical improvement.

The difference between the two periods, as we shall see, is explained as follows: from 1900 to 1924, the making of employment was not regarded as a federal government function; whereas, beginning with 1924, we have had, on an ever increasing scale, "economic planning" by our federal government, aimed at full employment!

II. EQUILIBRIUM CREATES PURCHASING POWER

When goods are produced in proper proportions, they clear the markets of one another. Wheat comes into the market as supply of wheat, but the same wheat comes into the market as demand for sugar, for automobiles, for textiles and for other things which the wheat producer wants.

Production itself gives rise to the income which supports consumption. Production and consumption expand together. The 135 million people in the United States consume vastly more than the 400 million in China, because they produce vastly more. The 20th-century world consumes vastly more than the 18th-century world consumed, because it produces vastly more. The problem is primarily one of keeping the different kinds of production in proper proportion.

This is accomplished under the capitalist system by the movement of prices and costs. Labor and capital tend to get out of lines where return is low and to move over into lines where return is better. The smooth working of this system calls for flexible prices, competitively

2. See the discussion below of the revival, 1921–1923.

worked out, which tell the truth regarding underlying supply and demand conditions. When production is well balanced, and prices (including wages and interest rates) are free to move and tell the truth, supply creates its own demand.

The Elements in Economic Equilibrium

Economic equilibrium involves a good many factors: (a) the proportions among the industries; (b) the balancing of prices among different kinds of products; (c) a proper relation of prices and costs so that profits are possible; (d) a proper balance in the international balance sheet (if foreign debts are very much heavier than they ought to be in relation to the volume of foreign trade, grave disorders can come); and (e) the money and capital markets must be in a state of balance. When there is an excess of bank credit used as a substitute for savings, and when bank credit goes in undue amount into capital uses and speculative uses, or when the total volume of money and credit is expanded far beyond the growth of production and trade, disequilibria arise, and, above all, the quality of credit is impaired. Confidence may be suddenly shaken and a countermovement may set in.

With respect to all these points, automatic market forces tend to restore equilibrium, in the absence of overwhelming governmental interference.

III. The Doctrine of Purchasing Power Versus the Doctrine of Equilibrium

There has arisen a dangerously strong body of opinion which, rejecting or not understanding the notion that purchasing power grows out of production, sharply separates production from purchasing power and sees the problem of full employment merely in terms of keeping purchasing power equal to or ahead of production.

Various proposals come from adherents of this notion. One of the commonest is that an abundance of cheap money will make active business and full employment. This was the doctrine of Lord Keynes in the 1920's. But in 1936 Keynes writes that he has grown skeptical of the adequacy of purely monetary policy, and expects to see the state take responsibility for investment.[3]

3. Keynes, *The General Theory of Employment, Interest and Money*, Harcourt, Brace, New York, 1936, p. 164.

Keynes is, of course, more sophisticated than many of the inflationists. He at least knows of the existence of the doctrine that supply creates its own demand, and he seeks, by arguments which I regard as wholly invalid, to discredit that doctrine. I discuss Keynes' arguments on this point in the Note following this chapter (p. 63).

The view of this school would now seem to be that with appropriate money-market manipulations, and appropriate variations in public expenditures of money borrowed from the banks, it is possible to maintain a steady level of commodity prices and a full volume of employment, regardless of the *quality* of money, regardless of the *quality* of credit, regardless of the state of the price and cost equilibrium, regardless of the foreign trade equilibrium, and regardless of the proportions among the industries.

Another view is that it is necessary to keep wage rates high, or even to increase wage rates, in times of depression, in order that purchasing power may equal or exceed production. We shall test these doctrines in what follows.

Prospects of Postwar Reaction

Should we expect a postwar reaction? It is clear that the end of the war has found our industries out of balance, calling for an immense readjustment in the proportions of our industries. We are turning now to peace production. A government-customer which has been spending $90 billion a year, much of which is borrowed money and much of which is money borrowed from the banks, will largely drop out of the market. It is clear that there must be a great readjustment of prices and of wages. We must find a new equilibrium in the proportions of the industries, in prices, and in costs. Not even a great inflation could avert this readjustment.

If we are flexible and if the markets are free, we can make our adjustment rapidly. If there are governmental interferences with the process of readjustment and, above all, if there is an effort to uphold the existing situation by powerful governmental pressures, by powerful trade-union resistance, by premature utilization of the funds the States and municipalities have held in reserve for public works, and by further deficit spending from Washington, we shall delay the readjustment. We shall turn it into a severe depression and we shall ultimately make worse unemployment.

Full Employment as an Ideal

We are faced by the demand that there must always be full employment, and that, if private industry does not give it, the government must take action to assure it. The demand is made on government to prevent any reaction in business or employment. There must never be any liquidation periods. There must never be any reduction in wages. To prevent these things, the government must plan, the government must direct the course of industry, the government must spend money, the government must increasingly take charge of the economic life of the country.

Now, I may observe, first of all, that the government of the United States has not yet demonstrated its ability, despite very heroic measures in governmental economic planning and a very heroic spending program, to prevent unemployment in peacetime, as shown by our table on pages 10–11.

But, second, let me say that the demand for full employment all the time, the demand that there shall never be any reaction or liquidation, is an erroneous demand. Of course we want full employment. But to strike directly at the symptoms of economic disorders, such as unemployment or liquidation, instead of taking measures that will straighten out the causes of the economic disorder, is a superficial and a dangerous procedure.

There must be temporary unemployment, there must be reaction, readjustment and liquidation. The reaction and the unemployment themselves may easily facilitate the prompt readjustment in the proportions of our industrial activities that the transition from war to peace involves.

The hysterical threat that if American business fails to give full employment throughout the transition period following the war, the laborers will demand that the government take over, is one which I do not think our recent history will justify. Our working population was patient when unemployment rose violently from 12 per cent in 1937 to 19 per cent in 1938.

Business Policy to Make Employment

The business community is planning, and the business community is being exhorted to plan, for full employment. This demand, laudable in intent, misses very important fundamentals. Having in my own mind the objective of full employment, I exhort the businessman to do something which he knows how to do and which he will understand, namely, to plan to make money in the postwar period. He understands that, and if he does it well he will give employment.

Now, the difference between the two approaches can be crucial from the standpoint of employment itself. If, overimpressed with his duty to make employment, the businessman decides to reject a new labor-saving device or a new technology, he may have more men for a time in his own plant than he otherwise would have, but he may also fail to make his main contribution to employment in the country at large.

Technological Progress and Employment

In 1921, we faced a new resource. There had grown up in the war a great body of technological ideas — the chemistry of explosives, the mechanics of aircraft, and a great variety of new things which were awaiting a peacetime application. During the period 1914–1920, businessmen had been so rushed that they had had little time to apply this new technology to peacetime uses. But in 1921 they had time and incentive to study and to plan. The result was a great spurt in the utilization of the new technological ideas in 1921–1923. There was an immense increase in output per wage earner measured in physical volume of production, accompanied by a great increase in the number of workers employed.

The following table tells the story:

GROWTH OF MANUFACTURING PRODUCTION IN THE UNITED STATES,
1914–1923

(Index numbers of physical volume of production, number of wage earners and per capita output)

Year	Physical Volume of Production	Number of Wage Earners	Output Per Wage Earner
1914	100.0	100.0	100.0
1919	127.7	124.5	102.6
1921	105.7	100.1	105.6
1923	156.3	130.3	120.0

Source: Mills, *Economic Tendencies in the United States,* National Bureau of Economic Research, New York, 1932, p. 192.

I think we should reflect a good deal on this. I believe that the future holds a similar promise of a new great spurt of technological improvement. I am afraid that there may be a degree of labor-union resistance to the new technology which did not exist in 1921. I am very much disturbed when I see a labor leader, Petrillo, able to force a great industry to delay the use of a laborsaving device on the ground that it takes work away from members of his union and, finally, in defiance of the President, to force the industry to pay tribute to his union for the privilege of using the device, and when I find the courts upholding him in this as within his rights under the existing laws of the United States. In our planning of general policies, I think we shall need to give attention and careful study to this case.

IV. How Much Do Wages Need to React in Crisis and Depression?

In 1913 Wesley Mitchell generalized as follows: "Wages also are reduced in seasons of severe depression, but in this case the reduction is less than that in commodity prices."[4] Mitchell points out, however, that labor costs are reduced much more than wages in periods of depression because the efficiency of labor increases, overtime ceases and overtime weariness ceases. The average quality of labor increases because the less desirable workers are not employed. Men value their jobs. "The heightening of the physical productivity of labor which results from these changes does more than the fall of wages to diminish the ratio between money cost of labor and money value of products."

Profits and Labor Costs

In this study Mitchell attaches high importance to variations in labor costs as affecting the ups and downs of business. The heart of the problem is business profits. When business profits look promising or are rising, production and employment expand. When business profits are threatened or are falling, production and employment decline. It is in the relation of prices to costs, of course, that the central problem of profits is found. And labor costs are a major factor in total costs. Mitchell's study covers the years 1890 to 1911. The importance of labor costs has obviously risen since the period covered by his studies.

4. *Business Cycles*, University of California Press, Berkeley, 1913, p. 563.

How large a factor direct labor costs are varies, of course, greatly from business to business. Businesses which work upon partially prefabricated materials have already paid wages indirectly in the purchase of their raw materials. Something of an over-all picture may be obtained, however, by showing the percentage of compensation of employees to total national income. This percentage in 1900 was 53.2 per cent; in 1909, 54.4 per cent; in 1914, 57.4 per cent; in 1920, 62.8 per cent; in 1924, 63.6 per cent; in 1927, 64.6 per cent, and in 1929, 65.1 per cent.[5] The percentage for 1929, taken from a Brookings Institution study, agrees very closely with the 1929 figures of the Department of Commerce studies shown in the table below.

NATIONAL INCOME PAID OUT BY TYPES OF PAYMENT

	Amount			Per Cent Distribution		
	1929	1936	1937	1929	1936	1937
	(In Millions of Dollars)					
Total income paid out	78,174	62,056	69,330	100.0	100.0	100.0
Total compensation of employees	51,204	41,250	46,728	65.5	66.5	67.4[a]
Entrepreneurial withdrawals	12,342	9,783	10,441	15.8	15.8	15.1
Dividends	5,969	4,573	5,010	7.6	7.4	7.2
Interest	5,089	4,378	4,656	6.5	7.1	6.7
Net rents and royalties	3,419	2,131	2,599	4.4	3.4	3.7

Sources: Statistical Abstract of the United States, 1937, p. 297; *Survey of Current Business,* June 1938, p. 13.

a. The percentage going to labor is much greater in the war years, 1941–1944.

Labor's Share in the National Income

This table does not tell us directly and simply what percentage of national income goes to labor. In the first place, not all laborers are employees, and not all employees are laborers. We must subtract that part of compensation of employees which goes to high-salaried officials. The total compensation of corporate officers, in 1929, amounted

5. Leven, Moulton and Warburton, *America's Capacity to Consume,* The Brookings Institution, Washington, 1934, p. 158.

to $3,337,000,000, and in 1934 was $2,171,000,000.[6] But much the greater part of this is essentially labor income. There are over 475,000 corporations, and most official salaries are small. The salaries of the president of a small mercantile corporation, who is himself behind the counter and who does part of the bookkeeping, and of the numerous minor executives even in great corporations, are a direct part of labor costs.

On the other hand a very big addition must be made to the percentage of compensation of employees if we are to get the total labor income. "Entrepreneurial withdrawals," amounting to 15.8 per cent of national income for the year 1936, represent the sums taken out of the business as individual income by the owners of unincorporated businesses. Much the largest item in this is what the farmer takes.[7] The farmer is an owner and a businessman and he has profits and losses, but he is also a working man, and a very big part of his income is compensation for his work. Another large element in the entrepreneurial withdrawals is found in the income of the boss barber or the master mechanic who owns his own establishment, and owners of the multitudinous unincorporated mercantile establishments.

I think it conservative to assume that a good half of the figures of entrepreneurial withdrawals represents labor income, rather than business profits, and that the total of labor income for the year 1936, and even more for 1937, runs high over 70 per cent of the national income. As against this, we would have in the form of property income the following items: For the year 1936, net rents and royalties, 3.4 per cent; interest 7.1 per cent; dividends 7.4 per cent, totaling 17.9 per cent. And if to this we add the other half of entrepreneurial withdrawals, we have a maximum of 25.8 per cent of income of all kinds that can be attributed to property ownership and to business enterprise.

A more exact study at this point would take account of that part of business profits which are retained for the expansion of the business and, very particularly, corporate profits added to surplus. But in the years 1936 and 1937, under the influence of the undistributed-profits tax, corporations in the aggregate paid out all their profits and more.

6. U. S. Department of Commerce, *National Income 1929–1936*, Government Printing Office, Washington, 1937, p. 29.

7. U. S. Department of Commerce, *National Income in the United States 1929–1935*, Government Printing Office, Washington, 1936, p. 52.

Labor Over 70 Per Cent, Profits 15.3 Per Cent of National Income

Profit income, as represented in our table, will be made up of 7.4 per cent dividends plus half of the entrepreneurial withdrawals, making a total of 15.3 per cent. This is the compensation of risk-capital and business enterprise. As against this 15.3 per cent of national income for profits, we have labor income exceeding 70 per cent of the total national income. (The developments of the war, of course, have increased the percentage of labor income very greatly.)

With these percentages, over 70 per cent for labor and not over 15.3 per cent for profits, we may reach some rough conclusions as to the extent to which wages may safely rise in a period of prosperity, and as to the extent to which wages need to decline in a period of reaction, in order to let profits emerge once more and business and employment expand once more. A sudden 10 per cent rise in labor income at the expense of profits would be over 7 per cent of national income, but would be half of the 15.3 per cent of national income in the form of profits. It would bring about a great disorder and force a great business reaction. On the other hand a 10 per cent drop in wages in a period when profits were rapidly falling might suffice to reverse the trend in profits. The percentage would vary in different industries and establishments. Relatively small variations in the great factor, labor income, can make tremendous variations in the minor factor, profit income. And it is profit income that is crucial in determining the ups and downs of business.

Douglas on Elasticity of Demand for Labor

I think that my conclusion with respect to this point is in harmony with the studies of Paul H. Douglas in his monumental book, *The Theory of Wages*. Douglas considers the question of the elasticity of the demand for labor. The demand for labor is highly elastic, increasing sharply with a moderate decline in wages, and falling off sharply with a moderate rise in wages, other things equal. Of course, when wages rise in response to increased demand, we have another story; but when in a given state of demand for labor an artificially high rate is set, employment falls off sharply. Douglas summarizes his conclusions with respect to this point in the following passage:[8]

The fact that the elasticity of the demand for labor seems to be between —3.0 and —4.0 indicates that where unemployment is caused by a wage rate which is higher than marginal productivity, a reduction of one per cent in the rate of

8. Paul H. Douglas, *The Theory of Wages*, Macmillan, Toronto, 1934, pp. 501–02.

wages should normally lead to an increase of three or four per cent in the volume of employment and hence to an increase in the total income of the workers of from two to three per cent. If wages are pushed up above the point of marginal productivity, the decrease in employment would normally be from three to four times as great as the increase in hourly rates so that the total income of the working class would be reduced in the ratio indicated above. It should also be noted that Pigou in his recent *Theory of Unemployment* arrives by almost purely deductive methods at an almost identical estimate of the elasticity of demand for labor during periods of depression, namely that it is "probably not less than —3.0."[9]

It does not follow, however, that the cause of unemployment is uniformly a wage which is in excess of marginal productivity. There are other causes of a seasonal, cyclical, and technological nature and in these cases a reduction in the wage rate need not invariably bring the greater expansion in employment.

I call special attention to Professor Douglas' qualification, in the concluding paragraph of the quotation above, and I would add other qualifications. The economic situation needs to be working toward equilibrium before a healthy revival can take place. The relation of wages to the marginal productivity of labor is a major factor in this equilibrium, but it is not the only factor, as we have seen above.

How to Raise Wages

The ideal, of course, is that wages over the years and over the decades should rise, and that the percentage of national income going to labor should rise. The way to bring about rising wages is to have a steady growth in the volume of capital, outrunning the increase in population, and rapid technological progress. When capital and natural resources are scarce and labor is superabundant, as in China, we can have interest rates at 4 per cent a month, land rents very high, and wages so low that it is cheaper to hire a man for draft purposes than to feed an ass.

Wage Policy in the Postwar Reaction

As applied to the postwar period and to labor policy in the postwar period, I think the conclusions of the foregoing analysis are very clear. If, when the $90 to $100 billion of government expenditure, based largely on borrowed money and to a great extent on money borrowed from the banks, is reduced to the neighborhood of $20 billion, and the source from which wages can be paid is to be found only in the gross

9. A. C. Pigou, *Theory of Unemployment*, Macmillan, London, 1933, p. 97.

income of businesses producing goods and services for the public, the demand for labor must be greatly reduced, while the supply of labor will be increased by the return of the soldiers and by the release of labor from the war industries. If, under these circumstances, labor-union policy, powerfully backed by government policy, should hold obstinately to existing wage rates, without reference to the ability of businesses to pay them, then we can have terrific unemployment.

If, in addition to this, a policy of high doles or WPA for the unemployed is adopted, we can make this unemployment chronic, as England did in the 1920's in the midst of a generally prosperous world. A country can have very heavy chronic unemployment if it is willing to pay for it!

But if government policy with respect to labor can be modified so that bargaining between labor and management is fair, two-sided bargaining once more, and if the labor leaders will be good merchants, making needed wage concessions promptly, the concessions on the average that labor will have to make in wage rates need not be very great, and the time can speedily come when the downward trend in wages can be checked and an upward trend resumed.

V. The Purchasing Power Theory of Wages

We still meet the fallacious notion that arbitrarily forcing up the wages of labor will increase general purchasing power, with a resultant increase in demand for goods and demand for labor, and the correlative theory that any reduction in wage rates will decrease purchasing power and precipitate business reaction and unemployment. Coupled with this is the notion that if hours can be shortened, with the same pay for the smaller number of hours, this will still further increase the demand for goods and labor. It is no longer necessary to discuss the theory of the matter. We have had very striking tests of the theory in the decade of the 1930's.

The Theory Tested

One case is that of France, where the introduction of the forty-hour week led to such a violent economic disturbance that the French government was obliged to undo much of what it had done. The law led, in one case, to a 30 per cent increase in personnel in a building. In a second case, where profits were already virtually at the vanishing point, it led to a 22.5 per cent increase in the total cost, and in a third case, in a factory, to a 60 per cent increase in labor costs which meant a 30 per cent increase in total costs. These cases, verified by the writer at the time, were typical. The resultant business reaction and unemployment were extremely severe.

The test of the rival doctrines (a) that arbitrarily increased wages make for prosperity and (b) that increased profits make for prosperity, under our NRA experiment in 1933, was dramatic and conclusive. We had had a very great rise in the volume of business between March and July of 1933 before the coming of the National Recovery Administration. The Federal Reserve Index of Industrial Production (old series) rose from 60 in March of 1933 to 100 in July of 1933. With the coming of NRA and the processing tax, this curve promptly dropped to 72 in the following November.

The following table tells the story.

NRA AND BUSINESS INDICES

	Preceding Establishment of NRA (March to July 1933)	Following Establishment of NRA (July to December 1933)
Industrial production[a] (adjusted)	+69	−25
Factory employment[a] (adjusted)	+23	+ 3
Factory pay rolls[a]	+35	+ 6
Wholesale prices[b]	+15	+ 3
Cost of living[c]	+ 5	+ 3
Food	+16	—
Clothing	+ 4	+21
Stocks of manufactured goods[d]	+ 7	+ 6
Labor costs per unit of output	−26	+54
Department store sales[a] (adjusted)	+23	− 1
Department store stocks[a] (adjusted)	+11	+ 8

Source: This table is taken from "The First Phase of the National Industrial Recovery Act, 1933" by Arthur Robert Burns, *The Political Science Quarterly*, June 1934. In cases where later figures have appeared to replace preliminary figures, revision has been made, except that the FRB Index of Industrial Production with the 1923–1925 base is used. The figures for "Labor costs per unit of output" are estimates by Professor Burns.

   a. Federal Reserve Board.
   b. U. S. Bureau of Labor Statistics.
   c. National Industrial Conference Board.
   d. U. S. Department of Commerce.

I call particular attention in the foregoing table to the figures showing the 26 per cent decrease in labor costs per unit of output preceding NRA and the 54 per cent increase in labor costs per unit of output which followed NRA. The decrease per unit of labor costs was due to the spreading of overtime costs over a much larger number of units of output. It did not represent declining wages.

The foregoing table shows, also, that during the half year of NRA a 3 per cent increase in factory employment and a 6 per cent increase in factory pay rolls took place. NRA did accomplish a modest increase in the purchasing power of factory labor.

Effects of NRA on Profits

But the effects on profits, as a banker talking with his customers could see it at that time, were disastrous. One large industrial organization, producing consumer goods, had had a 300 per cent increase in its volume between March and July. Its profits were large and it absorbed the increased cost of NRA and the processing tax, both of which affected it, without any difficulty, and went on with a large volume of activity. At the opposite end was a large organization, producing capital goods and equipment, which had been running a deficit of $3 million a year. It was not affected by the processing taxes, but was affected by NRA rules as to wages and hours. This industry had its deficit increased to $6 million. In between were the typical cases of businesses reporting that for the first time in two or three years they had had profits between March and July of 1933, but that, with the coming of NRA, and, in some cases, the processing taxes,[10] they found these profits largely wiped out or turned into deficits.

NRA was an antirevival measure. Through the whole of the NRA period industrial production did not rise as high as it had been in July of 1933 before NRA came in.

I may add that the purchasing-power theory of wages had been tested earlier when President Hoover in 1929, after the stock exchange crash, urged the business community not to cut wages, not to cut prices, and the business community, inspired by the fallacious doctrine of the "economy of high wages," made a prolonged effort to pro-

10. The processing taxes were taxes on certain agricultural products paid by the processor to provide funds with which to make "purchasing power" for the farmer. Both the purchasing power of labor and of farmers were raised in this period — at the expense of business profits. In the case of the farmers there was the additional factor of government advances of money, borrowed from the banks, in anticipation of the taxes.

tect wage *rates* and to "spread the work" at existing rates, without preventing the growth of unemployment and without protecting the annual income of labor.

We must have flexible wage scales as part of a flexible economy in order that we may make rapidly the readjustments needed in a rapidly changing world.

In this connection, I may add that the sharp and drastic rise in wages and in labor costs which came in 1937, as a result of the extraordinarily rapid growth of unionism following the passage of the Wagner Act and the election of 1936, was, in my opinion, an important factor, though not by any means the only factor,[11] in the great drop in business activity and employment which came in the latter part of 1937 and in early 1938. Unemployment, which averaged 6,372,000 in 1937 rose to 10,099,000 in 1938.

VI. OUR LAST NATURAL RECOVERY TO FULL EMPLOYMENT: 1921–1923

We had a clean-cut test of equilibrium doctrine versus purchasing-power doctrine in the years 1921–1923. There was an immense decline in the purchasing power of the people of the United States, including the laborers, between 1920 and 1921. The index number of commodity prices at wholesale dropped from 248 in May of 1920 to 141 in August of 1921. For most corporations, profits were turned into losses. Wage rates declined, but very much more moderately. Unemployment which had stood at 558,000 in 1920 rose to 4,754,000 in 1921. The aggregate purchasing power of labor was sharply reduced. Dividend income was radically reduced.

Re-establishment of Equilibrium

But in the hard year from August of 1920 to August of 1921, we were working rapidly toward the re-establishment of economic equilibrium.[12] And in August 1921, the tide turned and an upward trend be-

11. Another major factor was the demoralization of the stock market in 1937, discussed below in the section devoted to the stock market and the SEC. I discuss the 1937 crisis fully in a book, largely finished, on financial history, 1914–1945, which I hope to publish in 1945. I find no validity in the contention that this crisis was due to the increase in the reserve requirements of the banks, 1936–1937, and to the reduced federal government deficit.

12. See my discussion in the *Chase Economic Bulletin* of February 1921, called "The Return to Normal," for an analysis of the factors involved in the restoration of equilibrium.

gan. We reached full employment again by the beginning of 1923, in which year unemployment averaged only 749,000. On the basis of the Federal Reserve Index of Production[13] (base 1923–1925) physical volume of production had dropped from 89 in July 1920 to 65 in July of 1921. In August of 1921 this index began to rise. Through 1922 there was strong improvement, and the index reached new highs in early 1923, the figure being 103 in March and 106 in April of 1923.

Government Economic Policy, 1921–1923

The idea that an unbalanced budget, with vast pump-priming government expenditures, is a necessary means of getting out of a depression, received no consideration by the United States government in the period, 1920–1923. It was, rather, the business of the United States Treasury to look after the solvency of the government. The most important relief that the government felt that it could afford to business was to reduce as much as possible the amount of public expenditure, which had risen to great heights during World War I, to reduce taxes and to reduce public debt.

U. S. GOVERNMENT EXPENDITURES (NOT INCLUDING
PUBLIC DEBT RETIREMENT)
(*In Millions of Dollars*)

Fiscal year 1920	6,403
Fiscal year 1921	5,116
Fiscal year 1922	3,373
Fiscal year 1923	3,295

Taxes were reduced, but remained above expenditures:

ORDINARY RECEIPTS OF THE U. S. GOVERNMENT
(*In Millions of Dollars*)

Fiscal year 1920	6,695
Fiscal year 1921	5,625
Fiscal year 1922	4,109
Fiscal year 1923	4,007

13. I do not trust the revised Federal Reserve Index of Production. I agree with the criticism which General Leonard P. Ayres has made of it. I do not use it in this study.

The public debt was rapidly reduced, as the following figures show:

U. S. GOVERNMENT DEBT
(*In Millions of Dollars*)

June 30	
1920	24,298
1921	23,976
1922	22,964
1923	22,350

Nor was it felt necessary, during this period, to flood the money markets with a gigantic volume of excess reserves. The Federal Reserve Banks' rediscount rates during the crisis of 1920–1921 were 6 and 7 per cent. Necessary credit was extended to protect solvent enterprises. But nobody dreamed of interest rates such as we see today.

OPEN MARKET COMMERCIAL PAPER RATES IN NEW YORK CITY
(*Prevailing Rate on Prime Commercial Paper — 4–6 Months*)

	High	Low
1920	8	6
1921	7¾	5
1922	5	4
1923	5½	4½

Source: Federal Reserve Board, *Annual Report, 1927*, p. 96.

Nor did the government increase public employment with a view to taking up idle labor. There was reduction in the Army and Navy in the course of these years, and there was a steady decline in the number of civilian employees of the federal government.

This policy on the part of the government generated, of course, a great confidence in the credit of the government, and the strength of the gold dollar was taken for granted. The credit of the government and confidence in the currency are basic foundations for general business confidence. The relief to business through reduced taxes was extremely helpful.

Let the reader who still believes that government deficit spending is a sure cure for unemployment contrast the 1920–1923 policy of our government with the deficit spending policy of 1933–1939. The average unemployment, 1920–1923, was 5.2 per cent of the working force, or, eliminating 1920, 6.5 per cent. For 1933–1939, it was 18 per cent, or, eliminating the year 1933, 16.5 per cent. The best year of the whole period, 1937, showed unemployment at 6,372,000, or 12 per cent of the working force; 1939 showed over 9 million unemployed, or 16.7 per cent.

VII. INSTRUMENTALITIES OF ECONOMIC COORDINATION: MARKET VERSUS GOVERNMENT

Economic life guided by freely moving market prices needs no central brain. The partial insights of free individuals and organizations, competing with one another and seeking to gain advantages or to avoid losses, suffice. When government undertakes to coordinate economic life, there is required a central plan and a central brain. The process can no longer be unconscious and automatic. It is as if the human brain were consciously undertaking to regulate the beating of the heart, the digestive processes, and the metabolic processes in the human organism.

When a government at war is seeking to mobilize the whole economic resources of the country for war purposes, a good deal can be done in the way of intelligent coordination and control. The objectives are definite. But in peacetime, when the objectives are to produce goods the people want and are willing to pay for, in the right proportions, to bring them to the right places at the right times, and to sell them at prices to clear the markets and make way for more production to come, the government is hopelessly clumsy and ineffective.

U. S. Government Cannot Even Visualize the Problem

Government in the United States, as now organized, cannot even see what the problem of governmental economic planning is. An adequate economic plan must involve the various elements of economic life in their interrelations. We have a federal government with independent executive, judiciary, and legislative bodies. Our Congress has two houses working through special committees, each concerned with a different problem. There have recently been created temporary committees on postwar economic policy and planning, which can in principle look at all phases of an economic problem instead of merely looking at segments. This is an important step in the right direction.

In principle, the executive department at least ought to be unified. It has one head. But we have seen in practice continuous conflict of purpose and policy among the multitudinous executive offices.

Our federal government has become a jungle. I think no one mind can see it all. If the federal government as now constituted cannot understand itself, how can it expect to understand the complex economic life of 135 million people?

But our government is also made up of States and autonomous local governments. Effective economic planning would have to be preceded by complete centralization of our government. Democracy, local self-government, and individual rights protected by the courts would have to be done away with. The reconstitution of Germany's government under Hitler points the way — for those who wish to pursue it.

Government grows strong in time of war. In the Middle Ages and in the early modern period, governmental economic policy was primarily concerned with organizing nations for war against foreign enemies. In the century of comparative peace that followed the Napoleonic Wars, we broke away from medieval and early modern policies. Following the World War of 1914–1918 there came a great revival of these medieval and early modern policies, particularly as the great depression came on after the smash of 1929. Foreign trade restriction, price fixing, and currency debasement were stock-in-trade of medieval and early modern government.

Government and Prices — Just Price Versus Functional Price

From the standpoint of the economic student of markets, it is the function of prices to tell the truth about what is going on in the fields of production and consumption, to correct maladjustments, and to bring about a re-equilibration of the productive activities when they get out of balance. The facts which lie behind prices may be bad facts, but we do not help the situation by disguising them. Right prices, from this functional point of view, are prices that move goods. Right wages are wages that give full employment to labor. Right interest rates are those which equate the supply of capital to the demand for capital, keeping proper balance between saving and investment. But it is the essentially medieval notion of just price, rather than functional price, which dominates both juristic tradition and present-day government policy when governments touch prices.

Thus, the economist would *lower* public utility and railroad rates in a period of crisis and business depression in order to cause as much traffic as possible to move and to facilitate the general readjustment needed for business revival. But, in the last two great crises, we have seen railroad freight rates raised by the Interstate Commerce Commission at the beginning and in the course of the crises, once in 1920 just as the crisis began, and again in 1932.

It is reversion to medievalism when AAA formulates its policy on the basis of "parity price" — a just-price notion rather than a functional-price notion. The same unsound theory prevails when high hourly wage rates at which few men can be employed are substituted for functional wages — a policy to be condemned from the standpoint of the annual income of labor and the welfare of the laboring class.

It is my thesis that our gravest economic difficulties grow out of governmental interference with free markets, and that the solution of our postwar problem — to the extent that we solve it — is to be found in taking the strangling hands of government off the markets.

VIII. To What Extent Has the Free Market Disappeared?

There are not a few who would agree with the foregoing analysis in principle, and would much prefer the automatic workings of free markets, but nonetheless sadly acquiesce in a continued large measure of governmental control on the ground that the free market has disappeared. I wish to raise realistically the question of the extent to which the free market has disappeared and as to how recently the free market has disappeared.

And I wish to raise further the question as to whether the interferences with free markets are due to developments in industry itself, or whether they are due to governmental policies which can be and should be reversed. It is my thesis that the disappearance of an adequately free market is a very recent matter, and that it is wholly due to bad governmental policy and not to structural changes in industry.

Fallacious Theories Concerning 1922–1939

Space limits forbid discussion here of the theories of the sudden development in the period, 1920–1930, of structural changes making governmental interference necessary. I have elsewhere discussed the more important of these. The fallacy that technological progress is itself a cause of depression and general unemployment and that there was a great intensification of technological progress in the decade, 1920–1930, which made for progressive technological unemployment I have discussed in the *Chase Economic Bulletin,* Vol. 17, No. 2. The fallacy that oversaving is the cause of our troubles I have discussed in the *Chase Economic Bulletin,* Vol. 16, No. 2.

To those who hold that corporate consolidations are the cause of our disorders, let me say that there have been only two great periods of consolidations, 1899–1902 and 1924–1929, both periods of cheap money and excited stock markets. Such movements are harmful and should be prevented, but they are not inherent in the nature of industry itself.[14] The fallacious theory that the reduced growth of population, particularly between 1930 and 1939, has narrowed investment opportunities and should be offset by government spending, I have dealt with in an address before the American Economic Association,[15] December 28, 1939.

The theory of Adolf Berle with respect to the decade following 1922 that "something happened whose cause we may only vaguely attempt to assign" (*Liquid Claims and National Wealth,* page 69), and more specifically, on page 81, that the "instinct" for liquidity was suddenly intensified, is too superficial to require much comment. I was myself precisely assigning the cause, while the development was taking place, to the unsound policies of the Federal Reserve System and to the unsound high protective tariff policy of the United States government.[16] I may add that I am not encouraged by the biologists or the psychologists to believe in the sudden intensification of an "instinct."

I maintain that the serious impairment of free markets is a development since 1920–1923, and that it is wholly a matter of governmental policy. I shall discuss the governmental policies which have damaged the free markets in succeeding sections.

The Degree of Competition and Flexibility

In what has preceded, I have placed great emphasis upon the full,

14. See *Big Business: Its Growth and Its Place,* Twentieth Century Fund, New York, 1937, pp. 29–33, for the statistical evidence.
15. Published in *The American Economic Review,* Supplement, Vol. 30, No. 1, March 1940, pp. 247–50.
16. See *Chase Economic Bulletin,* August 1924, August 1925, November 1926, October 1927, June 4 and June 25, 1928, October 1928, and February 1929.

natural recovery from a great crisis which came in the years 1921–1923. Our markets were free enough then to do the job. If perfect competition and full freedom of prices in all industries and activities were necessary for the essential functioning of the market-mechanism, the case would be hopeless and would always have been hopeless.[17] But the mechanism can and does work adequately, despite many rigidities, *if only new ones are not continually being created.*

In 1920–1923, for example, we had a great long-term debt structure in industry. We had publicly regulated railroad rates which were increased at the wrong time in 1920, just as the great crisis came upon us, and which retarded the readjustment of costs to prices. We had noncompetitive public utility rates. We had labor unionism far stronger than it was in 1929. We had varying degrees of competition and varying price policies among our great industries, and unequal declines in prices and wages. We had to go through a break in commodity prices at wholesale from a peak of 248 in May of 1920 to 141 in August of 1921, and we had an immense shift in the direction of our industrial activity. We had to liquidate a vast volume of short-term commercial debt, and we had to transfer from banks to investors — at a price — a large volume of government war debt.

The mechanism worked. In thirteen months, from July 1920 to August 1921, we passed from a violent boom to the trough of a great depression. Then the tide turned, and the adequately free markets turned the great depression into revival and full prosperity, by the beginning of 1923.

IX. When Governments Play God

The recovery, 1921–1923, was our last natural recovery to full employment. Even as it was under way, the government was undermining it, by the sharp increases in our protective tariffs in 1921 and 1922.

This was not deliberate governmental economic planning. It was rather the application of an outworn political tradition by a very ignorant President, who could not be made to understand that our change from a debtor to a creditor position made adequate exports dependent

17. There were many more rigidities when Adam Smith wrote than there are today, and if some of Adam Smith's present-day critics would take the trouble to read his book they would see that it was, in large measure, a protest against the existing rigidities and interferences, and a kind of forecast of the immense economic progress which the nineteenth century enjoyed as it broke away from the rigidities against which Smith protested.

on low tariffs. The tariffs were raised, and the seeds of death were planted in the promising revival.

Our recovery in 1921–1923 was not assisted by improved conditions abroad. In 1920 the world as a whole went into crisis when we did. The tide turned in the United States without outside help. Prolonged difficulties continued in Germany, in France, in Japan, and in many other countries for several years after our revival.

Our tariff increases intensified the difficulties of the outside world. Our export markets, especially for agricultural products, turned bad, and in early 1924 a very sharp and sudden depression began.

Easy Money Policy

It was then that the government began consciously and deliberately to play God. The Federal Reserve System bought some $400 million of government securities between November 1923 and July 1924, flooding the money market, beating down interest rates to levels that then looked absurdly low, and generating in the course of the ensuing year an expansion of commercial bank credit of over $4 billion.

As this coincided with the coming of the Dawes Plan, which restored confidence upon the part of American investors in Europe, it restored a precarious equilibrium between agriculture and industry. We immediately began an enormous volume of foreign loans to Europe, loans which we could not have made in such volume if there had not been this great expansion of bank credit. We did not allow Europe to pay for American farm products by selling manufactured goods in our markets, but we did lend her the money with which to buy our goods.

The same flood of cheap money generated a strong speculative move in our securities markets, and here again the government assumed the leadership. We had the unedifying spectacle of the Secretary of the Treasury and the President of the United States acting as the "Capeadores of Wall Street,"[18] leading a bull market, and giving out encouraging interviews whenever the bull movement flagged.

The New Deal Under Coolidge and Hoover

The New Deal as a conscious and deliberate matter began in 1924, under the Coolidge Administration. The personal conduct of business

18. See Ralph Robey's brilliant and justly indignant paper, "The Capeadores of Wall Street" in *The Atlantic Monthly*, September 1928, for the details.

and industry by government officials, and the manipulations of money markets and other markets as part of "governmental economic planning" are the essence of the New Deal.

At first it worked. We went through five years of hilarious prosperity, with rapidly expanding bank credits, rising security prices, and gigantic new issues of securities, including foreign securities. We intensified the thing by a renewed cheap-money move following the conference of central bank governors in New York in the summer of 1927. Again the dope worked, and this time the intoxicated victim went wild. Stock prices rose to fantastic levels. New security issues, which had amounted to $4.3 billion in 1923, rose to $10 billion in 1929.

The quality of bank credit was impaired in the process. The volume of foreign debt was enormously increased and the annual debt service enormously increased. Meanwhile our tariffs remained as barriers to retard the payment by the foreigner of what he owed us. We, a creditor nation, continued to have a great export surplus, though we should have been having an import surplus.

Then came, in late 1929, the great smash in the stock market, followed speedily by an ominous decline in the prices of the great staples of international commerce. The stage was set for a very severe reaction. We were probably still strong enough at the end of 1929 to have gone through an orderly reaction and depression, and to have come through with an orderly revival, if the government had refrained from interference, and if, above all, the government had removed the worst of the restrictions that our tariffs imposed on foreign payments to us.

But the New Deal was in the saddle. The President of the United States, Mr. Hoover, the back-seat driver, called in the leaders of business, railroads, and public utilities to urge upon them the policy of not cutting prices, not cutting wages, and increasing capital outlay, and called upon the States and municipalities to increase public borrowing for public works. Purchasing power must be kept up! There must be no letdown!

Doping the Same Horse Three Times

And then, early in 1930, once more the Federal Reserve System resumed its policy of cheap money, buying government securities on a great scale, beating down interest rates, encouraging once more a speculative stock market and the flotation of foreign loans.

Once again the financial organism responded to the dope. Once again the stock market rose in early 1930. Once again the volume of new securities, including new foreign securities, rose. But the curve for industrial production did not rise. It sank steadily through 1930. Industry could no longer respond to financial stimulus. The third deliberate injection of financial dope failed. I may add that I know no race track where it is regarded as ethical to dope the same horse three times.

Late in 1929, moreover, the government began a further great interference with markets. The Federal Farm Board got into action, holding up the prices of various agricultural products with government money.

Trade Barriers and Gold

Finally, late in 1930, came the crowning act of folly of the Republican New Deal. In October we raised the tariffs again, and in reaction, the whole world began to raise tariffs and to erect strangling trade barriers of many different kinds. The international markets were so narrowed that export trade throughout the world fell to appallingly low levels. The burden of the payment of foreign debts, which should have been carried, primarily, by the movement of goods, fell heavily on gold.

When international trade lines are open and goods can move freely in payment of debts, there is plenty of gold. But when only gold is free to move in the payment of international debts, there is not enough gold in the debtor countries to make such payments possible. In the ensuing collapse of international credit, which moved fast in the tragic year 1931 with first Austria, and then Germany going down, and finally England going off the gold standard in September, there arose a great outcry against gold as the culprit. The fault was not with gold. The fault was with the strangling of the international movement of goods.

X. "My Father Also Chastised You With Whips but I Shall Chastise You With Scorpions"[19]

The Republican New Deal demoralized the markets and brought about the unprecedented depression and unemployment of 1932, when 12,478,000 men, or 24.9 per cent of the labor force of the country, was unemployed. The Democratic New Deal intensified the demoralization of the markets and perpetuated the depression and the unemployment.

19. I Kings, 12.

The New Deal Under Roosevelt

1. It continued and very greatly intensified the abuse of the money market and the artificial manipulation of the interest rate. 2. It broke the country's solemn promise, made by the Congress in 1900 and in 1913 and printed on every Federal Reserve Note and every government bond and every government bond coupon, to pay gold, at the existing standard of value, on demand. It left the dollar floating for nearly a year, and then anchored it precariously to gold, with a cut of over 40 per cent in the gold content. In doing this, it undermined financial confidence and destroyed credit everywhere in the world.

3. It undertook manipulations of the labor market under NRA, under the Wagner Act, and under the wage and hours legislation. 4. It greatly increased the manipulation of agricultural prices which Hoover's Farm Board had started, and it accompanied this by a great regimentation of agricultural activities. 5. In 1933 it destroyed the World Economic Conference which had offered promise of international monetary stability and of the relaxation of trade barriers, and it increased the trade barriers under NRA legislation and under the agricultural legislation. Inconsistently, in 1934, it finally gave to Secretary Hull, the one consistent statesman of the Administration, limited tariff powers which enabled him to fight valiantly, though with limited success, toward lowering trade barriers throughout the world.

Contradictory Policies — Special Interests

6. Totalitarian economic planning under a dictator with unimpeded powers, who also possessed clear objectives and superhuman intelligence, might make a consistent economic plan. Our democracy could not. AAA was designed to raise the position of the farmer in relation to manufacturing. But NRA lifted the level of manufacturing prices and wages as against the farmer. The New Deal has been characterized by steady conflicts between agricultural interests and labor interests. Often, too, special interests have combined their political power in raids in the general interest. The silver interest has been especially skillful and effective in this, and the bureaucratic interest in "Big Government" has been most skillful of all.

The inflation plans could have worked only if the markets had been free so that money could flow into them. But the New Deal closed the markets. The Johnson Act made foreign loans very difficult. The high trade barriers, in any case, would have prevented substantial foreign investment. The Securities and Exchange legislation largely closed the accustomed outlets for funds for investment in American industry. There was constant conflict of purpose within the New Deal.

7. The New Deal used taxation partly for revenue, but primarily to accomplish redistribution of wealth, imposing rates so high on larger incomes, and death duties so high on larger fortunes, that industrial investment by men of substantial means became hazardous in the extreme, and in the case of very large fortunes, almost impossible.

8. The New Deal introduced an incredible confusion. Drastic change after drastic change came with increased momentum. New government agencies were multiplied with extraordinary rapidity. Many assumed power to issue rulings with the force of law. Many assumed power to issue elaborate questionnaires which businessmen and others must fill out — "or else." The burden of paper work for businesses grew. Large corporations could create special departments which could handle the questionnaires. Small businesses were overwhelmed.

Lawyers and Tax Experts Replace Sales Managers and Engineers

In pre-New Deal days a businessman contemplating an expansion of his business could consult his engineer and his sales manager, phone his bankers, and give orders to go ahead. Today, he must first consult his tax expert, then his lawyers, then his bankers, then, if he needs further financing, the Securities and Exchange Commission — and with them he must consult many times — and then, finally, he may call in his engineer and his sales manager. But by this time his enthusiasm is sensibly abated.

The statistical record of the results of governmental economic planning under the New Deals, Republican and Democratic, is very disheartening. The record of employment and unemployment appears in full in our table on pages 10–11. The best year of the period 1930–1939, namely, 1937, was worse than the worst year, 1921, of the thirty years preceding. Another very illuminating set of figures with reference to the effect of the New Deal upon our industrial equipment is to be found in the figures of *The American Machinist* for the average length of life for tools and machines in our factories.

These follow:

PERCENTAGE OF METAL WORKING EQUIPMENT OVER 10 YEARS OLD

Year	Per Cent
1925	44
1930	48
1935	65
1940	70

We had idle labor of 9 million men in 1939. We had idle money on a colossal scale. We had idle technological ideas, as represented by the figures given above for obsolescence in equipment in our industries, on an appalling scale. War put them to work, but it took the war to do it.

XI. THE CAPITAL MARKET AND THE STOCK MARKET

Since the enactment of the securities legislation of 1933, the volume of new corporate securities issued in the United States has been appallingly low. I do not make my comparison with the wild years which began in 1924, when a vast flood of new bank credit was added to the ordinary volume of investors' savings and when new securities rose to fantastic levels, reaching a peak of $10 billion in 1929. I make the comparison rather with the year 1923.

There is no year since 1933 in which new corporate security issues have amounted to as much as 50 per cent of the issues of 1923. In 1934 new corporate security issues were less than 7 per cent, and in 1935 they were 15 per cent of the 1923 levels. In the more prosperous years, 1936 and 1937, new corporate securities rose to 46 per cent, falling again in 1938 and 1939 to 33 per cent and to 14 per cent respectively. During the war the drop even from the 1939 levels has been drastic.

Requiring Truth in Securities

I believe that federal legislation compelling truth in securities was called for. I sympathized with the purposes of the Securities Act of 1933. But the legislation was so extreme and so drastic that it was clear that it would stop normal functioning as well as prevent abuses. The business of issuing new securities became very pure but very sterile.

The British law requiring truth in securities is ordinarily satisfied by a prospectus which is brief, clear and readable. In contrast, the prospectuses issued under our Securities Act of 1933 as amended, and under the rulings of the Securities and Exchange Commission, are impossibly long things. Seventy pages are very common. The shortest which I have found is 23 long pages. I do not know of any investor who has read a prospectus before buying a security.

But in addition to the costly prospectus, which must be carefully examined by high-paid lawyers and carefully checked by certified accountants, there is the much more elaborate registration statement. The cost of registration could be very greatly reduced without sacrificing the reasonable objective that full disclosure of all material facts be made. Lord Kylsant was put in prison in England for failure to put into his prospectus a definite material fact. But honest men hesitate to assume responsibility for all the facts required by a 70-page prospectus and a much more elaborate registration statement.

I think there should be no registration statement required; that there should be only a sworn prospectus required and that the law should be so amended as to allow this prospectus to be brief. It should be a responsible document. It should be a document on the basis of which men may be sued in the civil courts or punished by the criminal courts if they falsify or if they omit material facts.

The Paralysis of the Stock Market

The New Deal had planned to make the stock market safe for investors. Radical measures were adopted to make sure that there be no repetition of the wild stock market boom of 1924 to 1929, and the violent crash of 1929. But the results were unhappy.

The Dow Jones industrials rose from 108.64 on June 1, 1935 to 190.38 on August 14, 1937 and then dropped to 97.46 by March 31, 1938. This approached the percentage break that we had in 1929 between the high of September 11th and the low of November 13th. This is not a brilliant record for a governmentally controlled, daily inspected, constantly managed stock market, designed to give protection to investors and designed to eliminate wide fluctuation in security prices.

The violence and the severity of this stock market break in 1937 were due to impaired efficiency of the stock market, growing out of governmental policy. The market had grown extraordinarily "thin."

The stock market, which in the past has been capable of absorbing an immense volume of selling with moderate recession in price, now saw moderate selling bring about large changes in price.

SHARE SALES ON DAYS OF DECLINING PRICES, RELATED TO NET CHANGES IN CLOSING PRICES OF THE INCLUDED STOCKS

Group of Thirty Common Stocks	Thousands of Shares Sold	
	Per One Per Cent Price Decline	Per $1 Price Decline
12 days, 1930–1931	13.1	23.1
12 days, 1936–1937	4.7	6.7
September 7, 1937	2.1	3.4

The Tax Factor

This "thinness" of the market was due to a variety of governmental policies. One was the extraordinarily high rates of income taxes, and especially the tax on capital gains, which was then a part of the general income tax.[20] These rates, applied to profits made in the stock market, meant that men of substantial means simply could not afford to engage in stock market trading.

Elimination of men of substantial means from the stock market, moreover, tends to eliminate informed trading in the stock market and to eliminate the courageous buying by informed men on bad days, which used to be a powerful steadying factor.

Securities and Exchange Legislation — "Insiders' " Trading

The securities and exchange legislation and the rulings of the Securities and Exchange Commission have added many burdens. In the past, insiders of a corporation, seeing its stock unwarrantedly beaten down in the market, would step in and buy, expecting to be able to sell again at a profit when the movement was arrested. This was very useful to the market and to the small investors in the corporation's stock.

The Securities and Exchange Act of 1934, Section 16-b, largely pre-

20. Even with the present capital-gains tax this remains true of transactions closed within a six months' period.

vented this. It provided that if insiders of a corporation should buy or sell their stock, and reverse the operation within six months and make a profit thereby, they would be liable to suit by any stockholder of the corporation to recover the profits for the corporation itself. The Congress had a commendable purpose in this legislation, stated as follows: "For the purpose of preventing the unfair use of information which may have been obtained . . . by a reason of relationship to the issuer. . . ."

However, the Congress recognized that not all such insider buying and selling was unfair in character, and in the same section it provided that exceptions and exemptions should be granted by the Securities and Exchange Commission. But even in 1944, ten years after the passage of the Act in 1934, the Securities and Exchange Commission has given no ruling which would permit this helpful action by insiders.[21]

The Securities and Exchange Commission is to be sharply condemned for this. It is easily possible to distinguish in objective terms between fair and unfair buying and selling by insiders. The typical unfair case is where the insider initiates a downward or upward movement because of information which he alone has, as for example where the chief executive, knowing that a dividend is to be cut or omitted, because he himself is making the decision, first sells his stock with a resulting break in price and then buys it back later after the bad news is out. On the other hand, the useful case for the corporation is where a break has occurred, not initiated by him, and where he steps in and steadies the market, or where a rise has occurred, not initiated by him, and where he sells the stock because he thinks it has gone too high.

The Securities and Exchange Commission should long since have exempted transactions by insiders which follow a break or a rise of a certain per cent, say of 5 per cent begun within a stated period of time, say three days, the first transaction by the insider being at a price 5 per cent below the highest price of the preceding three days in the case of a purchase, or in the case of a sale, 5 per cent above the lowest price of the preceding three days. This would be an absolutely definite rule that would eliminate the abuse and would preserve the good of insiders' transactions.[22]

21. SEC, *General Rules and Regulations,* February 15, 1944, pp. 1601–07.
22. See the address by W. W. Aldrich, *The Stock Market from the Viewpoint of a Commercial Banker,* October 14, 1937, issued by the Chase National Bank of the City of New York.

SEC Inquisitorial Practices

A further very important factor reducing trading by informed men of substantial fortune has been the frequent inquisitorial visits of agents of the Securities and Exchange Commission to brokerage houses when large transactions appear on the ticker or when substantial price changes occur. These agents demand full information regarding the name of the customer, and also the details of all of his other transactions for a period preceding, and in some cases then go to the customer himself. In any case the broker feels obliged to inform the customer of the visit. However legitimate their transactions, men do not welcome governmental inquiry into them. Many men simply withdraw from the market.

The Securities and Exchange Commission reaches out even where it has no power. In 1943 a wealthy individual, through his investment banker, publicly announced that he was offering, off the Stock Exchange, $25 million worth of stocks for the purpose of buying government war bonds. The offer was suddenly withdrawn. The Securities and Exchange Commission, however, denied that it had interfered. It had merely had inquiry made of the attorneys of the wealthy individual as to whether they had considered "the possibility of registering the proposed distribution with the Commission."[23] There was nothing in the law that required this registration. But this question put to the attorneys interrupted the transaction. The Securities and Exchange Commission is, in my opinion, an institution greedy for power, reaching out far beyond its jurisdiction, as laid down by Congress, in an effort to get more power.

SEC and Specialists

Further factors limiting activity in the stock market are the complicated rules which the Stock Exchange itself has adopted at the instance of the Securities and Exchange Commission, limiting the activities of specialists and floor traders. These rules create a great deal of uncertainty. It is often necessary in critical times, when quick action by specialists or floor traders is needed, for the specialist to confer with members of the Stock Exchange Committee instead of taking needed prompt action. The Securities and Exchange Commission has even erected a

23. *The New York Times,* October 28, 1943.

rule putting the burden of proof upon the specialist, requiring affirmative proof that the specialist's action is beneficial. It is not easy for a man to act quickly with such a burden of proof against him.

Margin Requirements

An additional factor intensifying the difficulties of the 1937 break was the high and inflexible margins required. The Congress, desiring to restrict the use of credit in the stock market, had given the Federal Reserve authorities control over margins required, a control that had previously been in the hands of bankers and brokers. The Federal Reserve authorities had raised requirements to a very high level. These high requirements meant that the margin trader's account was frozen the moment the market receded. He could not buy any more stocks on moderate declines nor could he withdraw any cash from his account. These margin requirements were made higher for specialists and floor traders on the floor of the Stock Exchange than for customers.

Now all this was benevolently intended. But it has very nearly ruined the safety and the efficiency of our great stock exchange machinery.

Radical Reform Called For

Sympathizing fully with the purpose of the Congress in demanding truth in securities and in forbidding stock exchange manipulation, I nonetheless believe that a radical change in the whole approach to this problem is called for. There is no more reason in the securities field than in any other field of private enterprise for constant governmental interference in the details of transactions. The securities business is in general a clean and sound business. Every day, transactions involving many tens of millions of dollars are made by word of mouth over the telephone. Transactions between brokers on the floor of the Exchange are made by a nod of the head without the interchange of written documents. A very high order of integrity is needed to make such a system work.

Occasionally, however, criminal acts occur as in every other field where human beings deal with one another. There is need for criminal law and punishment. In the interest of normal functioning we should set the business free, in a framework of definite law, and do away with the detailed interferences.

The existing rules and regulations of the Securities and Exchange Commission, together with the security and exchange legislation, should be thoroughly reviewed by the Congress with a view to eliminating most of the detail, and with a view to saving that part which is needed and valuable for the protection of investors and for the prevention of fraud and manipulation.

Free the Capital Market and Security Exchanges

There will be need for an immense flow of investment funds to corporations as we shift from war production to peace production, if our industry is to function well and if we are to have full employment. The Securities and Exchange Commission itself is of a different opinion. In the TNEC investigation it produced one-sided evidence that tended to show that our corporations needed little more financing. It has recently set forth figures designed to show that the corporations in the aggregate have so much cash that they will not need additional financing.

It is interesting that the Federal Reserve authorities considering the matter have reached a contrary conclusion. I myself thoroughly discount the Securities and Exchange Commission's figures. I am entirely sure that many corporations will need access to the capital market on a very substantial scale, if they are to make the transition and are to develop and grow as they should. I believe that there are few things more important in the whole program of postwar reconstruction than the freeing of the capital market and the security exchanges from unnecessary restraints and inhibitions.

XII. Government Finances, Money in Circulation, Bank Deposits, and Inflation

Extremely low interest rates at a time when the world was destroying capital on a colossal scale, and when the government of the United States was borrowing many tens of billions of dollars a year, were obviously an anomaly.

Apart from the expansion of bank credit, there are four normal sources of capital: (a) consumers' thrift; (b) business thrift, particularly the building up of corporate surpluses out of profits; (c) direct capitalization, where the farmer uses his spare time in building fences and barns, or allows his flocks and herds to increase instead of selling off the whole of the annual increase; (d) governmental thrift, where taxes exceed public expenditures and the government is paying down public debt, or is using taxes for other capital purposes.

New bank credit constitutes a fifth source of capital, safe enough when cautiously used and when kept in reasonable relation to the growth of the normal sources of capital and the growth of production in the country, but dangerous in the extreme when used to excess, as we saw in the period, 1924–1933.

Bank Credit in War Finance

Bank credit as a substitute for taxes and savings is particularly dangerous in wartime. It has been the typical breeder of wartime inflation. The classical case is, of course, that where the government leans directly upon the state bank of issue. The great expansion of bank notes is obvious, and pretty well understood by the people. But an expansion of bank deposits is in economic essence very little different from an expansion of bank notes. Notes and deposits are alike demand liabilities, and both are media of exchange. But the more insidious process of expanding bank deposits can be carried further without engendering popular distrust.

In World War I, between April 1917 and December 30, 1918, we expanded bank deposits by $5.8 billion, and bank loans and investments by $7 billion. This was enough.

In the period from June of 1922 to April 11, 1928, we expanded bank credit by $13.5 billion in deposits, and by $14.5 billion in loans and investments. This generated our immense boom, our wild stock market, and our stock market crash of 1929.

In World War II we have seen, as a result of the government's borrowing at low interest from the banks, an expansion of bank credit in the United States of $59.5 billion in deposits (demand deposits, "adjusted," plus government deposits) between June 30, 1939, and December 31, 1944 (from $28 billion to $87.5 billion), accompanied by a growth of the government security holdings of the commercial banks of $59.5 billion (from $18 billion to $77.5 billion) with an additional increase in government security holdings by the Federal Reserve Banks of $16.5 billion.

We have, moreover, seen an immense increase in money in circulation, chiefly Federal Reserve notes. This figure stood, at the end of June 1939, at $7 billion, and in April 1945 at $26 billion. Obviously, there are the very gravest danger signals here.

The Warning of the Federal Reserve System Ignored

We had already very greatly overdone government securities purchases by the banks and the Federal Reserve Banks between March of 1933 and 1940. The Federal Reserve authorities were greatly concerned. In a report to Congress on January 1, 1941, there was a unanimous recommendation by the Board of Governors of the Federal Reserve System, the presidents of the twelve Federal Reserve Banks and all twelve members of the Federal Advisory Council, urging the Congress to forestall inflationary tendencies (a) by increasing the power of the Board of Governors to raise reserve requirements of the member banks, (b) by ending the President's power to devalue the currency, (c) by repealing the power to issue $3 billion of greenbacks, and (d) by selling government securities directly to investors rather than to the banks.

This met no favor in Administration circles, and none in the Treasury. The Federal Reserve System, having made its protest, today lies supine. It imposes no brakes. It feeds the inflation of bank credit.

Alleged Safety in New Techniques

We are told that new techniques have arisen which make the policy safe. I see very little in the way of new techniques, and rather a very exaggerated use of old techniques.

We have first the purchases of government securities by the Federal Reserve Banks, replenishing the reserves of the member banks. In World War I, the Federal Reserve Banks did this in connection with each of the four great Liberty Loans, reducing the strain in the money market for a few days, while the loans were being floated, and then promptly selling the government securities again. The magnitudes were small — for the first three Liberty Loans a few tens of millions, and in the Fourth Liberty Loan something over $200 million — but only for a few days.

In 1924 and in 1927, the Federal Reserve Banks bought several hundred millions of government securities and held them for a good many months, in each case generating a very dangerous expansion of bank credit, and in the second case precipitating almost unmanageable difficulties.

In World War II, the Federal Reserve Banks bought government securities in terms, not of tens of millions or of hundreds of millions, but of many billions. The figure of their holdings stood at $2,184,000,000 on December 31, 1940, and at $20,720,000,000 in May 1945. This is no new technique, but the vast scale of its use makes one ponder.

In the first war, Federal Reserve Bank rediscount rates were well below the market rates, to facilitate war financing. But they followed the market up, as the war went on. The New York Federal Reserve Bank rediscount rate was placed at 3 per cent in 1917, moved up to 3.5 per cent at the end of the year, and to 4 per cent early in 1918, remaining, however, below market rates. At the present time, the Federal Reserve Bank rediscount rate is 0.5 per cent for advances secured by government obligations maturing in one year or less. Here again there is no new technique, but merely an extreme application of an old one.

The Federal Reserve authorities now have power to reduce the reserve requirements of the member banks, and they have already done this as far as New York and Chicago banks are concerned. But in the last war we reduced member bank reserve requirements by act of Congress in 1917 — to levels that made us great trouble in the period of the 1920's.

Finally, the Federal Reserve Banks buy government bills without limit from the member banks at a fixed rate, three eighths of one per cent discount, with a repurchase agreement. This is designed to make the member banks look upon government bills as ready cash, and to make them feel that it is not necessary to carry excess reserves. It may be granted that we have here a new technique. It is obviously a highly dangerous technique, and a highly inflationary one.

Using Up Ammunition Rapidly

In the process of this immense bank expansion, we have used up ammunition very fast. The reserve ratio of the Federal Reserve Banks to notes and deposits combined stood at 90.4 per cent in April 1942, and at 46.5 per cent on May 9, 1945. Excess reserves of member banks, which stood at nearly $7 billion in early 1941, dropped below $1 billion in 1944.

Moreover, the Treasury is borrowing chiefly on short term. Only a minor part of our vast public debt is outstanding in the form of long-term bonds. The so-called war savings bonds are in effect demand deposits after they have been held from two to six months. Insurance companies and certain other financial institutions have bought a substantial amount of long-term bonds. Individual investors have bought very few of them. The rates of 2 per cent on ten-year bonds, and 2.5 per cent on twenty-year bonds are simply too low to attract investors. The man who knows how to look at a bond table can see to what prices they would drop if the rate of interest should rise, and he can look back over the history of government bonds yields for the past twenty-five years, and see yields exceeding 5 per cent.

Inflation Policy in Last War

During our own participation in World War I, we held down inflation admirably. The great rise in prices in the last war came between December of 1915 and July of 1917, before our government war policy got into operation. Commodity prices at wholesale in July of 1917 stood at 187 per cent of 1913 prices. Under our war policy these prices receded to 182 per cent in October of 1917, and then rose slowly, under the extreme pressure of the war, to 207 per cent in November of 1918, after which they receded again to 197 per cent in March of 1919.

Our policy in World War I with respect to prices contained four elements: (a) the sudden, very heavy application of war taxation; (b) great concern that bonds be sold to investors rather than to banks; (c) a firm money market to hold down bank expansion. Commercial paper rates in 1918 stood at 6 per cent, though the government borrowed more cheaply. Rates were made, however, which would attract investors, and which could look reasonable over a long period of time. The First Liberty Loan was issued at 3.5 per cent, fully tax free, the Second Liberty Loan at 4 per cent, the Fourth Liberty Loan at 4.25 per cent, the last three Liberty Loans being partially tax exempt. (d) We had a limited amount of price fixing, applying to scarce essentials. We had retail price fixing only in the matter of scarce foods and fuels, and here not until after wholesale price fixing had been well established. We relied in the last war primarily on functional controls rather than direct controls, as far as commodity prices were concerned.

Price Fixing in World War II

In the second war, building up an immense inflationary flood by the expansion of bank credit and money in circulation, we have used, as our primary device for controlling inflation, price fixing, covering virtually all wholesale and retail prices and industrial wages.

It is quite clear that these price controls cannot be tolerated if we are to have a free postwar economy. Prices have work to do. Prices are to guide and direct the economic activities of the people. Prices are to tell them what to do. The prices must be free to tell the truth.

The bureaucrats will make a tremendous effort to continue price fixing and the other war controls in the peace. The Congress should watch this jealously, and with each renewal of wartime powers, should limit them to six months. Something may be said for the temporary continuation of price fixing, with rationing, in the case of a few very scarce essential commodities, but each case should be scrutinized carefully. The general idea that price fixing should be continued in peacetime for the purpose of preventing inflation must be absolutely vetoed. Inflation must be controlled, if it is controlled, by budget balancing and control of money and credit.

Eliminate Inflationary Money and Credit Policies Now

The existing low interest rates are made possible only by the substitution of bank credit for investors' savings. If bank expansion were to stop today, interest rates would forthwith rise. If, on the other hand, bank expansion is not stopped, we shall have a tremendous inflation. And then we shall see an immense rise of interest rates, the inevitable accompaniment of a great inflation. The choice is not between continuing low interest rates and not continuing. The choice is rather between a moderate and manageable reversal of policy in the near future, and an involuntary submission to very high interest rates at a later date.

Fund the Public Debt Now

I believe we should act as promptly as is now feasible, while we still have controlled commodity markets, and while we still have wartime motives to work with, in funding the government debt into long-term bonds at rates of interest which will attract investors' money. The magnitude of the operation calls, of course, for very aggressive bond selling on a patriotic basis, accompanied by neighborhood pressure. I believe that if we act promptly, these rates can be intermediate between those we paid in the last war, and those we are now paying.

We now have outstanding, as a result of the previous abuse of bank credit, an immense volume of idle money in circulation, and an immense volume of idle deposits in the banks. If these grew active, we should have an inflation that would blow us sky high. The thing to do is to pull them in and get them invested in government bonds before they begin to work actively in other fields.

I cannot, of course, set exact figures at which investors will take long-term government bonds. Only the market can do that. But this idle cash is a market factor of first importance, tending to hold interest rates down. I think the thing to do is to increase the interest rates on new government securities forthwith to levels at which investors' money will be forthcoming. This should be accompanied by a sale of government securities by the Federal Reserve Banks, to tighten up the money market correspondingly.

Higher Interest Rates and the Position of the Banks

Now, a moderate rise in interest rates would set in motion powerful counterforces, which would tend to hold the interest rates down. With rising interest rates, savings banks and other banks would find it worth while to offer attractive rates on savings accounts to the people, pulling in actual cash from circulation. And commercial banks would be interested in reducing or even dispensing with service charges on demand deposits, which would pull in a great deal of money from circulation. But this money coming in from circulation would ease the bank reserve situation and tend to hold interest rates down. Moreover, investors, attracted by higher yields on government bonds, would make a market for very many of the government securities now held by the banks. As the banks sold these securities to investors, investors would pay for them by checking against deposit accounts, canceling a great deal of the inflated deposits, and once more easing the money market situation by reducing the reserve requirements of the banks.[24]

There are two main objections to the policy which I propose: (a)

24. For an analogous situation, see my account of the money market in 1928, in the *Chase Economic Bulletin*, "Brokers' Loans and Bank Credit," October 31, 1928.

that it would involve dangers to the capital structures of those banks now too heavily loaded with long-term government securities; (b) that it would increase the tax money required to meet the debt service on the government's already enormous debt.

Let me say with respect to both these points that the problems grow progressively worse the longer we refrain from facing them.

To protect the banks in this change of policy, I have proposed that the banks holding long-term government bonds be allowed to exchange them for new issues at the higher rates of interest, at a discount of, say 2 per cent as compared with cash subscribers, leaving them with some loss but not with losses that would ruin their depositors. The FDIC needs a similar protection. Both banks and FDIC should be expected to take shorter maturities in making these exchanges. I have seen no other proposal for dealing with this that looks at all adequate. It cannot be solved by allowing the banks to carry these bonds at par on their books regardless of the market. Informed depositors would simply withdraw their funds from banks whose capital structures were impaired, and put them into banks whose holdings of government securities were predominantly short term. Nor do you solve any inflation problem by forcing the Federal Reserve Banks to take long-term bonds from the member banks at par.

The Interest Burden of the Public Debt

With respect to the interest burden on the government debt, let me say that this problem becomes progressively worse if we delay it. We can now fund the government debt at moderate rates of interest, as above indicated. If, however, we wait for inflation to come, interest rates will rise rapidly and the Secretary of the Treasury will sweat blood as Treasury bills and certificates fall due, as people cash in their war savings bonds, and as he has to borrow money on the rapidly rising money market — or else print, which would not help the inflation.

The notion that we can permanently hold the debt service on the public debt to a 2 per cent rate, that we can permanently service $300 billion of public debt with $6 billion of interest, is fantastic. We had best face the facts now. The facts are that our postwar budget is going to be very difficult to balance, and that we face the necessity for drastic economies in the postwar period. The facts are that proposals for expanding federal expenditures after the war must be fought all along the line. We do not create social security when we endanger the dollar in which social security payments are to be made.

XIII. Taxation and a Balanced Budget

We can balance the postwar budget by taxes if we hold down expenditures sufficiently. If we are reckless about expenditures we shall have chronic deficits, with an undermining of the credit of the government and with currency disorders.

1. Federal taxation should be adequate to cover both current expenditures and reduction of the public debt.

2. Taxation should be for revenue. We can no longer afford punitive taxes or experimental taxes.

3. Taxation should not dry up the sources of revenue.

4. This means that the reduction of wartime taxes should come first on revenue-creating activities.

5. The excess-profits tax should be promptly repealed, as soon as a decisive cut is made in war production. Nothing is more needed than that the lure of large profits should cause certain businesses to expand rapidly, as an offset to the contraction of businesses operating on war orders.

6. We should eliminate double taxation on dividend income. Dividends should be exempt from taxation in the first bracket, though not from surtaxes.

7. The corporation income tax should be greatly reduced.

Treasury Policy and Wealthy Stockholders

8. There should be a radical revision of law and Treasury policy with respect to the section of the Revenue Act concerned with the accumulation of corporate profits, where such accumulation makes possible the avoidance of high surtaxes by wealthy stockholders. Nothing could be more helpful to the country than the growth of new industries like Henry Ford's, built up by withholding dividends from wealthy stockholders. I have studied enough cases of Treasury action in connection with this section to be satisfied that the Congress should radically revise this section of the law. Corporations with a few large stockholders should have the same freedom here that corporations with many small stockholders have. If the avoidance of surtaxes is an

incident to the carrying forward of sound corporate policies, it should not be penalized.

9. We should retain and greatly reduce the rate of the capital-gains tax. We should thereby much increase the revenue of the government, since very many more such transactions would take place. Most of all, we should facilitate the rapid shifting of capital from one activity to another, which is necessary in a flexible dynamic economy and above all, in an economy making a shift from war to peace activities. I should also take off the six months' limitation on capital-gains taxes, especially as a means of helping to restore breadth and activity in the stock market, making an exception here for those men whose primary activity is trading in the stock market.

Income Tax in Upper Brackets

10. We should reduce personal income taxes in the upper brackets radically. Excessive rates in the upper brackets, coupled with the very high rates of the estate tax, have paralyzed the economic activity of many of the most productive brains of the country, turning men of great ability and economic knowledge and large investing power into timid men. We cannot afford the luxury of such taxation in the future. We must set such men to work again, and we must set their capital to work again in risk-taking, dynamic activities.

The Committee for Economic Development has made an admirable and thorough study of our postwar tax problem.[25] With much of their reasoning I am in agreement, but I do not think they draw the full consequences of their reasoning.

They estimate the total of incomes over $500,000 at only $120 million. Of this they would take in taxes $80 million, leaving only $40 million as retained income to the recipients.

I am sure that taxes like this would paralyze all initiative on the part of men who would be extremely alert and dynamic and useful in the economic life of the country if the taxes were lower. The $80 million of revenue to the government would be very highly paid for by a drying up of the sources of revenue.

Incomes of from $100,000 to $500,000 they estimate at $600 million. Of this they would have the government take $300 million and leave

25. Summarized in their document, *A Postwar Federal Tax Plan for High Employment*, Foreword, August 1944.

$300 million to the recipients. Here, again, I am sure the rates are too high. I should tax this group rather at not over 40 per cent, and the group above $500,000 at not over 50 per cent. Even more important is adequate tax relief for the $25,000 to $100,000 group, younger men, on the average, with more unspent dynamic energy.

The CED, discussing the rates which it proposes in its report (page 14), recognizes that they may be too high.

Income Tax on Small Incomes

11. At the opposite end of the scale, I think the CED goes too far. Assuming a national income of $140 billion, it proposes to eliminate $77.6 billion from personal income taxes, and to tax only $57.6 billion under the personal income tax.

Most of the $77.6 billion to be free from income taxes is received by the lowest income earners (page 27). One argument offered by the CED for this elimination of small incomes (pages 7, 9 and 27) is that it is undesirable to cut into mass buying power, from the standpoint of getting full production. I do not think that this is a valid reason. Money which the government takes from the mass of the people is not removed from aggregate buying power. The government itself is a good spender, and government employees are good spenders.

I should desire to reduce taxes on the smaller incomes as much as possible for humanitarian reasons. But the government's need for revenue requires that much be got out of this $77.6 billion. One per cent of it would give $776 million of revenue — more than the total of all incomes above $100,000 if they were taxed 100 per cent. We must tax where the income is.

"Incentive Taxation"

12. Various proposals have been made for "incentive taxation"; as for example, that taxes shall be lighter on corporations which buy new equipment than on corporations which do not. Taxation of this kind means the substitution of one governmental rule for the multitudinous diversities of policy which individual corporations and businesses, each studying its own problem, would otherwise work out. Some corporations ought to expand greatly; others ought to contract. The men who are closest to the affairs of the corporation are the only ones qualified to determine in the individual case. Taxation should be *neutral* as far

as possible with respect to business decisions, which must rest on the individual circumstances.

XIV. Our Postwar Foreign Economic Policy

The great job of the governments in postwar reconstruction is not economic or financial. It is political. Governments have had long experience and have acquired great skill in arms and in diplomacy. Their great job now is to make a lasting peace, and to put overwhelming force behind international law. Given a great peace in the world, a world of international law and order which men and markets trust, there is no need for international economic cooperation of a permanent sort.

Except in emergencies, we do not wish international cooperation in economic matters; we wish rather international competition. International cooperation means cartels and combines. It means a few great transactions made en bloc, with a mixture of political and economic considerations in the bargaining, instead of a multitude of transactions made piecemeal, with purely business considerations governing the bargains.

We do not wish international cooperation in monetary matters except in emergencies. We wish competition, with the central money market of each country obliged to protect its own position, and pulled up when it overexpands credit through the loss of funds to other money markets which are not overexpanding.

What follows rests on the conviction that we have gone much too far in the abuse of our government's credit, and that if we are to save our solvency and to save our dollar we must pull up drastically when the war is over, both in foreign and domestic expenditure.

Supply Creates Its Own Demand in Foreign Trade

It rests on the conviction, too, that there is no need for the generation of artificial "purchasing power" in either the foreign or domestic fields.

In foreign trade, as in domestic trade, supply creates its own demand, if the markets are reasonably free and if the proportions are kept right. The great importing countries are the great exporting countries. Exports and imports go up and down together. Goods and services pay for goods and services. The great need is for open markets.

Second only to the objective of a great world peace I would place the adoption of liberal trade policies, which will create wide international markets in which a multitude of different kinds of goods can be exchanged for one another in multilateral trade.

Reduce American Tariffs Radically

It is eminently desirable that our government should cooperate politically with other governments in bringing this about, but if no other government on earth should join us in lowering tariffs, in freeing exchanges, in abolishing quotas, we should still perform our greatest service to our own people and to the outside world in doing it alone. We should then get a great share of whatever foreign trade there was; our markets would be open, foreign nations all over would bring us what they had to sell and would take our goods in exchange.

Indeed, I think the present is an admirable time for us to lower our tariffs drastically, apart from any reciprocity, particularly on manufactured goods. Even though now we have entered the peace, Europe can send very few manufactures here until she has made a reconversion of her industry, and until she has made great purchases of foreign raw materials. Low tariffs could thus hardly complicate the domestic readjustment problem for any American manufacturing industry.

But the knowledge that the American market for manufactured goods is open to Europe would give Europe credit. American banks would then be justified in giving the stronger European industries credits for raw materials and for a certain amount of vitally needed machinery, having in mind that the raw materials could be worked up and returned here promptly in cleaning up the credits. A bank is justified in financing a round trip, where it is not justified in financing a one-way passage. These credits would, moreover, facilitate the export of American raw materials and machinery to Europe, giving us markets which we should otherwise lack in the readjustment period.[26]

A low tariff would also intensify and consolidate the position of our dollar as *the* "key" currency of the world. Business between two countries which distrusted one another's currencies would be done in our dollar.

26. We need not make the mistake that we made after the last war of fearing that depreciating exchanges are going to give Europe an advantage in the export trade. See the *Chase Economic Bulletin*, Vol. 1, No. 3, February 28, 1921, pp. 18–19, and Vol. 13, No. 2, May 9, 1933, pp. 6–7 and 13–15.

Our greatest duty to ourselves and to the world, moreover, in the matter of currency and finance is to balance our own budget and to make our own gold dollar unshakably strong.

How to Get Good Moneys in Other Countries

We want good money in other countries. They must have good money if they are to revive. But good money is primarily the responsibility of each country separately. In the postwar period, 1919–1926, we saw France and Belgium going through convulsive periods of monetary depreciation, and we saw each of them pull up, reverse unsound tendencies and stabilize its currency at a depreciated level, with its own resources. Either of them could have done it earlier at a higher level, had it seen fit to do so.

We saw Germany, Austria, Hungary and Poland all requiring outside help in getting back to good money. When they were ready to submit to the necessary conditions, the outside world, which meant chiefly the United States, helped them. We gave them stabilization loans, conditioned on drastic internal reforms, and accompanied by foreign supervision of their finances and currencies for a period of time.

These loans were not large loans. For Austria, Hungary and Poland, some tens of millions of dollars each sufficed. The largest loan was the Dawes Plan Loan to Germany of $200 million.

The effect on German economic life of the new sound gold-based currency and the fiscal reforms was magical. Germany had been utterly demoralized in a morass of inflation.

With a sound currency and with stable finance, German industry swung into a great boom with an immense increase in employment. Interrupted by a short-lived crisis[27] in the winter of 1925–1926, this prosperity continued, with good employment, into 1929.

Germany is, of course, a special problem after this war, and Italy may be, but for most of the stricken countries of Europe we can use this method, and with a few hundred million dollars give them sound currencies and stable finances again.

Given sound currency and stable finance, moreover, these countries would have credit with the outside world. Private credit would flow in for investment in their industries. Germany, in fact, got far too much

27. See the *Chase Economic Bulletin,* Vol. 6, No. 1, April 2, 1926, called "German Business and Finance Under the Dawes Plan."

private credit following the Dawes Plan, because of the great excess of bank credit being created in the United States through the cheap money policies of the Federal Reserve Banks, discussed in an earlier section.

It is probable, moreover, that France, Belgium, the Netherlands, and certain other countries of Europe will have enough gold and dollars of their own not to need stabilization loans in rehabilitating their currencies and internal finances.

Private and Government Credit to Foreign Countries

In the period of the 1920's we made these stabilization loans with investors' money placed through investment bankers — private funds. The governments interested themselves in studying the conditions of the loans, our own government acting informally but effectively.

In bureaucratic circles there is great opposition to private finance in foreign lending. The bureaucrats are very eager to do it themselves and to do it with government money. I think it probably desirable that there should be a governmental institution, an *American* institution, designed to share risks and responsibility with American investment bankers or with foreign governments, or with investment bankers in other parts of the world, in making stabilization loans of this character to stricken governments, conditioned on the adoption of the gold standard and on drastic financial reforms by the borrowing government.

Private finance in the United States ought to welcome this government participation in the placement of foreign loans, for its own protection. When a government institution, moreover, participates in placing foreign loans, the requirements of the Securities Act should not apply. The Johnson Act should be repealed.

The government institution might be empowered to take a major share, but the ideal case would be one where the government's participation was 5 or 10 per cent and the private participation was 90 to 95 per cent. I am especially desirous of having a preponderant participation by private finance in these transactions, to limit the amounts of money used, and to make sure that the loans are carefully considered from the business point of view. But the government, whether its participation is large or small, should have a veto.

We can straighten out the moneys of the world and restore the trade of the world with very modest outlays, if the foregoing program should be adopted.

Our Treasury has lost perspective, both as to its ability to lend to Europe, and as to Europe's ability to repay. First, it has a dangerous sense of financial omnipotence, growing out of the ease with which it borrows from the banks. Second, Europe can only repay with goods and services. We must not create a new fabric of foreign loans, governmental and private, which cannot be repaid, as we did between 1918 and 1929.

No Problems of Foreign Exchange and of Capital Movements

When several different countries are all on the gold standard, there is no problem of keeping exchange rates fixed among them. The ordinary machinery of the foreign exchange market will make the clearances.

When countries have sound moneys, moreover, adequately buttressed by sound fiscal policies, there is no danger of capricious outward capital movements breaking their exchanges. Capricious large-scale capital movements of "hot money" are the product of uncertainty regarding the future of the money of the country which is losing capital, or, as we saw after the Hitler menace grew in Europe, the product of fear of war and of confiscation.

Would Europe go along with us on a program of this sort? I am sure that the Continent of Europe would. The serious obstacle is England. But the French, the Swiss, the Dutch, and the Scandinavian countries would all, I am sure, much prefer gold in their own vaults to deposits in British banks, or American banks, or quotas in an international stabilization fund. They have been "fed up" with their experience since 1931 with sterling. The head of one Scandinavian central bank said to me in 1938, "I have lost money in sterling; I have lost money in dollars; I have lost no money in gold!"

The Tyranny of Hitler and the Tyranny of Gold

The temporary success of the German monetary and economic experiment led to the superficial generalization on the part of certain opponents of the gold standard that gold had been proved to be unnecessary, that Hitler had found a way to do without gold, and that the long tyranny of gold was over. Parenthetically, I much prefer the tyranny of gold to the tyranny of Hitler. Gold is not capricious.

All it requires of men and governments and central banks is that they be honest, that they keep their promises, that they keep their demand liabilities safely within the limits of their quick assets, and that they create debts only when they can see how these debts can be paid. Gold has no intuitions, and gold has very little imagination.

Futile to Stabilize Exchanges When Currencies Are Unstable

When currencies are stabilized on gold, there is no need to do anything about exchange rates. The effort, on the other hand, to stabilize exchange rates without first stabilizing currencies is an utterly dangerous and futile, and terribly expensive, undertaking. We tried it for something more than four months after the Armistice in 1918. Our government lent approximately $3 billion to our European Allies between the Armistice and June 30 of 1919. They used this money down to March 20 of 1919 in stabilizing sterling, francs and other exchanges. The stabilization broke down when Morgan "unpegged" on March 20, but after this they still used the money in supporting the exchanges. We developed a great export boom on the strength of it and went into our wild postwar boom of 1919–1920 and our great crisis of 1920–1921 as a result.

Meanwhile, the billions of credit to Continental Europe used in supporting the exchanges did no good. Indeed, they did positive harm. They made it unnecessary for the finance ministers of Continental Europe to pull up and reform their finances and their currencies. The finance minister could delay internal financial and monetary reforms so long as he could print paper money and the outside world would take it.[28]

The proposals of the Bretton Woods Conference for stabilizing the exchanges without stabilizing the currencies would repeat this episode. The credits proposed under the Fund are not to be accompanied by demands for financial and currency reforms and, above all, are not to be accompanied by demands for firm money markets to protect currency

---

28. See *Chase Economic Bulletin*, Vol. 1, No. 1, October 5, 1920, "Three and a Half Billion Dollar Floating Debt of Europe to Private Creditors in America," and Vol. 2, No. 1, January 12, 1922, "Artificial Stabilization of Exchange Condemned — Outline of a Fundamental Solution." See also the four addresses and articles listed in footnote 29.

reserves. On the contrary, the whole spirit of the plan is one of cheap money throughout the world. Lord Keynes, who originated the plan, definitely wishes to do away with the restrictive qualities of the gold standard, which restrains the overexpansion of credit, and the British appear to follow him in this.

Britain appears still obsessed with the theory that she can force full employment by further expansion of money and credit. With the pound blocked in the foreign exchanges, with the pound no longer valid even among the units of the British Empire, and with the certainty that a free pound would go very low in the foreign exchanges, the policy of postwar credit expansion on England's part does not look promising. Britain is more dependent on foreign trade, both import and export, than any other great country. She must buy so much from the outside world in connection with her domestic industrial activities that her ruined pound would not serve the purpose, even though made very abundant at home.

We want to help England. We must help England. But we shall not help England by going into a scheme which could easily pull our own currency down with hers.

I reject both the International Monetary Fund and the International Bank for Reconstruction and Development, on many grounds. I have discussed them, and my alternative constructive proposals, at length in recent publications,[29] and space limits prevent further discussion here.

Charity Rather Than Unsound Credits

The immediate postwar problem is, for many countries, not a problem of credit, but a problem of charity. We cannot support Europe; we can help her. Europe is still emphatically a going concern in agricul-

29. An address before the Los Angeles Chamber of Commerce, "Postwar Stabilization of Foreign Exchange," May 11, 1943, published in full in the *Commercial and Financial Chronicle* of May 20 and May 27, 1943, in *Vital Speeches* of June 1, 1943, and in *The Bankers Magazine* of May 1943; "Postwar Foreign Exchange Stabilization Further Considered," *Commercial and Financial Chronicle,* December 16, 1943; "International Currency, Gold Versus Bancor or Unitas," an address before the Chamber of Commerce of the State of New York, February 3, 1944, published in the proceedings of the Chamber, in *Vital Speeches* of April 1, 1944, and in the *Commercial and Financial Chronicle* of February 10, 1944; and "The Keynes-Morgenthau Plan as Revised by the Experts of Thirty Nations," *Commercial and Financial Chronicle,* May 4, 1944. Reprints of these documents may be obtained from the Economists' National Committee on Monetary Policy, 1 Madison Avenue, New York 10, and from the Capital Research Company, 650 South Spring Street, Los Angeles 14.

ture,[30] but important parts of Europe must have food from the outside as soon as we can get it in, until the next peacetime harvest. A great deal of manufacturing capacity remains in Europe, some active, some needing only raw materials to become active, some needing modest patching up to become effective again. There is a real basis for credit in these cases. With the war over and the people free to turn their energies to producing things to live on, they will need much less charity than many suppose. There may be need for charity rather than credit in certain vital instrumentalities of production where the bombing has been worst. Even as we give charity, we should insist on internal financial and currency reforms. Gifts, as well as loans, should do the recipient permanent good.

Life will be hard in postwar Europe, wages and standard of living must be low. A great deal of capital has been destroyed. Interest rates must, therefore, be high to compel economy in the use of existing capital, to invite foreign capital, and to encourage savings. Given peace, given settled governments, given the restoration of sound finances and sound domestic moneys, Europe can rebuild rapidly.

XV. Summary

The only effective economic planning which the government can do is planning to increase the flexibility of economic life; to restore freedom of movement of goods, capital, labor and enterprise; to take sand out of the oil. Neither in the foreign nor in the domestic field is it possible for the government, or chambers of commerce, or anybody else, to make one general plan. The job is a piecemeal job in which, in the foreign field, we deal with different countries, and with industries in different countries, separately. In the domestic field, it is a piecemeal job for each industrial establishment, separately studying its own markets, its own costs and its own sources of supply; for the workers, each seeking the best job he can get; and for the owners of capital, each seeking the best employment for his funds. The people must work it out.

30. See the studies, *Food for Postwar Europe: How Much and What?* and *Livestock in Continental Europe During World War II,* Food Research Institute, Stanford University, March and September 1944.

Note

A REFUTATION OF KEYNES' ATTACK ON THE DOCTRINE THAT AGGREGATE SUPPLY CREATES AGGREGATE DEMAND — BASIC FALLACIES IN THE KEYNESIAN SYSTEM[1]

Lord Keynes is the leading advocate of the purchasing power doctrine, and the leading opponent of the doctrine that supply creates its own demand. The present article is concerned with Keynes' attack on the doctrine that supply creates its own demand.

I regard Keynes as a dangerously unsound thinker. His influence in the Administration has been very great. His influence upon most of the economists in the employ of the government is incredibly great. There has arisen a volume of theoretical literature regarding Keynes almost equal to that which has arisen around Karl Marx.[2] His followers are satisfied that he has destroyed the long accepted economic doctrine that aggregate supply and aggregate demand grow together. It seems necessary to analyze Keynes' argument with respect to this point.

Keynes Ignores the Essential Point in the Doctrine He Attacks

Keynes presents his argument in his *The General Theory of Employment, Interest and Money,* published in 1936. But he nowhere in the book takes account of the law of equilibrium among the industries, which has always been recognized as an essential part of the doctrine that supply creates its own demand. He takes as his target a seemingly crude statement from J. S. Mill's *Principles of Political Economy* (Book 3, Chap. 14, par. 2) which follows:

" 'What constitutes the means of payment for commodities is simply commodities. Each person's means of paying for the productions of other people consist of those which he himself possesses. All sellers are inevitably, and by the meaning of the word, buyers. Could we suddenly double the productive powers of the country, we should double the supply of commodities in every market; but we should, by the same stroke, double the purchasing power. Everybody would

1. See page 14. This is an abridgement of my article, "Equilibrium Creates Purchasing Power," in the *Commercial and Financial Chronicle* of January 25, 1945. Reprints of the full article may be had from the Capital Research Company, 650 South Spring Street, Los Angeles 14, or from the Economists' National Committee on Monetary Policy, 1 Madison Avenue, New York 10. — *Benjamin M. Anderson*

2. I have not read much of this elaborate literature. Keynes himself I have studied with care. I think it probable that other critics have anticipated many of the points I make here, and I would gladly give them credit if I knew.

bring a double demand as well as supply: everybody would be able to buy twice as much, because every one would have twice as much to offer in exchange.' "

Now this passage by itself does not present the essentials of the doctrine. If we doubled the productive power of the country, we should not double the supply of commodities in every market, and if we did, we should not clear the markets of the double supply in every market. If we doubled the supply in the salt market, for example, we should have an appalling glut of salt. The great increases would come in the items where demand is elastic. We should change very radically the proportions in which we produced commodities.

But it is unfair to Mill to take this brief passage out of its context and present it as if it represented the heart of the doctrine. If Keynes had quoted only the three sentences immediately following, he would have introduced us to the conception of balance and proportion and equilibrium which is the heart of the doctrine. Mill's next few lines are as follows:

"It is probable, indeed, that there would now be a superfluity of certain things. Although the community would willingly double its aggregate consumption, it may already have as much as it desires of some commodities, and it may prefer to do more than double its consumption of others, or to exercise its increased purchasing power on some new thing. If so, the supply will adapt itself accordingly, and the values of things will continue to conform to their cost of production."

Keynes, furthermore, ignores entirely the rich, fine work done by such writers as J. B. Clark and the Austrian School, who elaborated the laws of proportionality and equilibrium.

The doctrine that supply creates its own demand, as presented by John Stuart Mill, assumes a proper equilibrium among the different kinds of production, assumes proper terms of exchange (i.e., price relationships) among different kinds of products, assumes proper relations between prices and costs. And the doctrine expects competition and free markets to be the instrumentality by means of which these proportions and price relations will be brought about. The modern version of the doctrine[3] would make explicit certain additional factors. There must be a proper balance in the international balance sheet. If foreign debts are excessive in relation to the volume of foreign trade, grave disorders can come. Moreover, the money and capital markets must be in a state of balance. When there is an excess of bank credit used as a substitute for savings, when bank credit goes in undue amounts into capital uses and speculative uses, impairing the liquidity of bank assets, or when the total volume of money and credit is expanded far beyond the growth of production and trade, disequilibria arise, and, above all, the *quality* of credit is impaired. Confidence may be suddenly shaken and a countermovement may set in.

With respect to all these points, automatic market forces tend to restore equilibrium in the absence of overwhelming governmental interference.

3. See the *Chase Economic Bulletin,* June 12, 1931.

Far from considering the intricacies of the interrelations of markets, prices and different kinds of production, Keynes prefers to look at things in block. I quote:

"In dealing with the theory of employment I propose, therefore, to make use of only two fundamental units of quantity, namely, quantities of money-value and quantities of employment. The first of these is strictly homogeneous, and the second can be made so. For, in so far as different grades and kinds of labor and salaried assistance enjoy a more or less fixed relative remuneration, the quantity of employment can be sufficiently defined for our purpose by taking an hour's employment of ordinary labor as our unit *and weighting an hour's employment of special labor in proportion to its remuneration; i.e., an hour of special labor remunerated at double ordinary rates will count as two units.*" [Italics mine.][4] . . .

"It is my belief that much unnecessary perplexity can be avoided if we limit ourselves strictly to the two units, money and labor, when we are dealing with the behavior of the economic system as a whole. . . ."[5]

Procedure of this kind is empty and tells us nothing about economic life. How empty it is becomes apparent when we observe that these two supposedly independent units of quantity, namely, "quantities of money value" and "quantities of employment" are both merely quantities of money value. If ten laborers working for $2 a day are dismissed and two laborers working for $10 a day are taken on, there is no change in the volume of employment, by Keynes' method of reckoning, as is obvious from the italicized portion of the quotation above. His "quantity of employment" is not a quantity of employment. It is a quantity of money received by laborers who are employed.[6]

Throughout Keynes' analysis he is working with aggregate, block concepts. He has an aggregate supply function and an aggregate demand function.[7] But nowhere is there any discussion of the interrelationships of the elements in these vast aggregates. Nowhere is there a recognition that elements in the aggregate supply give rise to demand for other elements in the aggregate supply. Purchasing power and production are sharply sundered.

The Function of Prices

It is part of the equilibrium doctrine that prices tend to equate supply and demand in various markets, commodities, labor, capital, and so on. If prices go down in particular markets this constitutes a signal for producers to produce less, and for consumers to consume more. In the markets, on the other hand, where prices are rising we have a signal for producers to produce more, for consumers to consume less, and a signal for men in fields where prices are less satis-

---

4. *The General Theory of Employment, Interest and Money*, p. 41.
5. *Ibid.*, p. 43.
6. See my criticism of the analogous procedure by Irving Fisher in his "Equation of Exchange," in my *Value of Money*, Macmillan, New York, 1917 and Richard R. Smith, New York, 1936, pp. 158–62.
7. *Ibid.*, p. 29.

factory to shift their labor and their capital to the more productive field. Free prices, telling the truth about supply and demand, thus constitute the great equilibrating factor.

The Function of the Rate of Interest

Among these prices is the rate of interest. The traditional doctrine is that the rate of interest equates supply and demand in the capital market and equates saving and investment. Interest is reward for saving and inducement to saving. The old doctrine which looked upon consumer's thrift as the primary source of capital is inadequate. It must be broadened to include producer's thrift, especially corporate thrift, and direct capitalization, as when the farmer uses his spare time in building fences and putting other improvements on his farm, or when the farmer lets his flocks and herds increase instead of selling off the whole of the annual increase. It must include governmental thrift, as when government taxes to pay down public debt or when government taxes for capital purposes instead of borrowing. The doctrine needs a major qualification, moreover, with respect to the use of bank credit for capital purposes.[8]

Keynes' Attack on the Interest Rate as Equilibrator

It is with respect to the interest rate as the equilibrating factor that Keynes has made his most vigorous assault upon prevailing views. Where economists generally have held that saving and paying off debt where possible are good things, Keynes holds that they are bad. He deprecates depreciation reserves for business corporations, amortization of public debt by municipalities, and additions to corporate surpluses out of earnings. His philosophy is responsible for the ill-fated undistributed-profits tax, adopted in 1936, which we abandoned with a great sigh of relief in 1938.

Keynes gives two reasons for his rejection of prevailing ideas with respect to interest and savings. The first will be found on pages 110 and 111 of his *General Theory*. I quote:

"The influence of changes in the rate of interest on the amount actually saved is of paramount importance, but is *in the opposite direction* to that usually supposed. For even if the attraction of the larger future income to be earned from a higher rate of interest has the effect of diminishing the propensity to consume, nevertheless we can be certain that a rise in the rate of interest will have the effect of reducing the amount actually saved. For aggregate saving is governed by aggregate investment; a rise in the rate of interest (*unless it is offset by a corresponding change in the demand-schedule for investment*) [italics mine] will diminish investment; hence a rise in the rate of interest must have the ef-

8. See my *Value of Money*, Macmillan, New York, 1917 and Richard R. Smith, New York, 1936, pp. 484 n., 484–89; my address before the Indiana Bankers Association, published in *The Chase*, the house organ of the Chase National Bank, November 1920; *Chase Economic Bulletin*, November 1926, and May 1936. See also my article on "The Future of Interest Rates" in the *Commercial and Financial Chronicle* of August 26, 1943.

fect of reducing incomes to a level at which saving is decreased in the same measure as investment. Since incomes will decrease by a greater absolute amount than investment, it is, indeed, true that, when the rate of interest rises, the rate of consumption will decrease. But this does not mean that there will be a wider margin for saving. On the contrary, saving and spending will both decrease."9

This is an extraordinarily superficial argument. The whole case is given away by the parenthetical passage "(unless it is offset by a corresponding change in the demand-schedule for investment)." The usual *cause* of an increase in the rate of interest is a *rise* in the demand-schedule for investment. Interest usually rises because of an increased demand for capital on the part of those who wish to increase their investments; on the part of businesses which wish to expand, speculators for the rise, home builders, and so on. Usually, when the interest rate rises, it rises because investment is increasing, and the increased savings which rising interest rates induce are promptly invested. Indeed, investment often *precedes* saving[10] in such a situation, through an expansion of bank credit, also induced by the rising rate of interest.

Keynes is assuming an *uncaused* rise in the rate of interest, and he has very little difficulty in disposing of this. But economic phenomena do not occur without *causes*.

Keynes' second argument against the prevailing doctrine will be found in his Chapter 14 (*loc. cit.*) called "The Classical Theory of the Rate of Interest." Here (with a diagram on page 180) he complains that the static theory of interest has not taken account of the possibility of changes in the level of income, or the possibility that the level of income is actually a function of the rate of investment.

Now it may be observed that Keynes is here introducing dynamic considerations into a static analysis. By this device one may equally destroy the law of supply and demand, the law of cost of production, the capitalization theory, or any other of the standard working tools of the static analysis.

The static economist has known all this almost from the beginning. He has protected himself in general by the well-known phrase, *"caeteris paribus"* (other things equal), and the general level of income has been among those other things assumed to be unchanged. Moreover, the static economist has concerned himself with infinitesimal variations in the region of the margin, a device which Keynes is very glad to borrow from static economics in his concep-

9. Harold G. Moulton, whose book, *The Formation of Capital*, was published at about the same time that Keynes' book appeared, independently presents essentially the same argument which Moulton calls "The Dilemma of Savings." I have discussed Moulton's view in the *Chase Economic Bulletin*, May 12, 1936, "Eating the Seed Corn."

10. The Keynesian reader will observe that I am using the word "savings" in the ordinary sense, and not in Keynes' peculiar sense. I am under no obligation to use Keynes' terminology, since Keynes himself, as shown in the first sentence of the passage quoted above, is discussing the usual view of the relation of the rate of interest to savings. To the extent that there is any shift in the meaning of terms in the course of the argument, it is done by Keynes and not by me. I use the word "savings" in the ordinary sense throughout.

tion of the "marginal propensity to consume" and in his initial conception of the "marginal efficiency of capital."

The Multiplier

Rejecting the function of the interest rate[11] as the equilibrator of saving and investment, Keynes is so impressed with the danger of thrift that he finally convinces himself in one of his major doctrines that *no part* of an increase in income which is not consumed is invested; that *all of the unconsumed increase in income is hoarded*. This major doctrine is the much praised Keynesian "investment multiplier theory." (*Loc. cit.,* pp. 113–19.) If an investment is made it gives a certain amount of employment, but that is not the end of the story. Investment tends to multiply itself in subsequent stages of spending. The recipients of the proceeds of the investment spend at least part of it, and the recipients of their spending spend part of what they get, and so on. How many times does the original investment multiply itself? Keynes gives a definite mathematical answer in which his investment multiplier rests solely on what he calls "the marginal propensity to consume." The multiplier figure rests on the assumption that the subsequent spending consists entirely of purchases for consumption. None of the unconsumed increase in income is invested. If any of the recipients of the proceeds of the investment should add to their expenditures for consumption any investment at all, the mathematics of the Keynes multiplier would be upset, and the multiplier would be increased. I am glad to find myself in agreement with Professor James W. Angell on this point.[12]

The Relation of Savings to Investment

The preoccupation with the varying relationship of saving to investment seems to me superficial in the extreme. Investment tends to equal saving in a reasonably good business situation, when bank credit is not expanding. In a strong upward move, when bank credit is readily obtainable, investment tends to exceed saving because men borrow at the banks and because expanding bank credit facilitates the issue of new securities. In a crisis and in the liquidation that follows a crisis, saving exceeds investment. Men and businesses are saving to pay down debts and especially to repay bank loans — a necessary preliminary to a subsequent revival of business. But the *reasons* for these changes in the relation of saving to investment are the all-important things. The relation of saving to investment is itself a very superficial thing. The *reasons* lie in the factors which govern the prospects of profits, including the price and cost equilibrium, the industrial equilibrium, and the *quality* of credit.

Keynes strives desperately to rule out bank credit as a factor in the relation of savings to investment. At one point he does it very simply indeed:

11. Keynes' own theory of interest I have discussed in my article, "The Future of Interest Rates," in the *Commercial and Financial Chronicle* of August 26, 1943.

12. James W. Angell, *Investment and Business Cycles,* McGraw-Hill, New York, 1941, pp. 190–91.

"We have, indeed, to adjust for the creation and discharge of debts (including changes in the quantity of credit or money) ; but since for the community as a whole the increase or decrease of the aggregate creditor position is always exactly equal to the increase or decrease of the aggregate debtor position, this complication also cancels out when we are dealing with aggregate investment."[13]

But bank credit is not so easily canceled out as a factor in the volume of money available for investment. The borrower at the bank is, of course, both debtor and creditor to the bank when he gets his loan. But his debt is an obligation which is *not* money, and his credit is a demand deposit, which *is* money. When he uses this money for investment, he is making an investment in addition to the investment which comes from savings.

On pages 81 to 85 of the same book, Keynes engages in a very confused further argument on this point.

"It is supposed that a depositor and his bank can somehow contrive between them to perform an operation by which savings can disappear into the banking system so that they are lost to investment, or, contrariwise, that the banking system can make it possible for investment to occur, to which no saving corresponds. But no one can save without acquiring an asset, whether it be cash or a debt or capital-goods; and no one can acquire an asset which he did not previously possess, unless *either* an asset of equal value is newly produced *or* someone else parts with an asset of that value which he previously had. In the first alternative there is a corresponding new investment: in the second alternative someone else must be dissaving an equal sum. For his loss of wealth must be due to his consumption exceeding his income. . . ."

But the assumption that a man who parts with an asset for cash is losing wealth, and that this must be due to his consumption exceeding his income, is purely gratuitous. The man who sells an asset for cash may hold his cash or he may reinvest it in something else. It is not "dissaving" unless he spends it for current consumption, and he does not have to do that unless he wants to. Indeed on the next page (p. 83) the man who holds the additional money corresponding to the new bank credit is said to be *saving*. "Moreover, the savings which result from this decision are just as genuine as any other savings. No one can be compelled to own the additional money corresponding to the new bank credit, unless he deliberately prefers to hold more money rather than some other form of wealth."

Keynes' confusion here could be interpreted as due to his effort to carry out a puckish joke on the Keynesians. He had got them excited in his earlier writings about the relation between savings and investment. Then, in his *General Theory,* he propounds the doctrine that savings are always equal to investment.[14] This makes the theology harder for the devout follower to understand, and calls, moreover, for a miracle by which the disturbing factor of bank credit may be abolished. This miracle Keynes attempts in the pages cited above, with, I think, indifferent success.

13. *General Theory*, p. 75.   14. *Loc. cit.*, pp. 61–65.

I take occasion here to protest against the dangerous identification of bank expansion with savings which is part of the Keynesian doctrine. (See *Chase Economic Bulletin,* June 1928, "Bank Expansion versus Savings.") This doctrine is particularly dangerous today when we find our vast increase in money and bank deposits growing out of war finance described as "savings," just because somebody happens to hold them at a given moment of time. On this doctrine, the greater the inflation, the greater the savings! The alleged excess of savings over investment in the period, 1924–1929, was merely a failure to invest *all* of the rapidly expanding bank credit. All of the real savings of this period was invested, and far too much new bank credit in addition.

The Wage-Rate as Equilibrator of the Supply and Demand of Labor

Keynes also tries to destroy the accepted doctrine regarding the rate of wages as the equilibrating factor between the supply and demand of labor. He attempts at various places to suggest that a reduction in money wages "may be" ineffective in increasing the demand for labor (*e.g., loc. cit.,* p. 13), but he nowhere, so far as I can find, positively states this. He does suggest (*loc. cit.,* p. 264) that a fall in wages would mean a fall in prices, and that this could lead to embarrassment and insolvency to entrepreneurs who are heavily indebted, and to an increase in the real burden of the national debt. On this point it is sufficient to say that the fall in wages in a depression usually follows, and does not precede, the fall in prices, and that it is usually more moderate than the fall in prices.

Keynes accuses other economists of reasoning regarding the demand-schedule for labor on the basis of a single industry, and then, without substantial modification, making a simple extension of the argument to industry as a whole (pp. 258–59). But this is merely additional evidence that he has ignored John Bates Clark's *Distribution of Wealth,* and the theory of costs of the Austrian School, for whom the law of costs, including wages, is merely the law of the leveling of values among the different industries. I think, moreover, that the studies of Paul Douglas, summarized in the text on pages 20–21, dealing with the elasticity of the demand for labor as a whole, constitute a sufficient answer to Keynes on this point.

But the practical issue does not usually relate to wages as a whole. The wages of nonunion labor, and especially agricultural labor, usually recede promptly and sometimes to extremes, in a depression. The issue usually relates to union wage scales held so high in particular industries that employment falls off very heavily in these industries, and that the industries constitute bottlenecks.

But Keynes does not come to the theoretical conclusion that a reduction in money wages could not bring about an increase in employment. He rather reaches the practical conclusion that this is not the best way to do it. Instead, he would prefer in a closed economy, i.e., one without foreign trade, to make such readjustments as are necessary by manipulations of money, and for an open economy, i.e., one with large foreign trade, to accomplish it by letting the foreign exchanges fluctuate (p. 270).

Chapter 3

FINANCING HIGH-LEVEL EMPLOYMENT

John Maurice Clark[1]

I. The Problem

TWO REVOLUTIONS

Within little more than fifteen years, this country has witnessed two momentous revolutions: one in economic thinking and the other in the economic functions of government.

In economics, it has suddenly become respectable to recognize that not all income is automatically and promptly spent, that the volume of spending does not take care of itself, and that its behavior is one of the chief active factors responsible for business ups and downs.

In politics the problems created by long-continued depression have become the primary peacetime concern of government. Throughout the nineteenth century the state had been conceived as a policeman, which in theory limited itself to telling people what they should not do; and left them free, within the bounds so defined, to pursue their interests as they saw fit. There was unquestioning confidence that this liberty was all the incentive that was needed (plus protective tariffs?) to develop our resources fully and effectively, in an economy organized on the basis of free exchange. This attitude persisted while the state grew increasingly busy restraining particular abuses.

Since the great depression of the 1930's, the state has been desperately trying to learn how to turn itself from a restraining into an energizing agency. The change is basic, fundamental; the methods used for one purpose may be inappropriate to the other, and some of them may have become liabilities for the new dominant purpose. Thus it is no wonder that there is confusion of counsel about how to do the new job. Most of us admit uncertainty, including uncertainty as to how far to trust the judgment of those of us who confidently claim to know the answer.

1. Professor of Economics, Columbia University.

War suspended the problem; but the coming of victory now brings with it the prospect of millions released from the armed forces and other millions from munition-making, dumping into our laps a problem of expanding peacetime production faster and farther than it has ever expanded before, if these millions are to be offered full-time jobs. And the general mood is: "They must be offered jobs, somehow — but we don't just know how it is going to be done."

This essay makes no claim to final knowledge as to the precise methods. Some of its conclusions must be labeled "tentative," but the time seems to call for a good deal of this kind of exposure of tentative conclusions to public criticism and discussion. Fortunately, the most fundamental and difficult parts of the problem are not the ones which have to be settled this year or next. They will in any case be settled by the processes of popular government, to which many proposals will contribute, and no one will emerge unmodified as the final program. Frankly tentative findings are still in order, though the proposer bears a responsibility for bringing them as near the blueprint stage as possible. In the present instance, I shall at almost every turn be drawing working conclusions about difficult questions on which years of intensive research might fail to yield certainty. There will be time for a good deal of research before the most crucial matters of policy have to be decided, but we can hardly hope to have reached certainty on all points even then. We should be satisfied if we can have reached a fairly clear judgment as to what course involves the least dangerous uncertainties.

GOALS AND STANDARDS

Methods Depend on Standards of Achievement

If the country sets for itself a rigorous standard of completely full employment, with no room for cyclical recessions of any substantial magnitude, and if this is an absolute and unconditional "must," the only system which can meet this test will be an outright collectivistic economy, and probably one of the centrally administered type. On the other hand, if the maintenance of a system of competitive private enterprise is an unconditional "must," then there are bound to be fluctuations, at least, involving spasmodic fits of underemployment; and we must adjust our requirements to what a competitive system is capable of producing. In general, unconditional "musts," settled in advance without investigating what they are going to cost, are likely to prove an expensive luxury.

It is tremendously important to decide, knowingly and deliberately, which things come first with us and which come second, and not to let this decision be made unconsciously, as a by-product of following lines of least resistance in what seem like minor matters. It should go without saying that the first thing is to come as near as we can to finding out what the possibilities are that are open to us, and how they are tied together. For example, Sir William Beveridge has said that his plan for social security can be financed only if employment is maintained at a fairly high level. It can provide for normal contingencies and fluctuations, but not for large-scale chronic stagnation.

If what we are aiming at is a level of employment high enough to make an adequate and comprehensive social security system feasible, it might be attainable with a system of prevailingly private enterprise; but if we insist on carrying the principle of "jobs, not money benefits" farther than that, and will not tolerate the prospect of having to rely to any very substantial extent on unemployment benefits in place of jobs, then it becomes doubtful whether any private or mixed system can meet the requirements. If we set our sights so high as to rule out all cyclical fluctuations of employment, the doubt becomes a virtual certainty. So it is important how high we do set our sights.

How Full Is "Full Employment"?

In the first place, what is employment? I hope it is not childish to stress the proposition that when one is employed, one is doing something. If the worker does not work, there is no employment, no matter what the employer does, or tries to do, to "give the worker a job." A job is not merely a possession of the worker; and it is not something which an employer by himself can "give" a worker. All the employer can give is a position and a promise of pay, which is properly contingent on the worker's performance. It represents an opportunity, and it rests partly with the worker to turn it into a job. I have known workmen who had jobs, but did not employ themselves at them.

The point, which need not be labored further, is that the idea of a right to employment is meaningless without some standard of performance on the part of the worker. The practical question is, of course, how it is decided whether a particular worker has failed to meet the minimum standard necessary to holding a particular job, and what happens to him then. "Full employment" must leave room for some right of discharge, as a last resort; though that right must not be exercised as irresponsibly and arbitrarily as it frequently has been in the flourishing days of individualism.

It is a matter of course that "full employment" does not mean that every would-be job-holder has a job all the time. It does not mean that every "employable" worker has a job all the time. It does not even mean that every employable worker has a job except when he has voluntarily left one or refrained from taking one that was offered. Over and above this, there are some kinds of unemployment which are actually useful, or are inseparable from useful changes or processes. In these cases, there is a responsibility somewhere to keep the amount to a practicable minimum, and to make just and reasonable provision for those on whom the burden falls. But an indiscriminate demand for complete removal is not helpful.

Seasons and Frictions

Fishing and harvesting are unavoidably seasonal; the manufacture of clothing is more so than necessary. Much can be done to make such jobs steadier or to dovetail different jobs together. Some of this is the employer's responsibility, some of it the worker's, and some is a larger matter of organizing the market so that reserves of labor may be pooled and not kept in separate compartments by particular industries or employers. Dock labor, for example, is casual, and for casual labor a well-organized market can reduce what would otherwise be an unnecessarily large surplus, and increase the number of days' work per year for the average worker.

Workers do some choosing between occupations, industries and employers, by a process of trial and error. This is their proper privilege though vocational guidance can help them to do it more efficiently and safeguard them from the danger of developing into chronic casuals. A domestic servant may decline an offer of a job, thinking that if she holds out a week or two longer, she may get one with a higher wage. That is her privilege, and it is no one's duty to hire her today.

An employer with a vacancy selects from among the candidates and may keep the vacancy open if no suitable candidate offers. That is his proper privilege, though the typical employer's idea of the number of candidates he would like to have to select from, and the standard of competence he would like to set, will need adjusting downward if employment reaches satisfactory levels. And he has an ultimate right of discharge, subject to similar adjustments. Some workers who are hopeless misfits in one establishment will fit elsewhere, others may not, and for them society has a responsibility.

Competition implies that some enterprises will decline or go out of business, while others grow, and the same thing may happen to localities. Then workers must shift, and if a worker does not want to move to a new community the question of rights and responsibilities becomes delicate. He has not an unqualified right to employment in his home town. General economic fluctuations add to these problems, and they cannot be completely eliminated, though they should be much reduced.

Progress in methods of production, and in products, implies some displacement. It should be minimized, and retraining and re-engagement facilitated, so that it would be a matter of turnover rather than of permanent "technological unemployment" for capable workers. But so long as there are competition, innovation, movement and free choice in the economy, there will be jobs coming to an end and others opening up, requiring shifts of employment which will not all be voluntary, and which will take time before a new job is found. So there will always be some unemployed. At the height of the war effort we had overemployment equivalent to more than ten million workers, including overtime, and there were still the better part of a million unemployed.

More Vacancies Than Applicants

Sir William Beveridge defines "full employment" as a condition in which there are more vacancies than idle workers looking for jobs. This is interesting as recognizing the vacancy side of the picture, and suggesting that unemployment might be reported as a net excess of idle workers over vacancies, if the number of vacancies can be measured. But there seems to be no obvious reason why it is either desirable or practicable that this net excess should be exactly zero. Perhaps the essence of the conception is that there should be no unemployment due to an aggregate shortage of job openings, as distinct from the unavoidable movements of a dynamic economy; but this hardly lends itself to measurement.

Another conception hinges on the length of time a worker is out of work. For instance, full employment requires that no qualified and willing worker should be out of work longer than it takes to canvass market possibilities thoroughly — say three or four months — plus the time it takes to retrain and qualify for a new kind of job, if the only available openings require retraining.

The "Float" of Unemployed

Perhaps the only practically usable standard is a statistical rule-of-thumb, which is framed with an eye to as many of these different conceptions as possible. It should be based on past experience, revised in the light of all the analysis that can be made of the types of unemployment that are included and their causes, and used elastically, with recognition that an economy which is in the midst of far-reaching shifts and readjustments actually needs a larger unemployed "float" than one which is more nearly stable. It would have both more unemployed and more vacancies. For this reason the normal "float" in this country during the postwar transition will be larger than a long-run peacetime normal. For the latter, three million does not seem too large, as a tentative first approximation, with the proviso that if private enterprise is kept, even with reasonably successful efforts at stabilization, there will be fluctuations which will raise the average, taking active and dull times together.

Of course, it is misleading to call this "full employment." The chief defense for using this term is the fact that it is probably too generally accepted to be dislodged, and is used to designate a standard which the country is determined to attain. It is dangerous, however, to leave the term unqualified because in that state it indicates something that is simply unattainable. A better conception, suggesting what is probably a better approach to the problem, is "high-level employment, as stable as it can be made."

Valuable Product and Fair Wage

"Employment" implies producing something worth producing, and statements of goals usually include also a fair wage. Both these ideas will take a good deal of defining. The "fair wage" cannot safely be defined simply as one we should like to see paid. It may perhaps be defined as a structure of wages about as high as industry in general is productive enough to support, with differentials giving sufficient recognition to differences in efficiency. This definition might be differently construed in socialistic and private-enterprise systems. In a socialistic system, there would be more discretion about the size of the differentials. In a system of private enterprise, they will create difficulty unless they come somewhere near making the hiring of a given grade of worker as cheap to the employer as other available ways in which he might get the same quantity and quality of work done. For some workers, this might mean undesirably low wages, and this creates a problem. The nation, for its own sake, may need to pay some workers more than they are "worth" by this test, and to do it as a "dole" has drawbacks, while to insist that industry should bear this load in its wage-costs creates another problem, and might be an obstacle to employment of these workers. These problems should be recognized and attacked with a combination of candor and ingenuity. In the meantime, we are on notice that the problems exist.

Income for the Sake of Jobs

One popular indoor sport is the game of estimating how big the national income will have to be, and how much we shall have to spend on consumption and capital outlays, in billions of dollars of current purchasing power, in order to give everybody a job, two or three years after final victory. The reader may use any of the available estimates he likes; they all alike call for a great deal more income than the country has ever produced before in peacetime. I have estimated, trying to be on the conservative side, that it calls for at least 20 per cent more real income per capita than we ever enjoyed before the war. The chief reason for being conservative is that the wartime production, which furnishes the basis for the biggest estimates of postwar output, has been gained largely by concentrating on industrial mass production on an unheard-of scale, while there are fewer people in things like domestic and personal service and small-scale retailing. That is, we have expanded the kinds of work in which product per worker-hour is high, at the expense of the kinds of non-mechanized, small-scale work where productivity is low. After the war, we shall shift back again, perhaps not completely, but to a very considerable extent.

Another factor mitigating our opportunity and necessity for unheard-of production and consumption is the depletion of some of our best natural resources; but with the miracles that are being wrought in synthetic substitutes, this depletion may not inconvenience us (or benefit us by making more jobs) very substantially. Another mitigating factor is the normal tendency to take part of an increased standard of living in the shape of shorter hours and more leisure, and only part in the shape of more goods. This will involve some problems, since there is already a notable disparity between hours in the factory and on the farm. Private employers, teachers and professors, doctors and lawyers, all will presumably work as long hours as before. And while there will presumably be a shortening of hours in domestic service, this is not likely to make more jobs in the single-family home, though it may in such places as hotels and restaurants. But there is considerable room for our great productive power to be used to buy us shorter hours which, while a valuable element of real income, do not figure in the dollar estimates.

At any rate, it seems that it is necessary for us to be rich, whether we wish to be or not. It is our duty to the rest of the world, in order that we may first help the rest of the world to their feet and afterward buy their goods, in order that we may send them ours (which they will need) without taint of charity. The rest of the world — or that part of it whose voice is audible in this country — appears to accept the idea that for us to be thus rich is the greatest service we can render them. If this makes us objects of the world's envy, even more than before, that is no part of the present study. Other writers will have to write other books about that.

The Make-Up of Stable High Employment

Into what kinds of products shall we put our increased income? One way to approach this problem is to start with something more modest. The first and most unquestioned objective is stabilization, and stabilization not by cutting down the peaks, but by building up the valleys. What should we need to do to stabilize employment and output at the level we actually reach in time of prosperity? One reason why the peak cannot be sustained is that it represents a concentration of construction and capital outlays generally, of inventory-building and purchase of the major consumers' durables. This concentrated rate of capital-building and investment in durables cannot continue without obvious overinvestment — it goes beyond any attainable long-run trend, and is out of proportion to current consumption. At the crest of a boom, the economy is unbalanced in the direction of too-rapid investment.

More Consumption or More Investment?

Merely to slow the rate of investment would pull down the boom, and might tend to stabilize activity at an average level. Then the fact of steadily available surplus resources might have some effect in causing them to be put to use; but this could hardly happen rapidly without starting a concentrated burst of capital outlays, and if this is prevented for fear of a subsequent slump, the process of absorbing idle resources would be slow. There would be unemployment, for which the boom-repressing policy would be responsible, and this would not be tolerated.

We do not want to reduce the rate of production at the peak — we could use it all with benefit — but we should like to balance it so that it might continue. And the key to balancing it lies in the fact that at the peak, when consumption reaches its maximum, we are still consuming less than our resources permit, because we are wasting some resources in an over-rapid accumulation of capital equipment and other durables. A balanced economy would call for more consumption than we achieve at the peak, and less investment.

Another and less obviously appropriate method of creating a stable balance would be to maintain the total flow of "investment" by additional public spending in dull times. It would have to be public spending over and above normal amounts — mere shifting of some of the normal public works from the peak to off-peak times would not do, if we are trying to stabilize at peak levels. It would only do if we are satisfied to average out the peak, and then face the dilemma just mentioned, of retarded expansion versus re-creation of unbalance. If the government is going to support stable prosperity at a high level, this means spending for the sake of making jobs more than it would spend for the sake of the roads, schools or other assets which it gets for its money. Many of these assets might be well worth having; and perhaps government does not spend as much as would be warranted in terms of the value of the end-products it creates — but most American citizens probably do not think so.

The illogic of this method lies in producing more public works when the people would rather have more income to use for themselves. In order that more workers may have wages to spend on things for their personal use, we build more highways instead of producing more things for the use of workers. That is, we produce one thing we do not want in order to get one thing we do want, instead of producing two things we want.

Besides this illogic, the policy has a logic. Economic expansion, unless reduced to an impossible uniformity, must involve some bunching up of capital outlays, though this has been overdone in the past. But the industries producing structures and durable equipment do render a service by putting some reserve productive power at industry's disposal when expansion is called for. Then if, as an incident to this stand-by service, they need to be kept going more evenly by some extra work in the off times, that price may be worth paying. But if we look at it in this way, we shall want to keep the price low, and not actually sacrifice consumption goods in order to have our capital goods produced in bunches instead of more steadily. After all, capital goods are worth having for the sake of consumer goods, not the other way around.

Chronic Private Underinvestment?

We have gone at the problem via the idea of stabilizing peaks of prosperity, but the principles of balance are the same, and the options as to generic methods are much the same, if it is a question of exceeding past or present peaks because they do not afford sufficiently full employment. For this and other reasons it is not necessary at this point to decide whether or not we are going to be faced with a tendency to chronic underemployment, in addition to short-term cyclical ups and downs. If we should encounter such a condition, and if it should appear to be due in part to remediable weakness in the flow of private business investment, then measures aimed to remedy this weakness would be added to the list of pertinent major lines of attack. For purposes of framing a policy, it is probably not necessary to give a definite answer to this question; and it seems reasonably certain that we are going to have to frame a policy and start it operating before we know the answer. What seems clear is that we *may* have to meet such a condition, that it *may* be due in part to business enterprise becoming less ready to take risks in making investments which pioneer ahead of realized and assured demand, and that if such a slackening of enterprising spirit exists, we may or may not be able to devise policies which will remedy it.

So long as answers are uncertain, wise policy will keep all doors open, so far as that is possible, and avoid policies that would commit us to something that would prove harmful if the answer which it presupposed should turn out to be mistaken. From this standpoint, the chief danger seems to be the possibility of going on the assumption that the vigorous and pioneering type of private investment is incurably a thing of the past. This might lead, consciously or unconsciously, to policies which amount to giving it up as a bad job and laying burdens on business (or failing to remove them) which would make sure that the spirit of vigorous, pioneering investment will not revive. That seems, to say the least, premature, at the present time.

METHODS OF PROMOTING HIGH-LEVEL EMPLOYMENT

Financing employment involves two questions: where the funds come from, and what makes them available for this purpose — that is, what makes people able and willing to use the funds in this way, acting on normal motives and on a basis that presumably satisfies their standards of sound conduct. The answer to the first question is simple when employment is stable and credit is neither expanding nor contracting. The funds are there and are merely circulated by payments for goods and services or by repayments of loans and the making of new loans.

But if people's present incomes were not expected to continue, or if their prospective incomes were sharply reduced, they would not go on spending as fast as they do now merely because they still had the same number of dollars in the bank. They also need to count on more dollars coming in to replace those they spend; and if the intake is checked, they will quickly develop parsimony. They might want to invest the part of their bank accounts which is out of proportion to their reduced rate of spending, but a general shrinkage of incomes spells a shrinkage of investment openings too, so the people as a whole could not do much in that direction. Therefore the availability of the funds depends on current incomes and on the expectation that they will continue.

Continuance of any given level of employment, at stable prices and wages, depends on the people as a whole spending (for consumption or capital outlays) the whole of the income they get from past employment. An increase in employment depends on their spending more. If they spend less, employment will shrink. This greatly oversimplified picture represents normal financing of employment.

How to Assure a High Level

To quite a number of persons, the answer to this question is very simple; only different people give different answers, and the different simple answers do not agree. Some of the answers are: (1) Government need only spend enough. It can raise the money: (a) by taxation more heavily progressive than we had in 1939, which will come mainly out of savings and will not check consumption, much, (b) it can lay special taxes on idle savings and cash balances, and then it will not have to spend so much, because people will spend their money to avoid the taxes, and (c) it can use the printing press, or its present-day equivalent. (2) Government need only set up a thoroughly competitive system, including competitively flexible prices and wages (how?). (3) Government need only bring about competitively flexible prices, wages being flexible only upward (how flexible would prices then be?). (4) Government need only combine spending with competitive price flexibility or, failing that, spend and put ceilings on prices and wages, to prevent the spending from being dissipated in inflation.

(5) Government need only stop hampering business, and relieve it (a) of taxes that discriminate against risk-taking enterprise, (b) of a network of harassing restrictions (just which should be repealed?), (c) of a general atmosphere of hostility and distrust, and the constant likelihood of fresh and unsettling burdens and regulations. (6) Government should encourage business to take risks and at the same time afford security to the workers whose incomes absorb the major part of business income. (7) Government should give up the idea that business will make bold and venturesome pioneering investments, and should fill the gap by itself making all the investments of uncertain value that may be needed to build up an adequate volume of spending. It should guarantee business risks involved in new enterprises or major expansions, or it should guarantee demand for products up to an amount that would put the requisite number of workers to work, and dispose of the surplus in various ways which would not spoil the regular market.

(8) Unions should be strengthened and wages should be high to increase demand for goods. (9) Unions should be smashed and wages

should come down whenever necessary to stimulate employment. (10) Costs and prices should be reduced to enlarge the sale of goods and thus make more jobs; and the way to do this is to increase productivity per man-hour. (11) Cost reductions which economize labor should be restrained to protect workers against being displaced from their jobs.

These are perhaps the main types of policies proposed. Some will fit together easily, some might be made to fit together, some clearly will not. They need to be tested against the requirements of a valid over-all program; and these may be summed up under two main heads. The first is that enough should be spent on current products, preferably on a balanced assortment of consumer buying and investment buying, and of durables and non-durables, so that the buying may have a chance of a fair degree of stability both in general and in the major divisions of production. The second is that the economic system should respond freely by putting people to work to make the things that are demanded in the amounts that are required, making whatever shifts and adjustments are called for, so that particular shortages are quickly met and do not turn into bottlenecks, and ample demand is not exploited and dissipated in inflationary increases in prices and costs.

These might be thought of as the energizing and the enabling conditions, or as spending and response. Past generations of economists thought the spending would take care of itself, and the enabling conditions were all one needed to think about. Most modern economists are inclined to make the opposite mistake. Actually, both kinds of condition are needed; neither is sufficient by itself. And neither can be trusted to take care of itself automatically.

II. THE APPROACH: POSTWAR TRANSITION

MEANING OF THE TRANSITION

We shall make our selection of policies in the setting of postwar transition, and this will decide the shape in which the problems will confront us. Our war effort spelled something in the neighborhood of 15 per cent above full employment, mostly in private establishments but nearly half of it financed by government purchasing. Government has paid its armed forces, bought supplies, and built most of the new war plants to the extent of some $15 billion. Of the money it has spent, it has taken back part in taxes and borrowed part from savings made in the economy (largely out of war-swollen incomes). The rest it has borrowed from institutions that expand the supply of circulating funds. This part represented the amount the government poured into circulation in excess of what it took back. There was enough of it to finance the employment of millions of additional workers and leave the people as a whole, after taxes and war bond subscriptions, with more free funds than there were goods for them to buy. If they spent the funds, that spelled inflation.

The transition from war to peace is the transition from employment financed by government to employment financed mainly by private business serving private demand. It is a transition from excess employment to something less — ultimately, we hope and intend, to a reasonably desirable level for a dynamic and progressive economy. And it is (or should be) a transition from a system of financing which left people with more funds than they could spend without inflation, to a system in which they can and will spend freely and get their money's worth in goods and services and deferred claims on future income.

These phases of the transition cannot be trusted to take care of themselves automatically, largely because there is so much shifting to be done all at once, and each shift takes time and means an interval between the stoppage of one job, drying up one source of income, and the starting of another to take its place. This starts the kind of mass disturbance which the markets do not iron out, but are more likely to intensify.

INITIAL POSTWAR RECONVERSION

After victory in Europe our war effort shrank, and there were some beginnings of reconversion. But this did not have time to reach substantial proportions before the coming of final victory. Thus we face the task of full reconversion substantially as a unit instead of in installments.

This brings increased difficulties; but as partial compensation we still have all the accumulated war-shortages to furnish great "backlogs" of demand for goods — shortages of miscellaneous hardware, furnishings and other minor durables, of automobiles and other major durables, and the great shortage of housing. The aggregate deferred demand for housing, automobiles and electrical equipment such as washing machines and vacuum cleaners overshadow all other "backlogs." Reconversion in these and other lines was given the go-ahead signal immediately after hostilities with Japan ended. The swifter the pace of reconversion the greater the help to the process of absorbing millions of men and women discharged from the armed services and workers released from war industries. A rapid changeover by business will probably encounter many technical and organizational obstacles but will spare us other, much more serious difficulties. Careful planning by government and business with courageous development and execution of their plans may avoid bottlenecks which otherwise would stall the process of reconversion.

The large cutbacks following V-J Day are compensated for only in part by "backlogs" of domestic demand. Additional compensation may be provided by the great demand of Europe, China and other war-torn areas of the world for food and materials to restore essential public services and some basic industries. Although the United States terminated lend-lease abroad simultaneously with the end of its military operations, the accumulated needs of countries ravaged by this war are sufficiently great and the machinery of financing such purchases is sufficiently well established that there need be little or no shrinkage of this demand. Its effectiveness will depend, of course, on whether the financial arrangements are actually forthcoming.

Total pay rolls will fall off, and there will be demands for wage increases to offset reduced hours and loss of overtime pay. To the extent that such wage increases might necessitate price increases, raising the cost of living, they would be fictitious and might start an inflationary spiral. Total disposable income, plus war-savings, will almost surely be enough to buy the goods the country can produce for private consumption for some time after the coming of peace.

The first year after final victory will witness the most concentrated reconversion and the greater part of the demobilization of men from the armed services. It will be a time of heavy transitional unemployment, which will not be as serious as it looks in the statistics. This is partly because there will be some temporary emergency workers who will soon leave the working force, partly because a revival is sure to follow and partly because the unemployed will be better financed than ever before. Nevertheless, consumers' incomes will shrink heavily, and the results may be cumulative if revival is too long delayed, making the job of revival that much harder.

As soon as possible, the specifications of a postwar tax system should be drawn up, not so much because of the needs of the current fiscal situation as to let business know what to expect, so that the uncertainties of its forward planning may be reduced by that much at least. Liberal benefits should be provided for the unemployed. This, plus some spending of war savings by many individuals, will help to sustain the demand for goods, on which the demand for workers rests.

For some things, like automobiles and housing, the demand will exceed the supply for some time, and continued controls will be needed to keep prices from going to levels that would hurt the general revival rather than help it. A world food shortage may persist, with wheat the outstanding exception. If demand in general exceeds supply while civilian production is still getting under way, that would tend to inflation, but this would be the lesser evil, as tending to avoid a cumulative depression. There is perhaps more likelihood that the chief discrepancies will turn toward deflation temporarily, especially in the case of a majority of the basic raw materials, other than food.

It goes without saying that the government employment services should be developed to the utmost possible efficiency, including aids to relocation, retraining and re-education. Normal public works should be promptly resumed, and preparations should be made for this at once; but large and lengthy projects should not be expanded to a point that could get in the way of private construction when that revives. For temporary support to the construction industry, projects should be selected which can be quickly disposed of. Private employers should employ as many as possible of their regular workers in reconverting their plants and should engage as many as possible in advance for the jobs that will open when the plants are reconverted.

The main objective is to come through this period with a minimum of temporary hardship, and especially without developing a cumulative depression or a depression psychology. There is enough general realization of the importance of this to afford considerable hope. This is likely to be helped by optimism bred of victory and of the sense of having shown the capacity to do the impossible when victory was at stake. Over against this is war fatigue, attrition of the will to cooperate, and exposure to a mood of cynical disillusionment if early steps are bungled and early expectations of speedy readjustment deferred or disappointed. These might diminish the energy of the subsequent revival. But a revival will come.

FILLING DEFERRED DEMANDS

For possibly two or three years after the initial postwar reconversion, our economy will have the stimulus of filling deferred demands of many kinds, automobiles being the largest single item. Housing and some other major construction undertakings will last longer. Exports to aid the reconstruction of war-shattered countries are likely to continue to be considerable for an uncertain time. Many new small businesses will be set up and will need structures, equipment, and stocks of goods and materials. New products may become an important factor after an interval, but not immediately. With all these elements of concentrated demand, the civilian economy should witness the most rapid expansion it has ever experienced. It seems entirely likely that by three years after the final end of organized fighting, we shall have something that could fairly be called "full employment."

The Danger of Recessions

But like any extra-rapid expansion, this will be a turbulent and uneven movement, made up of many parts with different timing. It would be a miracle if they all fitted together perfectly. To take a single example, the production of household equipment will probably be overcrowded, and some producers who go into this field may soon abandon it or contract their operations. The chief difficulty, however, is that the economy that takes shape in this rapid expansion will be unbalanced. It will be an extreme example of a temporary concentration on durable goods and capital outlays, far in excess of any conceivable long-run trend. There is a chance that some important new products will be just going into mass production at the time when output of automobiles tapers off; but it is obvious that we cannot count on any full and exact compensation of that sort. The situation contains the elements of a postwar recession, in which a decline of automobile production would be the main factor, and possibly another, later recession induced by a similar decline in housing and general construction. There will also be low spots in the demand for replacements in subsequent years, reflecting years of low output of new units, and tending to intensify business fluctuations. These will be the crucial tests of postwar economic policy. Fortunately, we have time in which to prepare to meet them, possibly as much as four years, and many leaders are taking the general problem very seriously. But thinking and planning will need to move very fast in those four years if we are to improve on our past performance as much as it needs to be improved on. For this purpose, we need to keep in mind not merely the goal of a *high* rate of economic activity but the requirements of a balanced economy which can keep going at a reasonably *stable* rate.

The Scheduling of Public Works

If the making good of deferred demands leads to such a boom that there is an actual labor shortage, then a move in the direction of balance would be to hold back some of the public works that would otherwise have been carried out in this period, as a reserve for a later recession. This is only common sense, but it is a kind of common sense that is almost impossible to put in practice when a prosperous period is actually in full swing and the temptation is to think that the specter of depression has been disposed of. If this temptation is resisted, there will still be only a limited amount of public works which are badly enough needed to make people willing to pay for them and still not so urgently needed as to make it undesirable to postpone them for a few years.

Therefore there will not be enough holding back of normal public works to provide a reserve large enough to take care of a considerable recession such as is likely to occur. Additional works should be scheduled for this purpose. As far as possible, they should be things worth doing for their own sakes, although done earlier than we should have gotten around to them were it not for the need of employment. (In practice, such a policy is bound to result in some net increase in the total of public works outlays over a term of, let us say, ten years.) The advance scheduling which the government is trying to do now against the first reconversion recession should yield experience of what to do and what to avoid later in the scheduling against a second recession; if we can only keep in mind that the second recession is a real threat and more serious than the first because it will lack the handy ladder of "backlogs" to climb out on.

Dealing With Chronic Underemployment

If the filling of deferred demands, including public works deferred by the war, does not give us a high enough level of employment within three years after final peace, then we shall be facing a problem that goes beyond stabilizing of cyclical fluctuations. Still more public works might provide more lift, but not without further unbalancing an economy that is already heavily unbalanced in the direction of public works and durable goods in general, as against current consumption. If the public works involve deficit spending, that, too, is naturally more serious than deficits that are limited to the troughs of business cycles. Perhaps the most important thing to do is to use the intervening time in earnest study of the various possible methods of dealing with such a situation, to pick out the methods with the least drawbacks and out of them build a coherent policy. None of the methods may suit us completely, but we cannot simply reject them all, because we are going to have to do something.

III. Adequate and Balanced Spending

GOVERNMENT SPENDING

The "obvious and simple" remedy for inadequate spending is for government to spend more, without simultaneously taking an equal amount of money out of private pockets by taxes. This is clearly an appropriate thing to do in case of a cyclical decline that centers in private capital outlays. If the government spends the money for the usual type of thing — "public works" — it supports demand in some of the industries in which it has fallen off most heavily; and it expects the need to be temporary. It can vary the amount of special support, or bring it to an end when the emergency is over, a good deal more easily than it could do the same with most of the other types of stimulative policy. There are numerous practical difficulties, but "in principle" the case is clear.

Government Investment Competing With Private Investment

One qualification is that, if the government's spending is to be a clear addition, it must not go into fields where it would compete with private business investment, without being pretty sure that it will not deter so much private investment that it would displace more capital outlays than it made. Then if the amount of public spending has to be very large, this limitation may lead to "leaf-raking."

If the government is to be called on to enlarge permanently its field of expenditures, it will need to consider whether it should, in carefully selected instances, undertake competition with monopolistic industries, or whether it should enter some well-defined field or part of a field of private investment, and keep to its part of the field, not competing with private enterprises, but using its capital outlays to help counteract irregularities in the flow of capital outlays in general. Public investment in an industry does not necessarily displace greater amounts of private investment, but it might. Private industry distrusts public competition as inefficient, but subsidized and therefore unduly dangerous. This distrust is something to be taken into account, and something which it may take some time to dispel. If numerous industries feel that the government may start competing with them in some uncertain future, private capital outlays are pretty sure to be retarded. This is no small part of the dilemma of very heavy public investment.

Cyclical and Chronic Shortages of Private Spending

This issue cannot and probably need not be rushed. But ultimately, if capital outlays are to be stabilized, either private industry must work out ways to do it, or government must occupy part of the field itself and time its part of the outlays so as to bring greater stability to the whole. Postwar policy should probably push experiments in both directions.

This problem of stabilization is sure to arise fairly soon. If we are fortunate and wise in our policies, the more difficult problem of chronic shortages of spending may not arise. If not, so much the better. But in case there does turn out to be a long-continued shortage of private spending, the government may have to consider continuous spending in large amounts, possibly as much as $10 to $15 billion a year above its otherwise necessary budget, if it is to bear the brunt of making the shortage good. Then we should be facing the real crux of the deficit problem.

One suggestion is that this can be done without deficits, by laying progressive taxes, which will come mostly out of the incomes, a large part of which would be saved, so that the taxes will not reduce spending materially. Of course, it is out of the question to make taxes more progressive than they are at present. What might happen is that, with the top-bracket rates lower than at present, they might still be enough higher than in 1939 to have the contemplated effect. This seems to presuppose that government bonds will not remain a tax-free refuge for the high incomes. This combination might do something to reduce idle savings, but hardly enough to dispose of any very large stagnant pool of this sort. Taxes, even though progressive, cut into spendings as well as savings; and this would cancel part of the effect of the public spending of the tax money. Very heavy taxes on the high brackets not only cut into savings, but also reduce the incentive to venturing capital in business undertakings. To be effective, the taxes must stop short of the point at which the second effect would neutralize the first.

Another proposal is to lay special taxes on idle hoards, not so much to raise revenue as to drive people to spend or invest. No detailed discussion of these proposals is possible here. They raise great difficulties, and in themselves they do not seem to assure that the money would be used in ways that would create demand for current products and current labor. These proposals should be further considered, but do not seem to have proved themselves at present.

Continuing Deficits and Mounting Debt

Is it true that the only bad thing about large continuing deficits and a mounting public debt is our habit of worrying about them? And that this worry rests on a mere superstition? And that all we need to do is to get rid of this superstition and take our deficits cheerfully? If the debt pays more than a nominal rate of interest, it seems that there is more than a superstition there. If the government lays taxes to pay the interest, when taxes are already very heavy, the added taxes may become a factor limiting investment and production. The idea of levying taxes to pay the interest may itself be a superstition, and actually meaningless if the deficits are continued. But even aside from tax burdens, the interest overhead would distort the distribution of the country's income in the wrong direction, if nothing else, tending to increase the idle savings which were the source of the trouble. If some countries have gotten on with even larger debt charges, relative to their national incomes, than ours is likely to be at the end of this war, it would take some demonstrating that their example has been happy enough to make us want to follow it, if it can be avoided. There is as yet no example, so far as I am aware, of a country which has taken Mr. A. P. Lerner's prescription[2] and gotten rid of the superstition completely, though the Hitler regime may have come close to it, leaving much of its debt not even formally recorded. That, however, is hardly a precedent.

We are thinking primarily of policy for the first ten years after the end of the war. Between now and then we shall need to get rid of enough superstitions to tax our capacity in that direction, but we are not likely to reach a point at which an endlessly increasing debt ceases to cause uneasiness that would be an obstacle to confident venturing in business. On the other hand, we are not likely to reduce our debt in that period enough to have serious deflationary effects on the economy. To the extent that holders of war bonds want to cash them in and spend the proceeds, the debt might be reduced without deflationary effects, but this does not seem likely to happen, because at the time the bondholders do most of their cashing in, the government will probably not yet be in a position to show a surplus. The real burden of the debt will be reduced slowly, if it stays the same dollar size while the national income increases. This increase may be physical, or due to an increase in the price level, or both. But continuing heavy deficits would jeopardize this process of automatic debt reduction.

Mr. Eccles has called deficit spending a last resort; and as a last resort, in default of maintaining high employment in other ways, it will be followed, and should be followed. But it should not be a last resort in the sense that we are satisfied to let the matter rest there. If it is necessary, it is because of an unbalance between spending and saving; and it does not cure that unbalance, but may make it worse, unless skillfully handled. It is a palliative, and the need of using it should be a sign of the need of finding something more like a cure.

BUSINESS SPENDING

The capital outlays of business are, of course, crucial factors in the spending that makes jobs. They are business' form of deficit spending (except where a business is plowing back its own earnings) but are intended to be "self-liquidating." Private deficit spending on business principles has outweighed any peacetime deficit spending of government in this country.

2. A. P. Lerner, "Functional Finance and the Federal Debt," *Social Research,* February 1943; also Lerner, *The Economics of Control,* Macmillan, 1944, Chap. 24.

As to what governs its amount, there is the view that it has ceased to be an independent initiating force and simply follows demand, providing in the most economical way for the demand which is actually in sight. Those who hold this view tend to discount the importance of favorable or unfavorable conditions, other than demand for goods. Accordingly, they think of public spending as increasing private investment by increasing the demand for goods. Others think the other factors bearing on confidence are important, and that the only reason why investment has followed demand somewhat passively of late is that these other conditions have been bad. Among these bad conditions are heavy taxes and uneasiness over continuing public deficits and a mounting public debt. Thus public spending may have some tendency to confirm the disease (decay of bold business pioneering in advance of realized demand) for which it is prescribed as a remedy. From this stand point, the logic of the situation calls for giving business investment every facility and every reasonable stimulus, and removing deterrents as far as possible.

Obstacles to Private Investment

Facilities include access to credit, especially for the many ex-servicemen who want to start small businesses on their return. The most tangible obstacle lies in the tax system, and here reform is definitely in order. These things we may take for granted, though of course they contain plenty of problems.

Among other obstacles, simplification of government regulations and reports would be an obvious blessing, but it is not easy to think of any major department of public control which could be dispensed with — not even the SEC, which has been charged with operating to the disadvantage of small business. The antitrust laws probably prevent some combinations which would incidentally involve some capital outlays; but unrestrained monopoly would do much more to check investment in improved methods. It may be true that, if business and labor interests were to get together and devise a joint plan for regularizing capital outlays as a whole by putting some of them in otherwise dull times, some features of it would need special dispensation from the antitrust laws — which would be well worth granting. The issue may be faced when such a plan comes in sight. Initial steps could be taken without requiring collective action between competitors in the same industry, since the kernel would lie in relations between different industries, and between employers and organized workers.

Perhaps one of the really important deterrents is intangible. There has been an atmosphere or "climate" of hostility and faultfinding which may detract somewhat from the human rewards of outstanding business success — but then, the individualists and buccaneers of the mid-nineteenth century must have made plenty of enemies, of a different sort. Now that big business has become a quasi-public function, the businessman learns the joys of exposure to defamation, like the candidate for political office. Also, between government and nationally organized labor, businessmen often feel that they do not own their own businesses any more. It is true, they do not have the old absolute type of ownership, and will not regain it. And it may be that some of the rights or powers which they really need, in order to do their job properly, have been impaired. Some redefining of rights and powers may be needed, in which organized labor as well as business may need to recognize its quasi-public character. But it may turn out, so far as business management is concerned, that its safety in the troubled times ahead lies in accepting the role of buffer between the various interests, rather than acting solely as representative of equity ownership. It is not self-evident which of these roles is more favorable to business spending for employment.

Plans to Stimulate Business Investment

If the stimulus of an open field is not enough to bring about vigorous business spending for employment, what kinds of positive stimulus can be offered? The outstanding type of plan at present is that government should guarantee business risks, or demand for products. Crucial points in the plan would include the working out of a national budget of goods that would be bought by consumers and producers, out of the income which high employment would furnish, and the production of which would in turn create high employment. If the goods were not all bought, the government would take them over at a nonprofit valuation, and dispose of them in some way which would not interfere with regular sales.

This plan might work if the main thing needed is a push to get over a sort of dead center in which business employment waits on demand and demand waits on the income that comes from business employment. But if there really is a strong tendency for the economy as a whole to fail to spend its entire income, there would be a consistent and large balance of unbought goods to be disposed of. Then avenues of disposal might be overtaxed. The possibilities of food stamp plans are limited. Foreign markets might not be receptive to large surpluses, having employment problems of their own. No country wants to be a dumping ground. Even the much advertised Hottentot might not afford a satisfactory market, and the destruction of goods has not gained in popularity during the wholesale destruction of war.

The present mood of business offers a good prospect that there will be no initial dead center of the sort suggested. In that case, it is not an urgent matter to decide at once whether to adopt some form of the plan or to reject it. There is time to weigh it, and perhaps adapt some part of the principle to an experimental trial on a reduced scale.

CONSUMER SPENDING

The same mechanistic theory which holds that business investment follows demand holds that consumers' spending follows income, and that the only way to affect it is through income. To accept this at its face value would discourage any attempt to bring about a real balance between consumer spending and investment, in case a lack of balance here is part of our trouble. This would shut off some of the most promising lines of effort, because they would undertake to change the amounts that consumers will spend out of a given income.

Saving Habits

If there is this lack of balance, it may simply result from the bunching up of capital outlays and the buying of durables in boom times. But a more stubborn form may result from the fact that, when people get well enough off to save, they want to turn part of their income into deferred claims to goods instead of goods now. Then if business or government or someone does not take these funds (or an equal amount) and turn them into demand for goods now — for example, by building a factory or making some other capital outlay — then the income will not all be spent, and the next round of income (derived from the spending of this round) will be that much smaller. This is something which is inherently likely to happen to a growingly rich country; and the automatic correctives, such as a reduced rate of interest, do not appear powerful enough to make sure that income will all be used.

We may escape this kind of difficulty in the postwar years, or we may not. If we do not, then anything that would stimulate consumer spending would be the most pertinent remedy. One of the simplest methods in principle, is publicly subsidized consumption for those who would not otherwise consume enough of certain things for their own good, chiefly because they do not have money enough. This means an extension of the sort of thing represented by school lunches, assisted services of health and recreation and food stamp plans. This, of course, is public spending, but it is more directly useful public spending than some of the less urgently needed "public works."

Ways to Reduce Excessive Saving

Another suggestion is that there would be more spending out of the same total income if the income were more equally divided between the rich and poor. This points to making taxes more progressive, the limit being set by the point at which the rich man is discouraged by the high rates, so that he shrinks his capital outlays by one dollar or more for every dollar that is added to total spendings because the poor man has more money to spend than he had before. Incidentally, it probably takes the shifting of, for example, five dollars of income from rich to poor to increase total consumer spendings by one dollar.[3]

Low interest rates are usually thought of as stimuli to investment, but they might have as much effect in reducing long-run net savings, if they became low enough to drive the ordinary middle-class saver into buying annuities instead of holding his principal intact and spending only the income. The effect would be much greater if the government offered the annuity, and did not accumulate actuarial reserves, but used most of the early intake for current expenses. Ultimately, intake and outgo for annuity payments would roughly balance. In short, extend the principle of social security without orthodox reserves, and perhaps on a voluntary basis, to persons who do more saving than the average wage earner.

A social security system which is compulsory, and is accumulating

3. For example, if those whose taxes are increased reduce their savings by forty cents and their spendings by sixty cents per dollar of change in their disposable income, and the others increase their savings by twenty cents and their spendings by eighty cents, then a shift of $1.00 increases spendings by twenty cents. This seems an optimistic estimate.

large reserves, has just the opposite effect: it increases the amount of saving, partly at the expense of present consumption. By varying its reserve policy, social security can be a very powerful instrument to increase net spending or decrease it. If too many people want claims to future goods instead of goods now, the government can give them their future claims, and put their money to work now instead of letting it stand idle. The price is some unorthodox financing of a sort that need involve no real danger.

These are merely illustrative. If the general idea is accepted, there is enough inventiveness available to evolve many improvements on the crude suggestions made here. The main point is that the volume of consumption from a given income is something that can be influenced, and is one of the most logical and promising areas in which to work.

IV. The Cost-Price Structure as an Enabling Factor

THE THEORIES ON THE SUBJECT

The cost-price structure extends to matters of hours and output, but we may start with the question: "From the standpoint of the largest possible volume of productive employment, how is it desirable that wages and prices should behave?" On this question economists have done surprisingly little work, and what they have done needs to be re-examined to make sure that it is pertinent to the problems of policy we shall be facing after the war.

Allocation and Full Use of Resources

They tell us in general terms how prices and wages should be adjusted in order that productive resources should be properly allocated between different products. That is, they tell us how to be sure that we never use any part of our resources producing commodity X when a little of the resources could be shifted to producing commodity Y and produce something that would sell for more. To be sure, when one tries to go beyond the conveniently abstract X and Y and think about steel, wheat and bituminous coal, beefsteaks and packing-house by-products, ready-made clothing, retailing and radio programs, and services of health and education, one runs into qualifications and exceptional features at every turn; nevertheless, one has at least some guiding principles. But these principles do not give us any clear message as to how to keep as many as possible of our "resources" — that means mostly people who need jobs — producing something, and as few as possible producing nothing.

When this question comes uppermost, it tends to dwarf the importance of close calculations of whether those resources that we do employ get directed into precisely the most productive openings. Since this last is what orthodox accounting is supposed to tell us when it tells us whether a product is worth what it costs, the result is equivalent to dwarfing the social importance of orthodox accounting, when it insists that the dollar values of products must cover their monetary costs of production.[4] This requirement cannot be ignored, for various practical reasons, especially where production is carried on by private business. But it cannot claim to be a socially correct answer unless resources are so fully employed that idle plants and idle workers do not constitute a substantial problem.

Conservative economists cannot, naturally, deny that unemployment exists. They have, however, habitually claimed that there is at least a tendency for a competitive economy, under the guidance of its appropriate scheme of values and costs, to bring idle resources into employment, if it is not unduly disturbed or interfered with. But as to how and why this mechanism works, how prompt and how powerful it is, and what conditions it requires; these problems turn out to have been sadly neglected, and no really convincing answer to them has been produced and put in general circulation.

How the Mechanism Is Supposed to Work

One early answer was too simple. Based on "Say's law," which stated that there could be no general overproduction, because supply of one thing constitutes demand for other things, it concluded that the only problem was that of producing the right things in the right proportions. Another answer adds that prices and wages must be flexible, always ready to be reduced until the demand absorbs the supply. On examination, it appears that the success of this adjustment must hinge on its being needed only now and then, not continuously.

To work, drastic deflations must be limited to intervals of weakened

4. The cost of production consists of the market values of the resources used; and these market values are supposed to be based on what the resources could produce in the best readily available alternative uses. Unemployment reduces this last to zero.

demand, and must be capable of bringing about a revived demand which would permit prices and wages to rise again while demand still absorbed supply. It would not be necessary that prices should rise precisely as much as they had fallen; but a continuous and fairly rapid decline in wages and prices would hardly afford a favorable condition for continuous prosperity. Falling prices lead to inventory losses, and tend toward a niggardly policy of hand-to-mouth buying. Moreover, the prices and wages are not merely the costs which buyers must pay; they constitute also the incomes out of which the buying must be done. The result is that incomes and costs would decline together; and the net effect is not simple and easy to predict.

Offhand conclusions are frequently drawn, based entirely on one or the other side of this two-sided aspect of wages and prices. Some say that wages must be maintained to prevent a decline of employment, or even raised to increase employment by increasing diffused purchasing power. This ignores the fact that wages are also costs; and that it is inherently possible that some wages might be high enough to be obstacles to expansion of production from the cost side. Others insist that the laws of supply and demand must operate in the usual way in this case, and that therefore the way to increase the number of workers hired is to reduce the wages they ask. This focuses on the fact that wages are costs, and ignores the fact that they are also purchasing power. These two one-sided views simply cancel one another.

Modern Theories of Wage Flexibility

It is only very recently that pioneering efforts have been made to produce a more conclusive answer to this really baffling problem. Pigou, in his *Theory of Unemployment* (1933), held that labor could always increase employment by reducing its wage demands. Lord Keynes, in his *General Theory of Employment, Interest and Money,* credited Pigou with the "first attempt to write down the classical theory of unemployment precisely," but found his theory faulty. Keynes held the idea that the slashing of wages in a depression is a futile method of maintaining employment under ordinary conditions.[5] Accordingly he favored the stabilizing of money wage rates in depressions. In the long run, he is inclined to favor taking the gains of increased technical efficiency in

5. *The General Theory of Employment, Interest and Money,* Harcourt, Brace, New York, 1936, pp. 269–71, and appendix immediately following.

the shape of a stable price level and rising money wages, rather than stable money wages and falling prices.

Pigou, in a later book, *Employment and Equilibrium* (1941), comes closer to Keynes' method of treatment. He still believes that a flexible price-wage system is capable of bringing about full employment, and holds that, statistically, it worked fairly well up to about 1914. His mechanism, like Keynes', seems to hinge on the stimulative effect of reduced interest rates.[6] This does not appear to be a strong enough stimulus to do the job that is required of it, for reasons that will appear later.

Still more recently, Professor Oscar Lange has attacked the same problem and reached the conclusion that, while flexible prices and wages may have tended to stabilize production and employment in an earlier and more generally competitive condition of the American economy, they cannot be counted on to operate in this way in the present economy, which contains various sticky and semimonopolistic sectors. Under existing conditions, he favors stabilization, not of all prices, but of some key price or price element, particularly wage rates.[7]

This brief sketch of the theoretical literature of the subject has at least indicated what a limited amount of serious work has been done on this crucially important problem.[8] The most substantial work has been done by mathematical economists, with the result that it is, for all practical purposes, shut out from the understanding of everyone else. It is not safe to accept the results as guides to policy unless their processes and assumptions are checked by the kind of person who is familiar enough with actual practices to be in a position to judge whether the assumptions and processes are pertinent. If these results are pertinent guides to policy, it is tremendously important that the policy makers should get the benefit of them; but this cannot happen unless they are translated into language that makes them accessible to

6. Paul A. Samuelson, "Pigou's Employment and Equilibrium," *The American Economic Review*, Vol. 31, pp. 545, 550. Cf. also Pigou, "The Classical Stationary State," *The Economic Journal*, Vol. 53, pp. 343–51 and L. A. Hahn, "Compensating Reactions to Compensatory Spending," *The American Economic Review*, Vol. 35, p. 35, footnote.

7. O. Lange, *Price Flexibility and Employment*, Cowles Commission Monograph, No. 8, Principia Press, Bloomington, 1944, p. 90.

8. Samuelson, *op. cit.*, p. 545, states that when Professor Hicks wanted to discover the classical theory of what determines the volume of employment, he was reduced to the expedient of imagining what theory he would hold if he were a classical economist.

this kind of checking, most of which would have to be done by persons not initiated into the higher mathematical mysteries.

TWENTY TENTATIVE PROPOSITIONS

In the meantime, and because the results so far available seem so uncertain and inconclusive, it is well worth trying different methods and different approaches, including different ways of formulating the problem. The need is urgent, time presses, and no one need apologize for contributing what he can. The studies just mentioned attacked the question whether a thoroughly fluid system of prices and wages will suffice to maintain full employment, and how their effects on employment operate. This is typically thought of in terms of a general rise or fall of prices or wages or both. This is a good question to ask, but not the only good one that can be asked. In what follows I shall suggest answers to some different questions. They are not all new, but taken together they may represent a different approach to the question of a desirable price-wage structure, from the standpoint of a high level of employment.

Wage-Price Behavior Cannot Cure Cycles

1. No conceivable behavior of prices and wages would in itself iron out those cyclical fluctuations of prosperity and depression which take place over intervals of ten years or less; particularly the cycles which last on the average about forty months in this country. Whatever unemployment is necessarily involved in these cycles cannot be cured in this way. This does not mean that complete and universal rigidity is desirable.

General Deflation Is a Dubious Remedy

2. As a remedy for a possible disease of chronic underemployment a general deflation of wages and prices would have to be progressive, at a substantial rate. The benefits of such a remedy are dubious, to say the least; and whatever its economic effects might be, it is not thinkable that it should be voluntarily adopted, or that it should come about by itself, in the kind of an economy we have at present.

In the past, our economy has shown great capacity both to develop increasing productive powers and to put the increase to work. This proves that there is some set of mechanisms or forces which act to assimilate increases in productive power. They have worked, as a matter of long-time trend, when prices and wages were rising and when prices were falling — and also when money wages and real wages were falling, so far as there may have been considerable periods of this sort.[9] This proves that it does not depend wholly on whether prices and wages in general are rising or falling. But since the days of adequate statistical records we have never succeeded in assimilating all of the productive powers we had developed; and the decade of the thirties made the poorest showing yet. This poor showing is correlated with a puzzling complex of historical changes, some combination of which is presumably responsible.

Correct Wage-Price Behavior May Be Part of the Cure

3. Assuming that the behavior of prices and wages cannot cure either cyclical or chronic depression, it still is not a thing that can be safely ignored; because if it could not cure things, it might make them worse. Provisionally, then, reasonably correct behavior of prices and wages (if we can find out what that is) may be necessary to a cure of underemployment, though not by itself sufficient.

Proper Wage and Price Policy as an Enabling Factor

4. The effectiveness of proper wage and price policy can best be considered, not as something by itself, but in connection with whatever other policies may be used. By itself it cannot succeed; but it may enable other measures to succeed, or it may defeat them.

General Competitive Price Flexibility Is Hardly Attainable

5. Whether or not complete competitive flexibility is the correct answer, solely on the basis of the economic effects which it would have if it prevailed, it is not going to prevail as the generally ruling state of affairs. This is only partly on account of "capitalistic" monopoly. The government's efforts to maintain competition in this area may encounter hard sledding, of course. But we should not have a thoroughgoing competitive system, even if the government were to succeed to perfection in its attempts to combat monopoly in the areas of business and in-

---

9. There has been some uncertainty whether real wages were rising or falling in the last quarter of the 19th century.

dustry where it does combat it. There are too many areas in which competition has been deliberately dethroned, with public aid or approval.

When wages, plus prices of some agricultural raw materials, plus freight rates, plus the cost of electric power and probably after the war the price of bituminous coal, are all determined in noncompetitive fashion, there is only a limited amount of room within which the prices of manufactured products can be competitively flexible. Even in the final merchandising, competition may be restricted in states which have fair-trade laws. The manufacturer's profit margin is, on the average, a secondary factor in the series that makes up the total selling price. When anyone recommends general competitive price flexibility as the correct economic policy, it is fair to expect him to offer at least a glimmering as to how this is to be brought about.

Certain Monopolistic Prices or Wages May Obstruct Full Employment

6. It is clear that particular prices or particular wage rates of a monopolistic character may be so high as to be obstacles to full employment. Arguments in favor of stabilization of prices and wages are misused if they are used to support the pegging of these particular prices. In this case the movement of a number of particular prices or wage rates may be a more effective way of stimulating employment than a general movement in which all prices and wages move together and their relationships do not change. If the stimulative effect of a universal deflation of wages and prices is an affair for academic speculation, the obstructive effect of a selective assortment of monopolistic wages and prices is a highly practical matter.

Restrictive Practices May Do More Harm Than Monopolistic Prices or Wages

7. In the case of monopolistic and semimonopolistic situations the height to which the price or wage rises above a competitive level may, within ordinary limits, be less important than the restrictive tactics which are used to maintain and protect the monopolistic position. Production may be directly curtailed and workers may be directly kept out of jobs. If it were only a matter of raising prices, especially if workers get a wage increase as their share, then, after the movement has become general, things would be much as before. The first industry to raise prices would suffer a reduced volume of sales, but perhaps only until

the others followed suit, after which money demand would have approximately caught up with increased money prices. But the process of doing this, industry by industry, may have different results from a simultaneous increase such as economic theorists commonly envisage. This is especially true if the increased prices and wages are fortified by restrictions on entry into the industry or trade. These restrictions may survive after the increase has become general, and may directly interfere with mobility of resources and with full employment.

Rules restricting labor's output might also survive, and have the effect of reducing product and real income. Such restrictive rules are very generally due to fear of losing the job. So they constitute a vicious circle, which may be broken if the insider's fear of losing his job can be relieved.

Wage Cuts Ineffective in Consumers' Goods, May Stimulate Capital Outlays

8. Different policies may be appropriate to different kinds of products. In the production of consumers' goods of the kinds wage earners buy, wage earners as a whole would hardly be warranted in consenting to a cut in their wages in order to reduce the prices of their products and so promote sales and increase employment. If the full amount of their wage reduction were passed on to the consumers in lower prices, the income available to buy the goods would be reduced by about as much as the aggregate asking prices of the goods, and the total physical volume of sales, and of employment, is not likely to be very much affected. But the workers in these industries would carry the whole burden, and share the benefit with workers in other industries, and other persons who bought part of these same goods. The workers who took the cut would have smaller real incomes, and others larger. If the employer, in consideration of the workers' cut, takes a cut himself, *which he would not otherwise have taken,* then the original workers may lose nothing and employment may be slightly increased. This might happen but seems like a rather exceptional case.

Capital goods — things like steel, machinery and construction materials — furnish a different kind of problem. The demand for such things, especially in dull times, is sure to be decidedly inelastic, responding little to reductions of price, if that is the only stimulus that is used. This would be particularly true of any one product taken singly, since it would be only one element in the cost of a capital installation; but it would also be true to a less extent of general reductions in this field. A wage reduction in this field, taken by itself, would be a loss to the workers and would do little to stimulate employment.

But it would have some stimulative effect, whereas in the consumers' goods industries it would probably have none. And if it were part of a well-rounded program for inducing the building up of capital outlays in what would otherwise be dull times, the whole program might be effective enough to be worth undertaking, and to make it worth while for the workers to contribute their bit along with all the other interests involved, with proper safeguards to make reasonably sure that their total earnings, on the average of good and bad times, would be increased rather than reduced. If employment were made steadier, there is every likelihood that the result would be an increased total volume, on the average of good and bad times, though probably not to the level of "full employment" for a working force of the size these industries use during booms in capital construction.

Advantages of Controlled Price Cut

9. An administered or controlled movement of prices, up or down, can have one advantage over an uncontrolled, competitive movement. It has at least a chance to get rid of the reverse effect which often causes a reduction in price to reduce sales for awhile rather than increase them (because it leads buyers to think that prices are going lower and that they will do better still if they wait). A well-managed reduction in price, especially if it were planned by buyers and sellers in consultation, might be handled by one cut, large enough to make it worth the buyer's while to buy now, after which there would be little likelihood of further reductions. A single large producer might be in a position that would enable him to carry through a reduction of this sort.

Public Works Hamper Private Investment by Keeping Costs High

10. In so far as the government might be a partner in sustaining demand in the field of capital goods — for example, by using public works to maintain output and employment in the construction industry — it cannot avoid influencing the price-wage structure in one way or another. Influencing it for the worse is almost certainly easier than influencing it for the better. Existing rules frequently result in the gov-

ernment buying construction materials at openly quoted prices which are higher than large private buyers regularly pay in their unpublicized negotiations, and paying for labor at nominal union rates which few contractors follow on private work in times of slack business. This is carrying the principle of stabilizing prices and wages to irrational and harmful lengths.

There are reasons for these rules, and a change to greater administrative discretion might open the door to some abuses. But these abuses do not look so serious, comparatively speaking, as they did before this generation came face to face with its dominating economic emergency. In terms of stabilizing employment at a high level, this kind of pricing and wage policy influences the price-wage structure in precisely the wrong way. It furnishes standing notice of government support for precisely those price and wage structures where flexibility could do some good. Even if these wage and price structures are monopolistic, they are nevertheless protected against the only force that is likely to break them down: namely, the pressure of hard times.

This tends definitely to prevent private business from scheduling its capital outlays at dull times, by removing the incentive it normally gets from being able to get the work done cheaper at such times. The capital goods and construction industries are central in the problem of depression and prosperity. In following policies of stabilization, the last thing the government should wish to do is to hamstring any private efforts at stabilization, and make certain that government will have to bear the entire load.

Price Movements Mean More Than Price Levels

11. The question whether prices as a whole should be low or high is relatively unimportant, provided the foreign exchanges adjust themselves to the relative price levels in different countries. What is more important is the direction in which prices are moving, and how large a fraction of the price goes to profits.

Low Profit Margins May Be the Best Policy for Business as a Whole

12. The policy of large sales at low unit profit margins is unquestionably the correct policy for the economy as a whole. The more thoroughly business will voluntarily follow this policy, within the range in which it has discretion to choose a policy, while pushing the expansion

of investment vigorously, the better for the volume of employment. This is the profitable policy for any business enterprise which has strong competition to meet, or which would stir up more formidable competition for itself if it were less enterprising or if it tried to exploit the market with a policy of high prices and high margins per unit of sales.

We need waste little time on the question whether the low-margin policy is advantageous for a given industry taken as a unit. That is the same as asking whether it is to the interest of a secure monopoly to carry a low-margin policy as far as it would be in the public interest to have it carried. The public instinct would not willingly trust any monopolist with that discretion; and the public instinct would be right. But the interest of business as a whole is a different matter, and it might conceivably lie in the same low-margin policy that is in the public interest.

Lower Profit Rates Are Probably Inevitable

13. Will a policy of low margins increase the volume of sales enough to yield high annual rates of return on investment? Probably not. It is more probable that the low-margin policy will serve the interests of business only in the sense that the trend toward lower rates of profit on larger investments is inevitable; and that business will suffer less by accepting this trend and adjusting itself to it, than by resisting it. If it does resist, and does its pricing for high profits, it may end with restricted sales, a restricted field for investment, idle funds that earn zero profit and stagnant business. Then it may face the alternative of public deficits or heavy taxes to support great non-self-liquidating public works, or heavy bills for unemployment relief, or both.

In the past, the percentage division of the value created in the processes of production between profits and wages seems to have remained surprisingly stable. This has been true in spite of a progressive increase in the amount of capital per worker. The adjustment has been made by very much higher wages per worker and somewhat lower rates of return on investment. In the future, if the country produces the income which it must produce in order to employ its workers, it will be so rich that the flow of savings which *must* find investment will naturally tend to increase in a sort of geometric progression, unless something happens to change our past trends of saving relative to income. This means a progressive increase in the volume of investment; and if it earns an undiminished rate of return, it will necessarily be absorbing an increasing percentage of the total income, leaving a smaller percentage for wages even if wages increase absolutely. The only escape from this would be for productivity to increase at an ever increasing rate — a geometric progression that could hardly be kept up forever. The alternative would seem to be a reduced rate of return on investment as a whole.

Profits as Source of Saving and as Incentive to Invest

14. In a general way, it seems likely that the total amount of profits in an economy such as ours is subject to both maximum and minimum limits. Both are presumably rather elastic and capable of shifting with changes in business psychology and business risks, and in the spending-saving habits of the population. The minimum is the amount necessary to afford sufficient incentive to invest. The maximum is the amount beyond which people and businesses receiving these concentrated incomes will undertake to save more than can be invested, with resulting idle funds and shrinking total income and employment. The interesting question is what will happen if the maximum gets below the minimum: if, in order to avoid oversaving, total profits must be so low as to afford insufficient incentive to invest, by current business standards. In a very rich country, this dilemma seems entirely possible. In that case, something would have to give; and the thing that could give with the least serious results would be the business investor's idea of the rate of return he has to have to make him willing to invest his funds in ways that increase the country's supply of productive equipment. This, of course, is easier said than done.

Efficiency of Weaker Competitors Needs Raising

15. Furthermore, the most serious deterrent to free and vigorous investment consists in the large percentage of enterprises which at any given time are making losses instead of profits. If new enterprises are to be started in large numbers, the prospect of profit must outweigh the prospect of loss; and this can hardly be true if many will fail and if the successful ones are limited to small or very moderate profits. To a less

extent the same thing is true if established enterprises are to be willing to take chances on far-reaching modernizations and bold departures, such as are necessary if industry as a whole is to maintain a healthy state of development and progress. One of the things that is most needed is a tax system which does not unduly discriminate against the taking of risks; but this could easily mean merely that successful concerns could keep larger rates of profit, rather than enabling industry as a whole to get on with more moderate rates. For the latter purpose it is more important to help the higher-cost concerns to raise their efficiency closer to that of their lower-cost competitors. Only then could they be strong enough to keep the profits of their lower-cost competitors down to moderate levels, without ruining themselves in the process. And only then could average profits be reduced without increasing the percentage of failures to a point that would prohibit bold risk-taking.

Another thing needed is to develop sound ways in which industry can raise larger amounts of equity capital from many personal investors in the general market. At present, too many concerns feel they must earn enough to furnish their additional equity capital out of plowed-back earnings, thus building up a margin of safety on the basis of which they can go into the general market for loan capital only. This is too much like earning two returns, one to divide and one to plow back. It requires the industry to earn more than the cash return which the personal investor receives. Not that there is anything wrong with plowing back earnings; the difficulty comes when it is incorporated into industry's idea of the necessary return, in addition to cash distributions, and when this idea persists into a period when the rate of return which industry as a whole can soundly earn seems likely to shrink to a point at which it would not support this practice as a general standard of sound financing.

It is the more successful concerns that can afford to plow back earnings on a large scale; and if they should all suddenly be converted to a policy of giving this margin to the consumer in the shape of lower prices, the result might be to put many of their less successful competitors out of business; and this would be a doubtful benefit. If a change of this sort takes place it would, as already noted, need to go hand in hand with a raising of the efficiency of the weaker competitors and would need to be gradual enough to permit this raising of efficiency to keep pace with it.

Competition and Business Responsibility for Low-Price Policy

16. There is probably no danger of the gospel of large sales at low margins spreading fast enough and in extreme enough form to do serious harm. Anything that business can be induced to do in this direction will be so much gained. The danger is rather that business self-interest, with whatever enlightenment it may be applied, will not carry this kind of policy as far as the welfare of the economy requires. A lively sense of the potentialities of competition is probably a better incentive to low-price policy than business self-interest of the sort that calculates visible and tangible quantities. Over and above this is a growing sense on the part of the more progressive business leaders that the most important job of business in the postwar period is to make itself into an effective instrument for promoting a high level of employment. This is in the interest of business, and it is a more important interest than the kinds that figure in tangible calculations of dollar profits and losses.

The Cooperation of Organized Labor Is Necessary

17. Organized labor also is recognizing that business must not only be asked to furnish ample employment but enabled to furnish it, and that the enabling conditions include willingness of labor to meet business halfway. This great joint interest needs to be implemented in every way possible, especially by groups representing the various particular interests which have a vital concern in this matter. Policy leadership by such groups can be a powerful force. In particular, the great federative labor organizations should be able to express the interest which all their members have as consumers and job-seekers in opposition to the kind of partnership in monopoly in which a union wins concessions from an industry and the industry charges the cost to the public in higher prices.

Low Interest Rates Have Limited Power to Stimulate Investment

18. A low rate of interest can be a material stimulus to investment in some important areas where maintenance and depreciation are low, risks are moderate and interest is a really substantial part of the cost incurred on account of an investment of capital. This is pre-eminently

true of hydroelectric installations and is broadly true of housing. But in the general field of industry and trade, low interest rates cannot accomplish as much as many economic theorists give them credit for. Interest alone is a minor part of the total cost or sacrifice involved in a capital outlay, especially in a dynamic industry, where equipment gets obsolete long before it is worn out and the allowance for obsolescence alone dwarfs the element of interest.

Heavy Taxes May Channel Investment in Wrong Directions

19. Among other things, heavy taxes can outweigh the stimulating effect of any feasible reduction of interest rates. Then capital may enter only openings where its yield is extra high, because the tax has to be paid out of it, when the situation requires that capital should be flowing into openings where the yield is moderate or low, in order to find productive uses for the country's large and growing flow of savings. And it is better for capital frankly and knowingly to go into low-yield openings than to hunt for high yields by duplicating existing investments in high-yield fields and crowding them with excessive facilities until the actual yield of the additional investment is a minus quantity for the economy as a whole.

The Wage Structure May Affect Employment

20. The structure of relative wages may be more important than the general level of wages in determining whether industry, acting on "sound" business principles, can furnish the opportunity for employment to virtually everyone. In fact, the question whether a particular increase or decrease of wages is desirable, from this standpoint, is likely to hinge on whether it shifts income to people who are more likely to use it (for consumption or investment) than the people from whom it is shifted, or vice versa. But there are other angles which may be equally important.

When minimum wage standards push up the lowest wages, one natural reaction in peacetime is for other wage rates in the same industries to rise so that the customary differentials for the better workers are more or less restored. Then prices are likely to be higher than they otherwise would have been, especially in industries in which low wage rates were particularly prevalent; but there is not likely to be any great effect on employment. Under wartime wage controls, with a general rise in wages restricted, the effect of an increased minimum wage is to squeeze the differentials together. Under war conditions, with a man power shortage, this has little or no effect on employment. But if some part of this squeezing together were to hold over into peacetime, it might not only react on the workers' incentives, but also have a tendency to make the poorer workers unprofitable to the employer and to make it harder for all of these poorer workers to find jobs. Then instead of increasing the total amount of pay going to these lower-paid workers, the effect might conceivably be to reduce it.

It will not work like a simple sum in arithmetic. The lower-paid workers may be employed on the simpler and less skilled operations, most of which nevertheless have to be done in a given quantity for a given total amount of product. Increased wages for this group of workers might make it economical to mechanize these operations, or to carry mechanization farther than it had been carried previously. This would first increase employment in the machine-making industries, and then reduce it in the processes that have been mechanized. The best or most adaptable of the former low-paid workers would be trained and promoted and some new workers of a different class might be brought in. But there would naturally be less work in this industry for this group of workers after the change.

Another possibility is that, without mechanization, more attention might be paid to training these workers and increasing their rate of output. In many cases, substandard wages are an index of the inefficiency of the employers more than that of the workers. Such employers might succeed in raising their efficiency or might lose business to others who are more efficient, thus raising the average level. This would be in the line of progress; but the workers who could not benefit by the training or improved conditions would remain "problem children" in the employment market. The problem of inadequate pay would have been replaced by the problem of relative unemployability at statutory wage rates, for some — perhaps a minority — of the workers whom the minimum wage is aimed to benefit. This is not a condemnation of minimum wages. It merely indicates that if they are carried very far, they may create a problem of employability for which private industry is not responsible and which it may not be in a position to handle with complete success.

Akin to this is the problem of the standard union wage rate, paid to workers of different quality without differentiation. The effect of this is again not a simple problem in arithmetic. To some extent the union assumes responsibility for certifying the efficiency of the workers. In some cases there is a standard maximum day's work (formal or informal) which matches the standard pay and enables the less capable workers to do as well as the others. And in some cases the poorer workers have gravitated to employers who do not pay the union rate. This affords a loophole, but it grows smaller as an industry approaches complete unionization, and complete unionization would close it completely. This would change the effect of the standard rate. The same rate which worked without ill effects as long as the loophole was open, might be too rigid after the loophole is closed. Thus the spread of unionization may lead to a need for greater elasticity in union wage systems; otherwise some of the poorer workers might become unemployable at union rates and thus be priced out of the market.

The general proposition which sums up this discussion of relative wage structures is that, as they become noncompetitive, the altered differentials are likely to make it harder for particular groups of workers to find employment, and may in effect price some of them out of the market.

Tentative and Yet Strategic

As to the entire twenty propositions bearing on the effect of wage-price structures, they have raised more problems than they have solved, and most of their conclusions are tentative, indicating what might happen rather than what must happen; but enough has been pointed out to indicate that if either government or private industry were to underwrite a high level of employment without regard to what the wrong kind of wage-price structure might do to defeat them, they would be inviting trouble and probable failure.

EFFECT OF HIGH-LEVEL EMPLOYMENT ON THE COST-PRICE STRUCTURE

So far we have been asking about the effect of the wage-price structure on the volume of employment. Equally pertinent is the effect of a high level of employment on the wage-price structure. Normally, the two move together. If cycles of prosperity and depression continue after the war, we may expect this tendency to continue, but in a modified form.

Wage Rates Raised During Expansion and Maintained During Contraction

In recessions, wage rates will resist deflation more strongly than before, the position of organized labor being stronger in the bargaining arena, while wage deflation would be almost sure to be considered contrary to public policy, so that bargaining power would be backed by political pressure. But if wages are pegged when production and employment decline, prices of industrial products cannot fall far — they seem bound to follow the pattern of wages, or at least to show increasing stickiness. Thus the pattern may be established under which wages will rise during industrial expansion and hold their gains during contraction. If the net rise of wages during a cycle is equal to the gain in productivity over the same period, prices may merely fluctuate slightly around a stable trend-line. If wages gained more than productivity, prices would be forced up by the increase in costs, unless some rather far-reaching adjustments were made to enable business to absorb the increase in costs and still retain the vitally necessary power to expand.

This is the kind of pattern we may expect to see if private business remains the governor of the rate of economic activity. Even if it succeeds in holding a high average level and in keeping fluctuations moderate, it is not in the nature of private industry to run with perfect steadiness. That is, not unless the economy were to become thoroughly cartelized, in which case industry would no longer be private. But suppose the government enters in with supporting policies, the simplest being direct public spending, thereby guaranteeing that when business gets prosperous it will stay prosperous, and that when employment reaches a high level it will remain high; how would that affect the pattern?

One group of theorists say that there will be no price-wage "inflation" until we reach "full employment." So unless we go beyond that level, which is not likely, there will be no inflation. Others, more realistic about the behavior of the labor market, forecast the possibility of an endless inflationary movement of wages and prices, and conclude that if we are going to spend our way to full employment and do not want to suffer from endless inflation, we shall be forced to maintain ceiling controls over wages and prices as a permanent peacetime measure.

Which is right — or is the truth something less simple than either hypothesis?

Wage Rates Rising Before Full Employment Is Reached

In normal times, as we have seen, wages and prices tend to rise while economic activity is on the way up from depression to prosperity — that is, while there are still idle workers and idle plant capacity. Perhaps this rise is not "inflation" but merely "reflation" from unduly depressed levels — we shall not quarrel over names. If it goes no farther than it does in a normal business revival, the mere extent of the rise need not trouble us, the only disquieting question being whether it contains internal maladjustments which are bound to lead to a relapse.

More pertinent, perhaps, is the experience of this country in the defense drive and war effort of 1940–1942, since this was an expansion induced by government spending, and one which was intended to utilize our productive capacity to the full. At the start, in June 1940, there were 8.6 million unemployed, and not until April 1942, was this number reduced to 3 million, which might be taken as a normal "float," equivalent to full employment. By this time strong inflationary pressures had been developing for a year. The cost of living had risen some 15 per cent and wholesale prices about 30 per cent, and the General Maximum Price Regulation had become necessary to hold the movement in check. This is a far greater increase than accompanies a normal business revival. The suggestion is that a deliberately stimulated expansion may be expected to bring on inflation considerably before full employment is reached.

However, there are reasons why a peacetime program, aimed at high-level employment for its own sake, would not naturally bring on such a steep price movement. The armament drive, it was clear from the start, would not stop when "full employment" was reached, but was certain to keep right on until an acute man power shortage was reached. More important perhaps is the fact that it required an urgent and drastic redirection of production into new products, calling for new equipment and new skills, and in many cases for movement to new localities; and therefore was bound to develop many more bottlenecks than a peacetime program would encounter. In the peacetime program there would be no need to restrict production and purchases for private consumption — the more the better and the less burden on the government program. There would be no need to draw off or sterilize income which consumers were eager to spend on consumption or which producers would invest in producing to satisfy consumers' wants. It would be only the income that consumers and private business would *not* use in these ways that government would be concerned to acquire and set moving, or to compensate for.

Weighing the pros and cons, it appears that a publicly supported full-employment program would bid up wages and prices probably as much as they rise in a normal business revival and possibly more, but not to the extent that they rose in 1940–1942. This rise might be mitigated by shrewd and businesslike negotiation on the part of government in administering its own spending, but opinions will differ as to how successful government is likely to be in this direction.

Gradual Progressive Rise in Prices

The serious question would be: what next? Would the wage-price increase continue in a progressive inflation, would it flatten out into approximate stability, or would it perhaps lead to a contraction of private production and a decline of the price-wage structure, due to its own internal inconsistencies? No one can say for certain. But the probability would seem to be that if a really high level of employment were maintained — if unemployment were approximately stabilized at a "float" averaging not more than three to four million — there would be a tendency to a gradual progressive rise in prices of the sort that is pushed up by increased money costs. If various powerful groups were to act as if the government's program were a Christmas tree or a grab bag, the inflationary tendency could go far enough to do harm. If the groups follow a statesmanlike policy, the tendency might be kept within harmless limits. Whatever happens, much will depend on whether these powerful groups develop a sense of responsibility in the exercise of their power, and something approaching economic statesmanship.

Something should be said of the considerations on which this tentative conclusion rests. One central question is: do wages rise because employment is high, or because it is rising? In the latter case, we should expect stable wages at full employment, except for a slow upward trend due to advancing productivity. In the former case, we should expect a continuing inflationary increase. Probably each has some effect. Commonly prices and wages stop rising at the crest of a wave of prosperity, when expansion ceases and many employers find that they are paying about as much as they can afford. But would they stop if continued high demand were virtually guaranteed, including a guarantee against shrinkage due to increased costs and prices? (Here the form of the government's commitment is important, and the kinds of measures it undertakes to employ. These might or might not have the effect of a virtual guarantee.) Or would prices and wages keep on rising?

Union Wage Policies and Monopoly Prices

Factors tending to continued rise include the likelihood that public spending would fortify existing monopolies, and that employers and workers might join forces and charge the bill to the public. This may be furthered by the fact that there are always vacancies in the labor market, even when there is a considerable amount of unemployment. When there are three million unemployed, there may be at the same time, for example, a million vacancies. If labor is unorganized, ten unemployed can perhaps outweigh ten vacancies in their effect on the relative bargaining power of employer and employee. If labor is strongly organized, with union-shop contracts and a restricted membership, operating under a tight seniority system which does not leave the employer free to hire any qualified worker who may happen to be unemployed, then ten vacancies might fairly easily outweigh thirty or forty unemployed, enabling the union to insist on a wage increase while the older workers who are influential in determining union policy would still have assured jobs and some elbow room in the labor market, being able to change employers if they wished, without fear of unemployment. Thus employers might be competing for labor more actively than workers are competing for jobs.

Add to this the fact that union leaders are under pressure to produce a gain for their membership every now and then, to earn their salaries and to justify the union dues and overhead. Available methods include keeping a close watch on the employers' earnings and the method of directing initial demands at concerns that can most easily afford to grant them, after which others may be forced to follow suit. This may necessitate a price increase, especially since the gains that might be made out of increased productivity are hampered by output-limiting practices. This combination of powers and methods has been growing and developing to a point at which gradual but progressive wage-cost inflation may well be within the discretion of union leadership.

Against this it can be argued that the fortifying of private monopolies would result from public spending only if it is bungled. If it is shrewdly handled, it could be a lever for extracting concessions, even from groups with some monopoly power. It can further be contended that the above argument exaggerates the extent to which wages are insulated from the forces of supply and demand. The observed tendency of wages and prices to rise before full employment is reached can be explained on the ground that they have been forced to abnormally low levels by the pressures of depression, including not only an excess supply of labor, but the inability of many businesses to pay more; and they begin to recover as soon as the pressure is eased, and business can afford a more adequate wage. It can be argued that strong demand and a reduced "float" of unemployed will aid wages to rise as long as business can afford to pay the increases, but no longer. And increased productivity affords a fund out of which labor leaders can secure a gradual flow of gains to their members, without the necessity of raising prices. Where productivity has increased, employers can absorb a wage increase. Even where no prior increase in productivity has taken place, a wage demand may prod the employer into making an improvement which will enable him to absorb it. This progressive increase in productivity is not entirely prevented even where it has to take place in a setting of output-limiting practices.

FINANCING WAGE INCREASES BY INCREASED EFFICIENCY

The reducing of production costs through increased productivity is pretty universally regarded as the unquestionably sound way to finance wage increases. Yet the simultaneous existence of output-limiting practices at least suggests that there may be two sides to that question.

Increased Productivity of Labor and Technological Unemployment

Increased productivity means turning out the same amount of product with less labor. When the gains are passed on to the customer in reduced prices, a 10 per cent reduction in price almost necessarily means more than a 10 per cent reduction in the number of man-hours represented by a physical unit of product. This would be more markedly true if the gains are shared with the workers in the particular industry in the form of increases in wages. Unless the reduction in price causes more than a 10 per cent increase in the number of physical units purchased, the whole change will mean fewer jobs in this industry than there would otherwise have been. And if the reduced price increases sales more than 10 per cent, then it is likely to mean that the customers will spend less for other things. Is it not then true that reducing costs to increase sales is no remedy for idleness, since reduction of costs through increased productivity per man-hour means displaced labor, somewhere, for someone, and cannot mean anything else?

The answer is basically simple. Increasing efficiency by reducing labor costs does displace labor unless the economy is ready to make active use of the increased total power of production which the improvement has given it. This would normally mean some increase in the buying of consumers' goods and some increase in capital outlays by productive establishments. This kind of adjustment is actually made, but may or may not be made in sufficient amount to absorb the increased productive power, and rapidly enough to absorb it before some other improvement displaces more labor which will have to be absorbed. This type of unemployment can be written down as due to a lagging of the adjustments that absorb increased productive power behind the improvements that increase it.

Adjustments Necessary for Reabsorption of Displaced Labor

Does this mean that, ideally, we should cut the speed of technical progress to fit the speed of the expansion of our demand for products?[10] No, it does not. The case for retarding improvements does not apply to the kind of progress that introduces new or improved products, merely to the kind that reduces costs of producing products substantially identical with those we are already producing. But the two cannot always be sharply distinguished. And if an employer can be nudged by a wage demand to improve his efficiency of production, a nation with many unsatisfied wants can also be prodded into spending some of its ingenuity in finding ways in which the satisfaction of the wants can be financed. And when it has gone as far as it wants to go in

---

10. We may pass over the answer some unions might make: namely, to limit output or reduce the working week without reducing weekly wages, until the problem is solved by eliminating all reduction in cost of production. This is too clearly a wrong answer.

that direction, it can turn the same ingenuity into shortening its average working week (which is easy) and making the (not-so-easy) adjustments which are necessary to cause this shortening to take the shape of an equitably diffused benefit for the people in general instead of a concentrated misfortune or calamity for some of them.

To block the introduction of improvements is an economic error; but some retardation may be, on economic grounds, a lesser evil, unless we do something effective about these adjustments, without which improvements can be a calamity to some as well as a benefit to others. During the past hundred years and more, we have been too generally content with the first of these truths and have failed to recognize the second truth, which qualifies the first; or we have consoled and justified ourselves with the false idea that these adjustments take care of themselves. What is needed first is to recognize that neglecting these adjustments weakens or undermines the case for unchecked technical improvement; and that they do not take care of themselves, but constitute far-ramifying problems which will not be easy to solve.

A Working Code of Principles

Next, we should take steps toward developing a working code of general principles applying to these matters. The code drafters must know the actual impact of improvements, and must somehow incorporate the valid substance underlying the divergent traditional attitudes of employers, of employees and of economists. But the only persons from either of these three groups who are qualified to take a useful part in the actual drafting of the code are persons each of whom realizes that the traditional attitudes of his own group represent only a partial truth. Each must not only be prepared to make adjustments, but he must recognize that adjustments are right and proper, and are not a mere matter of expediency. He must not be saying to himself: "Of course, I am right, but I must compromise with the unwarranted demands of these others, because otherwise they won't go along." Such a compromise is better than war, but it produces only unstable truces instead of stable bills of rights which are accepted as equitable and not merely as necessary. And it is stable bills of rights that we need, with the qualification that stability includes capacity for development, such as our political constitution has shown, and does not mean unchanging rigidity.

IS AN UPWARD TREND OF WAGES AND PRICES HARMFUL?

Assuming a gradual upward drift of prices, how much harm does it do? The answer is that the increase in itself does no clearly demonstrable balance of harm, if it is gradual enough. The thing that might do harm would be pushing prices up from the cost side in noncompetitive fashion, when demand is not strong enough to invite the increase and sustain it. This may conceivably lead to reduced output and idleness, where an increase induced by strong demand would add a secondary stimulative element of its own. And if the bargaining power which pushes up the cost-price structure is based on practices interfering with the free use of productive resources — new processes, plant facilities or idle workers — which could pay their way if used, then employment is directly interfered with.

In so far as such practices are part of the picture, the evil would not be cured by attempting to maintain ceilings on prices and wages after the war. Once more, much will depend on the good sense and community responsibility with which those at the heads of great corporate and group organizations exercise the enormous powers which the modern organization of industry places in their hands.

V. Concluding Reflections — A Responsible Economy

ADEQUATE AND BALANCED SPENDING

In the matter of total spending, the chief conclusion reached is that the financing of a high level of employment is not merely a matter of where the money is coming from, but needs to take account of where it is going to and for what it is to be spent. A desirable balance between consumption and investment may ease the burden on outright public spending and may save the economy from the necessity of making one thing it does not want in order to get one thing it does want, enabling it instead to make two things it wants.

If there is a problem of people wanting to save more than the economy requires for investment, desirable balance means, among other things, an increase of spending for current consumption. Ways of bringing this about, while still providing for individuals' future needs, are less obvious and simple than an increase in public works, but the ultimate results are more satisfactory. Sheer increased public spending will probably have to be employed, and a regular policy of intermittent increased spending in slack times is logical as a measure to stabilize economic fluctuations. Beyond that, it is to be looked on as a palliative, to be used while measures looking to a more naturally balanced economy are being investigated and experimented with.

THE COST-PRICE STRUCTURE

To sum up the provisional findings on the cost-price structure is not easy. Some of them look to the maintenance of competition, with especial emphasis on reducing inequalities in efficiency between competitors. Some look to a high level of policy leadership by those who are strategically placed to exercise it — usually heads of great nationwide organizations. Some look to bringing together members of different economic groups. They might undertake general policy leadership — such as the Johnston-Green-Murray declaration — or more specific policy commitments — such as might be formulated with respect to the annual wage or other methods of paying wages. In some cases they might undertake actual business commitments — as where the different interests involved in construction might agree to share the burden of a price concession, with the help of which some definite expansion of construction or additional off-peak construction could be made economically practicable. The impression resulting from these varied recommendations may be of a collection of proposals which is incoherent or perhaps even inconsistent. Something should be done to bring these elements into a more unified picture.

Competition should be maintained wherever it can be made to work in a reasonably effective and healthy way. The fact that in every particular case it is either mixed with monopolistic elements or otherwise imperfect, does not condemn it. Imperfect competition is the only kind possible; and some grades of "monopolistic competition" probably come nearer to the economist's ideal of "perfect competition" than "pure" and unmitigated competition does, since that so often goes (or used to go) to ruinous cutthroat lengths, driving the participants into various kinds of protective arrangements.

This principle applies not only to business but in the field of labor organization, where we have recognized the harmful and "cutthroat" character of unmitigated competition among individual workers and have sanctioned "democratic collective bargaining." Under this heading we have accepted, without too many qualms, arrangements involving degrees of noncompetitive action and unified power and control such as would unquestionably be prosecuted under the antitrust laws if business did the same kinds of things. This acceptance is not necessarily wrong; in fact, a considerable degree of it is not only inevitable but necessary to enable the workers to protect themselves with any approach to equality. Because the individual worker is more helpless than the individual business enterprise, he needs more liberty for joint action.

But we must not forget that matter of degree, nor the responsibility that goes with any considerable degree of freedom from competitive pressures. Both are of the essence of the case. In both business and labor, some degree of discretionary power over the markets is inevitable; and in the case of labor and agriculture it has public approval and support. Such discretionary power may be called "monopolistic" if one wishes to use a colored word, but that word does not do justice to the competitive forces that remain, and may well be reserved for some of the more aggravated degrees which can do so much damage that they need to be restrained or publicly supervised in the interest of the community. There are degrees which require formal restraint; but if formal restraint were used in every case in which there is something wrong, then we should really be headed toward a totalitarian system. A free system requires and implies a large area in which people make decisions and are under obligation to make them responsibly.

We must write off as obsolete the theory that the institutions of a laissez-faire system harness economic selfishness so perfectly that it can do no positive harm and therefore can safely be left free of further responsibility. Along with this should go the inconsistent idea that a free system must be competitive (which is true) and that competition is not "true" (or "perfect") unless it is of a sort that standardizes conduct with such coercive power that it eliminates all real freedom on the part of the competitor. These old theories had a workable (though sadly imperfect) relation to a simple economy of many small units. But we cannot turn the clock back to this simpler stage if we wished. Therefore it is past time for us to abandon our long-cherished illusion that we live in a world which is safe for the irresponsible pursuit of self-interest.

Big business, big organized labor, big organized agriculture, are more than bargaining agencies. They are all also forms of government.[11] They are not supreme, but they have so much power that the political government is not exactly supreme over them either, as a practical matter, despite its theoretical supremacy. They have become a working part of our system of "checks and balances." They exercise a considerable degree of the generic kinds of power which are the earmarks of government. And we live in an age in which government, in enlightened countries, must be responsible to the governed. This responsibility must be implemented, but the implementation must stop short of complete subjection to the coercive power of political government. And the lesser degrees of this responsibility must remain private and personal. If we are not capable of developing this sense of personal responsibility in economic affairs, then we simply shall not weather successfully the storms that are coming.

This does not mean that altruism must replace self-interest in economic affairs; though critics from both sides — socialists and old-fashioned individualists — will read this into my position for purposes of refuting it. Altruism means looking out for others' interests for their own sakes, in addition to one's own or instead of one's own and without regard to whether these interests of others are bound up with one's own in any way other than the fact that one feels altruistically. Altruism connotes a motivation which, so far as it exists in most of us, is too palely intellectual to exert much force in the rough-and-tumble of material affairs. But the motives we are dealing with here are anything but palely intellectual.

One is the impulse of self-preservation, or more exactly the impulse to defend what one feels to be the most basic things about one's environment and way of life. Farsighted businessmen realize that, if private business does not make a better employment record in the future than it has in the peacetime past, something fairly drastic is pretty sure to happen. Another is the impulse to be self-supporting — not only to pay one's legal debts, but to be able to justify one's income by service rendered. This criterion is not satisfied when one party's comfortable income comes out of a two-sided relationship out of which the other

11. Cf. the present writer's *Social Control of Business*, 2d ed., McGraw-Hill, New York, 1939, pp. 517–18. The point is the main theme of an unpublished paper delivered in 1931. Cf. also B. Ruml, *Tomorrow's Business*, Farrar and Rinehart, New York, 1945, especially p. 51.

party fails to get the minimum conditions of tolerable existence, by the accepted standard of the time.

The impulse of self-support compounds with the sense of justice and the necessity of being a member of a community, where the community must at least be broad enough to include those with whom one comes face to face in one's dealings. Ultimately, it has to be broad enough to include all those whom one's dealings affect in a substantial way. Though the manual worker's immediate ties are to other manual workers, and the business manager's are to others in his own class, to stop there is to accept the implications of class war. Most of us are now consciously rejecting these implications, with an awareness sharpened by our contacts with various totalitarian systems; and the thinking ones are paying fresh attention to the fact that if we do not want our economic relations to be settled for us by governmental coercion, we must learn to settle them among ourselves. This means getting together, each group accepting responsibility for doing its part to make a workable whole; and each recognizing, at least in general terms, that the others have basic human needs which must be met, plus functional requirements without which they cannot do their parts successfully.

This method cannot do everything that needs doing to ensure adequate opportunity for employment. Its clearest field of operation lies in the adjustments of the system of costs, prices, hours, output and forms of wage payments; and even in this field it has its limits. If monopolistic units persist in following a restrictive and exploitive policy, it may be necessary to attack them formally. But such cases should be exceptional. Granted a general acceptance of the idea that the most crucial product of industry after the war will be jobs, that the cost-price structure can be a favoring condition or a hindrance, and that the responsibility for making it a favoring factor lies on all concerned, much should be accomplished without formal public intervention. More specifically, much may be done in checking the shortsighted exercise of the lesser degrees of power over prices and wages afforded by the partial and limited shelters from the rigors of competition which are nowadays so prevalent. Neither altruism nor intelligently calculating self-interest will alone do what is needed. No combination of motives will do all that an idealist might wish. But associative action on a really broad base seems the most promising approach.

Chapter 4

ECONOMIC EXPANSION
THROUGH COMPETITIVE MARKETS

Howard S. Ellis[1]

I. BASIC OBJECTIVES

The economic philosophy which underlies the policies outlined in this essay for the period after the war is strongly liberal, individualist, equalitarian, and internationalist. Protracted debate in the abstract concerning the merits of competition versus planned or totalitarian economic orders is indeed bootless. But it is dangerous to venture into policy-making over a broad field without at least a brief consideration of basic objectives. The careless use, in much current discussion, of such terms as "private enterprise," "profit system," and the like serves to obscure issues and to invite a patronizing attitude on the part of those who believe a competitive system moribund.

To be explicit: by *liberal* I mean the reliance upon a competitive price system as against political authority for the largest part of economic control. By *individualist* I mean an emphasis upon individual "rights" or liberty as against the negation of such liberties in an omnipotent state. By *equalitarian* I mean the advocacy of a degree of equality of income approximately as great as that contemplated by liberal socialists.[2] By *internationalist* I mean favoring the abandonment of all efforts directed toward the insulation of national economies, except limiting immigration, sometimes defensible on both sociological and economic grounds.

Since competition itself is invested with nearly every possible meaning, it is necessary to say that the term is here used to mean the existence, among both buyers and sellers, of effective rivalry, together with reasonably adequate (but not necessarily perfect) mobility and knowledge of market conditions. In this sense a competitive price system has,

---

1. Professor of Economics, University of California, Berkeley; Assistant Director, Division of Research and Statistics, Board of Governors of the Federal Reserve System.
2. Such as Hobson, Durbin, Lange, Lerner, and Mossé.

briefly, the following advantages: (a) economic resources tend to be supplied to those uses which promise to yield the most profit; (b) price will be high enough to evoke and maintain supply in equilibrium with demand for each good; (c) no owner of productive resources can materially increase returns by withholding supply; (d) the distribution of jobs and resources amongst possible claimants depends upon an impersonal mechanism; (e) economic power, while not distributed equally, is diffused.

A Competitive System Does Not Mean "Hands Off Business"

The underlying cause of most misgivings as to the advantages of competition is inherited wealth; but the power and earnings which it brings are not part of a truly competitive system, and nearly all economists, past and present, believe that it should be reduced to small proportions by inheritance and gift taxes. It should be emphasized, moreover, that under modern conditions, the competitive system does not admit a laissez-faire policy: it requires outside interference to turn its powers toward full utilization of resources. Nor is a competitive system incompatible with extensive "social services." With these warnings (rather than "exceptions") the traditional arguments for a competitive price system as set forth in the preceding paragraph will be seen to be substantially valid. Most of the wastes commonly ascribed to competition are actually those of monopoly and monopolistic competition.[3]

With the removal of large inheritances of wealth, a competitive system need not differ much from a liberal socialist system[4] in which state-owned enterprises compete for the use of labor, materials, and capital in order to satisfy the market demand for various goods and services resulting from free consumer choice. The chief advantage of either, especially in view of the present trends toward concentrating power in national governments — bureaucratic, collectivist, or totalitarian — is its lack of dependence on authoritarian or highly centralized control. A competitive price system, by and large, governs in a "rational" way without preconceived plan and avoids the insoluble question as to who

3. Frank D. Graham, *Social Goals and Economic Institutions*, Princeton University Press, Princeton, 1942, p. 52, and Joan Robinson, *The Economics of Imperfect Competition*, Macmillan, London, 1933, *passim*.

4. Cf. A. P. Lerner, "Economic Liberalism in the Postwar World," *Postwar Economic Problems*, ed. S. E. Harris, McGraw-Hill, New York, 1943, Chap. 7; and F. M. Taylor and Oscar Lange, *The Economics of the Socialist State*, University of Minnesota Press, Minneapolis, 1938.

has a right to impose his plan. Besides being impersonal it provides a decentralization and balance of economic powers. Business has been indicted as a "system of power," and so it is under monopoly control; but let us not forget that the state possesses the greatest of all monopolies — the monopoly of force.

The state has always and presumably always will participate in economic activity in order to enforce certain generally accepted rules of fairness in the market, to offset the inherent instability of the competitive system, and to perform economic functions ill suited to production for profit. Persons who declare that a "mixed system" is impossible make as great an error as those who imagine there was ever an unmixed system, e.g., complete laissez faire. As society becomes more complicated through more intricate techniques, through accelerated transportation, and through new forms of monopolistic restraint, the role of the state becomes more extensive. But this does not signify, as some people infer, a necessary attenuation of the competitive field. There are simply more social and economic functions to be done, including that of maintaining the effectiveness of the competitive mechanism.

Unemployment Not Inherent in a Private Competitive Economy

To advocate a liberal economic system as the goal of postwar policy requires at least brief comment upon the idea that reasonably full employment is impossible in a private-enterprise economy.

1. Economists have thoroughly repudiated the idea that a downward course of economic activity necessarily generates self-corrective forces before it reaches disastrous levels. One does not need to be either a Keynesian or a Marxist to accept this view. Hence we cannot expect to solve the problem of cyclical unemployment without state action. In fact, responsibility for preventing cyclical decline of incomes and employment rests squarely upon the state. If it is true that no "single business leader of national prominence" is willing to accept this proposition,[5] dire consequences will follow. While the efforts of business enterprises to master the business cycle are essential, responsibility cannot attach to them singly or collectively, because they possess neither the unity of action, compulsory power, nor resources, commanded by the state. It does not follow, however, that we must turn to some form

5. Thus Lawrence Stern, in the *Magazine of Wall Street*, January 9, 1943, pp. 333–35 and 387–88.

of collectivism; there are a number of appropriate means of controlling business cycles in a capitalistic system which have not as yet been fully utilized.

2. The suggestion that capitalists have a lively interest in maintaining unemployment as a means of controlling labor does not bear close examination.[6] The fallacy of this argument lies in its supposing that the entrepreneurial class — witness the profits of our present full-employment economy — is not as much interested in continued high levels of activity as the workers. Why should we attribute to capitalists a psychopathic Samson-and-the-pillars complex?

3. It is likewise difficult to follow the reasoning of those who abandon the private-enterprise system because of its monopoly elements. Even a liberal socialist system would need to cope with the danger of restriction of output and there is no certainty that the remedies would be effective. If the alternative to capitalism, on the contrary, is a totalitarian or dictatorial form, it is passing strange to fly from the perils of "monopoly capitalism" into the arms of really complete and absolute monopoly. The problem of developing adequate policies to deal with monopoly presents no less a challenge to liberals than the struggle for the survival of political and economic liberty.

4. Before we leave the question as to whether full employment can be attained in a private-enterprise system, we need to consider a fourth line of argument, to the effect that private enterprise cannot possibly provide investment sufficient to maintain high-level employment.[7] This argument, generally known as the stagnation thesis, has received so much attention in recent economic literature that it merits discussion at some length.

The Oversaving Explanation of Unemployment

The stagnation thesis was launched in England by Keynes under the caption of "equilibrium with less than full employment" and elaborated in the United States by Professor Alvin Hansen. It has persuaded most of its numerous followers of the eventual demise of private enter-

6. Cf., for example, M. Kalecki, "Political Aspects of Full Employment," *The Political Quarterly*, Vol. 14, No. 4, October–December 1943, p. 325.

7. This characterizes the National Resources Planning Board's *Report for 1943*, Part I, *Postwar Plan and Program;* cf. Myron W. Watkins' review, *The Journal of Political Economy*, Vol. 51, No. 5, October 1943, pp. 397–414, especially pp. 408–09; also Robert R. Nathan's *Mobilizing for Abundance*, McGraw-Hill, New York, 1944, p. 94 *et passim*.

prise, though its chief authors do not go farther than to suggest that a large part of investment will for the foreseeable future have to be carried on by the state. Both Keynes and Hansen found the immediate cause of unemployment in a supposed excess of savings in relation to the profitable uses of capital. A somewhat involved theoretical analysis lay behind this conclusion; but for purposes of the general reader this can be considerably simplified — without injustice to the position I hope — under the convenient headings of the technological, psychological, and institutional obstacles to investment.

Under the first, Keynes found the demand for capital to be limited and inelastic because of a prospective lack of new uses for capital and the possibility of capital-saving inventions. Even so, investment might absorb savings at rather low interest rates were it not for two psychological blocks: (a) savers refuse to invest at low interest rates when by choosing instead to hoard money they can escape business risks; (b) laborers refuse to submit to a reduction of money wages, and this downward inflexibility of money wages limits the earning prospects of capital. Keynes had little to say on the score of institutional obstacles. This element was elaborated by Hansen, who emphasized the restrictive influence of monopoly and the reduced incentives arising from the disappearance of the frontier and from the declining rate of increase in population.

We cannot foretell the future course of technology, but the present scene is bright with promise.[8] Other considerations also may have counseled a retreat from the technological stagnation thesis. But industrial innovation causes technological unemployment, and creates business risks. On balance it would be difficult to assert whether technological progress in the future will aid or impede the flow of investment under private enterprise. The case is speculative and completely inconclusive.

As for the psychological obstacles to investment, hoarding presents a serious problem, but one which can be attacked through eliminating some of the institutional obstacles to investment.[9] Indeed, it would be

8. See, for example, the great variety of new investment channels contemplated by industrialists, businessmen, and scientists in William R. Kuhns, *The Return of Opportunity*, Harper, New York, 1944.

9. Incidentally pessimistic expectations (impending political or military defeats, declining birth rate, miscarriage of production plans) on the part of the management of a planned economy could produce unemployment, unless it were decided to keep people out of mischief by what seemed at the time to be purposeless production.

impossible to explain continued pessimism and hoarding unless the objective or institutional obstacles played an important role. The other subjective factor — the refusal of labor to accept reductions in money wages — plays a curious role in Keynes' own theory, since he proposes to expand employment by reducing real wages through the covert device of a (mild) price inflation. Perhaps because this policy seems rather Machiavellian, and because it is completely inconsistent with policies to stimulate consumption through raising real wages, Hansen minimizes the tendency of increased money flows to reduce real wages, preferring to direct attention to their expansionary influence on production.

With respect to the institutional obstacles to investment, the stagnation school moves on ground quite familiar to other and less "modern" economists. Unemployment is explained by monopolistic restriction, taxes which bear upon enterprise, obstacles to the free international movement of goods and capital, unjustifiably high interest rates in certain areas, and the discouragement to investment from the recurrence of depressions — subjects which appear subsequently in these pages and need not be pursued here. But it deserves explicit emphasis that the greater the role which is assigned to the institutional obstacles, the more rational is the policy which concentrates upon increasing investment rather than upon decreasing saving. Savings which are successfully incorporated in capital goods increase the welfare of labor through making goods more widely available and through increasing the productivity of labor itself.

The sections which follow propose numerous lines of government action intended to be internally consistent and to work powerfully through their mutually re-enforcing action toward economic expansion and the preservation of individual liberty. If a moral is to be drawn from these pages, it is the gospel of low price to the consumer and the horrors of a race between monopolistic restriction and Treasury expenditures. If a motto were taken, it would be the words of President Roosevelt, who looked forward to "a program whose basic thesis is, not that a system of free enterprise for profit has failed in this generation, but that it has not yet been tried."[10]

10. Message from the President of the United States to the Congress, April 29, 1938; reprinted in *Final Report and Recommendations of the Temporary National Economic Committee*, TNEC Doc. No. 35, p. 20.

II. THE SHORT-RUN PROBLEM OF SUSTAINING THE NATIONAL INCOME

At some unpredictable time in the postwar period, the government will undoubtedly face the necessity of direct measures to support income and employment as a whole. Over a longer run, the economic liberal believes, reform of our institutions would permit a gradual shrinkage of direct participation of government in economic activity. Through exploiting and extending the advantages of a competitive price system, we may succeed in bringing about a full and stable use of economic resources. But the cataclysm of war and its aftermath demand more (or at least protracted) government control in order eventually to have less. Engineering the economy through the reconversion period with only an inescapable minimum of frictional unemployment is thus doubly imperative: first, for its own sake, and then also for the sake of longer-range plans, such as the reduction of international trade barriers and liberation from domestic monopoly, which could scarcely be undertaken in the midst of deep depression.

THE MAGNITUDE OF THE UNDERTAKING

Businessmen, Congressmen, and journalists are increasingly aware of the importance of such broad economic aggregates as the national income, savings, employment, and total government outlays. Estimates of the probable relationships among these aggregates must play an important part in the formulation of public policy in the years to come.

In 1944–1945, with a gross national product of $200 billion we had 52 million persons in civilian and 11 million in military occupations, or 63 million employed. By two years after the war (say, 1947) the available labor force — in view of population increases and the permanent retention of some 2.5 out of 6.5 million new war laborers — will be about 60 million. Making allowance for increased productivity and for a frictional unemployment of 2 million, it will require a gross national product of about $180 billion (1943 prices) to absorb the total of 58 million laborers.[11]

11. Cf. estimates of E. A. Goldenweiser and Everett E. Hagen, "Jobs After the War," *Federal Reserve Bulletin,* May 1944, pp. 424–31. Subsequent to publication, the estimate of full-employment gross national output was increased by the authors from $170 to $180 billion. Cf. also S. Morris Livingston, *Markets After the War,* Bureau of Foreign and Do-

In estimates of this sort one of the most hazardous elements is the assessment of productivity increases through the war years and their applicability to the immediate postwar years, when productive effort will be devoted to civilian purposes. The Department of Commerce estimates the annual increase of output per man-hour for the period 1929–1941 at 2.5 per cent, compounded annually. If this were projected through the years 1940 to 1947 it would amount to nearly 20 per cent; but an efficiency increase of only 10 per cent was assumed in the preceding paragraph as the basis of the gross national product necessary to full employment. It deserves explicit emphasis that if this assumed increase of productivity proves to be excessive, all of these magnitudes will be smaller; and the private-enterprise sector will encounter a less formidable amount of potential technological unemployment.

The nature of the policies followed in the transition period will play an important part in determining whether the full employment induced by war will be followed by serious depression. The Swedish economist Gunnar Myrdal has voiced his conviction that America's conversion period will turn into depression. I do not share his feeling of inevitability, but we need to be prepared for the necessity of government support to the total demand for goods and services. To this we now turn.

PUBLIC WORKS AND CONSUMPTIVE EXPENDITURES BY THE GOVERNMENT

Stimulating Consumption Does Not Imply a Campaign to Reduce Saving

If in the long run it appears that we face a problem of "oversaving," the cure is an onslaught, not against savings, but against the institutional obstacles to investment. As long as the material welfare of the lower income groups leaves much to be desired, as long as vast quantities of capital can be used for slum clearance, hospitals, schools, etc., for the benefit of the broad masses of people, it is a cruel myth that we have "too much saving." To remedy unemployment arising from uninvested saving by attacking saving is analogous to reducing mortality from diabetes through lowering the birth rate. Extreme advocates of the

---

mestic Commerce, 1943; A. H. Hansen and H. S. Perloff, *State and Local Finance in the National Economy*, W. W. Norton, New York, 1944, Chap. 2.

oversaving thesis do not hesitate to go this far in fact: it is even dangerous, according to a recent utterance of Keynes, to permit people to work and earn as much as they naturally would, lest they save too much. Common sense, I believe, revolts at this particular route to an "economy of abundance." We need to recall once more the truth that real wages are raised by increases in the complement of capital goods: savings, effectively applied to production, contribute to the economic welfare of the masses.

Consumption is the purpose of economic activity; and a much more equal sharing in total consumption is the purpose of a democratic economic program. A more equal sharing is an end in itself to be achieved by a whole gamut of measures — progressive taxation, confiscatory death duties, a national minimum per capita income, free or at-cost provision of many essential services, and equality of opportunity through free public education and through a general relaxing of monopoly restriction. An onslaught upon savings can only withdraw the material foundation of consumers' and producers' capital goods upon which a high income economy, including the welfare of its poorer members, rests. Finally the goal of liberty, another ultimate value, is at stake. "It is the democratic dogma that the people themselves shall decide how much they will consume . . . and how much they will set aside for additions to capital," writes the *Economist*. "A democratic full employment policy must attain its goal while obeying these instructions."[12]

The Legitimate Grounds for Stimulating Consumption

The main emphasis, in planning a program of public spending to combat a postwar recession, should be on the adequacy of total spending. Public works and government expenditures to encourage consumption will both, I believe, quite properly be used, despite a general presumption favorable to consumptive expenditures. This presumption arises from two maxims of a liberal economic policy: (a) to permit to the individual a free choice of expenditures except for the limited sphere of socially harmful consumption, such as opiates and the like; and (b) to leave to private enterprise as large a segment of production as possible.[13]

12. The *Economist*, London, June 3, 1944, p. 738.
13. The thesis is ably argued by John H. G. Pierson, "The Underwriting of Aggregate Consumer Spending as a Pillar of Full Employment Policy," *The American Economic Review*, Vol. 34, No. 1, Pt. 1, March 1944, pp. 21–56.

Among the various methods of state spending upon consumption, only the policy of a "national minimum," the provision by the state of a certain minimum money income for every person, would embody both advantages. As the great liberal economist John Stuart Mill wrote: "Since no one is responsible for having been born, no pecuniary sacrifice is too great to be made by those who have more than enough, for the purpose of securing enough to all persons already in existence."[14]

A national minimum would be a simple and direct way of dealing with a depression without adverse effects on private production and without requiring paternalistic control of consumption. Certain conditions, however, would have to be observed. Membership in labor unions and other organized groups would have to be freely open. The minimum itself would have to be low enough so that there would be no incentive to loaf rather than to work, yet high enough to ensure enough purchasing power to maintain full employment. And, finally, the scale of payments would have to be related to the cost of living in different regions. These conditions would be difficult to achieve. Organized groups would be loath to relinquish their "right" to exclude members; and the marked regional and racial diversities of the United States would make the establishment of equitable minima a highly complex problem.

A practicable approach to the national minimum is an inclusive program of social security. Measures such as the Beveridge Plan in England or the Wagner-Murray-Dingell bill in the United States are surely justified as part of a long-run program to improve material welfare. During periods of recession, they would not only contribute to the relief of unemployment, but would also help to maintain employment through supporting purchasing power. But neither the size of the benefits nor the duration of unemployment payments bid fair to cope with the possible dimensions of a postwar depression.[15]

The unemployment benefits of the "G. I. Bill of Rights" are subject

14. J. S. Mill, *Principles of Political Economy*, Ashley ed., reprint, London, 1936, p. 363.

15. Estimates of the Tax Foundation for Wagner Act payments are $1.4 billion in 1945, rising to $8.5 billion by 1950, $9.8 billion in 1955, and $11.1 billion in 1960 — and these are thought to be rather high estimates. Lawrence R. Klein, "The Cost of a 'Beveridge Plan' in the United States," *The Quarterly Journal of Economics*, Vol. 58, No. 3, May 1944, pp. 423–38, presents estimates of $13 and $15.6 billion as the expenditures resulting from an application of the Beveridge Plan to the United States on an assumption of 7 million unemployed in 1945 and 1965. In place of 1945 the reader is apparently supposed to substitute a year with this much actual unemployment.

to the same limitation, and its other features — the $2,000 per capita loans, the construction of veterans facilities, and the four-year educational grants — while contributing effectively to aggregate demand, may do so under boom conditions as well as depression. Proposals to increase greatly the appropriations for the Federal Employment Service, even for covering the transportation costs of regionally displaced laborers, are well conceived, since they also contribute simultaneously to adjustment and to aggregate demand.

Desirable Character of Public Works

Despite the "general presumption" in favor of direct outlays for consumers, an extensive public works program should be planned for a postwar recession because (a) social security and similar expenditures do not promise to be large enough, (b) the federal government should utilize otherwise idle war plants (which will presumably require improvements and adaptations) to compete with monopolies, and (c) in some cases, private enterprise does not under existing institutions provide enough investment to care for certain "social wants." Other contributors to the present volume, I am confident, will supply authoritative estimates of the probable necessary magnitude of public works outlays, and I shall comment only upon the place of such a program within a general policy of fostering a competitive price-controlled economy.

If we are to bring about an orderly transition to a satisfactory level of economic activity after the war, immediate action must be taken to prevent an excessive postwar boom, to shape our tax laws favorably to enterprise capital, to open up international trade and finance to expansion, and finally to withdraw the bases of monopoly in all fields. Measures such as these, if successfully carried out, would eventually make possible a reduction in public spending to support the economy. But a public works program must play an important part until the effects of these basic reforms begin to be felt. Accordingly, it should be carefully planned in advance and vigorously executed when the need for it appears.

The direction of public investment should be governed by long-run productivity. For example, to cure a chronic surplus capacity in certain agricultural staples, public works should partly take the form of projects favoring diversified agriculture — experiment stations, schools, etc. The location of public works should again be determined by long-range productivity. Other things equal, labor should move to the project, not vice versa, in order to help correct regional oversupply of labor and discourage "pork barrel" appropriations. In the nature of the case this rule must be reversed wherever the public works are designed specifically to serve concentrated populations themselves, such as slum clearance, city center redevelopment, multiple dwelling units, and the like, as contemplated in the Thomas and Wagner bills. If public works are oriented toward long-run productivity, eventually even to long-run profitability, toward restoring competition in monopolized fields, and toward fields not well covered by private competition, and if they are timed to operate in a direction opposed to the business cycle, they will strengthen — not jeopardize — the system of private competitive enterprise.

GOVERNMENT SPENDING, TAXATION, AND DEBT

What we have been saying is that, in view of its responsibility to maintain employment, the government must spend enough to close any gap between private (and business) spending and the total spending necessary to maintain full employment. This principle collides directly with the declaration — nowadays in danger of becoming a shibboleth — that "we want no public spending for its own sake and no projects merely because they support purchasing power in general."[16] However much the advocate of a liberal economy may hope for basic reforms which will eventually reduce the need for public spending, he cannot intelligently counsel economy and caution. The principle is simple arithmetic. Since reforms necessarily proceed slowly, private and government outlays must at any time add up to full use of resources. Naturally this offers no defense of purposeless or wasteful use of public funds.

Orientation of Taxation to the Flow of National Income

On the basis of the gross national product of $180 billion (national income, $150 billion) assumed to be necessary for full employment two years after the war, taxes under present revenue laws — assuming the repeal of the excess-profits tax and excluding pay roll taxes —

16. Thus Beardsley Ruml in the symposium "A Postwar National Fiscal Program," *The New Republic*, February 28, 1944, p. 265.

would yield about $35 billion.[17] Upon the most probable assumption that federal expenditures, after the more immediate transition period, may run between $20 and $25 billion (excluding expenditures of trust funds), tax reductions of at least $10 billion would be possible with a full-employment national income of $150 billion.

With a national income of $130 billion, the yield of present taxes would fall to about $27 billion. Expenditures would be higher at the same time, so that a balanced budget would permit little or no tax reduction. As long as the magnitude of national income and employment permits tax reduction, the appropriate order would be: first, repeal of the excess-profits tax and the drastic cutting of excise taxation; next, the elimination of double taxation of dividends and a moderate reduction of personal income taxes; and finally, the drastic reduction of all tax revenue if unemployment is severe. This procedure on the revenue side would follow the pattern of "compensatory" fiscal policy, which requires a parallel increase of "spending" on the other side of the budget.

Drawbacks of Deficit Financing

Without a thoroughgoing program of institutional reform to favor competitive enterprise and venture capital, I would expect continued resort to deficit financing to carry us along to a fascist or socialist state. The increase of the public debt is dangerous to private enterprise from several angles. For one thing, it adds to the amount of fixed income and thus concentrates risk upon fewer incomes, indeed increasingly upon the entrepreneurs or active capitalistic class.[18] Those economists who regard the increase of the national debt with complacency argue that the service of even a large debt would represent a relatively small fraction of national income. But they fail to ask another appropriate question — how large is the service of the debt in relation to incomes on venture capital alone?

If the federal debt reaches $300 billion by June 30, 1946, the service on the debt in that month will amount annually to about $6 bil-

17. This estimate and those which follow were made by Richard Musgrave.
18. Emphasis upon precisely this aspect of public debt is to be found with Frank D. Graham, *Social Goals and Economic Institutions*, Princeton University Press, Princeton, 1942, p. 160; and with Norman J. Silberling, *The Dynamics of Business*, McGraw-Hill, New York, 1943, p. 679.

lion. This would represent only 4.2 per cent of a full-employment national income, but it would exceed the total of interest on private debt plus rents and would equal one fourth of total business income (dividends plus income of unincorporated business plus agriculture).[19] The purpose of this comparison is not to emphasize the amount of taxation, ascribable to the debt service, which falls upon property incomes. It points rather to the fact that, in an economy subject to ups and downs, the risk of fluctuating national income is the more concentrated upon venture capital income the larger the proportion of fixed capital income to total income. Since the ratio of genuinely entrepreneurial and business income to the total national income, is already small — say 10 per cent — an increase of the fixed public debt charges from one per cent to only 4 per cent of the national income may spell a substantial increase of the concentration of risks upon venture capital, upon which we rely as the mainspring of the economy. Of course the "fixed charges" of the debt may themselves be absorbed by deficit financing, but this is not possible secularly, and there are political limits in cyclical depressions.

Furthermore, a large national debt renders monetary management difficult. Given such a debt, it is almost impossible to control inflation without a depreciation of government securities and extensive direct interferences in the capital market. Finally the debt entails a heavy social cost, despite its being "owed to ourselves." Consider, for example, the burden of any kind of taxation upon economic motivation, the wastes of tax litigation, and of collection, and the costs involved in Congressional wrangling over revenue acts. Nor can we afford to forget the political drawbacks of a large *rentier* class. With interest absorbing a third of the federal postwar budget, these considerations are extremely important. On the other hand, proposals to convert a large part of the debt to non-interest-bearing form cannot, in our present institutional milieu, be seriously considered;[20] though interest payments to banks now appear to be excessive, and the limitation of banks to low-yield maturities could be carried farther than it is at present.

19. Cf. Tax Foundation, *Postwar Business Taxation and Jobs,* New York, 1944, and *Survey of Current Business,* July 1944, pp. 15–20. In 1943 private debt was 40 per cent as large as public, but interest rates were probably roughly twice as high in the former.

20. J. Carl Poindexter, "Fallacies of Interest-free Deficit Financing," *The Quarterly Journal of Economics,* Vol. 53, No. 3, May 1944, pp. 438–60.

Postwar Budget Deficits

The amount of debt incurred for war dwarfs the prospective magnitude of debt which, over a three- to six-year period, might result from public spending to combat a serious postwar recession. The war debt, with all its drawbacks, is something which we must now accept. It would be penny-wise and pound-foolish to bridle over another 10 per cent increase (or even more) which might successfully put the economy into running order after the cataclysm of war.

For the immediate future more serious monetary and fiscal problems will arise from the management of the debt — securing a structure of rates and maturities to induce public holding without further bank-credit support — than from the increments. For the longer future, a continued increase in economic productivity would progressively ease the debt burden by permitting larger national money incomes without inflation. Whether this increase actually appears, whether after a recuperative transition profit system will provide a level of output to utilize our capacity, depends upon the progress of basic reforms to realize a genuinely competitive economy.

III. Monetary Controls and the Business of Banking

The overwhelmingly important fact in postwar monetary matters, the prospective shrinkage of federal expenditures within a few years from $100 billion to a fourth or fifth of this sum, tells us nothing as to the sequence of future events. Must we be prepared for a postwar boom like that which followed the last war? Perhaps not. With widespread apprehensiveness as to the future, with victory in Europe preceding the end of the Pacific war by only a few months, with an expeditious shifting of production, with enormous surpluses to be liquidated, and with a steady decline in federal expenditures, there may be no force to engender a postwar boom. We may witness, instead, a short "shock" depression in the reconversion period, recovery induced by backlogs of demand, and finally the playing-out of deferred demand, and depression.

Whatever the precise sequence of events, several things seem reasonably certain. We shall have to cope with frictional, sectional, and particular industry unemployment, whether prices as a whole move upward or downward. Secondly, we must be prepared for the eventual appearance of inadequate demand. There is only a chance that inflationary pressure may develop before that juncture.

But we cannot afford to ignore the possibility of a postwar boom. What monetary measures could be applied in such a situation? Looking farther ahead, will monetary controls be superseded by direct controls to solve the long-run problem of achieving economic stability at high output levels? Finally, what will be the future roles of commercial banking and of central banking in the American economy?

CENTRAL BANK CONTROLS AND A POSSIBLE POSTWAR INFLATION[21]

The only absolute control of inflation is direct limitation of spending; rationing, price ceilings, and War Production Board priorities on the use of materials are therefore indispensable for the first postwar years. Many unsatisfied wartime demands will appear as simple physical needs (housing, household appliances, automobiles), and many others as a part of a decent American standard of living. Furthermore there is the constant pressure of particular interests — witness the cotton growers' victory in the early summer of 1944 — to raise or abolish price ceilings.

Factors Involved in a General Price Rise

As ceilings and rationing are withdrawn, four factors compatible with sustained economic activity might play a part in preventing a general rise of prices: the growth of production for civilian use, surpluses in the federal budget, the repayment of business and private debt, and continued large holdings of cash relative to income. Rapid conversion would help to restrain prices but would be impotent against strong inflationary pressure; there is virtually no prospect of budget surpluses in the immediate postwar years; and even the great liquidity in war years has induced only a small reduction of private debt.[22] Thus, if price controls are relaxed, the course of prices will depend largely on the attitude of the public toward spending. Will individuals and business firms be disposed to hold their money, bank deposits, and govern-

21. To associates in the Board of Governors of the Federal Reserve System, particularly Roland I. Robinson, Woodlief Thomas, and Carl E. Parry — who are not answerable for my contentions and errors — I am indebted for substantial aid.
22. During the years, 1941–1943, total private debt fell from $119.5 billion to $111.7 billion, or by 6.5 per cent; cf. "Wartime Debt Changes in the United States," *Survey of Current Business,* July 1944, pp. 14–20.

ment securities, or will they proceed to sell securities and spend money? If they should choose the latter course, an enormous volume of purchasing power could be set loose.

ESTIMATED HOLDINGS OF PRINCIPAL LIQUID ASSETS BY
INDIVIDUALS AND CORPORATIONS
(*In Billions of Dollars*)

	December 31, 1939	December 31, 1944	Increase During Five Years
Currency	6.2	23.3	17.1
Demand deposits	21.3	54.7	33.4
Time deposits	26.3	38.9	12.6
U. S. government securities	12.1	76.7	64.6
Total liquid assets	65.9	193.6	127.7

Source: Federal Reserve Bulletin, June 1945.

Note: Figures exclude currency, demand and time deposits, and United States government securities, held by banks, insurance companies, savings and loan associations, all governmental bodies, educational and charitable institutions, other nonprofit associations, and foreigners.

During five years of national defense and war (1939–1944), the public's liquid holdings have increased *by* (not *to*) 194 per cent. It should be noted that the "public" in this tabulation excludes those sectors not apt to dishoard or to sell securities before maturity. For the public, so defined, the inclusion of government securities in the totals is warrantable if the Federal Reserve stands ready to convert the entire body of government securities to cash rather than permit a decline in their prices.

Selective Credit Controls

What steps could be taken to restrict spending in the event of threatened inflation? The selective credit controls which now apply to the purchase of securities on margin and to consumer buying undoubtedly exercise strong restraints in these markets. These controls could be tightened to bring about the complete elimination of credit buying in both fields. A boom in agricultural land values could probably be held in check by the termination of "parity" and other measures which disproportionately increase farm incomes. Aside from such fundamental changes, special legislation to increase the down payment on land purchases[23] would be superior to attempting to improvise a special tax on speculative gains as proposed in a recent bill.[24] Differential taxation of "unearned" income or gains is dangerous and inequitable unless carried through to all cases; but this presents almost insuperable difficulties.

Such selective controls may eliminate some spending altogether; but if the inflationary movement should prove to be really strong, they would be quite insufficient since they pertain only to borrowing, leaving the mass of existing purchasing power untouched.

Depressing the Prices of Government Securities

The usual method of checking inflationary price advances is for commercial banks to restrict loans to customers, and for the Federal Reserve Banks, acting as a central banking system, to restrict their loans to commercial banks. The table on page 142 shows, however, that private individuals and business can, if they are so disposed, bring about an inflation without any borrowing through drawing upon their enormous cash reserves and redeeming or selling short-dated securities. Similarly, commercial banks can help to create an inflation without borrowing from the Federal Reserve Banks. On January 31, 1945, commercial banks held $72.6 billion in United States government marketable securities. Of this total, only 1.4 per cent had maturities over 20 years, 4.7 per cent from 10–20 years, 28 per cent from 5–10 years, 65.4 per cent within 5 years, and 36.6 per cent within one year. With so large a volume of short-term assets, and without higher rates of interest on the part of the Federal Reserve and Treasury, the banks could expand their reserves and loans simply by holding the securities to maturity.

Thus the ultimate, and indeed the only, recourse is an advance of

23. It has been suggested that Presidential emergency powers could be used to limit speculative developments in agricultural land through an emergency construction of the private individual mortgagee as a bank, bound by rigorous requirements as to margins, amortization period, etc.

24. E. C. Johnson, "The Farm Real Estate Market," *Federal Reserve Bulletin,* March 1944, p. 232.

interest rates and a consequent depreciation of government securities not redeemable on demand. This would tend to discourage sales of these securities by holders seeking to convert into cash, since a prospective seller would face a capital loss on the transaction. It would not, at least formally, break faith with investors, since they would be paid full values at maturity dates. The decline in the prices of government securities would have to be held to moderate proportions in order to prevent a panicky wave of selling on the part of banks and other holders of "governments." Undoubtedly this is chiefly a "psychological" matter. Almost any departure from the antecedent policy of complete support of security prices might dislodge the avalanche. The results would be disastrous not merely to the relatively weak or poor holders of securities and to Treasury financing, but also to bank credit, entrepreneurial expectations, and employment.

General Credit Controls

If a moderate decline in government securities did not check the price inflation, it would be necessary to resort to other credit controls, with higher discount rates as the first step. Admittedly this would not directly prevent security or commodity speculation; but margin requirements, which would probably persist even if price ceilings had gone by the boards, could probably check a runaway stock market, while the higher bond yields would cut off some long-range planned investment upon which part of the speculation would rest.

Raising reserve requirements should be held until last. Excess reserves, which have in the past presented an obstacle to central bank control, will probably disappear in the next year or two, and there cannot be much doubt as to the eventual potency of higher reserve requirements. But a straight increase would fall with uneven severity on individual banks, and growing banks might find their leading activities unduly restricted. To avoid these difficulties, banks could be required to provide one hundred per cent reserves for all additional deposits above a certain amount.[25] Existing reserve requirements could be retained for deposits beneath the ceiling, at least for the time being. The new "ceiling reserve" requirement would not cause any bank to be short on re-

25. In the United States this proposal was inaugurated by Dr. E. A. Goldenweiser of the Federal Reserve Board. It was suggested earlier by Fritz Machlup in the German edition (1931) of *The Stock Market, Credit, and Capital Formation*, Macmillan, London, 1940, p. 240.

serves and thus be forced to sell securities or borrow; but credit expansion would be definitely stopped.[26]

Since it is unfortunately impossible to count on other devices against a possible postwar inflation, central bank controls over the aggregate supply and availability of credit must be retained. The fact that the English and Canadian authorities seem to have committed themselves definitely for an unlimited time to the present low rates,[27] does not necessitate a similar course in the United States. Swings in business activity have always been more violent here and the controls must consequently be more severe. Furthermore the diversity of our population and the lack of sophistication and rationality about financial matters in our Congress make our monetary policies volatile and unpredictable.

If the direct controls over inflation stand in jeopardy from the very character of democratic government, it is important to preserve the defenses which do not depend upon popular caprice. The Federal Reserve should keep its own counsels, continuing for the present to give complete support to the market for government securities, but not committing itself irrevocably for the future. Thus it achieves the "delicate balancing of confidence and fear" which Professor Whittlesey recommends,[28] and which is an essential aspect of successful monetary administration.

INFLATION CONTROLS AFTER THE TRANSITION PERIOD

Despite demagogic phrases about perpetual prosperity and an economy of abundance, and despite a categoric imperative to avoid recession and unemployment, the monetary authorities will have in the future to cope with cyclical inflation. Indeed, this will continue to be an absolute prerequisite for avoiding downturns. What are the prospects for effective monetary control and what have we learned from our current experiences?

26. A plan by Lawrence H. Seltzer, "The Problem of Our Excessive Banking Reserves," *Journal of the American Statistical Association*, Vol. 35, March 1940, pp. 24–36, to require a reserve in special "reserve privilege" bonds issued by the Treasury would also effectively establish an absolute limit for bank credit, but with considerably more apparatus than the ceiling reserve plan would involve.

27. Cf. the White Paper on Employment Policy, H.M. Stationery Office, and Macmillan, New York, 1944, Sec. 59; and Bank of Canada, *Annual Report to the Minister of Finance and Statement of Accounts*, Ottawa, February 10, 1944, statement by Governor Towers, p. 5.

28. C. R. Whittlesey, "Problems of Our Domestic Money and Banking System," *The American Economic Review*, Vol. 34, No. 1, Pt. 1, March 1944, p. 256.

Selective Credit Controls to Combat Cyclical Inflation

Margin requirements for security purchases will certainly be retained; and other existing "selective" controls, augmented by some device to curb speculative prices for agricultural land, might well be held in abeyance after the termination of postwar inflationary pressure for future contingencies. These methods are less extreme than a drastic raising of discount rates; they impinge at the proper places; and they do not need to be selective in any very great degree.

Whether the selective credit controls should eventually be extended in scope to apply to the bulk of staple commodities, as sometimes proposed, is more than questionable. It would involve the danger that the apparatus might become genuinely selective, i.e., discriminating through its distortion of price relationships from those of a free market. The temptation to utilize discriminating credit requirements for various "ulterior" designs, i.e., for adjusting relative prices to fiscal, welfare, foreign-trade-strategy purposes, makes this variety of selectivity unsuitable to a private-enterprise economy. On the other hand, if the selectivity pertained not to particular commodities but to particular types of consumer credit, there would be every reason for its use against really inflationary developments. Service credit, single-payment loans, and charge accounts follow no cyclical pattern; but installment credit most surely does. For the purpose of checking cyclical inflation, "selective" controls — aside from margin requirements for securities — should therefore be restricted to installment credit after the transition period; and within this field it should be limited to the quantitatively important installment-credit commodities, such as automobiles. Power to extend the controls to other types of consumer credit might, however, be retained as a precaution against evasions of installment regulation.

The Problem of Excess Reserves

If American export surpluses persist and if the Treasury continues to buy gold, we may again some years hence witness the piling up of excess reserves. The best solutions of this problem would be a downward revision of our tariffs, the maintenance of employment and incomes, and the granting of loans within and outside an international stabilization fund and investment bank. If these fundamental corrective measures are not pressed with sufficient zeal, the Treasury may again need to sterilize gold as it did in 1936–1938. It might even sterilize existing gold stocks by purchasing gold certificates from the Federal Reserve Banks out of Treasury funds raised by taxation or borrowing in the market. Approximately the same results would follow from a mere transfer of Treasury deposits from member banks to Federal Reserve Banks, which would involve a corresponding decrease in member bank reserves at the Reserve Banks. One writer has emphasized this as an unexploited device available in the future to help manage excess reserves.[29]

The Board of Governors of the Federal Reserve System possesses more flexible powers than the Treasury for the restraint of price inflation, since fiscal action — aside from two examples just cited — depends upon the typically slow-moving action of Congress. Excess reserves of sufficient magnitude can, of course, render all but the "selective" controls inoperative; and upon these grounds larger discretionary powers ought to be vested in the Board with respect to member bank reserves.

I shall not now venture upon an appraisal of a number of proposals from one quarter to another for implementing this added power.[30] In brief compass, the simplest and most effective reforms would be Congressional enactments widening the zone of discretionary authority for the Board over fractional reserves, and legalizing the use of ceiling reserve requirements. To avoid hardships for a growing member bank and general deflation through the failure of some banks to utilize all their reserves while others pressed upon the limit, it would be necessary to provide for periodic reallocation of ceilings. Since the ceiling reserve puts an absolute limit to credit expansion it is superior to fractional requirements — even very high ones — in checking strong inflationary movements. By the same token, the device would presumably not be utilized in more normal times.

In the long run, the strength of the banking system depends much

29. E. C. Simmons, "Treasury Deposits and Excess Reserves," *The Journal of Political Economy,* Vol. 48, No. 3, June 1940, pp. 325–43.

30. These include: debentures to be issued by the Federal Reserve Banks in order to augment the resources of the Open Market Committee (Goldsborough Bill, H.R. 10517); "100 per cent reserves"; reserve-bonds (Seltzer); velocity reserves; and capital-deposit ratio stipulation (cf. Mead Bill, S. 3867; so far as capital regulation influences bank loan and investment policies, the subject is touched upon later, pp. 150–52). I am indebted to Lt. Col. Victor M. Longstreet for permission to use unpublished material regarding "Proposals to Control Bank Reserves," and to Dr. E. A. Goldenweiser similarly with regard to his "Ceiling Reserve Plan."

less upon the capacity of the central bank to master inflation — which by and large I believe can be presupposed — and more upon the role which banking can play in helping to maintain high levels of saving, investing, and producing.

BANKING AND VENTURE CAPITAL IN THE LONG RUN

Commercial banking, especially in the United States with its fourteen and a half thousand unit banks,[31] fits well into a preponderately liberal competitive economic system. Despite limited local monopoly,[32] particularly in the West and South, commercial banking still remains a fairly competitive business. If we want to encourage a shifting of responsibility for investments from the state toward private enterprise, we shall probably want to encourage commercial banking.[33] This requires certain changes in the economic setting and certain internal reforms within the institution of banking.

Changes in the Economic Setting Favorable to Banking

Like all other businesses, banks would gain from policies aimed toward sustained high levels of national income and the discouraging of monopolistic practices in all fields — industry, agriculture, and labor. Furthermore, the elimination of double taxation upon income from stocks (as compared to bonds) would benefit the earning prospects for banks in their investments. Improved earnings would attract capital; and for reasons set forth presently, higher ratios of capital to assets would react favorably upon risk-taking by banks.

Investment, savings, and commercial banks have been adversely af-

31. There can be little doubt that we would retain the competitive advantages of large numbers and gain substantially in the quality and safety of banking if this number continued to shrink, particularly through the spread of branch banking.

32. In communities typically served by only one bank or by relatively few banks, and where at least limited monopoly could prevail in the supply of credit, bank earnings from loans appear to be much higher than in communities served by larger numbers of banks, where competition would presumably be more effective. For example, in the Kansas City and Dallas Federal Reserve districts, characterized by one bank or relatively few banks in a community, the largest number of banks was found (in 1938) in the bracket 8.0 to 9.9 per cent interest receipts on loans, allowance being made for bad debts. In Boston, New York, Philadelphia, and Cleveland districts, characterized by several banks in a community, the most numerous bracket was 5.0 to 5.9 per cent. A part of the difference in gross interest receipts on loans, of course, is explained by the higher costs entailed by the smaller loans typical of small banks.

33. The term "commercial" is used in a broad sense to designate the common mixed type of banking in the United States.

fected by the channeling of savings into life insurance companies. This development has had a number of undesirable effects: the progressive concentration of economic power, the artificial extension of the demand for riskless investment including government securities, and the fact that insurance companies are acting as middlemen for savings — a function for which they are ill suited.

Insurance companies now control the disposition of funds equaling the total of savings accounts in commercial banks and mutual savings banks. This has resulted partly from an increased popular interest in insurance; but it also has been furthered by the sale of "fancy" policies (endowment, educational, etc.) having very little to do with term insurance, the essence of real insurance. Thus, the funds controlled by insurance policies comprise a mixture of true insurance reserves and savings; and the "gilt-edged" investment policies appropriate to the former have been applied also to the latter. Critics have agreed that these policies lead to a stagnation of investment. But the insurance companies have, on the whole, refused to be persuaded to buy equities, on the ground that what people want in insurance is as near absolute safety as possible.[34]

Unless insurance companies were to establish as many local offices as there are now commercial banks — a development which would involve needless duplication of existing facilities — they must continue to miss the small fellow, the local venture, and even sizable regional enterprises. The alternative is the continuance of institutions with disproportionate masses of capital for their real function, inevitably biased toward big businesses, monopolies, and the state — all for the sake of safety.

An escape from this dilemma will probably require, on the one hand, that insurance laws and commissions permit wider recourse to high-grade direct investments, and to agricultural and industrial loans, especially when protected in whole or part by federal or state guarantees. On the other hand, legal limitation of new policies to straight life insurance may be also worth considering. Such a change would be slow working; but the main thing is the disposition of new savings, of which a certain additional portion would be directed toward the stock exchanges, investment trusts, and banks.

34. Of course, a certain automatic outflow of funds may be expected in a decade or so when the recent growth of insurance will begin to result in a greater flow of benefit payments. Even so, the funds held by insurance companies will continue to be enormous.

Another long-range undertaking should be a reorganization of the numerous federal loan agencies to articulate with commercial banking more effectively. The proliferation of these agencies was a by-product of the last depression, and undoubtedly the net effect was to prevent further deflation and even to expand bank credit.[35] Where these agencies clearly duplicate facilities offered by the banks, the interests of a private-enterprise economy now require withdrawal by the government. But commercial banks must demonstrate their ability to meet the varied credit needs of business at reasonable rates. If they succeed, we may expect to see an almost automatic shrinkage of government agency banking. A step in this direction is the extension of Federal Reserve Bank powers to guarantee industrial loans by commercial banks, as contemplated in the Wagner-Spence bills.

Internal Banking Reforms

Reforms in commercial banking could help to bring about a shift of active risk-taking from the state to banks, to businesses, and to individuals. These reforms should be aimed at reversing certain recent tendencies, as shown in the asset and liability position of banks: the growth of deposits from mere hoarding by the public, the decline of "other securities" and loans in favor of government securities, and the reduction of capital relative to total liabilities.

Bankers cannot be expected to launch into more risky investments and loans by spontaneous resolution or from exhortation. The demand for bank credit must be increased through antirestrictionist measures in the economic scene generally, through government policies to sustain employment, through taxes favorable to equity financing, and through limitation of insurance companies to the insurance function. The result would be a rise in bank profits. Increased earnings are not desired because of a present inadequacy,[36] but in order to permit two fundamental reforms — the requirement of higher ratios of capital to total assets, and of reserves to deposits. The increase of these two ratios

35. Neil H. Jacoby, "Government Loan Agencies and Commercial Banking," *The American Economic Review*, Vol. 32, No. 1, Pt. 2, March 1942, pp. 250–60.

36. Net profits, as a ratio to total capital accounts, for member banks moved in the range of 10.4 per cent to 7.1 per cent from 1919–1929, fell to minus 7.3 per cent in 1933, but equaled 6.3 per cent in 1939, and rose to 8.8 per cent in 1943 and to 9.7 per cent in 1944. Cf. Board of Governors of the Federal Reserve System, *Banking and Monetary Statistics*, pp. 264–65; *Federal Reserve Bulletin*, July 1943 and May 1945.

PERCENTAGE DISTRIBUTION OF ASSETS AND LIABILITIES OF ALL OPERATING
COMMERCIAL BANKS IN THE U. S. AND POSSESSIONS

	June 30				
	1920	1929	1937	1942	1943
Assets					
Cash and amounts due from banks	17.2	14.7	26.4	27.9	24.9
Obligations of U. S. government	7.9	8.0	25.7	32.9	50.3
Other securities	10.1	14.0	13.2	9.4	6.3
Loans and discounts	59.6	57.7	30.7	27.3	16.9
Fixed and miscellaneous assets	5.2	5.6	4.0	2.5	1.6
	100.0	100.0	100.0	100.0	100.0
Liabilities					
Total deposits	77.4	79.3	86.9	90.1	92.3
Miscellaneous liabilities	10.9	6.6	1.3	0.7	0.6
Total capital accounts	11.7	14.1	11.8	9.2	7.1
	100.0	100.0	100.0	100.0	100.0

Source: Annual Reports of the Federal Deposit Insurance Corporation.

in conjunction with continued higher absolute dollar earnings would
permit and induce the assumption of higher risks without sacrifice of
safety for the depositor or bank.[37]

Capital-Asset Ratio and Reserve Ratio

The ratio of *capital to total assets* fell from 14.1 per cent in 1929 to
9.2 per cent in 1942, that is, by one third. This thinning of the owners'
equity lessens the pressure on banks to seek an asset distribution bringing high yields. The process can be reversed by expanded earnings, increased investment in banks by their owners, and greater emphasis on
loans and securities which afford higher returns for higher risks. Spread
over a broader capital base, these greater risks imply no sacrifice of
traditional banking standards. Explicit legal requirement would be necessary to raise the capital-asset ratio, and this should be complemented

37. The reforms imply a revision of standards of bank examination favorable to more
risky loans and investments; but the increase of the two ratios would prevent a deterioration of liquidity and solvency.

by differentiation of the requirement according to the risk category of assets.[38] Putting the measure into effect now during a period of credit expansion and high profits in the banking business would appear to be reasonable.

A complementary measure, eligible as soon as war-engendered deficit financing is ended, would be the segregating of bank holdings of government securities and a gradual reduction of interest paid on these types of securities. This would induce the banks to support their earnings through loans and investments in private industry.

An increase of the required minimum ratio *of reserves to deposits* would bring two substantial gains from a social angle. Without impairing bank liquidity, it would augment the pressure from increased capital requirements to force the bank to seek more venturesome and profitable loans and investments. In the second place, a contraction of bank credit could not cause as large a deflation in a period of economic recession. A flight into currency would of course still be possible, but the bankers' own desire for liquidity could no longer play as large a role. In other words, we approach closer to government control of the volume of money, which is, I believe, one of the essential conditions for full employment in a liberal economy.

Deposit Insurance and Loan Insurance

Another reform which would induce banks to riskier loans and investments without sacrifice of safety would be the extension of both deposit insurance and loan insurance. Deposit insurance now covers 97 per cent of depositors; but the $5,000 limit and the refusal of some banks to insure restricts it to less than 50 per cent of total deposits. The principal shortcoming is not so much the vulnerability of large depositors as it is the risk of destruction of purchasing power in depression. Since the activities of supervisory agencies, such as the Federal Deposit Insurance Corporation, tend to diminish the number of failures, and since an actuarial basis converts risks of failure to calculable losses, deposit insurance signifies to a very large degree the elimination of risk, rather than a transference of risk to the government.

Much the same analysis is applicable to loan insurance. It is simply not true, as some people have maintained, that the insuring banks are

---

38. R. I. Robinson, "Capital-Deposit Ratio in Bank Supervision," *The Journal of Political Economy*, Vol. 49, No. 1, February 1941, pp. 41–57.

"relieved of all loss absorption."[39] For the uninsurable fraction of loans, the bank bears the risk of loss absorption; and for the insurable fraction, the bank absorbs a small certain loss in preference to the risk of a large one. For neither portion does the government assume risk. But the commercial banking system can pursue more venturesome loan and investment policies without increasing risk over its magnitude before insurance.

THE ROLE OF COMMERCIAL BANKING IN A LIBERAL ORDER

Through providing larger supplies of venture capital, the commercial banking system can play a modest but integral role in strengthening the vitality and employment possibilities of a liberal economic order. This depends upon the realization of external and internal reforms, such as those contemplated here, rather than upon a direct onslaught on interest rates through increasing the quantity of money and credit. For the short run, monetary stimulation is effective, and may even be indispensable. As a long-run matter, continued injections of credit would be a fatuous policy: lagging costs overtake prices, lenders anticipate the depreciation of money, interest rates rise. Stabilization of the value of money thus has significance in a full-employment program. It cannot be made a fetish and be allowed to block emergency public spending to prevent a collapse of employment. But it is through reforms to induce the smooth passage of savings into investment that full employment can finally be reached without inflation on the one hand and without the whole gamut of price controls and rationing on the other.

IV. COMPETITION AND EMPLOYMENT IN FOREIGN TRADE

During the great depression of the thirties, international trade lost its liberal character. In place of free choice by exporters and importers, limited only by the relatively mild restraint of protective tariffs, governments — with a few notable exceptions — intervened to secure the home market for home producers and home laborers. This discriminatory intervention has not unjustly been called "the exporting of unemployment." Looking toward the postwar scene some economists, following a tradition since the time of Adam Smith, reject the idea that in

39. J. Brooke Willis, *The Functions of the Commercial Banking System*, Columbia University Press, New York, 1943, p. 185.

the long run unemployment can be reduced through adventitious export devices, and call for concerted international action to reduce trade
barriers. Others regard the achievement of full use of resources in the
United States as largely a domestic problem, with international trade
playing a quite minor role. Depending upon the time element, there is
point in both these positions.

SHORT-RUN AND LONG-RUN ASPECTS

American Employment in the Transition Period

During the transition period, American employment will depend in
small measure upon the state of international trade, but international
trade will in large measure depend upon American employment. In
the decade before the war our exports represented only a small fraction (varying from 3.1 per cent to 5.3 per cent) of our gross national
product, but a much larger fraction (varying from 12.6 to 15.6 per
cent) of total world exports.[40] On the basis of past trends, the Department of Commerce estimates that with a gross national output of $175
billion in 1948, we may — upon certain assumptions — expect something like $6.3 billion in imports and $7 billion in exports.[41]

Thus our foreign trade is small in comparison with our domestic
production. But there are other grounds, in the view of some economists, for regarding international trade and the reduction of trade barriers as of relatively little importance for the United States. American
imports have been demonstrated to be closely correlated with variations in the level of industrial output and not much room seems to be
left for a responsiveness of imports to price or rate of exchange variations.[42] Tariff reduction appears to be blocked by decades of popular
and Congressional immunity to the arguments of the economists; and
international collaboration to eliminate or modify direct restrictions
on trade — bilateral clearing, quotas, exchange control, subsidies, state
trading, and the like — seems a long and tortuous way. Russia will not

40. The latter comparison seems a fairer basis of judging the weight of the United States
in international relations than, for example, a comparison of national incomes, of which
the United States' share was half the world total in 1929.

41. August Maffry and Hal B. Lary, *Foreign Trade After the War,* U. S. Department of
Commerce, Bureau of Foreign and Domestic Commerce, Economic Series, No. 28, October
1943, *passim.*

42. Hal B. Lary, *The United States in the World Economy,* U. S. Department of Commerce, Bureau of Foreign and Domestic Commerce, Economic Series, No. 23, May 1943,
p. 39.

depart from a government monopoly of her foreign trade. Britain will not lightly surrender the strategic bargaining position attending international indebtedness, which was demonstrated by the German exchange control of the thirties, and which accrues to Britain from the Empire blocked balances. South America, China, and India aspire to industrialization behind protective economic walls. We cannot rely upon a movement toward freer trade, they say.

In view of these uncertainties, it is concluded, let each country solve its own unemployment problem; and, because Great Britain and the United States dominate world trade,[43] let them maintain full employment, and international exchange will not fail to flourish. Reducing trade barriers might indeed help, they concede, but it supplies no very important force toward expansion.

For the transition period and with reference to such great and nearly self-contained economies as the United States and Russia, this reasoning seems to me to be substantially valid. But it has very little meaning even in the short run for a country highly dependent upon foreign trade such as Great Britain, and it rapidly loses its force as we think ahead to the future of the United States.

American "Full Employment" in the Long Run

Though conceivably achievable without a parallel development of international trade, prosperity in the United States alone would be an unstable state of affairs.

The major factors involved in this conclusion are three: (a) domestic expansion in the United States not paralleled by an expansion in foreign trade would release several forces working toward investment stagnation; (b) even when complemented by an extensive foreign lending program, domestic expansion would not be sustained if restrictionist practices on the part of private monopolies and governments persisted in the field of international trade and finance; and (c) these restrictionist practices continually threaten to divide the world into economically armed camps and to break down all efforts at political and economic cooperation. Exchange controls, bilateralism, discriminatory exchange rates and the like face in the direction of one particular solvent of unemployment, and that is war. This is the most

---

43. Their combined share of world imports varied between 27.9 per cent and 25.7 per cent, and of world exports between 22.1 per cent and 26.3 per cent, in the decade before the present war.

potent argument against pursuing a purely nationalistic full-employment policy.

It is no mere coincidence that the most protracted and devastating depression of modern capitalism occurred during the decade of the thirties, when, for the first time since 1870, the volume of international trade and the volume of manufacturing production failed to follow parallel trends.[44] It is not clear whether internal or the international trade collapse took causal precedence, since the two elements combined variously in different countries. But our depression was certainly deepened and protracted by the international economic situation, despite the relatively small fraction of our own total activity involved in foreign trade.

Aside from cyclical depressions, the secular development of the foreign trade of the United States may well spell the difference between success and failure for our domestic policies. We shall in the next few years be working out new functions and a realignment of functions for government and private enterprise; during this process, the successful disposition of our flow of savings would be facilitated by really substantial foreign investments. Even during our vaunted foreign lending boom of the late twenties, the largest net capital outflow was reached in 1928 with $1.2 billion or 16.4 per cent of our net national savings (Kuznets). We have indeed barely scratched the surface of the productive utilization of capital in industrially undeveloped regions such as China and India, which with 40 per cent of the world's population account for 2 per cent of its manufacturing and 8.4 per cent of its imports of manufactured goods.[45]

However much we bolster our domestic measures for achieving stable and full use of our resources by foreign loans, we shall only be preparing for a debacle unless we move rapidly in the direction ultimately appropriate to a large international lender: receiving the service of these loans in real imports. The alternative is a permanent policy of capital gifts by the United States to foreign countries.[46] First-rate statesmanship, it is conceded, would have converted lend-lease to outright war contributions from December 7, 1941 onward, treating our

44. League of Nations, *Industrialization and International Trade*, in process of completion.

45. *Ibid.*

46. Cf. C. P. Kindleberger, "Planning for Foreign Investment," *The American Economic Review*, Vol. 23, No. 1, Pt. 2, March 1943, p. 351.

allies at least as well as mercenary soldiers; and second-rate statesmanship will retroactively cancel these debts as war expenditures. But it would be no statesmanship at all to demoralize foreigners, outrage our own needy classes, and expose our country to scorn for a permanent inability to cope with domestic problems except by continuously giving away our labor and resources, by refusing to receive payment of interest and principal in the form of imports.

The Immediacy of Long-Run Factors

Although the success of a full-employment program in the United States during the first few postwar years depends primarily on domestic measures, the fate of a long-run program to expand international trade will be determined during that period. A unique opportunity will be provided for an extensive lowering of our tariff barriers, since the war has completely changed the nature of our foreign trade, and since in addition our domestic production has been extensively converted from ordinary purposes. As industry reconverts to peacetime production, the emphasis should be placed on products in which this country has a competitive advantage and does not require the protection of high tariffs or the assistance of export subsidies. Such a shift in production could be accomplished with virtually the same effort as a return to prewar productive patterns. A wholesale lowering of tariffs under these conditions would be relatively "painless," and the result would be a greatly expanded volume of trade and employment. If the American Congress turns its back upon the several plans for promoting freedom, expansion, and stability in international trade and finance, it will have dealt a body blow to our domestic full-employment prospects a decade hence.

But a liberal regime does not mean laissez faire: foreign trade and finance will for the foreseeable future require even more control than domestic activity for a number of reasons. (a) Unless a collective security pact promises to guarantee peace, nations will prepare to meet military aggression by economic self-sufficiency. (b) Because business cycles do not follow precisely the same pattern throughout the world, nations are exposed to unwelcome booms and depressions from the outside. (c) Some countries which are extremely dependent on the exportation of one raw material (or of only a few) seek diversification against the risk of having all of their economic eggs in one basket. (d)

As long as agriculture is more competitive than industry, predominantly agricultural countries tend to be especially vulnerable in periods of depression. (e) Large countries, particularly those with sources of supply and export markets not concentrated upon a few trading partners, can, by threatening to break off trade with a smaller country, secure adventitious economic and political concessions. (f) Under some conditions, international commodity and capital movements lead to prolonged maladjustments which cannot be corrected without government intervention.

All of these factors combine to justify more interference with the profit system in international than in national affairs. But these differences afford no justification for most of the restraining and discriminating devices which flourished in the thirties, nor for tolerating them after the war. In the next section we will examine briefly some of the special problems of important trading regions to discover to what degree peculiar balance-of-payments problems are amenable to "liberal" solutions, and to what degree interference is necessary.

COMPLICATIONS IN THE POSTWAR TRADE OF PARTICULAR REGIONS

The United States and the "Shortage of Dollars"

Most countries will experience a scarcity of dollar exchange after the war for a number of reasons: their need for rehabilitation and reconstruction, their reduced foreign investments and foreign exchange reserves, and the strong export position of the United States. Many commentators believe that this shortage will give rise to an intensification of the national foreign trade controls which characterized the thirties. But foreign countries do not need to cope with a shortage of dollars by relying on exchange control or import quotas, except perhaps for a transition period following the end of hostilities. Other alternatives will be open to them. A persistent unfavorable balance of payments can in many cases be ameliorated by a downward revision in the country's rate of exchange.

Some economists go much further and demand freely fluctuating exchange rates. There are dangers in this solution, however. In some cases, exchange depreciation tends to intensify itself, for example in the case of difficulties in meeting a fixed monetary obligation in a foreign currency, and in the case of economies confronted with inelastic demand for their exports. Moreover, if it is left to the country, acting upon its own responsibility, to regulate its exchange, it may succumb to the temptation of maintaining too high rates for the sake of favorable terms of trade or too low rates for the sake of undercutting on export sales.

In any case, as recent monetary history has shown clearly, it is very difficult for a country, acting unilaterally, to adjust its exchange rate to precisely the appropriate level. If the currency is overvalued, for example, the country's exports are penalized and its imports are stimulated. This usually leads to the introduction of overt or concealed export subsidies and other devices intended to encourage exports and check imports. Perhaps worst of all, it is likely to result in bilateral clearing arrangements, which are inevitably discriminatory and restrictive in nature.

The International Monetary Fund

The only solution is international supervision over exchange rates, as provided by the International Monetary Fund, to secure an equilibrium adjustment of currency values. Under this arrangement, direct limitations on trade, such as quotas and the rationing of foreign exchange, would be proscribed. Continuous revision of exchange rates would, however, be administratively impossible; and, furthermore, frequent revisions would be upsetting to trade and adverse to international loans, particularly to long-term loans. Consequently the Monetary Fund apparatus provides for (a) occasional revision of exchange rates to correct maladjustments, (b) in the meantime (i.e., between revisions) short-term loans by the Fund to bridge over balance-of-payments difficulties, (c) the emergency resort to direct limitation of imports by individual member countries to help correct a situation in which the Fund's supply of a given currency approaches exhaustion (exchange control to prevent a capital flight being always permissible), and finally (d) recommendations by the Fund, to countries with balance-of-payments problems, as to appropriate domestic measures to avoid repetition of the exchange-rate revision.

The prospect for relieving a world shortage of dollars depends finally upon whether these recommendations will actually be followed. The responsibility falls both upon foreign countries and upon ourselves; but since at the end of the war we shall be by far the most rich and powerful industrial nation, it can be argued that our duty is greater.

What steps could be taken by the United States in order to bring the supply of and demand for dollars to equilibrium? Since a "shortage" indicates an excess of demand for dollars over the supply, it would presumably disappear through one or another of the following circumstances: (a) a rise in the value of the dollar relatively to other currencies; (b) a rise of our prices or a fall of prices abroad; (c) an increase in our money incomes in comparison with incomes abroad; (d) a reduction in our tariffs; (e) a spontaneous increase in our demand for foreign goods or a decrease in their demand for ours; and finally (f) American loans.

Six Ways to Attain Equilibrium

(a) On purely objective grounds an increase in the value of the dollar (in terms of foreign currencies) would work in the right direction. American producers of export goods would probably resist the change; but since in many lines we enjoy a strong competitive advantage anyway, adverse effects on exports would not be serious. Whatever loss of markets did occur, however, would be a genuine economic cost, justifiable as a contribution to re-establishing equilibrium. But since some people would apprehend this cost, and since there obtains a strong popular conviction against "tampering with the currency," the measure cannot be viewed as promising.

(b) If American prices rose more rapidly than prices in our chief trading countries, we would have an approximate equivalent of a higher dollar rate; and popular opposition to "moderate" inflation is weak. But if foreign inflations were marked, as they may well be, both public sentiment and the facts would combine against a policy of outstripping the rise of prices abroad. We can predict neither the state of foreign finances nor the course of prices, and consequently we cannot rely upon this adjustment.

If the United States should (c) maintain or increase money incomes without price inflation more successfully than foreign countries, and thus experience the reduction of export balances characteristic of our prosperity periods, the dollar shortage might disappear. But if this were attained without (d) a reduction of American tariffs, our prosperity would be less apt to be communicated to foreign countries through our import demands; and by the same token, our prosperity would be less apt to be maintained.

As for (e) spontaneous changes — not induced by variations in exchange rates, tariffs, prices, or incomes — the postwar reconstruction needs of Europe and Asia will probably far outweigh any increase in our demand for foreign products, such as American travel abroad; indeed, the resumption of peacetime trade may unfortunately not include the importation of certain natural products such as rubber, if our synthetic industries enforce a demand for protection.

Thus we arrive at the only remaining offset to our export surplus, (f) American loans. There are indeed overwhelmingly forceful arguments for a large outflow of capital from the United States on the supposition of productive investment: it will help to maintain employment both at home and abroad, and it will contribute to foreign long-run productivity and our long-run real income. But the condition for the service and gradual amortization of these loans is the development of larger imports and eventually an import balance by the United States. Unless our tariffs are reduced, the proposal for an International Development Bank thus becomes tantamount to a proposal for a charitable fund. It is to be hoped that, when the time comes for the members of Congress to weigh the advantages of a multilateral program for tariff reduction, they will take a long-range view of American self-interest.

Great Britain and the "Scarcity of Dollars"

At the end of the European war, England had lost half of her overseas investments, amounting to £4.6 billion in 1939, and contracted an unfunded debt in the form of blocked sterling balances of £3 billion or more. To her the "dollar scarcity" problem appears as the converse of our own: how to export sufficiently to command food and other necessaries from abroad and at the same time amortize her debts. Her problem will be greatly eased if other countries, especially the United States, pursue policies aimed at an expansion of international trade. She will certainly be in need of reconstruction loans. But just as we may be reluctant to lend without limit, so the English may not want to launch upon indefinitely protracted borrowing.

Conceivably England could meet her "dollar shortage" problem by pursuing policies the reverse of those appropriate for the United States. But by no means all of these policies would be economically desirable or politically feasible. Thus (b) a decline of the general level of prices, and (c) a shrinkage of money income are both too intimately associated with depression to be entertainable. Furthermore a decrease of imports, whether (e) spontaneous — "Buy British" — or (d) forced by higher protective tariffs, would not be compatible with a long-run increase in British exports without difficult changes in lines of production and techniques. In addition, it would mean a reduction in the standard of living unless (and perhaps even if) wartime measures to equalize income were continued.

But promising alternatives still exist. The first would be a general increase in British productive efficiency or conversion to newer and more profitable types of exports; the second would be a devaluation of the pound, provided the demand for British exports proves to be elastic; and the third, domestic measures to reduce imports selectively. Concerning the first not much needs to be said, for its desirability is self-evident; and since the extension of exports by devaluation and the economizing of luxurious imports have quite definite limits, the increase of productive efficiency is the only ultimate solution which Britain herself can work out. The efficiency of British industry cannot, however, be increased overnight nor can it probably be increased sufficiently in the period of drastic postwar adjustment. If England follows the advice of the Federation of British Industries and some of her more vociferous young economists, she will resort for the next decade or more to one or another or perhaps the whole gamut of direct restrictions on foreign trade.

Devaluation Versus Exchange Control

It is sometimes argued that the pound cannot be devalued without reducing real wages, and that this is a political impossibility. But if unemployment prevails and if, as one may reasonably suppose for a country like England with highly diversified industrial exports, the foreign demand for British products is quite elastic, the total foreign currency value of British exports will rise. Increased profits and production in the export trades would operate toward a general rise in employment and money wage rates. Whether real wage rates rose or not would depend upon whether this spontaneous movement of money wages, supplemented perhaps by trade-union action, offset certain forces set afoot by devaluation which raise the cost of living — the greater cost of imports, the higher price of exported goods included in a workingman's budget, and a rise in costs of production elsewhere through competition with export industries. With a presumptive gain in employment accompanied by a distinctly favorable outlook for higher real wages, it is scarcely conceivable that the British Labor Party, remembering the twenties, would fail to insist upon devaluation.

Reliance on exchange control, as an alternative to devaluation of the pound, is sometimes defended on the ground that it is more humane to close a gap in the balance of payments by excluding luxuries than by leaving the matter to free market prices. This argument implicitly assumes an inelastic foreign demand for British products. Some such reasoning apparently underlies the permission given by the Monetary Fund to individual countries not only to ration a currency which becomes scarce to the Fund, but to ration it in any way they choose. Luxury imports can, it is true, be excluded by sumptuary legislation, avoiding altogether the discriminatory and restrictive perils of exchange controls, but this method would not always suffice. To justify exchange control of imports, however, as against devaluation, it would have first to be established that the demand for British products really is inelastic, or that the difficulty is merely temporary.

I will not dwell upon that small but vocal part of English opinion which, utterly despairing of all the equilibrating forces treated in the present and preceding subdivisions, regards exchange control, export subsidies, discriminating monopoly, multiple exchange rates and the like as "the *conditio sine qua non* of progressive internal policies."[47] Fortunately for Great Britain, whose destiny depends upon a flourishing state of international trade more than any other great nation's, her government has thus far ignored these voices and has taken a strong initiative in plans for liberalizing international trade and finance.

Germany and Reparations

If reparations were to be as badly managed as they were after the last war, not only the vanquished but also the victors would be better without them. But with reasonably good management, German reparations can be justified, not upon grounds of retribution, but of economic reconstruction for the pillaged nations. In any event Russia and other coun-

47. Thomas Balogh, "The Currency Plans and International Economic Relations," *The Political Quarterly*, October–December 1943, p. 347; cf. *idem*, "A Case for Export Subsidies," *The Banker*, August 1943, pp. 71–5; and equally extreme: E. F. Schumacher, "Export Policy and Full Employment," *Fabian Research Series*, No. 77, London, 1943.

tries have signified their intentions of collecting reparations, and so the problem is with us. The United States will not, it is assumed, make substantial claims; but because we shall be involved in the economic and political consequences of reparations, we must have a clear policy.

If it were thought that future world security could not be guaranteed except by "rendering Germany economically impotent," the only effective way of doing so would be to ruin the country completely. Any limitation of this policy to "strategic" or specifically military production would, immediately after the war, be tantamount to "killing a dead horse"; whereas in the long run the selective control could largely be circumvented. Collective security must be achieved by other than economic means.

The most appropriate economic precaution — as far as it goes — against a renewal of war by Germany would be the abolition of her food self-sufficiency. If the removal of the high grain tariffs were written into the peace treaty, it would be difficult for Germany to wage war on any scale because she would have to depend on initial conquests even to ensure adequate food supplies for further warfare. Moreover the abolition of the artificially fostered grain culture in Germany would make impossible the maintenance of the East Elbian estates. Thus it would destroy the economic foundation of the Junker class, with its baleful influence on German domestic and foreign policies.[48] Finally the reform would secure a substantial and natural market for the agricultural exports of the Americas and southeastern Europe. Once the German economy had become adjusted to the lower tariffs, the standard of living would, of course, be raised by cheaper foodstuffs. A rejection of this outcome would scarcely be compatible with a cosmopolitan interest in the welfare of the working classes.

For the future peace of the world much more depends upon political alliances with Germany and upon her internal political movements than upon the immediate economic impact of the war, including reparations. The central position of Germany in the midst of the European continent, together with her highly developed industrial and commercial traditions, would seem to assure her of an important position in the European economy in the future, unless Draconian measures are taken

48. Cf. Alexander Gerschenkron, *Bread and Democracy in Germany,* University of California Press, Berkeley, 1944. It goes without saying that direct restrictions on grain importations, as well as the traditional high tariffs, should also be abolished.

with her boundaries and resources. Otherwise, in relation to Germany's probable "capacity to produce," quite sizable reparations would not place an intolerable strain on her economy. Total payments of, say, 120 billion marks (at 1938 prices) over a twelve-year period would represent an average annual annuity of 11 per cent of her 1938 net national output,[49] or not more than one or two per cent of the net national outputs of the prospective reparation claimants.

The Danger of Bilateralism

But Germany can "pay" reparations only through her capacity to develop an adequate export surplus, and it is in this connection that the real difficulties of the reparations problem arise. Indeed, it is at this point that the interest of the United States is most intimately involved. There are several strong factors favorable to the evolution of bilateral clearing with Germany. If the postwar trade of Germany proceeds through clearings, this will almost certainly mean that bilateralism will be fastened upon her trading partners in Continental Europe, and hence probably also upon England and South America. In these circumstances the United States would find its traditional freedom of trade position completely stultified.

To avoid this outcome, the military occupation authorities in Germany should not be tempted even temporarily to make use of the Nazi clearing system, since, once set out anew in this direction, trade will tend to settle there permanently. Furthermore it will be necessary to resist two outside interests which would otherwise probably have recourse to clearing as a method of collecting their claims: (a) countries having an export surplus to Germany — in general, countries to the east — who could refuse to sell except for immediate payment through the clearing account, and (b) countries having an import balance from Germany — countries to the west — who could, as in the thirties, attempt to secure payment on reparations as a condition for their meeting obligations on current account. The second contingency would arise only if the period of reparations extended past the direct control of the German economy by reparation-claimant countries. In this event great inequities would be entailed if only countries of the second category could enforce their claims for reparations. The only course would seem

49. These figures are given only as illustrative of relative magnitudes, not as an estimate of Germany's "capacity to pay."

to be for the military government of Germany to provide a small initial commercial credit for German trade, and thereafter to refuse to tolerate bilateral trading arrangements. The importance of this principle is in no wise reduced by the agreement of the United Nations at Yalta to levy the reparations "in kind." A debtor of Germany on current account aside from reparations can — in the absence of direct controls — utilize bilateral clearing to force payments no matter in what they consist.

Russia and State Trading

If Russia conformed to the scheme of a liberal socialist economy, with production determined by prices answering to free consumer choice and economic costs of production, and with each productive establishment buying and selling "on its own," capitalist countries could trade with her with no more difficulty than among themselves.[50] But though some beginning has been made on comparative costing in Russia, the heavy flat turnover tax introduces a large measure of arbitrariness into prices;[51] and still more important, foreign trade is a state monopoly. Other countries have less to fear from the selling than from the buying activities of this monopoly, since Russia controls the supply of only minor trade items, but the magnitude of her purchases — at least potentially — places the outside private seller in a distinctly vulnerable bargaining position.

It has sometimes been proposed that the only recourse for private enterprises abroad would be to allow their governments to conduct trade with Russia on similarly monopolistic lines. But the danger is great that those trading monopolies outside Russia would launch upon discriminatory policies amongst themselves if no further steps were taken. Furthermore, if individual state monopolies were to deal bilaterally with Russia, each for itself, the possibility of discriminatory treatment by Russia would remain, and would become the more dangerous the larger Russian imports were in the world market.

Another proposal — to secure from Russia a minimum global purchasing commitment unallocated by countries — falls afoul of the same difficulty. How much Russia purchases from the outside world in the

---

50. B. F. Hoselitz, "Socialist Planning and International Economic Relations," *The American Economic Review*, Vol. 33, No. 4, December 1943, pp. 839–51.
51. Abram Bergson, *The Structure of Soviet Wages*, Harvard University Press, Cambridge, 1944, Chap. 3.

aggregate depends upon whether she looks forward to peaceful expansion and a rise in the standard of living; but this choice cannot be determined by trading requirements. Furthermore, the unallocated minimum import quota would still leave the division among countries to be solved; and each country in isolation would prove impotent against so important a buyer.

An eligible defense against the development of bilateralism in this context would be a multilateral agreement rationing the Russian purchasing schedule amongst the various exporting countries, with a further allocation carried on by each government separately to its own individual exporting firms.[52] Such a device, as Gerschenkron admits, would be awkward with regard to its initial quotas and never thoroughly satisfactory even afterward. Yet it involves no more bargaining than a series of separate bilateral agreements with Russia would entail, and it would certainly move more rapidly toward free multilateral trade than purely bilateral bargains. Eventually after a large volume of trade with Russia had developed in close approximation to a multilateral pattern, the device would become superfluous.

South America and Industrialization

At present many South American countries utilize exchange control as a hedge against inflation. On the one hand, foreign exchange rates are prevented from falling, in anticipation that such a course would have to be retraced when the flood of war buying from abroad abates; and on the other, exporters are paid only a part of the value of their bills in cash, the rest being paid in government securities. Such an anti-inflationary exchange control probably contributes to long-run stability and employment.

It is, however, argued that these countries will need to retain exchange control after the war to lift the economies out of their primitive agricultural or extractive phases. This cannot be done by security flotations within the countries because the capital markets are undeveloped; and it cannot be done by government subsidies, since the system of taxation does not yield enough. Consequently the only recourse is seen in large-scale central bank loans, inflationary pressure, officially main-

---

52. Alexander Gerschenkron, *Economic Relations with the U.S.S.R.*, Committee on International Economic Policy in cooperation with the Carnegie Endowment for International Peace, New York, 1945, pp. 37–41.

tained overvaluation of exchange, and selective control of imports. Even foreign loans are sometimes objected to as an alternative because they "take the profits abroad" and "give control to the foreigners."

The general interest in free multiangular trade, as well as the special interest of the United States in Latin American markets can, however, ill afford to accept these conclusions. Furthermore they proceed, at almost every step, from lazy logic. Extracting savings from an already generally indigent population by means of inflation can scarcely be better than even a poorly devised tax system. The objections to foreigners' profit and control probably arise fundamentally from resentment against monopolistic exploitation, something more apt to be intensified than relieved by exchange control. Aside from this, the suspicion against foreign capital per se belongs to the same category as the superstition against foreign goods.

CONCLUSIONS

This brief review of the complexities which immediately beset international exchange reveals with sufficient force the necessity of extensive international collaboration. It does not establish a case for "complete planning" in international economic matters.[53] We must move toward expansion and stability on a number of fronts, both domestic and foreign.

Stability is to be achieved by domestic measures to control cyclical fluctuations and by international agreements to outlaw beggar-my-neighbor methods of combating depression. With respect to the former, the United States has the worst record among all nations. From 1929 to 1932 our imports fell from an index of 100 to 30, compared with 42 for all countries and 44 for European countries; and during the same period the supply of dollars to foreigners, under the combined influence of our reduction of imports and withdrawal of capital, declined by 68 per cent![54] With respect to cutthroat foreign trade measures against depression, we must assume responsibility for the adverse foreign repercussions of our having devalued the dollar below its equilibrium level, though it was the "others" who resorted to direct quantitative restrictions on trade. With respect to both the domestic

53. Carl Landauer, *Theory of National Economic Planning,* University of California Press, Berkeley, 1944, pp. 123–24, 132.
54. Lary, *op. cit.,* pp. 5, 187.

and international aspects of stability, diverse and persistent efforts are required: there is no unique and once-and-for-all cure.

Expansion in the international field is to be achieved by a general policy of relaxing trade barriers and by extensive foreign loans. Of the present international plans to achieve the dual ends of stability and expansion, the most important and crucial is probably the proposed multilateral commercial convention. This would be designed not only to reduce tariffs, preferences, and discriminations, to limit the resort to subsidies, exchange control, and quotas, and to cope with state trading, but also to establish an international commercial policy organization. Continuous oversight by such an organization will be necessary to distinguish, for example, between exchange control as a legitimate emergency device, as an unfair offensive weapon, and as a cover for the perpetuation of domestic policies which are incompatible with international stability. Without continuous supervision it is difficult to see how bilateralism can be suppressed in the dealings of Russia with capitalistic countries, in the eventual liquidating of England's empire-blocked balances, and in the transferring of reparations. In no single case are these problems soluble by individual national action.

This is also true of the field to be covered by the International Monetary Fund. Its four chief functions — supplying loans to meet temporary balance-of-payments difficulties, deciding whether proposed exchange-rate changes make for long-run equilibrium, passing upon requests to institute direct trade and exchange controls, and finally recommending suitable national action to achieve equilibrium — all of these cannot, from their very definition, be solved by individual countries. Again, continuous supervision is the essence of the process. The case for collaboration in an international investment bank and in a primary products stabilization plan is similar. Separate efforts by countries individually can go far toward the objective; but there can be no doubt that collaboration increases both the possible extent and the consistency of operations. In the aggregate these international agencies would represent a powerful attack against the institutional basis of investment stagnation and unemployment.

V. Taxes and Enterprise After the War

Preceding sections of the present essay have recognized the responsibility of government for the maintenance of employment. In the short run this implies that any deficiency in private outlays upon consumption and investment below the level necessary to maintain a high level of employment must be made good in the sector of public outlays. In the long run — and this is the phase with which many current discussions seem too little concerned — it implies a vigorous program of fostering private enterprise, unless we are content to accept some form of collectivism.

TAXATION AND EMPLOYMENT

The short-run principles for taxation should be the following two. First, in a situation of inadequate employment, no tax should be levied until the alternative has been considered as to how the volume of private output and employment would be affected by not levying or by abating the tax. Second, in a situation of reasonably adequate employment, no tax should be levied until the alternative has been considered as to what inflationary pressures might develop if disposable income were not reduced. Together the two principles should underlie the taxation aspect of compensatory spending by government.

The long-run principle implies the modification of our existing tax structure along lines which we propose to examine in order to encourage enterprise.

But beyond the application of these short- and long-run policies I do not believe we can venture far in orienting fiscal and tax policies toward the achievement of full employment. Many proposals of "incentive taxation" for this purpose seem to be ill conceived, either in failing to accomplish the objective or in entailing undesirable by-products. As an example, the many devices which have been invented for penalizing hoarding are open to both objections. Taxes upon bank balances could be evaded by a flight into cash, and schemes for the automatic depreciation of cash could be evaded by a flight into jewels, land, and other nonemployment-creating forms of wealth. Besides, since money-holding is almost always the intermediate stage in a process of applying savings to investment, a penalizing of money-holding might adversely affect the natural and necessary process of private saving and investing. Another "incentive taxation" proposal, the tax exemption of bond issues for new construction, while it would surely encourage investment and employment in the construction industry and possibly in the aggregate, would be open to the general objection to tax-exempt securities that they favor the higher income and wealth strata.

As traditional tax theory has always argued, to the degree that taxes can be levied upon pure scarcity incomes and monopoly profits, the tax burden can be made correspondingly lighter upon commodities and services of which the supply would shrink if net income were reduced. It is this criterion specifically which has justified the imposition of death duties, taxes on the unearned increment of land values, and — in conjunction with the moral argument for lessened inequality — the progressive personal income tax. Taxes of this character tend to minimize the adverse effect of a given revenue load upon economic motivation and thereby to enhance the output and employment level of the economy.

But, aside from these quite general forms, it is doubtful whether incentive taxation can be pressed far without running afoul of the difficulty that differential treatment of incomes as to source or kind denies the very freedom of choice which is the chief recommendation of a competitive price system.[55] Furthermore — and this is still more important — before we venture to create differential or discriminatory taxation in order to favor private enterprise, larger outputs, and employment, we should make sure that nothing significant remains in the way of tax reforms to remove present discriminations in the tax structure unfavorable to these ends. The following proposals are made conformably to this second purpose. A large majority of economists would favor some such program of tax reform designed to encourage private enterprise, particularly competitive and innovating ventures.

PROVIDING A MORE EQUITABLE DEFINITION OF INCOME

For reasons which will later appear, first importance in our list of tax reforms is not assigned, as it frequently is, to shifting the burden from corporate to personal income taxation, but rather to a more equitable definition of income. Taxes have to be paid annually, but any businessman or accountant realizes that the only thing which can be known with certainty is the total income of a business retrospectively over its entire

55. This point has frequently been urged by Professor Henry C. Simons of the University of Chicago.

life. The arbitrariness of allocating income to any particular year should induce the Bureau of Internal Revenue to considerable tolerance with respect to the reporting of annual income. Furthermore, an attempt at a meticulous annual reporting is adverse to (a) firms with markedly fluctuating incomes, (b) new firms, which can succumb to losses in the first few years, and (c) enterprise in general, since businessmen are probably more sensitive to losses than to profits.

For these reasons private enterprise, and particularly new and venturesome businesses, would be benefited by a definition of income involving an implicit averaging over a number of years. Deducting present years' losses from past profits by amending previous income tax returns ("carry-back"), now permitted to two years, might well be extended, particularly through the reconversion period, to five or six years. Carrying forward present years' losses to the future ("carry-over") should "theoretically" be permitted indefinitely.[56] Because of certain administrative complications, however, it would be more practical to extend the period of permissible carry-over from the present two years to ten in order to cover the possibility of a major depression.

For similar reasons, Treasury restrictions on the deductions of capital losses should be liberalized. At present, capital losses can be deducted only from capital gains, and then only within limits. It is perhaps unnecessary to permit unlimited offsets to all income if the capital loss can be completely applied against capital gains and, to a limited extent only, to dividends.[57] The same considerations also require that an unincorporated business, if it is not to continue at a disadvantage relatively to others, should be permitted under the personal income tax to claim a credit or refund on the basis of what the tax would have been on a five- or ten-year average, with certain exceptions to avoid numerous small refunds as suggested by Simons and Groves.[58] Finally, and consistently with a longer-run and broader concept of income for tax purposes, firms should be allowed rather wide latitude in the method and timing of depreciation and obsolescence charges.

---

56. As urged for example by the National Industrial Conference Board in *Effects of Taxes Upon Corporate Policy,* New York, 1943, p. 74.

57. Cf. Lewis H. Kimmel, *Postwar Tax Policy and Business Expansion,* Brookings Institution, Washington, 1943, p. 38. See, however, p. 175 below.

58. Harold M. Groves, *Production, Jobs and Taxes,* McGraw-Hill, New York, 1944, pp. 85–86, who credits Simons with the suggestion.

REMOVING THE EXCESS-PROFITS TAX

There is a virtually unanimous demand for the elimination of the excess-profits tax, after a possible postwar inflationary pressure but before a possible reversal into deflation. Of course this does not mean abandoning the renegotiation of contracts as one way of preventing excess profits in the special wartime setting.

In a war economy the excess-profits tax helps to check inflation, provide revenue, and distribute the burden of the war. Theoretically it might have a place in a peacetime budget, if it could be applied differentially to monopoly gains. But actually, if new and small businesses earn profits, they usually show a larger return on equity capital than older firms and consequently the excess-profits tax penalizes "venture capital" at its tenderest stage. It adversely affects all firms, whether new or old, with fluctuating income and thus it reduces the return for risk-taking. Finally, aside from fluctuations, it treats all income over a certain level as excess, whether monopoly or competition prevails; when monopoly is not present, it again encumbers the riskier ventures. Even if it appropriates monopoly gains, it does not thereby abate the output and employment restrictions caused by monopoly.

The repeal of this tax should be complemented by permission to apply unused excess-profits-tax credits to a limited "carry-back" period. The moral obligation of government to proceed directly against monopoly restriction is, of course, increased if this tax is no longer to be levied.

COORDINATING THE CORPORATE AND PERSONAL INCOME TAXES

A strictly rational tax system would not include any taxes upon business. This does not mean that any tax on an artificial person is preposterous. Windows, dogs, and waxworks are sometimes and not necessarily irrationally taxed, and all taxes, including those on business, are paid from capital or income belonging ultimately to natural persons. Furthermore in the absence of progressiveness of personal income taxes, it would be difficult or impossible to demonstrate a difference in the burden upon investment, particularly active risk-bearing, between the two types of income taxes; taxation in either form undoubtedly costs something in economic motivation. The real reason for eliminating business taxes is that they defy any attempt to relate the tax to be paid by an individual to his income. Consequently any argument for progressiveness — equalitarian policy, encouraging consumption, etc. — becomes per se an argument against business taxes.

But there are two strong reasons for carrying through a reform of business taxation without abolishing it, both particularly cogent in the situation after the war. In the first place, the general public, erroneously identifying corporate taxation with "soaking the rich," would resent a sharp turn to personal income taxes, just at a time moreover when maintaining adequate taxation will be difficult anyway. In the second place, labor unions, taking as self-evident something which is actually doubtful, would regard the abatement of taxes on corporate income as a windfall profit and as a justification for wage demands, just at a time when downward wage revisions will be called for in many sectors.

The really serious flaw in the present tax situation is not the taxation of business income per se, but the fact that interest payments are, but dividends are not, deductible as costs in arriving at net taxable corporate income. Thus despite the virtually unanimous agreement of experts in corporation finance that equity financing is preferable from the angle of both firm and public in an economy subject to business booms and depressions, the tax system favors fixed debts. The double taxation of dividends can be eliminated either by retaining the corporation income tax and permitting the shareholder to deduct the tax — already paid at the source — from his personal income tax, or by exempting corporations from the income tax on dividends and catching the dividends in personal income taxation. Appropriate adjustment of rates can make the two procedures yield arithmetically identical results for the individual taxpayer.[59]

Beyond the double burdening of dividends, the present taxation of corporations urgently requires revision with regard to the treatment of undistributed profits and capital gains and losses. The present law imposes no special tax on undistributed profits and thus permits an individual to avoid the personal income tax upon such an accrual of wealth indefinitely. Devising an equitable method of taxing undistributed

59. Both methods of eliminating double taxation of dividends differ categorically from the proposal made by a group of Minneapolis–St. Paul industrialists to exclude 40 per cent of dividends from personal gross income for tax purposes! Cf. *The Twin Cities Plan: Postwar Taxes,* Twin Cities Research Bureau, St. Paul, June 1944, p. 16.

profits is fraught with great complexity, and we cannot here enter into a discussion of the merits of competing proposals. Suggestions include the treatment of corporations as partnerships, the revival of an *ad hoc* undistributed-profits tax, the imposition of a penalty tax on "unreasonable" accumulations, attempting annual evaluations of common stocks with profit or loss counted as income, and taxing appreciation when realized by stock sale.[60] A simple and equitable solution would be to continue to apply a normal corporate income tax to all income including undistributed profits, and, in conformity with the solution of the double-taxation problem, to give credit to individual stockholders for taxes paid on distributed earnings.

In line with these proposals, it would be possible to follow the suggestion made by Professor Simons to tax capital gains as all other income; but, where capital gains result from corporate reinvestment, in order to avoid double taxation of undistributed profits, to apply taxes paid on the latter as a deduction against personal income taxes.[61]

ABATEMENT OF TAXES ON INCOME FROM NEW VENTURES

A progressive income tax tends to have a discouraging effect on new ventures. It may reduce the compensation for investment in such enterprises below an adequate level, at least in those cases in which the returns before taxes are barely large enough to compensate for the higher risks involved. Furthermore a new business cannot take advantage of the "carry-back" in offsetting losses against earlier gains. Finally, a new business is less apt to have "other income" against which to offset losses.[62] For these reasons, the demand is being made rather widely for abatement of taxes, both personal and corporate, upon income from investment in new ventures.[63] Of course this raises questions as to the definition of a new venture, the duration of abatement, and its degree. The answers would have to be partly arbitrary; but this is not sufficient reason for rejecting a measure which, without going much farther than

60. Cf. Eustace Seligman, "A Post-war Program for the Taxation of Corporations and their Stockholders," *Proceedings of the American Philosophical Society,* Vol. 88, No. 1, June 16, 1944: "Symposium on Taxation and the Social Structure," pp. 60–67.

61. Groves, *op. cit.,* p. 81.

62. On the general importance of loss offsets, and particularly to new businesses, cf. E. D. Domar and R. A. Musgrave, "Proportional Income Taxation and Risk Taking," *The Quarterly Journal of Economics,* Vol. 58, No. 3, May 1944, pp. 388–423.

63. It would of course be necessary to take precautions against tax evasion through the holding of the stock of new firms by other corporations.

to offset the relative tax handicap of the new firm, promises much to encourage active investment, innovation, and competition.

The foregoing proposals should be supplemented by further limitation of tax-exempt securities by a federal tax on state, county, or municipal tax-exempt bonds. With reference to the tax systems of local governments, there is also pressing need of unification with federal taxes in order to avoid double taxation of corporate incomes. Indeed, from numerous angles a thorough overhauling of state and local finance should be undertaken with a view to the articulation of all units of government (including the federal) in a unified system. Shortcomings and specific reforms are exhaustively set forth by Hansen and Perloff in *State and Local Finance in the National Economy*.

It is not necessary to treat of numerous other evils of our tax laws — the deductibility of mortgage interest by occupant owners of homes, the avoidance of higher federal income taxation by persons in community property-law states, etc. — since these are indiscriminate inequities rather than special obstacles to investment and employment in the postwar period.

On the whole, the prospect for enhancing the profitability of private enterprise and competitive production through relatively few and clear lines of tax reform is promising. The proposals which have been outlined in the present section would be agreed upon by virtually every specialist in the field. Since the most conspicuous shortcomings seem to proceed from legislative blundering rather than from vested interests, the obstacles to reform should not be serious. Furthermore since the changes would improve business expectations, economic adjustment to the new tax structure would be nearly frictionless. There is every reason for emphasis upon the recommendation made in the Baruch-Hancock report that the main outlines of postwar taxation be expeditiously formulated.[64]

VI. The American Monopoly Problem and Employment

The phenomenal increase of production in the United States during the defense and war years — more than twofold since 1939 — may be ascribed in some part at least to the temporary release of our economy from the trammels of monopolistic restriction. Of course, many causes

64. S. Doc. 154, 78th Cong., 2d sess.

combined to expand output. But it is significant that while the index of industrial production increased to 222 by December 1943, the index of industrial capacity increased to less than 150 and man power in industry only to 202 over the same period (1939 = 100).[65] The wartime denial of the right of monopoly to withhold resources probably had much to do with this margin.

MONOPOLY AND STAGNATION

Even though we can attribute a large measure — perhaps much the largest share — of unemployment and idle funds to monopoly, this does not imply that we should aim at some theoretically "perfect" state of competition. The competition which we can reasonably hope to preserve and restore is rather a "fairly healthy and workable imperfect competition."[66] It is not essential that we have competition with costless and frictionless movement of labor and capital and perfect knowledge of the market. Nor do we require "pure" competition, in which products are not differentiated by various selling devices and each firm's output forms a negligible fraction of the total. Nor, finally, do we need complete price flexibility, if effective competition obtains with regard to the quality of the product. Upon the basis of such a conception, not all monopolistic elements are necessarily bad: price discrimination, price rigidity, price leadership are not always and necessarily contrary to public interest.[67] In any situation we can be sure that the greater the ease of entry into production the closer is the approach to a workable competitive norm.[68]

But monopoly restriction of output works cumulatively,[69] for monopolistic sellers of a given commodity may also become monopolistic buyers of the materials and resources entering into its production. They restrict output not only against consumers but additionally against the owners of the materials and resources in order to keep down their own cost of production. Labor, capital, and other resources excluded from

65. For industrial capacity see *Federal Reserve Bulletin*, January 1944, pp. 4–7; manhour figure computed at Board of Governors.

66. J. M. Clark, "Toward a Concept of Workable Competition," *The American Economic Review*, Vol. 30, No. 2, Pt. 1, June 1940, pp. 241–56.

67. *Idem*, "Monopoly in Law and Economics," *The Yale Law Journal*, Vol. 47, No. 1, November 1937, pp. 34–49.

68. E. S. Mason, "Methods of Developing a Proper Control of Business," *Proceedings of the Academy of Political Science*, Vol. 18, No. 2, January 1939, pp. 40–49.

69. W. H. Hutt, *Plan for Reconstruction*, Routledge, London, 1943, p. 73.

use by monopolies are dumped upon the competitive market, where their prices fall so low as to induce their owners to refrain from supplying them. This restricts income and reduces effective demand all around.

Monopoly adds to unemployment also by increasing risks in the aggregate. The threat to firms in competitive segments of the economy resulting from forays by would-be monopolists is greater than the corresponding risks resulting from ordinary competitive forces; thus monopoly increases the risks of competitive enterprise. Furthermore, these risks are heightened by the ability of monopoly in time of depression to control prices and output and thus to concentrate the decline of expenditures upon competitive industries.[70]

And finally, though the advantage of large economic units in carrying on research and technical improvement is great, the tendency of monopolies is to suppress technological improvement wherever it would weaken the monopoly or involve a large capital loss through obsolescence.

IS MONOPOLY INEVITABLE?

It is not possible to venture here into the long debate as to whether there has been a secular increase in monopoly, in the degree of industrial concentration of control. In general the conclusion, reached by some of the most careful students of the problem, is that at the present we simply do not know.[71] We can, however, be reasonably certain that the immediate economic scene includes several institutional forces working potently in the direction of monopoly. Under pressure of time during the war, the Army and Navy have negotiated contracts with larger producers, leaving the "small fry" to the vicissitudes of subcontracting. During the reconversion period this tendency may well be enhanced since many plants to be sold by the government will involve huge sums possessed only by the largest companies. If the war is followed by depression, this will add further opportunities to the well-established firm, to the large unit, and to the monopolistic concern to absorb competitors; and public works, again involving government

70. In times of prosperity the price margins established by monopoly controls undermine the markets necessary for sustained activity.

71. For example, Donald H. Wallace, "Industrial Markets and Public Policy: Some Major Problems," in *Public Policy*, ed. C. J. Friedrich and E. S. Mason, Harvard University Press, Cambridge, 1940, p. 73; and Mason, *loc. cit.*, cf. note 10.

buying, characteristically strengthen the larger firms.[72] The emphasis is placed upon technological rather than upon financial savings of large-scale operation, since for the most part the latter are not social economies but adventitious private gains arising from bargaining position and amenable to institutional equalization.

Concerning the supposed technological savings of monopoly the various TNEC investigations showed that in important industries increases of output have been taken care of by reduplicating productive units rather than by building larger ones.[73] The monograph on *Competition and Monopoly in American Industry* concludes that "in nearly every case in which monopoly persists, it will be found that artificial factors are involved."[74] The staff report on the result of the entire investigation says: "It is sometimes asserted, or assumed, that large-scale production, under the conditions of modern technology, is so much more efficient than small-scale production that competition must inevitably give way to monopoly as large establishments drive their smaller rivals from the field. But such a generalization finds scant support in any evidence that is now at hand."[75] If we accept these conclusions, we are thrown back for an explanation of most monopoly to nontechnological factors — deliberate product differentiation, unfair competition, adventitious bargaining position, collusion, legal monopoly through patents, other government-fostered monopolies, and the various factors underlying "fewness" of sellers and buyers.

NONTECHNOLOGICAL BASES OF INDUSTRIAL MONOPOLY

One of the most important causes of monopoly is what economists call "product differentiation" — the common phenomenon of a firm's attaching a portion of the market to itself through advertising, salesmen, distinctive packaging and the like. Undoubtedly these outlays contribute some benefits to the consumer, for the most part ephemeral in nature (e.g., the "exclusive" atmosphere of a shop or restaurant)

72. Wesley C. Ballaine, "How Government Purchasing Procedures Strengthen Monopoly Elements," *The Journal of Political Economy,* Vol. 51, No. 6, pp. 523–38.

73. Cf. the summary of TNEC findings upon this point by George J. Stigler, "The Extent and Bases of Monopoly," *The American Economic Review,* Supplement: "Papers Relating to the Temporary National Economic Committee," Vol. 32, No. 2, Pt. 2, June 1942, pp. 1–23, esp. pp. 8–13.

74. Clair Wilcox, TNEC Monograph 21, p. 315.

75. *Final Report and Recommendations of the Committee,* TNEC Doc. No. 35, p. 89.

and of small value in relation to their cost. The monopoly power conferred by such practices may vary from virtually complete control to a situation in which monopoly profits vanish through a crowding in of other firms with similar products.

Product Differentiation and Unfair Competition

Much of the waste carelessly attributed to competition actually arises from deliberate product differentiation or from attempts to achieve it.[76] Extravagance and reduplication of effort in the distribution of products is not the whole story. Some of the economies of large-scale production may be needlessly lost, if the splitting-up of the market among rival firms goes so far as to make the physical production units smaller than they would be without a multiplicity of brands. And the high technical costs entailed by these less-than-optimum plants are probably seldom paralleled by qualities in the product which the consumer, especially if he were well informed, would seek in the items he buys.

Furthermore, product differentiation may lead to oligopoly (fewness of producers) or monopoly because enormous outlays upon advertising and selling campaigns may be necessary to break into a national market of the size of the United States. In some lines of production, no doubt, local markets may suffice to realize all the economies of scale; but in others this will not be true and here the problem assumes serious dimensions. Where entry into the industry is impeded only by the requirement of a large accumulation of capital, however, the capitalist system has not shown itself sorely ineffective; and the maintenance of monopoly or oligopoly merely by the arts of sellers' persuasion is probably one of the less serious monopoly problems.

A part of any concerted attack upon monopoly should be a thorough overhauling of the ineffective, contradictory and sometimes perverse features of common and statutory law with respect to unfair competition. Patently indefensible on any grounds are the unholy practices such as false advertising, misbranding, misrepresentation of competitors' goods, molestation, inducing breach of contract, and some forms of the boycott. Other practices, such as price discrimination, tying agreements, local price cutting, and the like are unfair if the effect is substantially to reduce competition. Indeed, as in the case of the federal and state retail price-maintenance statutes, the law itself some-

---

76. Cf. A. P. Lerner, *The Economics of Control,* Macmillan, New York, 1944, p. 183.

times artificially creates a category of alleged unfairness and thereby actually strengthens monopolistic tendencies.[77]

Government Policies Favorable to Monopoly

Among the remaining nontechnological bases of monopoly, the activities of government are especially important. Compared with other aspects of the monopoly problem, these cases are relatively simple in their theoretical character; but politically they are frequently the most formidable because they often indicate the capitulation of democratic government to special economic interests. Perhaps the most conspicuous instance is the recent wave of resale price-maintenance laws, for which an apology in terms of economic welfare is not yet forthcoming. Similarly in the National Recovery Act codes, fortunately a closed chapter, industrial monopoly celebrated a field day in devising restrictive arrangements, under legal sanction, for application under the aromatic label of "self-government in industry." Closely related to such measures are the instances of legislative support of labor-producer collusion to restrict output and raise prices.[78]

So manifold, indeed, are the contributions of government to monopoly that the present context permits only the cataloguing of a few additional — but in some cases permeating — restrictive policies and devices. Most notorious of these is the American high tariff policy, which has permitted special groups to carve out for themselves profitable and restricted markets behind a wall of tariff protection and has obstructed international commodity and capital markets, as an earlier section has illustrated. Our system of taxation, as another section indicated, frequently penalizes the small producer and the new venture as against large and established firms. Our own patent and copyright laws, and the complete lack of uniformity between countries, have supported — particularly in the chemical and electric apparatus fields — some of our most oppressive national monopolies and international cartels, as the TNEC investigations amply demonstrate. Even this impressive list must be supplemented by mention of large subsidies to producers, interstate trade barriers, and government purchasing policy during the war.

77. Milton Handler, "Unfair Competition," reprinted from the *Iowa Law Review*, Vol. 21, No. 2, January 1936, in *Readings in the Social Control of Industry*, ed. by Hoover and Dean, Philadelphia, 1942, pp. 76–179.
78. Cf. below, pp. 182 ff.

LABOR AND RESTRICTION OF OUTPUT

Up until the present Administration, the labor-union movement in the United States was not strong; but in the period before the war it increased its powers rapidly. It is probably impossible to determine how much restriction of output is attributable to union activity. We know that barriers to entry were erected by some of the older craft unions. We know that union demands concerning seniority, piecework, hours, vacations, hiring, etc., frequently resulted in limitation of output, not always showing itself in unemployment. We know further, that overt "restraint of trade" is involved in some union contracts which (a) prevent the utilization of new techniques and machines, (b) prohibit the use of goods and materials upon which certain labor operations had been carried on outside the immediate locality, and (c) require the hiring of superfluous labor.[79] No doubt some protection of the individual laborer from technological unemployment is warranted in the form of dismissal wages and the like, and yet the enumerated practices — clearly in restraint of trade — cannot be defended, and any antimonopoly program will include their elimination. Finally, there is the vexed question as to the extent to which wage rates secured by union action restrict output and employment.

Union Wage Policy

The economic and political power of the unions in and after the war raises the fundamental issue as to how far wages can be advanced, by collective bargaining or otherwise, without producing unemployment. I think there can be no doubt that in certain industries where very high current rates were paid during the war to move labor rapidly into the field, downward adjustments should and will come about. But in considering the question of the general level of wages, we must take into account three situations: (a) the existence of monopoly profits in the industry; (b) technical progress; (c) lack of both.

Wages Rising With Monopoly Profits

The presence of monopoly profits in a particular industry or even firm is apt to persuade the union, and sometimes even economists and

---

79. Corwin D. Edwards, "Public Policy toward Restraints of Trade by Labor Unions: An Economic Appraisal," *The American Economic Review*, Vol. 32, No. 1, Pt. 2, March 1942, pp. 432–48. Cf. also Sumner H. Slichter, *Union Policies and Industrial Management*, The Brookings Institution, Washington, 1941, *passim*.

regulatory authorities, of the justice of a wage increase. In fact, however, such a wage increase has precisely the same outcome as collusion between producer and employee against the consumer, which would clearly violate the antitrust laws and which represents the acme of all-round restrictionist mentality. Even so, some well-meaning "friends of labor" demand this procedure as a political necessity in a world where the more indirect processes of industrial monopoly regulation and monopoly taxation seem to move slowly and uncertainly. But this action would certainly make the industrial monopoly problem insoluble.

Once employee participation in monopoly profits is sanctioned in a particular firm or industry, two movements are set afoot which tend to reduce employment. In the first place, rates on similar kinds of labor in other industries may be forced up by union action seeking to universalize the gain in the original monopoly-profits industry. But if the other industries are competitive, advances in wages may be attained only at the cost of lessened employment. In the second place, there is nothing to prevent a monopolist, if compelled to pay higher wages on these grounds, from reducing employment and output still further in order to maximize profits under the new conditions of increased labor costs.

Wages Rising With Technological Progress

With a general improvement in techniques or management, a good case can be made for permitting the gain to accrue to labor by a combination of approximately stabilizing the prices of consumers' goods and permitting money wages to rise parallel to the average increase in efficiency.[80] The workers employed in the firms or industries where efficiency has advanced are not to be the favored beneficiaries of the progress in the technical arts, but all-round wage increases commensurate with the average growth of productivity in the economy and supported by appropriate monetary policy should ensure the widest possible distribution of the additional real income.

Such a combination of wage and monetary policies would have several advantages, as compared with a policy of permitting productive gains to show themselves in falling prices of consumer goods. It would have an equalitarian effect, since laborers characteristically belong to lower income groups than consumers in general. Secondly, it would

---

80. The requirements of this situation are carefully described by D. H. Robertson, *Banking Policy and the Price Level*, P. S. King, London, 1926, Chap. 3.

permit the gains to accrue in a way which answers better to the character of collective bargaining. It is, for example, difficult to imagine long-shoremen striking because the price of rubber tires does not decline. In the third place, the policy lightens the burden of the debt relative to money incomes without appreciating or depreciating it in absolute or real terms.

Applied to the postwar period in the United States, the policy would, because of the cumulation of technological and managerial economies during the war, probably speak against a general reduction of wage rates.

Wages Rising Through Militant Bargaining

Where neither monopoly profits nor windfall gains from improvements exist, an increase of wages could come about only from militant exaction by labor monopoly. Extremists sometimes seem inferentially to justify such increases from the fact that a forced transfer of income from higher to lower brackets increases the aggregate propensity to consume and thus expands markets and employment. It may readily be granted that this effect might follow inheritance or progressive income taxation; but a forcing of wages above the economic value of the work in competitive industries acts as a direct tax on employment.[81] Measures to increase consumption in the aggregate and measures to secure a more equal distribution of income must proceed by taxation and by the costless or subsidized provision of education, social security, housing, medical care, etc., and not by monopolistic wage increases, unless we are willing to accept chronic unemployment and investment stagnation.

In a competitive enterprise economy, wage rates should tend to be settled for each occupation on the basis of free entry and a price that "clears the market" (i.e., absorbs the supply of laborers offering to work at that wage). The benefits of progress, accumulation, and equalitarian measures should accrue to labor as a "social dividend" and should be divided upon some rational basis or other, but not upon the artificial scarcities created by labor monopolies. If we really desire a competitive market economy, this principle of clearing the market must occupy a central place in the national wage policy.

81. A. C. Pigou and D. H. Robertson, *Economic Essays and Addresses,* P. S. King, London, 1931, pp. 126–27.

Unions in a Liberal Economic Order

The supply-and-demand principle pertains to relative wages. It does not imply that cutting the general level of wages is the way out of depression. Nor does it preclude exceptions for "substandard" or "sweated" labor markets (minimum wage laws), for extensive subventions to aid in the movement of labor from regions of relative oversupply, to provide technical education, or for other general welfare expenditures for labor.

Extreme measures with respect to labor unions are inappropriate to the character of the liberal competitive order or "guided capitalism" which most Americans seem to desire. It would be folly to propose the elimination of unions, in view of their many legitimate and socially beneficial activities — the elaboration of working agreements as to safety, work day, discipline, vacations, dismissal pay, grievances and the like. We must also take into account union activity on behalf of "substandard" wage groups. Nor must we forget that unions are symbols of achievement and hope of further economic advancement to the working classes generally.

On the other hand, the danger of "syndicalism" (in the Italian sense of economic and political governance by producers) as envisaged by Simons[82] cannot be gainsaid.

The best guarantee against this perversion is ultimately a developed public sentiment and more immediately a responsible union leadership. Labor leaders must recognize that "we cannot all get rich by restricting production," and that this principle must be applied in every specific case, i.e., that the wage which "clears the market" with free entry for qualified applicants in each classification is the socially justifiable wage.

The trial-and-error method in working out these relative wage rates by collective bargaining remains, despite its frequent abuse, the best available means of putting such a policy into effect. Its efficacy in a liberal economic order depends upon the abandonment of the philosophy that a "victory anywhere on the labor front is a victory everywhere," by employees and employers alike. Its efficacy also depends upon whether, by an appropriate combination of policies, reasonably

82. Henry C. Simons, "Some Reflections on Syndicalism," *The Journal of Political Economy,* Vol. 52, No. 1, March 1944, pp. 1–26.

full employment is achieved, since the risk of mass unemployment and the loss of markets for particular skills undoubtedly induce unions to restrictive devices as a precaution against bad times.

Now that peace has come it is probable that general and direct government regulation of wages will end, as incompatible with a market-controlled economy. Chief reliance for nonrestrictive union policies must rest upon cessation of industry warfare against unions as such, an improvement in the personnel and outlook of union leaders, and the intervention of government to arbitrate disputes, prosecute outright restraint of trade by unions, and prevent employer-labor collusion. It remains to be seen whether the militancy of companies and unions will necessitate universal compulsory federal arbitration. Whether these tribunals should be tripartite or wholly public depends upon the course of events. During the course of the war the tripartite panels undoubtedly played an important educative role for all parties; but since minority dissent is apt to follow industry-labor lines, the rulings carry less authority than a completely public tribunal.

INTERNATIONAL LIMITATION OF PRODUCTION

For the most part the restriction of international trade has been national and unilateral, by means of tariffs, quotas and exchange controls, discussed in an earlier section. There is, besides, the wide field of restriction on output, exports, prices and the like imposed by international agreement, either private or governmental. In this general field we can distinguish three main categories: (a) agricultural raw materials and foodstuffs, produced for the most part competitively; (b) minerals and metals, usually more or less monopolistically controlled; and (c) fabricated products, for which monopoly by patent is quite common. But what can be said of an international-buffer stock arrangement, of an international commodity authority, and of cartels from the present viewpoint of monopoly restriction of output?

The Buffer-Stock Proposal

The buffer-stock proposal — striking directly at one of the most potent causes of protracted depression, the perverse response of agriculture to low prices in producing more rather than less — cannot lightly be dismissed. Working ideally it would absorb surpluses in depression and sell them in boom years, stabilize agricultural prices and incomes, and thus go far to reduce the industrial cycle. In the case of the great agricultural staples such as rubber, cotton, wool, wheat, tea, coffee, cocoa, and sugar, the efficacy of this action would depend in large degree upon concerted international action.

As applied within one country, the buffer-stock or over-normal-granary scheme has met three great difficulties: (a) the inadequacy of the operation actually to stem the depression of agricultural prices; (b) the difficulty or impossibility of distinguishing cyclical from secular surpluses; and (c) the tendency of price-maintenance to preserve or increase the underlying surplus capacities. On an international basis buffer stocks would reduce the first difficulty, but they would make the third still more serious. To date the collaboration has not extended past the purely negative device of setting export quotas and prices.[83] Quite aside from the delicate question of quota allocation and the difficulty of raising an international fund of sufficient magnitude, any advance beyond this essentially negative and restrictionist phase encounters the practically insoluble question of inducing national measures to move resources out of the protected field and into useful production, i.e., to serve the ultimate interests of consumers.

It would not be difficult to devise methods of financing an international commodity corporation,[84] although in practice there might be obstacles to the actual raising of the funds. Nor would it be impossible to invent mechanical devices to prevent the indefinite accumulation of stocks by such a corporation. Thus it might be directed to make its purchases at a certain margin (say 20 per cent) under a base price computed as a ten-year moving average.[85] Furthermore, in depression the net losses of the corporation could be reduced and the real income of unemployed or relief sections of the population could be increased by "two-price" or other discriminatory price policies.

We should not hesitate at the prospect of a larger amount of imme-

83. The Wheat Agreement of June 1942 also set maxima on stocks. Cf. International Labour Office, *International Commodity Control Agreements,* Montreal, 1943.
84. The question has already been explored in official circles.
85. Any such mechanical device, perhaps necessitated in order to withstand pressure groups, is ideally inferior to discretionary authority, since not only historical but also prospective market conditions are relevant.

diate control, if this promises less control in the foreseeable future. Thus, buffer-stock agreements, carefully formulated and adequately surrounded with safeguards, might help to correct conditions of chronic oversupply.[86] In the present scene, however, all-round reduction of trade barriers would seem to be the more promising approach from a political angle. Large sums would not have to be entrusted to an outside agency; and, to the extent that trade expansion did eliminate surplus productive capacity, nations would not be required to surrender part of their sovereignty through agreeing to shift economic resources out of the protected fields.

International Commodity Agreements

Misgivings with regard to the great agricultural staples would seem to be even more justified when we consider tin, copper, chrome, steel, aluminum, zinc, and the like. Whereas net losses of public funds in the stabilization of farm products usually benefit mostly the lower income groups,[87] this would not be so true in the case of iron, steel and nonferrous metals which are largely characterized by monopoly. In the immediate postwar scene there will be areas of intense oversupply and overcapacity; and it will be in the public interest to prevent a complete collapse of prices for the sake of income maintenance in general. But the danger of an international organization's being captured by monopolistic producers is so great that direct national subsidies, coupled with domestic measures to move resources from these war-inflated industries, would seem to be the saner course.

International Cartels

The dangers inherent in international commodity agreements apply with even greater force to international cartels of private producers. The investigations of the TNEC and the Senate Kilgore Committee have revealed the perniciously restrictive influence of cartels in controlling prices, impairing quality, allocating territory, subjecting supply to quotas by country and even by concern, restricting productive capacity, limiting the use of inventions, and various devices to harass

86. Cf. Joseph S. Davis, "International Commodity Agreements in the Postwar World," Chap. 18 in *Postwar Economic Problems,* ed. by S. E. Harris, McGraw-Hill, New York, 1943, pp. 305–21.
87. In the case of coffee, rubber, and sugar especially, this requires obvious qualifications.

and weaken independent companies. This says nothing concerning their sinister political powers to thwart national laws, carry on espionage and propaganda, and finally under private auspices to set up a system of private protection.[88]

The activities of cartels are not, of course, entirely unacceptable from the point of view of the public welfare. Occasional benefits may result from the interchange of technical knowledge, if not accompanied by patent-based exclusive territory agreements, or from the artificial limitation of output, if accompanied by measures to remove excess capacity. But this acknowledgment is very far from an acceptance of the institution of international cartels as a part of the "wave of the future."[89] Both of these desirable objectives can be achieved without cartels. Thus the general availability of technical information can be greatly furthered by compulsory patent licensing (as a part of a uniform national patent act for all countries) and by extension of publicly supported technological research. To cope with the immediate impact of wartime excess capacities, direct subsidies, coupled with measures to convert plant, can be undertaken by national governments without cartel action.

If this really honest procedure should prove politically unacceptable, it is argued sometimes that temporary import quotas conducted by governments would be less dangerous than quotas conducted by private monopolies.[90] But the certain evidence of the history of government-fostered or "regulated" cartels appears to be that there is no significant difference between their policies and straight monopoly practices. On the other hand, an international convention with respect to the prohibition of undesirable cartel practices would form a part of a liberal international program.

A PROGRAM TO REDUCE RESTRICTION OF OUTPUT BY MONOPOLY

Some economists regard the inflexibility of monopolistic prices as the chief cause of unemployment.[91] With equal ardor others maintain

88. Corwin Edwards, *Economic and Political Aspects of International Cartels,* 78th Cong., 2d sess., Kilgore Committee, Monograph No. 1. Cf. also TNEC *Hearings,* Pts. 2, 3, 5 and 25 (Cartels), and Monographs 6 and 40.

89. Cf. Julius Hirsch, "Legal Cartels, U. S. Style," *Barron's,* June 19, 1944, p. 3.

90. Cf. Edward S. Mason, "International Cartels," *Foreign Affairs,* July 1944, pp. 604–15, especially p. 606.

91. For example, Gardiner C. Means, *Industrial Prices and Their Relative Inflexibility,* S. Doc. 13; 74th Cong., 1st sess., 1935.

that achieving flexibility would do nothing toward remedying the situation.[92] My own conviction is strongly that there is an element of truth in both positions. If the setting is a cyclical downswing, the flexibility thesis would seem to imply a downward revision of administered prices toward or to the level of competitive prices; but the pessimistic outlook engendered by general price recessions may make this process self-perpetuating within undesirably wide limits. Combating cyclical depression is more effective through raising the low to the high prices than through beating down the inflexible segment.

But it is not possible to deduce from this that "if it is a question of the full utilization of resources, perhaps it [trust busting] is not the primary objective or, rather, not the primary instrument to get this objective."[93] This chain of reasoning would require one to believe (a) that trust busting would actually succeed so rapidly as to engender in the public the desire to withhold purchases in the expectation of still lower prices, in the manner which characterizes cyclical depression, and (b) that the monetary authority could not easily offset the mild downward drift of prices produced by a gradual loosening of monopoly restriction. It is precisely the different results reached by "fiscal and monetary policies" without trust busting and the results of fiscal and monetary policies to sustain demand and output with a balanced program against monopoly restriction which constitutes the central theme of the present essay. An onslaught against the "inflexibility" of monopoly prices is misleading because it suggests a falling general level of prices. It is not the inflexibility of monopoly prices but monopoly restriction of output which is at issue.

Until we have exhausted available devices against monopoly restriction of output and employment, we cannot legitimately conclude that an economy governed by planners or commissars rather than by competitive prices is "inevitable." An enumeration of such available devices serves to set in bold letters the manifold and varied character of such a program. Judicial antitrust procedure forms an important and integral part, but the whole field of action is several times as extensive as this one segment. Policies to combat monopolistic restriction of output are:

92. For example, Oscar Lange, *Price Flexibility and Employment,* Cowles Commission, Monograph No. 8, Bloomington, 1944.

93. Jacob Marschak, "Price Flexibility and Income Maintenance in the Transition from War to Peace Production," *Proceedings* of the Conference on Price Research of the National Bureau of Economic Research, New York, May 5–6, 1944, typescript copy, p. 155.

1. Direct government measures to facilitate the movement of savings into private competitive fields
    a. Fiscal and monetary policies designed to maintain national income
    b. Measures to move resources from sectors of chronic oversupply
    c. Encouragement to new, small, and competitive enterprises*
2. Government research and economic education
    a. Concerning the structure of industries
    b. Concerning "business conditions"*
    c. Research and publication in productive techniques
    d. Consumers' education
3. Public and private efforts to develop a higher plane of economic ethics
4. Removal of government or legal support of monopoly
    a. Reduction of protective tariffs
    b. Reform of taxation hindering small and competitive businesses
    c. Repeal of Miller-Tydings and state price-maintenance acts
    d. Patent reform*
    e. Removal of barriers to trade between the states*
5. Antitrust action
    a. Strengthening the antitrust agencies*
    b. Unification of law as to unfair competition
    c. Enactment of federal incorporation law*
    d. Federal supervision of corporate mergers, trade associations, and interlocking directorships*
6. Government regulation of "natural monopolies"
7. Government ownership and operation
    a. Of government ventures to compete with certain monopolistic producers*
    b. Of certain monopolized industries

* Policies recommended in *Final Report and Recommendations of the Temporary National Economic Committee*, TNEC Doc. No. 35, pp. 24–40.

Anything approaching adequate treatment of these subjects would, of course, require an entire treatise. We can attempt no more here than to indicate the main outlines of a programmatic attack upon monopoly restriction which will require a decade (or two or three) to be really effective. Furthermore, since preceding sections have included parts of this program, only a few portions now require explanation.

1. *Direct government measures to facilitate the movement of savings and investment into private competitive fields:* The economic philosophy represented in these pages denies the desirability of government investment merely as an "outlet for savings" and unaccompanied by far-reaching reforms favorable to a competitive price economy; but it would be fatuous to suppose that during the process of reform, general

"spending" programs could not materially aid the attack upon restrictionism itself. Fear of unemployment supplies an important motivation of trade-union policies concerning wage and entry; the fear of depression moves business to monopoly price policies, and arrival of depression permits the strong to absorb the weak. In other words, full use of resources — even if secured by essentially superficial devices — eases the way for fundamental correctives in the system.

Moreover, until this correction has progressed rather far, it will require direct government action to supplement the faltering action of our present market structure to care adequately for outstanding cases of chronic surpluses. In contrast to the over-all savings-investment problem, this question of surpluses pertains to particular markets and does not yield to — though it may be facilitated by — general expansionist devices. What is essential, as we have seen in the analysis of international raw materials, is the temporary resort to subsidies to prevent a demoralizing of the market, complemented by direct national action to redistribute resources to other fields. War is the great propagator of these intense oversupplies, and after the war we must simply face the necessity of more control in order eventually to have less. National governments will need to display great ingenuity in securing diversified agriculture to supplant mono-culture economies, for example. We must also bear in mind the fact that budgetary burdens incurred not to perpetuate oversupplies but to reduce them may have added justification from the angle of supporting income as a whole.

The perennial threat to established monopolies from new industries and new firms should be greatly furthered. Indeed, many authors see in the new techniques developed during the war one of the most promising avenues toward fuller employment. But since these techniques may be subjected to patent-based restriction, the reform of the patent laws as recommended by the TNEC should be carried out immediately. Prompt action favorable to the new entrant is also possible in the field of taxation along lines already described. This action would go only so far as to remove the present tax handicaps upon new firms, without differentially favoring them; but with careful precautions against administrative arbitrariness, the policy might be pressed further. In the reconversion period, the federal government can, if it chooses, favor new industries and independent firms by refusing to sell war plant to monopolies. Many of the policies suggested elsewhere in the present essay regarding banking, research and tariffs, ease the way for the innovator and the new competitive firm.

2. *Government research and economic education:* Cases of monopoly which rest upon mere fewness, rather than upon other institutional bases amenable to fairly clear remedies, can only be dealt with industry by industry according to the peculiarities of each case. Sufficient knowledge is frequently lacking for the formulation of appropriate policies. Intensive study over a decade by a corps of experts, utilizing among other things the rich experience of the OPA, is necessary in many instances to reveal industry and market structures as the basis of antirestriction measures.

Scientific research bearing upon products and productive processes could be subsidized still more extensively by federal and state governments to offset the superior financing resources of large firms. The advantage of size and long life and experience of large and monopolistic firms can also be compensated by the extension of present government research in the general course of business — savings, investment, price and income effects on demand, etc.

Finally, the ultimate remedy against the wastes involved in deliberate product differentiation — selling costs and production in plants smaller than the technical optimum — is consumer education. Instruction in the common schools could undoubtedly arm the average citizen against the worst pitfalls; grade labeling and the accurate and clear description of physical characteristics of products might well be made compulsory.

3. *Public and private efforts to develop business, labor, and professional ethics:* One of the reasons why collectivist or "planned" societies appear attractive is that we frequently know about them only through literary description of their ideal or pure form, whereas we know private enterprise firsthand in its far-from-ideal actuality. Thus the beguiling character of planned economies rests often upon the postulate of wise, perfectly informed, and incorruptible administrators and boards. Pursuing this line of thought, would it not be more reasonable to attempt to raise the standards of economic illumination and morals in the world about us than to pin our faith on some formal utopia? At bottom any system is conditioned by the morals of its members. It does not appear more difficult to develop the morality necessary to the beneficent working of a competitive price system than to the

beneficent working of fascism, socialism, or a planned economy —
quite the contrary. If our aim is a competitive system that is free of some
of the worst defects of the present economic order, we must remove
the social stigma from the "profit motive" as such and attach it to monopoly gains and living from inherited wealth or other adventitious
position. Thus what now passes as professional ethics of the American
Medical Association, the Farm Bureau, the CIO, and the AF of L are
as relevant to the effective working of private enterprise as the animus
of the American Association of Manufacturers, and the United States
Steel Corporation. In the present scene, the preservation of American
ideals of liberty, opportunity, and justice depends immediately and ultimately upon whether these large aggregates of power turn toward restriction or toward full use of resources. There exists no formal or mechanical substitute for economic morals.

4. *Removal of government or legal support of monopoly:* The reduction of tariff protection and the reform of taxation have already
been touched upon; the removal of interstate trade barriers and price-
maintenance acts must be left to speak for itself; and the specific details
of patent reform must be passed over with a mere reference to the
TNEC recommendations of compulsory licensing, unrestricted licenses,
limiting the patent monopoly period, and forfeiture for violations.[94]

5. *Antitrust action:* Any serious program against monopoly involves
a strengthening of the antitrust agencies by providing adequate budgets
for the Antitrust Division of the Department of Justice and the Federal
Trade Commission. It should include, further, the explicit endowment
of the latter — in accord with the intent in the Act — with power to
establish findings of fact, and effective collaboration — also as originally intended — between the two agencies. An aroused public sentiment against monopoly restraint of employment would, of course, be
paralleled by a general program of prosecution of collusive agreements
and other restraints in place of the limited sporadic descents of the Department of Justice, imposed by its limited personnel. In order to purge
away some of the actual defense of monopoly involved in certain FTC
rulings, Congress should codify the law of unfair competition into a unified statute; and in order to enforce national standards of business practices, it should enact a federal incorporation statute. Finally, beside the

94. Cf. TNEC *Hearings,* Pts. 2, 3 and 30; Monographs 31 and especially 35, pp. 36–37.

stiffening of penalties and the extension of liability for violating the antitrust laws to corporation directors recommended by the TNEC, there would be good reason in this age of the "managerial revolution" to apply the liability to the top management as well.

6. *Government regulation of "natural monopolies" and*

7. *Government ownership and operation:* As set forth in an earlier section devoted to income maintenance in a potential postwar slump, government incursions by yardstick plants into monopolized fields would represent one of the most intelligent public investment policies. To the degree to which plant in obviously overexpanded industries can be converted to compete with monopolies, three birds are killed with one stone: the overcapacity here, the monopoly restriction of employment there, and the reduced flow of money income generally. Against these advantages, the promise of Congress not to use war plants to compete with private industry needs to be reinterpreted or abrogated: the promise was not a guarantee of immunity to private monopoly.

Whenever it becomes clearly established that one productive unit is more efficient than a plurality for the naturally defined market (national or local) the industry should be publicly regulated, operated, or owned. Acceptance of this principle does not imply hostility to mere size as such but makes a "natural" tendency toward monopoly the criterion. It also repudiates a number of schemes for dealing with monopoly which would virtually but not explicitly amount to government ownership, operation, or regulation.[95] Thus it is compatible with a gradual transition to a liberal socialist regime, if and to the degree that monopolies prove to be founded upon real economies.

If a valedictory word is in order, however, it would be this: most of the institutional (as opposed to the technological) origins of private monopoly are problems which would have to be met and solved also by a liberal socialist society. We may not now possess the knowledge of markets and control techniques sufficient to cope with all monopolistic

---

95. E.g., general price control, of J. S. Bain, Jr., "The Normative Problem in Industrial Regulation," *The American Economic Review,* Vol. 33, No. 1, Pt. 2, March 1943, pp. 54–70; "counter-speculation," cf. Lerner, *op. cit.,* pp. 55, 85, 94; government forward contracting, of M. A. Copeland, "Business Stabilization by Agreement," *The American Economic Review,* Vol. 34, No. 2, June 1944, pp. 328–39; the "industrial expansion" scheme, of Mordecai Ezekiel, *Jobs for All Through Industrial Expansion,* Alfred A. Knopf, New York, 1939.

restriction. But with available courses of action we can go very far in the direction of the fundamental cure of unemployed capital and men. Whether this course results in a capitalism realizing the postulates of laissez faire or a liberal socialism is no great matter: it will in either event secure high standards of living and high levels of employment under the economic governance of a competitive price system and not of the subjective judgments of planners and of other less benevolent tyrants.

VII. Concluding Observations

Current discussions of economic developments in the United States in the immediate and longer postwar period reveal a very general preoccupation with the future of consumption in the aggregate, with economic security, and with planning by the government. These terms are sufficiently general and vague to cover genuine social values which no one can deny; but there is also an acute danger that they cover a multitude of questionable proposals. It may be worth the while to point to the implications of earlier pages.

In an essay which runs counter to the current mode on the subject of consumption, it is probably necessary to repeat that the end of economic activity is consumption, and one aim of a democratic economic order is the increase of consumption by lower income groups. But to conclude from this that a settled public policy should be to encourage consumption and to discourage saving is an error, as long as additions to investment increase the total available for consumption. In fact, very many of the proposals for increasing low income consumption — slum clearance, public health centers and hospitals, technical education, etc. — themselves require large investments. To reduce savings because a part fails to arrive at productive investment is to throw the child out with the bath.

A democratic economic system leaves the decision as to saving and consuming to the income receivers; it interferes only — along lines previously indicated — to assure the utilization of saving in active investment. One reason for leaving this decision to individuals is to secure a maximum of free choice in the economy; but another is the lack of any objective criterion as to what is a "correct" amount of saving. Deflation affords objective evidence of too little spending but no evidence of how much of the spending should be investment, how much consumption. In a word, policies to encourage productive enterprise also encourage consumption; antimonopoly and equalitarian policies make for "fair sharing" of consumption; but policies to promote consumption at the expense of saving cannot be relied upon to contribute to either objective. The most that should be done with regard to saving itself is to try to establish an economic system in which saving is not motivated by a fear of periodic depressions.

Increased economic security is another social value which is reached better by indirection than by direct measures. Actually, as these pages have frequently reiterated, the only kind of security of the one group or interest compatible with the security of others is the security which accrues to all members of the society through a high and sustained level of national income. The safety of the individual achieved through monopoly, special privilege, or successful resistance to changes required by shifting demand and progressive technique is a beggar-my-neighbor kind of security. Undoubtedly we are confronted here with a vicious circle: cyclical variations of income induce the individual to take refuge in restrictive measures to protect his investment, trade, or class of labor; and these restrictions in turn contribute to the violence of economic downswings. Public policy has therefore to proceed simultaneously against economic security via monopoly and favorably to economic security through a high-level and stable aggregate demand.

Conversion to peacetime outputs now requires extensive planning— of reconversion in the narrow sense, of price ceilings, rationing and priorities, of monetary and fiscal measures, of public spending, and of international economic relations. We have seen that this planning can be so constituted as gradually to attenuate itself, in place of propagating itself and approaching collectivism. All too frequently the case for deliberately formulated and timely policy is subtly identified with a case for far-reaching economic government by a master plan and by master planners. In contrast, we can turn government action into the direction of realizing an equalitarian competitive regime, where obedience is owed not to persons but to laws.

America has much for which to be thankful and little to justify morose misgivings as to the future. Even our severest trials leave room for hope. We withstood the greatest depression of modern industrialism without civil disorder or political breakdown, and we were groping toward effective remedies. The problem of racial minorities is severe, but most Americans have faith in nonviolent solutions. Our international isolationism has cost dearly, but increasing numbers of our citizens recognize the error.

The other side of the balance is heavier. We have had no wars on our soil for eighty years; and relative to other great nations, we have paid lightly in blood and suffering in the world wars. Not within living memory have we experienced the devastating costs of serious inflation. We have not suffered from famines or great epidemics. Our national politics are not threatened by class wars or by extremist movements; our political parties show no signs of disintegrating into contentious and factional parcels; and our Congress has never reached a legislative impasse such as sealed the fate of German and Austrian democracy. Our sense of national unity is strong and balanced, without dangerous sectionalism on the one hand and without aggressive nationalism on the other. The sentiments of democracy, of the worth of the common man, of the dignity of labor are lively and real. We benefit from a rich endowment of natural resources and the cross-fertilization of racial stocks and cultures.

Such a society can be the master of its economic fate. If, as it would appear, the broad masses of our people cherish the ideals of individualism and liberty, economic governance must for the most part consist in the impersonal mechanism of competition and competitive prices. By not taking thought we shall fail to reach this goal: it requires a militant public sentiment and aggressive, manifold, and persistent action by the state. The American way requires this — rather than collectivism or economic government by planners — for the achievement of the ideals of full employment, material progress, and equality of opportunity.

Chapter 5

STABILITY AND EXPANSION

Alvin H. Hansen[1]

I. THE REVOLUTION IN ECONOMIC THOUGHT

Among the many contrasts between World War I and World War II nothing is more remarkable than the profound change in economic thinking, and in the climate of public opinion throughout the world. Following World War I it was generally accepted that the main purpose of postwar economic policy was to reconstitute as rapidly as possible the automatic forces in economic life. The drive all around was a return, in the broad essentials, to laissez faire.

After the First World War

By and large, there were no serious apprehensions about the future. Cycles of prosperity and depression were regarded as more or less an inevitable part of the modern system of production and were accepted as not too painful by-products of a dynamic and progressing economy. The century-old optimism born of the great era of growth and expansion of the 19th century — notably the era between the introduction of the railroad and World War I — still dominated public opinion everywhere. The prewar trends, it was thought, would rapidly be resumed. The war had been an unhappy interlude. The problem was how to get back to the prewar order. The task was approached not indeed with enthusiasm but at any rate without serious apprehension.

These high hopes suffered devastating disillusionment in consequence of the experiences between the two world wars. The international gold standard was bit by bit reconstituted — Germany in 1924, England 1925, France 1928 — and so throughout the world. But it was short lived. Already by the end of 1929 it began to totter. By 1931 it was shattered for good.

International monetary and economic conferences were held. These strove to restore the prewar economy. But everywhere in Europe coun-

1. Littauer Professor of Political Economy, Harvard University.

tries were confronted with mass unemployment. In England a group of economists wrote a report entitled "Third Winter of Unemployment."[2] The problem persisted, however, and subsequent volumes of a similar character appeared dealing with the hard and persisting core of unemployment. Ameliorating palliatives were offered, but in general the discussion proceeded in an atmosphere of fatalism and resignation. In such an atmosphere the dole was the best that could be offered. Of all the British developments in the first postwar decade, it most vividly portrays the consequences of confused thinking; indecision whether to go back or forward; inability to understand the new problems; a dying hope that things would somehow right themselves if nothing were done; a fear of new policies.

It was a decade of disillusionment, resignation and bewilderment. There was nostalgic looking back to prewar days but there were also grave doubts that these days would ever return. But what to do about it? To strike out along new lines was regarded as dangerous. Better hew close to the old financial and economic moorings. Time might, after all, set things right. Such was the intellectual climate of the first postwar decade.

The Great Divide

The great depression beginning in 1929 must be set down as one of the most profoundly explosive events in all world history. It has shattered the old patterns of man's thinking in a thousand ways, and particularly in respect to economic institutions and economic policy. The imperious necessity of doing something about a situation that had everywhere become intolerable, at long last overcame the counsels of timidity. Everywhere it became apparent that inaction was dangerous. Everywhere energies were at last galvanized into action. Whatever knowledge and ingenuity were available were concentrated on the task of developing the best positive programs that could be devised. It was no longer a question of perfectionism, of waiting until scientific inquiry had cleared up every dark nook and corner, until there were no unknowns in our equations, until agreement could be reached all around with respect to the remedies to be applied. The swift rush of events — bankruptcy, mass unemployment, the threat of starvation — in the three years of cumulative and accelerating deflation beginning with

2. *The Report of an Enquiry Undertaken in the Autumn of 1922*, P. S. King, London, 1923.

1929, brushed aside timid men and timid counsels and forced a program of action.

History will, I think, show that the economic upheaval of the great depression constitutes a "great divide" in economic thinking and economic policy. We have entered upon new territory. We are confronted with the great task of exploration. This task involves implementation, adaptation, and improvement of new instruments of management suitable for the functioning of a society so extraordinarily complex as that of the modern world.

While England at the end of the last war faced problems that she did not understand with a policy of inaction and indecision, there is reason to believe that the experiences of the two decades between World War I and World War II have given her a new direction and a new purpose. There is a profound difference between the utterances of British statesmen today and the utterances of British statesmen after World War I. One gets the impression that they now know where they are going and what to do. The bewilderment, hesitation, and fatalism so evident after the last war are gone. There is a feeling abroad that the community as a whole can be the master of its own economic destiny. There is a positive belief that mass unemployment does not have to be accepted as an act of God. There is a confidence that productive resources need not be wasted in idleness, that the high standard of living which modern technical progress has made possible can in fact be achieved. Indeed, in the recent White Paper on Postwar Employment Policy, presented by the Minister of Reconstruction to Parliament, the responsibility for averting a slump is accepted as a function of government. The White Paper recommends that the British Government accept as one of its primary aims and responsibilities the maintenance of a high and stable level of employment. This is the most basic and fundamental of a series of postwar plans issued by the British Government.[3]

The Economic Experience of the United States

The intellectual climate in the United States after World War II is likely to be somewhat different from that in Great Britain. The reasons

3. The Murray Full Employment Bill of 1945, if adopted by Congress, would become the American equivalent of the British White Paper. It is probable, however, that Congress is not now prepared to go as far as the Murray bill or the British Employment Paper. Leaders in both parties are, however, committed to federal responsibility for a full-employment program.

for this are not difficult to find. After World War I the economic experience of the United States was markedly different from that of England. England was confronted with a seemingly immovable core of mass unemployment. The United States, on the other hand, was entering a new phase of the dramatic century-old process of spanning a great expanse of territory with transportation facilities. Beginning in the early 19th century with the building of canals, later the construction of railway lines up and down the country, then the connecting up of the country with telegraph and telephone lines, there now emerged the stupendous job of laying hard-surfaced roads throughout the vast stretch of the American continent.

Bound up with this development and basic thereto was the building up from scratch of a dozen gigantic industries associated with the rise of the automobile. Throughout our history the development of transportation and communication has played a large role. The vast expanse of territory in relation to the size of the population has profoundly fixed the economic pattern in the United States and has in large measure determined the scope and volume of investment opportunities. In addition there was the growth of the chemical and electrical industries, together with the effect on construction and the consumers' goods industries of the largest absolute growth of population in our history.[4] But when this vast expansion came to an end the United States swiftly sank into a slump more devastating and destructive than England's postwar unemployment.

The recovery in the United States in the thirties fell far short of the levels which the growth of the labor force and ever increasing technical progress should have made possible. Thus in 1939, with total real income slightly above that of 1929, we had about nine million unemployed. Striking an average through the two decades between the two world wars, the American economy with its expanding boom of the twenties and the devastating depression of the thirties fell as far short of reaching its potential as England with its stagnant twenties, its depressed early thirties, and its substantial recovery in the late thirties — a recovery supported in no small measure by the cheap foodstuffs and raw materials which she was able to import from the depressed primary producing markets.

4. Equaled in only one former decade, that of 1900–1909 — also a decade of great expansion.

American Public Opinion

The vigorous expansion of the twenties and the terrifying depression of the thirties have left the American public opinion uncertain and confused. Thus our pattern of thinking at the end of World War II is in some respects similar to the pattern of thinking in England at the end of World War I. There are, to be sure, important differences but there is at least this similarity: just as English thinking after World War I was uncertain whether a new world had really arrived — a world which called for new policies — so we are uncertain today. Did not the boom of the twenties show that the old order was fundamentally all right? And if we resurrect it now as far as possible and turn our backs upon the new and unproven economic ideas, will not all again be well? Yet there remains the dread of the aftermath of the boom of the twenties. Why did not the prosperity last? Should we indeed again experience a new resurgence comparable to the twenties, what assurance that there may not lie beyond an even more devastating depression than that of the thirties?

These are the hopes and fears that confront the United States today. We are far from sure of our future yet we are ill prepared to take the measures needed to ensure that future. We are by no means convinced that we can indeed be masters of our economic fate and we are undecided whether to trust to luck and hope for the best or to embark upon a positive and planned program.

This climate of public opinion no one will deny presents for us grave dangers. It is not even a climate in which the automatic processes can work to good advantage. It is not a good climate for the expansion of private investment. Some of the uncertainties now confronting us, I believe, we shall indeed rapidly resolve. It should not be too difficult or indeed too controversial a matter to arrive at a satisfactory program with respect to the cancellation of war contracts. The disposal of government surplus of supplies and equipment of all kinds is more difficult but again soluble. A knotty problem is the disposal of our vast government war plants either by lease or sale in a manner which will promote productivity and employment and avoid the danger of strengthening monopoly. It will not be easy to reach a satisfactory solution.

Difficult as some of these problems are, I do not think they are among the most serious problems that confront us. They are not the problems that basically will determine whether in fact we shall succeed in becoming masters of our economic destiny.

THE UNITED STATES FACES THE POSTWAR WORLD

The really vital problems about which our future turns are, I think, twofold. One, what role are we prepared to play in cooperation with other countries to solve the great economic problems that concern the world family of nations? Political internationalism stands in the gravest danger of being rendered ineffective by economic isolationism. The modern world cannot function unless we are ingenious enough and wise enough to set up international economic institutions suitable to the kind of world we live in. American public opinion is uncertain and confused. Why is there any need, we ask, for an international monetary fund? Why do we need an international investment bank? After World War I America turned isolationist on political lines. We are now convinced that this was a great mistake. We are now prepared, I believe, to go along on a political world federation designed to maintain the peace of the world. But are we prepared to back up such a world political federation with appropriate economic institutions which can render it workable and permit it to endure? This is one great question that now confronts us.

The second main question is, shall we be able to maintain full employment in the United States? The answer to this question is important not only for ourselves but for the entire world. Indeed, the United States cannot cooperate effectively in international economic institutions, or even in an international political institution, unless it does succeed in a domestic full-employment program. In laying our plans for a durable peace and for a secure international world, we cannot afford to overlook the threat to the stability of any international arrangements, whether political or economic, that would arise if this great country experienced a recurrence of deep depression and prolonged mass unemployment.

America's Role in the World Economy[5]

It is precisely the uncertainty with respect to the future of the American economy that looms up as a major disturbing element in the post-

5. See my recent book, *America's Role in the World Economy*, W. W. Norton, New York, 1945.

war outlook throughout the world. Canada, the Latin American countries (and other primary producing countries from whom we import so heavily) and Europe, whose prosperity is both indirectly and directly affected by conditions here — all have every reason to fear the economic impact of the United States upon world affairs if we continue to have (a) a high degree of instability, or (b) chronically depressed conditions.

Undoubtedly countries everywhere eagerly desire international cooperation with the United States. And the great majority of Americans, there is good reason to believe, earnestly desire that this country shall play a constructive role. But adherence to international arrangements is not enough. We cannot effectively cooperate with other countries in monetary, trade, and world development programs unless we do a good job of managing our own economy. Upon this depends, in no small measure, world security and world peace. Never was it more true that "charity begins at home." Never was it more true that "we help others by helping ourselves." Prosperity and full employment in the United States are basic prerequisites to the successful functioning of international political and economic institutions. This is true because high prosperity in the United States means a good market in this country for the products of the entire world. When business activity is at a high level in the United States, our mass production industries consume vast raw materials imported from abroad; we buy luxury imports; and we spend vast sums abroad in tourist travel.

Thus it is doubly tragic that we face our own future without assurance and confidence. We have as yet reached no agreement among ourselves as a nation on postwar domestic plans.

Postwar Plans

I do not wish to exaggerate. Much constructive research and planning have been done. We have before us well-considered plans relating to reconversion, social security, public health, urban redevelopment, housing, resource development, agricultural programs, public roads, and we have done a limited amount of planning in standard public works. There are widespread public interest and discussion. The National Resources Planning Board (before its decease) issued useful reports on social security, transportation, urban problems, and reconversion problems. The Baruch-Hancock report, the Treasury Study on

Inter-governmental Relations, the work of the Truman, George and Colmer committees in Congress, and innumerable special studies in various government agencies, the reports issued by the National Planning Association, the Committee on Economic Development, and by labor organizations, indicate that much constructive thinking is going on. On an international economic program we are farther along than in our domestic program — witness the formation of the United Nations Relief and Rehabilitation Administration, the International Conferences on Food and Agriculture at Hot Springs, and the International Monetary and Financial Conference at Bretton Woods. It should not be too difficult to agree upon definite plans, if the nation could decide in what direction we wish to go.[6]

Nevertheless, to show how far we are from having achieved the status of a truly responsible government — one that is united on a constructive program of action which could give substantial assurance of stability, full employment and a rising standard of living — it is necessary only to list some major problems that inescapably will confront us. We shall, in fact, be compelled to deal with these problems whether by the haphazard method of improvisation or by competent planning. They are as follows:

The fiscal operations of the federal government
The financial problem of our cities and towns
Postwar tax structure
Management of the debt and internal stability
Wage adjustment and price stability
An international monetary and financial program

II. The Fiscal Operations of the Federal Government

I believe it to be a fair statement that responsible thinking in England, the Scandinavian countries, Australia, Canada, and increasingly in the United States, is tending to the view that economic stability and high levels of income and employment require the adoption by government of a compensatory and developmental fiscal program — one that adjusts expenditures, taxes and borrowing according to economic

6. An indication of the uncertainty with respect to the direction in which we are going can be seen in the last challenging articles of Wendell Willkie in which he sought to persuade the Republican party to abandon a policy of negation and to adopt a positive program concerning social security, fiscal policy, taxation, federal-state-local relations, labor, and international relations.

conditions. The word "compensatory" emphasizes stability; the word "developmental" emphasizes growth and expansion. Thus, a compensatory and developmental fiscal program seeks not only to iron out fluctuations, but also to promote rising productivity and higher living standards.

PUBLIC INVESTMENT AND A STABLE ECONOMY

A Compensatory Fiscal Program

The recent British White Paper on Employment Policy declares that the "Government accept as one of their primary aims and responsibilities the maintenance of a high and stable level of employment after the war."

In Sweden information is assembled from private business at the beginning of each year in order to get a tolerably clear picture of the probable volume of private investment during the next twelve months. This enables the government to plan public works and public improvement projects, so as to bring the total volume of capital outlays, public and private, up to the required level. Such a procedure may be described as responsible fiscal policy. In this country the Department of Agriculture annually obtains from farmers a report on their "intentions to plant." Similarly, we might get from business a report on "intentions to invest," i.e., to make outlays for construction work, new capital equipment, and installations.

In the British White Paper reference is made to the statistical information needed by the central authority in its planning for the country as a whole. This includes regular information relating to projected capital expenditure by public authorities and, as far as possible, by private industry. It is recognized that spontaneous variations in expenditures are likely to be greatest with respect to private capital outlays. Accordingly, it is urged that public investment, both in timing and in volume, be carefully planned ahead so as to play a balancing role. It is urged that the government be prepared in the future to accept responsibility for taking action at the earliest possible stage to arrest a threatened slump. To this end the government must make sure that public investment expands when private investment is declining.

Let me emphasize that a compensatory fiscal program is not a "temporary expedient." It is not a "palliative." It is not a "shot-in-the-arm."

It requires continuous adjustment from phase to phase in the business cycle. At times it calls for restraint and curtailment; at times it calls for stimulation and expansion. In a surging investment boom, taxes should exceed expenditures; national debt should be reduced. In depression useful and productive expenditures should be made. Moreover, in the depression phase the standard[7] income tax rate, now collected at the source, could be reduced to stimulate private spending. Taken by itself alone, tax reduction would be relatively ineffective; but as a supplement to the main program it could reinforce the effect of increased public expenditures.

Unbalance in the Cost-Price Structure

It is sometimes objected that fiscal policy may prevent us from correcting distortions and unbalance in the cost-price structure. I am convinced that this view is wholly erroneous. It is, of course, true that fiscal policy is not enough. It is true that wage and price policies are vitally important. It is true that restrictive practices constitute a serious menace to full-employment opportunities and to the achievement of rising living standards. It is true that we cannot achieve a balanced full-employment economy if business firms pursue a pricing policy which permits them to "break even" at, say, 60 per cent of capacity. There are signs that many of our corporations are headed in this direction, having learned how in the depressed thirties. It is, however, my conviction that a lack of balance in the cost-price structure, wasteful allocation of resources, and restrictive practices both with respect to price and output, can be attacked and removed far more successfully in an environment of expansion than in one of contraction. It is not easy to get rid of the restrictive practices of building tradesmen when construction activity is low. It is not easy to reduce tariff restrictions on trade when industries competing with foreign imports are confronted with a seriously depressed domestic market. We have learned that it is not easy to abandon restrictions on agricultural output so long as urban pay rolls and urban purchases of farm products are low. It is not easy to achieve a balance in the cost-price structure when industry is running at half capacity.

Balance and flexibility seriously deteriorate if depression is allowed to run its course. Once lost, they are hard to restore. For this reason it is

---

7. By "standard" is meant the rate which applies to the first bracket of taxable income.

of the utmost importance that we use fiscal policy to prevent serious depression. It will not do to wait until we have reached bottom, and then at long last undertake an expansionist program. If we so wait, we shall find ourselves encumbered with all manner of distortions, rigidities, and restrictions which will be hard to remove.

Equally, a compensatory fiscal program cannot allow expansion to run on into a price inflation. If this is permitted, new distortions will afflict us. A truly compensatory policy must unceasingly be "on the job," holding the economy in balance — fighting both inflation and deflation.

Reform in Governmental Machinery

To achieve this result — balance, full employment and economic stability — it will be necessary to improve our governmental machinery. Mistakes will be made and the results will be far from perfect. But the task is inescapable. It cannot be carried out without governmental machinery which permits quick action when necessary. A flexible compensatory policy requires that close attention be paid to the timing of expenditures and to changes in the basic income tax rate. Having authorized a long-range public investment program, Congress could set the limits within which the expenditures could be timed according to the requirements of stability and also the limits within which the standard tax rate could be varied.

A number of suggestions have been made to promote fiscal flexibility. The one made by Ruml and Sonne[8] has, I think, great merit. It is suggested that there be created in each branch of Congress a fiscal and monetary committee. This committee would consist of the chairmen of the various existing committees now dealing with expenditures, taxation and monetary problems. On the administrative side it is suggested that an agency be created under the immediate direction of the President to give directives in the fiscal and monetary fields in so far as the executive branch has jurisdiction in this area. This agency would be in continuous contact with the Congressional committees on monetary and fiscal policy, thereby achieving coordination between the executive and the Congress on these important factors. Such an arrangement would, in my judgment, greatly promote a flexible fiscal program.

8. B. Ruml and H. C. Sonne, *Fiscal and Monetary Policy,* National Planning Association, Pamphlet No. 35, Washington, 1944.

The Murray Full Employment Bill of 1945 would create a Joint-Congressional Committee to which the President's reports and recommendations relating to employment policy would be sent, and which would be responsible to Congress for the formulation of an over-all employment program.

The Dynamic Role of Investment

Why is the British Government, in the White Paper on Employment Policy, so greatly concerned with the volume of expenditures on capital goods? Why have business cycle theorists placed such stress upon investment? The reason is that investment or capital outlays, while relatively small, are of extraordinary importance. This is true, first, because it is new investment that makes possible a rising productivity[9] and, second, because the level of income and employment is peculiarly determined by the volume of new investment.

Let me illustrate the dynamic power of investment from the great depression which began in 1929. The essence of that depression, as indeed of all depressions, can quite simply and plainly be stated. There occurred a decline of private capital outlays from the annual rate of $17 billion in 1929 to $2 billion in 1932. This decline of $15 billion in private capital outlays caused unemployment in all the heavy goods industries, and in turn induced a decline in consumption expenditures amounting to about $30 billion. Thus the fall in investment had a magnified effect upon the economy causing a fall in income not of $15 billion but of some $45 billion. The national income, in fact, fell from around $85 billion in 1929 to around $40 billion in 1932. Had investment been maintained at $17 billion, as in 1929, we can be sure that there would have been no important decline in consumption expenditures. Here we see then the great role of investment or capital expenditures. A relatively small fall in investment will induce a tremendous decline in income and employment. Investment is the dynamic and energizing part of the income flow. Unfortunately, however, as the record of a hundred years shows, the flow of investment expenditures is a highly uncertain and undependable quantity.

Consider how a compensatory public investment program might

---

9. Many other factors involving little new investment may raise productivity, including improvement in management, plant layout, better labor relations, advances in medical knowledge and in the science of nutrition and general education.

have been used in the depression beginning in 1929. The $15 billion decline in private capital outlays was unprecedented in amount, exceeding anything ever before experienced. The decline, once started, proceeded in a cumulative manner, each drop inducing a further drop. As income and employment fell, there was less and less inducement to invest. Suppose now the government had been prepared with an adequate compensatory investment program to counter the decline — by useful public works and development projects. Had this been done, it cannot be doubted that private capital outlays would have fallen by much less than $15 billion. The cumulative downward spiral would have been stopped. Private capital outlays might have fallen by no more than $6 or $7 billion, while consumption expenditures would have fallen but little, if indeed at all, had the total level of investment been maintained. A comparatively small amount of public investment outlays, boldly thrown in on a sustained basis, could have held the line and prevented the ever widening breach which brought our railroads, banks, farmers, and home owners close to bankruptcy. A good case can, indeed, be made out for the thesis that a positive compensatory fiscal program will mean in the end less government action than a negative policy.

PUBLIC INVESTMENT AND AN EXPANDING ECONOMY

Developmental Investment and Private Enterprise

We need not only a *compensatory* policy but also a *developmental* public investment program designed to ensure an expanding economy. Let me illustrate in the international field. Everyone is agreed that there is scope for great industrial development in China, for example. Such development includes highways, port facilities, power plants, and the like, much of which involves public investment. Without this basic development, a general program of industrialization becomes quite impossible. Our own past history affords numerous illustrations of the fundamental importance of a developmental investment program.

But, does not a public investment program mean the end of private enterprise?[10] I think there are strong reasons for believing precisely the opposite. A well-conceived public investment program will enlarge the opportunities for private enterprise. The role of government under

---

10. It should be noted that the public projects in question would be constructed under private contract.

such a program would be a marginal one. It would operate in a small but important area in the whole economy — an area which could not be undertaken effectively by private enterprise. The government would not enter the general production field at all. That would be the job of private enterprise.

The question, however, is often asked why may not private enterprise do the job if the government can economically make these investments? The answer is that only the government can take the larger view. Only the government can take adequate account of the effect upon the economy as a whole. The Tennessee Valley development has demonstrated its profitableness from the standpoint of the whole economy. It has opened up new private investment outlets in the area involved; it has raised productivity; it has contributed to an increase in the income of the region and of the nation as a whole. It may not directly return one hundred cents on the dollar to the federal Treasury, but the repercussions of the project upon the whole economy make it, nevertheless, a profitable venture.[11] Private enterprise cannot undertake a development which does not offer an adequate direct return. The government alone can look beyond the limited direct return to the larger benefits accruing to the economy as a whole.

In place of our 19th-century western frontier we can, if we look for it, find and develop a great new frontier in our own "back yard." We can have an expanding and dynamic economy. But it will not come automatically. It is not easy to conquer mass unemployment. Our forefathers could exploit virgin resources. Our task is more difficult. We need to develop and improve our resources. That requires ingenuity and planning. We need to discover and develop areas for public investment which can open up private investment opportunities, increase our productivity and add to the nation's purchasing power.

THE NEED FOR A PLANNED PROGRAM

We have thus far made very little headway with a rational compensatory and developmental program. The spending program of the thirties was in large measure a salvaging process. We salvaged the

---

11. Indirectly the Treasury benefits from the higher national income through larger general tax receipts. Thus while the TVA accounts might not show a profit directly to the Treasury, the venture may well return more than one hundred cents on the dollar if account is taken of the larger general tax revenues.

banks, we salvaged the railroads, we salvaged agriculture, we salvaged home owners, we salvaged millions of unemployed with work relief. There was, however, the beginning of a positive program. Consider in this connection such projects as the Tennessee Valley Authority, the Rural Electrification Administration, the Farm Security Administration, the Public Works Administration, the United States Housing Authority, and the Federal Housing Administration.[12] We need now to undertake a systematic and well-planned compensatory and developmental program. Yet we have thus far made no adequate preparations to cope with a national depression.

A Flexible Federal Budget

If the federal budget is to act as a balance wheel to the economy, it must vary inversely with fluctuations in private capital expenditures. Fluctuations in the normal functions of government are not possible to any considerable extent, and indeed in most cases should not be tolerated. The item of government expenditures that can and should be fluctuated is that for public works and public development projects.

The view has been ably advanced by Beardsley Ruml that variations in the volume of public construction cannot be expected to carry the whole load of stabilizing the entire economy. This, I think, is a sound position. Mr. Ruml urges that variations in the value of public construction be used for the more modest goal of stabilization of the construction industry as a whole. This would indeed make a tremendous contribution to stability.

In the good years, 1925–1929, the average volume of construction was $10.6 billion. In the depressed years, 1931–1935, it was $3.7 billion. On the face of it this would seem to indicate that public projects should have been increased by $7 billion in the bad years in order to iron out fluctuations in construction as a whole. But this, I think, is an exaggeration. A well-planned public investment program would have sustained employment, income, and total effective demand so that private construction would have fallen by far less than, in fact, it did.

A flexible postwar federal budget is presented below, not as a forecast, but as an aid in our analysis. This includes federal aid to states and localities.

---

12. It should be added that the Works Progress Administration, despite the limitations under which it operated, can show a substantial record of construction and achievement.

FLEXIBLE POSTWAR FEDERAL BUDGET

(In Billions of Dollars)

Military outlays	5
Interest on public debt	5
Public works, urban redevelopment,[13] international loans, and re- source development (including agriculture)	5
Social expenditures:	
Social security, health, education, welfare, agricultural programs, and veterans' benefits	12
Residual overhead administration	1
	—
	28

In this budget it is assumed that public construction would vary according to fluctuations in private construction (business plant and housing). Adequate preparedness demands a long-range reserve far in excess of probable requirements. We should have at hand, planned ahead through the blueprint stage, a reserve of $50 billion of public projects, federal, state and local, short-term and long-term, so as to ensure both adequate volume and flexibility.

It is true that other measures will need to be taken to offset fluctuations in private expenditures. One means would be to fluctuate the standard income tax rate. A reduction in the rate could add a considerable amount to the volume of spending of employed workers. Such action, taken in conjunction with an increase in public construction and other measures, could be calculated to have a powerful counter-deflationary effect. In addition, as suggested in the British White Paper on Employment Policy, social security contributions paid by employers and employees might be varied in sympathy with the state of employment.

Moreover, a developmental program would tend to reduce cyclical fluctuations. A sustained long-run program, by promoting a steadily rising national income, would tend to raise the ratio of consumption to income and at the same time encourage a stable rate of investment.

13. Public housing is not here included since it is assumed that it would be financed by bonds issued by the local housing authorities.

The Burden of the Debt

There is a firm basis for confidence that an all-out compensatory and developmental fiscal program would not result in an ever increasing tax burden.[14] A secular increase in the public debt would lead to difficulties only if the fixed charges on the debt should rise at a faster rate than the national income. It requires no proof to see that if the national income remains constant while the interest charges continue to rise, the tax rate will keep increasing until it approaches the absurd magnitude of 100 per cent. The result is entirely different, however, if the national income increases at some minimum constant percentage rate. If now the debt each year increases by a certain fraction of the total income, it can be shown that the tax rate will not continue to rise, but will approach a definite limit. The magnitude of that limit, the maximum tax rate, depends on the percentage rate of growth of the national income (R) ; the percentage of income borrowed every year by the government (P) ; and the interest rate paid on government bonds (i).[15]

From what we know of the savings-investment problem, we may assume that a compensatory and developmental program would not absorb, as a maximum limit, more than half of the annual flow of savings. (Thus, if total saving amounted to say 12 per cent of the national income, we might assume, for purposes of illustration, that P = 6.)

The rate of growth of real national income in the period 1879–1929 was about 3.3 per cent.[16] An examination of its behavior gives an impression that it was slowly declining. The decline in the rate of growth of our population was probably the most important single factor in this secular decline. The per capita rate of income growth averaged around 1.5 per cent. In at least one half of the 50-year period, however (particularly the two decades before World War I), the per capita rate of income increase was about 2.5 per cent. A 2 per cent rate of in-

14. E. D. Domar, "The 'Burden of the Debt' and the National Income," *The American Economic Review*, December 1944.

15. The expression $\dfrac{1}{\dfrac{R}{P}+i} \times i$ shows the limit which the tax rate approaches.

16. Simon Kuznets, an unpublished revision of Table 2 in *Uses of National Income in Peace and War*, Occasional Paper No. 6, National Bureau of Economic Research, New York, March 1942, p. 31.

crease, if we provide in future adequate funds for scientific research, may be regarded as a conservative assumption. (Let us assume, therefore, that R = 2.)

Finally, a rational management of the public debt and of monetary policy should make a 2 per cent average interest rate on government bonds a reasonable expectation. (Thus, i = .02.)

A $300 billion debt at the end of the war is above present expectations. Full employment, it is generally agreed, would give us a $140 billion annual income in the first years after the war. On the basis of these various assumptions, the following table shows the magnitudes of the ratio of annual debt charges to income at stated intervals, together with the final asymptote or limit reached.[17]

RATIO OF DEBT CHARGES TO NATIONAL INCOME

Year	Ratio of Interest on Debt to Income
1950	4.1
1960	4.4
1970	4.6
1980	4.8
1990	5.0
2000	5.1
2050	5.5
At the limit	5.7

Note: Table shows the effect of a continued rise in the national income on the debt burden under the assumed increases in national debt and other conditions as stated in the text.[18]

17. The assumption that the government borrows an average percentage (6 per cent) of the national income may meet with the objection that in times of emergencies, such as wars, a much greater percentage will have to be borrowed. But anyone interested in making some simple mathematical computations can conclude for himself whether the limit (asymptote) for the ratio of fixed charges to income, reached on the basis of varying assumptions with respect to future wars, is tolerable or not. Having made these computations, he is likely to reach the conclusion, I believe, that future wars present intolerable problems, not in terms of finance, but in terms of the destruction to populations and resources involved. Consider, for example, the effect of the two world wars on the age distribution of the German population. Finance is manageable, but the inroads which wars make on a nation's population and resources cannot be repaired.

18. P = 6; R = 2; i = .02.

The Growth of the National Income

It is wholly unrealistic to assume in the foreseeable future a static national real income.[19] Technical progress means either a growth in national income or else rapidly growing mass unemployment. The figures presented indicate that once a growth in income is admitted, a given percentage rate of national income borrowed by the government will not lead into ever increasing difficulties, as is often superficially assumed. Instead an asymptote or limit in the ratio of interest charges to income is reached. With a moderate and reasonable volume of borrowing, this limit represents a quite manageable tax burden.

It should be emphasized that a purely theoretical model such as that presented above in no way implies that the management of a large public debt is a matter of no concern. No country with a large public debt can hope to achieve economic stability without competent and responsible management by the fiscal and monetary authorities.

Responsible management of the public debt involves, among other things, the following: (a) the maintenance of the value of government bonds, (b) prompt cash payment to every bondholder whenever the bonds mature, (c) the preservation of the purchasing power of money (prevention of inflation and deflation), and (d) measures to promote a steady rise in the national real income.

The statistical model given above, together with the assumptions made, has a value only as a means to illuminate the problem. It is in no sense to be taken as a forecast. The figures suggested can, however, be regarded as setting the outside limit for borrowing. A well-managed compensatory and developmental fiscal program, together with other measures, would indicate a much lower volume of loan financing. Moreover, as we make gradual progress toward a higher-consumption economy,[20] the savings-and-investment problem will gradually diminish. We should accordingly achieve a better balance in the economy as a whole. While no spectacular change can be expected in the short run, a higher-consumption economy is the goal toward which we should work.

19. Money income should rise proportionally with real income so as to maintain a substantially stable price level.

20. A high-consumption economy is one in which the ratio of consumption to income is high.

A developmental program, involving a wise use of the public credit and promoting a rise in the national income, *is wholly consistent with the goal of achieving a progressive fall in the ratio of national debt to national income.*

THE SAVINGS-INVESTMENT PROBLEM

In order to round out the discussion on a compensatory and developmental fiscal program, it is necessary to consider in some detail the savings-investment problem[21] as it presents itself in the United States.

The national income is generated by a stream of expenditures. Apart from government expenditures, the magnitude of the national income depends on the volume of (a) net private investment[22] (outlays on new capital goods) and (b) private consumption expenditures.

The Propensity to Consume

So far as the private sector of the economy is concerned — the overwhelmingly major part — it is important to raise both private consumption and private investment so that the total effective demand will be adequate to employ all our labor force (transitional unemployment considered) with the best equipment which technical progress can provide.

Private consumption expenditures can be raised by better income distribution, minimum wage legislation, higher wages in substandard industries, general wage increases commensurate with over-all increases in labor productivity, price reductions in industries enjoying more than the average rate of increase in technical progress,[23] adequate social security programs, and finally, progressive income taxation.[24] These measures act like an "irrigation system" distributing mass purchasing power throughout the economy.

21. By this is meant the problem of ensuring that whatever purchasing power is taken out of the income stream through the savings process is again returned to the income stream through the process of investment.

22. Including net foreign investment.

23. Many economists have rightly been concerned about the apparent growth of monopoly in our economy. Monopoly operates to raise prices and profits. It therefore restricts the volume of consumption expenditures on the one side, and on the other, increases the volume of savings. Moreover, by restricting output it tends to reduce the volume of investment. Thus, all around, the savings-investment problem is intensified.

24. Advertising performs an important social function in so far as it tends to intensify wants and so to stimulate private consumption expenditures.

For the first few years immediately following the war two factors will tend to strengthen the propensity to save. The first is the sudden jump in the level of real income compared with the relatively low prewar years. Following a sharp advance, a lag is likely to occur before consumption standards have caught up with the new level of income. The second is the uncertainty with respect to the future which will confront people in the first postwar years. A third factor — the widespread accumulation of wartime savings — may operate partly in one direction and partly in another. On the one hand, many may acquire an appetite for more saving, once a small nest egg has been started; on the other, such a nest egg may induce many people to spend more freely out of current income. The net effect of this third factor is difficult to appraise.

All the measures to raise consumption will at best operate slowly and gradually. Accordingly, neither quick results nor revolutionary changes are likely to occur in the consumption-savings pattern. After all feasible measures have been taken to raise the ratio of consumption to income, we shall in all probability be confronted for a long time with a savings-investment problem in the United States. This means that the propensity to consume is too low (or, in other words, the propensity to save is too high) in relation to investment opportunities.

The Propensity to Save

Let us see how our traditional saving pattern works out. What volume of saving does our society tend to generate at full-employment levels? The volume of saving which we choose to make at full employment may exceed the volume of gross capital formation which private investors find it profitable to make.

If we take the high income years (virtually full-employment years) 1923, 1926, and 1929 we find that the ratio of realized private gross savings per annum to gross national product was 18 per cent. If we take the average for the relatively high years, 1925–1929, it was 17 per cent.[25] Assuming that gross product at full employment in the first postwar years will be $170 billion, this means $28–$30 billion of gross business and personal savings.

---

25. 1919–1928: Preliminary estimates by Marvin Hoffenberg, U. S. Bureau of Labor Statistics, 1929, *Survey of Current Business,* May 1942, Table 2, p. 12.

Estimates of savings so derived may be on the high side. Let us assume that individuals in planning their savings take account of income after taxes — disposable incomes. By concentrating upon "disposable income" we can isolate, more or less, the effect of higher taxes (relative to prewar) upon savings. In the high income period, 1925–1929, we find that individuals saved 10.5 per cent[26] of their disposable income. In 1940 they saved 10 per cent.[27] Assuming income payments in the postwar period of $137 billion (national income $140 billion) and direct personal taxes (federal, state, and local) of $12 billion, we arrive at a disposable income of $125 billion. Applying the same ratio of saving to disposable income as in 1925–1929 and 1940 we obtain individual savings of around $13 billion for the postwar period. If now we add to this, $3 billion of net corporate savings and $10–$12 billion[28] of business depreciation and other reserves, we arrive at total gross savings of from $26–$28 billion.

Investment Outlets

The savings-investment problem must also be considered in terms of the probable volume of profitable investment outlets. How far will private investment outlets be adequate to absorb the flow of savings generated by a full-employment income?

It is evident that the rate of gross private capital formation depends upon (a) the replacement demand for capital, and (b) the new demand for capital. The former is roughly a function of the capital stock and is related to the level of the national income; the latter is related to growth which is dependent partly upon the increase in population and partly upon technical progress. The growth factor in capital formation obviously stands in some relation to increases in the national income incident to changes in technique and in available resources and to increases in the labor force. In particular, it needs to be emphasized that the more rapid the rate of technical innovations, the more rapid will tend to be the possible rate of growth of income and of capital formation. Thus, if both *level* of income and anticipated *growth* of income

26. Louis J. Paradiso, Business Statistics Unit, U. S. Bureau of Foreign and Domestic Commerce, unpublished estimates.

27. *Survey of Current Business*, April 1944, Table 12, p. 14.

28. In 1943 business depreciation and additions to reserves amounted to $10 billion. See *Survey of Current Business*, April 1944, Table 13, p. 14.

are considered, it may be affirmed that there is in some sense a correct rate of gross capital formation — which rate is dependent upon income, or more narrowly upon consumption. Interpreted in this sense, Malthus was right when he asserted that a correct proportion must exist between capital formation and consumption.

Put in common-sense language, the volume of new private productive facilities that can profitably be added to the existing stock, year in and year out, is far from limitless. Beyond a certain amount, these productive facilities would become so excessive as to reduce the yield on an additional increment to an unprofitable level. We could not continue to build office buildings, hotels, houses, etc., at the rate we did in the twenties without bankrupting the owners of these types of property. As we have seen, the volume of gross capital formation which is economically feasible depends upon income considered both with respect to its level and its growth, as determined by the rate of technical progress and the growth of population. The spirit of capital formation in the boom years exceeded the normal rate of growth.

The rate of capital formation which takes place in boom years cannot continuously be maintained. The rate of capital formation as we have known it in boom years in the past quickly outruns the requirements both of the level and the growth of income. Thus the boom dies a natural death. It would be a grave mistake to take the past statistical ratios of gross capital formation in boom years to national income or gross national product and assume that such ratios can be a guide to the volume of private capital formation which is economically feasible year in and year out without limit. No such rate of private capital formation could continuously be made without destroying existing property values.

The Flow of Savings

In analyzing the outlets for private savings — business and personal — it will be helpful to indicate the categories into which these savings can flow. They are as follows:

Business plant and equipment (including agriculture)
Business inventories
Residential construction
Net foreign investment
New government issues (budgetary deficit)

On the savings side we may analyze gross savings into component parts as follows:

Business depreciation and additions to reserves (corporate and unincorporated)
Business net savings (including agriculture)
Personal savings (excluding entrepreneurs)

Business Savings and Business Investment

Now the first thing to note is that almost the whole of business investment in plant, equipment and inventories is financed from depreciation and other reserves and from the retained earnings of business. A relatively small part is financed from new capital issues. Thus in 1929, gross business savings (depreciation and other reserves and retained business earnings) amounted to $10.9 billion while the total investment of businesses of all kinds — corporate and unincorporated — in plant, equipment and inventories amounted to $13.3 billion.[29] Personal savings (excluding entrepreneurs) flowed mainly into urban residential construction, farm mortgages, and foreign loans, with a small part going into new capital issues.

As indicated above, internal business savings finance, more and more, the replacement of plant and equipment and also new facilities and inventory accumulations. Indeed, depreciation and other reserves (and even maintenance) ordinarily not only are adequate to maintain productive capacity but even to increase it on a substantial scale. When a machine is worn out it is typically replaced by a better and more productive machine. It is a sobering thought that in the entire decade, 1931–1940, more than 90 per cent of the investment in business plant and equipment taken as a whole was replacement. There was relatively little net investment.[30] Nevertheless, we know that the productive capacity of American industry was enormously greater at the end of the decade than it was in 1930. We know this because, were this not so, it

29. The estimate of gross business savings is based on data in *Survey of Current Business,* May 1942, Table 4, p. 12 and Simon Kuznets, *National Income and Its Composition, 1919–1938,* National Bureau of Economic Research, New York, 1941, Vol. 1, Table 39, p. 276.

The figure for total investment was taken from *Survey of Current Business,* May 1942, Table 2, p. 12 and June 1943, Table 11, p. 32.

30. Simon Kuznets, *National Income and Its Composition, 1919–1938,* with estimates for 1939 and 1940 added. The figures are as follows: *Net* capital formation for the entire decade in business plant and equipment was $4.7 billion, while *replacement* capital formations amounted to $54.7 billion.

would have been quite impossible for the American industry to produce the output which, in fact, was produced in the years 1941–1942 — an output achieved on the basis of the plant and equipment available at the end of the decade. During the decade of the thirties nearly $60 billion had been expended on plant and equipment, mainly on replacements and renewals. These replacement outlays were sufficient to provide the highly productive machine which made possible the miracle of the war output. But this investment absorbed very little net saving.

In 1929 gross business savings ($10.9 billion including unincorporated business and farmers) financed the bulk of the $13.3 billion invested in plant, equipment and inventories. Individual savings (entrepreneurs excluded) found only a very moderate outlet in business investment. New productive corporate issues amounted to only $1.7 billion.[31] In 1940, indeed, gross business savings amounting to $10.9 billion were adequate to finance the whole of the gross investment in business (including agriculture) plant, equipment and inventories ($10.7 billion). Thus in 1940 individual savings (entrepreneurs excluded) could find an outlet only in residential construction and new government issues.[32] The same analysis holds for 1941. This year gross business savings of $15.4 billion adequately financed the whole investment in plant, equipment and inventories amounting to $14.9 billion. Again individual savings (entrepreneurs excluded) were invested mainly in housing and new government issues.

The Future Savings and Investment Aggregates

Let us approach the problem from the standpoint of probable future investment and savings aggregates. In the postwar period gross business saving in high income years may reasonably be expected to approximate the following:

	(In Billions of Dollars)
Business depreciation and other reserves	10–12
Corporate net saving	3
Entrepreneurial net saving	2
	———
Total	15–17

31. Alvin H. Hansen, *Fiscal Policy and Business Cycles,* W. W. Norton, New York, 1941, p. 385.
32. It is of course true that individual savings are in the first instance largely invested in savings banks, insurance companies and other financial institutions. These institutions in turn must seek an outlet in real-estate mortgages, new government issues, federal, state and local, and such new corporate issues as may be available.

This volume of annual business saving would require an annual investment in plant, equipment and inventories of around $16 billion per annum as follows:

	(In Billions of Dollars)
Business plant (including agriculture)	5
Business equipment (including agriculture)	10
Inventory additions	1
	—
Total	16

These figures in fact represent approximately the same ratio to the assumed gross national product of the postwar years as the actual ratio of average investment in each of these three categories to gross national product in the period 1921–1941, inclusive. It is not probable, however, that any such volume of investment in productive facilities as $16 billion per annum can be maintained year in and year out without creating vast excess capacity. In 1923–1929 the average investment in business plant and equipment was $8.7 billion per annum.[33]

In this connection it may be noted that the total present value of privately owned manufacturing plant and equipment is only about $40 billion, or less than three times the annual investment here indicated.[34] There are, of course, other important business investment outlets including transportation, public utilities, trade and agriculture.

In the figure of business savings we have included $2 billion of entrepreneurial net savings. Deducting this from the estimated $13 billion of individual savings in the postwar period there remains $11 billion of personal savings to find an outlet in residential construction, new government issues, and foreign loans. If there were no new government issues, housing and foreign loans would have to absorb the whole $11 billion year after year — a figure which exceeds by a wide margin the most optimistic expectations.

These data are sufficient, I think, to indicate that it is not possible to be complacent about the savings-investment problem that will confront us over the long run in the postwar period. Fifteen billion dollars may, indeed, in some years be invested in plant and equipment, but hardly year in and year out. Yet, even though we assume that this were possible (thereby finding an adequate outlet for business savings)

33. See *Fiscal Policy and Business Cycles*, p. 26.
34. *Statistics of Income for 1939*, Pt. 2, p. 22. Add to this the $2.5 billion of privately financed investment during the war.

there would still remain the problem of finding outlets for $11 billion of individual savings (excluding entrepreneurs) in residential construction and in foreign loans, if we assume a balanced budget and therefore no new government issues.

All the various measures designed to lift the "consumption function" are likely to operate slowly and within fairly restricted limits. The traditional savings pattern in the postwar period is not likely to be markedly different from the prewar years. Thus, however much we may strive to raise consumption, an inescapable problem will remain to find adequate investment outlets for the people's savings. Yet if we do not do so, we cannot maintain full employment.[35]

The Need for Public Investment

If public investment projects are wisely chosen they can open up new private investment not otherwise available. This would help to solve the savings-investment problem. The kind of projects best adapted to this purpose are, I believe, regional resource development, urban redevelopment, and transportation.[36]

The public investment projects selected could and should be highly productive from the standpoint of the economy as a whole. In considerable measure they would indeed be "self-liquidating." A capital budget might wisely be set up for such projects. The capital outlays required could be financed from new issues.[37] Operating expenses and capital charges would as far as possible be met out of income from the project.

35. Investment each year must in fact exceed the savings made out of "disposable" income in Robertson's sense, in order to make possible a rise in income commensurate with rising productivity. This excess of investment would normally be financed by an increase in bank credit, which in a growing society must occur in order to provide sufficient circulation media to transact the ever growing volume of trade at stable prices and in addition to provide sufficient money (currency and demand deposits) to ensure the necessary degree of liquidity required to maintain a low rate of interest.

36. See discussion of urban redevelopment and other public improvement projects under Section III, The Financial Problems of Our Cities and Towns.

37. It is highly probable that the flow of institutional and mass savings, seeking investment in government bonds, once normal peace conditions are restored, will amount to several billions per annum. And once we have gotten past a temporary period of excess liquidity, we shall want a further increase in our money supply to match the growth in the economy. Roughly our money supply has doubled every twelve years. With a somewhat slower rate of growth the required increase in money supply would be less. Nevertheless, it will remain very large. Private borrowing at the commercial banks and bank investments in private issues are not likely (considering the low volume under modern conditions of commercial loans and new capital issues) to be adequate to give us the needed increase in money supply. There would thus be a basic need, from the long-run standpoint of monetary management, for some volume of government borrowing from banks.

But, nonliquidating projects may be equally valuable. A project should be judged by its over-all productivity for the economy as a whole, and not necessarily in terms of its direct earnings. Public free roads and port facilities may be far more productive in terms of increased national efficiency than directly self-liquidating projects.

Public investment, wisely chosen, can have a magnified effect in opening outlets for the people's savings. We must consider not only the direct outlet which government issues for public development and improvement projects afford, but even more the induced new private investment outlets which these basic public projects release.[38]

An ever growing, expanding economy is both a goal in itself and a necessary condition for the achievement of full employment. Only in an expanding economy can investment outlets be found. If we are to have such an economy, our technology must be progressing all the time.

Rapid technological progress requires two things:

1. Inventions
2. Application of new technical knowledge to the productive process

In the nineteenth century inventions were made by curious individuals and their appearance was to a great extent a matter of chance. At present they are largely the results of systematic, scientific and industrial research carried out by private business, universities and various governmental units.

Government Participation in Research

Our total expenditures on scientific and industrial research remain, however, pitifully small. In 1940 private business spent about $300 million, while our universities spent perhaps $50 million including research in the social sciences. Federal expenditures on scientific and industrial research amounted in 1938 to $52 million, the largest share going to the Department of Agriculture.[39] Thus, total expenditures on research in 1940 were probably around $400 million. With the coming of the present war, federal expenditures on research have shown a

38. Consider a simple but illuminating illustration recently given by Senator O'Mahoney, namely, the development of a harbor or a lake adjoining a city. This may stimulate and promote the formation of boating, yachting, and racing clubs. The ramifications of such a public improvement project obviously extend to a great many private industries.

39. National Resources Committee, *Research — A National Resource, Vol. 1 — Relation of the Federal Government to Research*, Washington, 1938. National Resources Planning Board, *Research — A National Resource, Vol. 2 — Industrial Research*, Washington, 1941.

sharp increase due to the urgent need for new methods of national defense. But new methods of warfare may or may not point to new and more efficient methods of peacetime production.

We must realize that scientific and industrial research represents a most important national resource, and that it should be developed in every possible way. It is doubtful that this can be done by private business alone, without government support. Many research projects are extremely important for the development of science, but lack immediate profit prospects; others may require larger funds than private business is prepared to lay out; finally there are those (such as medical research) which represent no interest for private business at all. Federal participation in scientific and industrial research is imperative.

Senator Harley M. Kilgore of West Virginia has twice introduced a bill to provide for a systematic federal participation in research.[40] He proposes the establishment of a central organization (Office of Science and Technology) in the federal government to coordinate research carried out by other federal agencies; to offer universities and private laboratories subsidies for specific research projects; and finally, to undertake research on its own accord. The office would offer scholarships to promising students in the sciences to ensure an adequate research personnel; it would also take active part in the dissemination of scientific and technical information.

All patents owned by the government (except those essential for national defense) should be offered to individuals and businesses on reasonable terms. Moreover, we need a reform in our patent laws. While the inventor is entitled to a reasonable royalty to be paid by all users, the results of scientific discoveries should be made available to all business, big and small alike, on equal terms.

III. The Financial Problems of Our Cities and Towns

One of the most serious problems confronting this country is the deterioration, both physical and financial, of our urban communities.

SLUM CLEARANCE AND URBAN REDEVELOPMENT

The poison of slum and blight is spreading in ever widening circles. It is sapping the strength of the healthier sections. It is weakening the

---

40. S. 2721, 77th Cong., 2d sess. and S. 702, 78th Cong., 1st sess. A revision of these bills is being undertaken at present.

fiscal position of our cities. Local government problems are reaching a crisis in many urban communities.

The Cost of Maintaining the Slums

One third of our urban population live in slums, substandard and deteriorating areas. They comprise around 20 per cent of the total residential area. The incidence of fire hazards, major crimes, juvenile delinquency, social disease and tuberculosis is far higher in the slum areas.

A study of a slum area in Cleveland disclosed that the per capita cost of fire protection was 7 times that of the city as a whole; murders per capita were 8.5 times the average; social vice 10.5 times; tuberculosis deaths 5 times; police protection 3 times the average.[41] The cost to the city to maintain the slum area (fire department, police, garbage collection, street cleaning and lighting, sewer maintenance, health department, education, welfare) was 6 times the real-estate taxes collected from the area, and nearly 9 times, if community fund and other relief agency expenditures are added. The total cost of maintaining the section in 1932 was in fact $1,972,000, while real-estate tax receipts were only $225,000. The operating loss involved in maintaining the area was $78 per capita or $315 per family. A similar operating loss ($79) per capita was found in a Boston survey in 1933. A second Boston survey in 1934 covering the entire low rent residential area disclosed a per capita operating loss of $48.[42]

Other surveys indicate in general the fact — now generally recognized — that cities sustain a considerable financial loss in the slum and blighted areas. The slum dwellers are in fact subsidized, but they are subsidized to live in slums.

The indirect cost of slums cannot easily be calculated. Disease and crime, bred in the slums, spread and infect the whole community. The disease and crime rates are higher in non-slum areas than they would be if it were not for the slums in the heart of the city. The social and financial costs of slums cannot be measured by the slum area alone.

In Cleveland[43] a wide belt encircling the central slum district and comprising 40 per cent of the total residential area is becoming blighted

41. See Regional Association of Cleveland, Bulletin No. 17, December 1943.
42. Alvin H. Hansen and Harvey S. Perloff, *State and Local Finance in the National Economy*, W. W. Norton, New York, 1944, pp. 108–12.
43. Regional Association of Cleveland, *op. cit.*

or is threatened with blight. To prevent its progressive decay into blight and finally slum, protective and curative action must be taken. There is no thoroughgoing solution of this problem except to clear the slums and redevelop the areas in accordance with a comprehensive urban redevelopment plan. Unless this is done, the blight will spread, urban land values will continue to decline with serious consequences for the financial position of the local government. In Philadelphia taxable real estate has declined 28 per cent from 1930 to 1942;[44] in Boston 27 per cent; in St. Louis 19 per cent; and in Chicago 53 per cent. Broadly the same trends appear throughout the country.

The Obstacles to Slum Clearance

A large-scale program of urban redevelopment involves the purchase and assembly of land. Two obstacles stand in the way. One is financial, the other is legal.

Let us first consider the legal obstacle. Cities must obtain from state legislatures adequate powers to purchase and assemble land, and to control land use. Specifically, a local authority must be given the power (a) to acquire land, by condemnation when necessary, anywhere within the urbanized area and around the outskirts, (b) to hold, use, lease or sell such land, and (c) to control the use to which all land within the metropolitan area may be put, in accordance with a master plan.

Consider now the financial problem. It relates (a) to the high cost of slum and blighted land, and (b) to the amount of redevelopment which can profitably be undertaken.

Why is the acquisition cost of slum and blighted land so high? The answer in large part is to be found in the high density — the intensity of land use. There are few open spaces. Some decades past, in many of our cities, the alleys between existing structures were built virtually solid with new dwellings. Such "sweating" of the land means high land values. But the community pays the price in the financial and social costs of maintaining the slum population. The owners of the slum properties are in fact being subsidized.

All this has happened with the consent of the community. The conditions of land use have not been properly defined. For this the community itself is to blame. On the other hand, it cannot be denied that

44. Bureau of the Census, *Financial Statistics of Cities.*

local sanitary and health regulations have very generally been violated and have not adequately been enforced. Failure to enforce these regulations is due partly to the pressure and influence on local government of special interest groups, but it is also, and I believe fundamentally, due to the lack of any constructive program with which to attack the problem. Substandard houses that violate health ordinances could not be closed, since there was a housing shortage for low income groups. There was no place to put them, and so the obsolete structures have remained occupied.

The whole thing is a vicious circle. Recriminations and abuse of the individuals involved — persons who have operated within the framework of a hopeless and impossible pattern — are not likely to help us out of the mess. A constructive attack on the problem by the nation as a whole, operating through all the levels of government — federal, state and local — is necessary.

The Policy of Slum Abandonment

It has been argued, notably by Mr. Nathan Straus[45] (whose pioneer leadership in slum clearance deserves high praise) that the solution to the high cost of slum land is to let the centers of our cities rot, build public housing in the suburban areas, draw the slum population out, and thus crack the high land values at the center. I cannot convince myself that this is the best solution.

It cannot be denied that the land in slum and blighted areas is frequently valued at an unjustifiably high level. This is partly due, as we have seen, to over-sweating of the land and excessive population density; partly to failure to enforce local sanitary and health regulations; partly to over-zoning of land for business use which gives a speculative value to the land; partly to the hangover of values based upon rates of population growth that no longer exist; and partly to a reluctance of city officials to reduce the valuations for tax purposes. All this explains the excessive cost of land acquisition in slum and blighted areas.

The suggestion that the proper solution is to flee to the suburbs and let the slums decay until all property values are destroyed is attractive to many persons. But I am convinced that it is a short-sighted view. A policy of developing outer areas, without at the same time having a program for redevelopment of the slum and blighted areas, would be

45. Nathan Straus, *The Seven Myths of Housing,* Alfred A. Knopf, New York, 1944.

a self-defeating policy. Such a policy would increase the blight and therefore increase the ultimate cost to the community. A process of abandonment of the central portion of a city is far from costless to the community in either financial or social terms. Moreover, the physical mess in which it would leave our cities for a generation could not, I think, lightly be contemplated. Once the process was completed, the city would have been reconstituted around the abandoned shell in such a manner as to have rendered impossible a master plan designed to make the best use of all the land, including the central portions.

It is, of course, true that a comprehensive urban plan, making appropriate use of all the land, both central and suburban, will frequently involve a large suburban development no less than a redevelopment of slum and blighted areas. Population density in slum and blighted areas (Baltimore, Philadelphia, Boston, Cambridge, for example) is so great that proper land use, with adequate open spaces, parks, and playgrounds would result in a large-scale decentralization of the population. There is accordingly no contradiction between the redevelopment of slum and blighted areas and suburban development. The proper balance between these two programs can be achieved only by making a comprehensive master plan in which account is taken of the best use that can be made of all the land in and about the city.

A Land Acquisition and Housing Program

Accordingly, it is my view that a sound plan of urban development and redevelopment requires two things: (a) a program of land acquisition, and (b) a large-scale housing program, both private and public.

A land acquisition program is necessary in order to assemble the land under one single ownership so as to make large-scale redevelopment possible. The program is also necessary in order to finance the loss, that must somehow be covered, between the acquisition cost of the land and what it is worth to private enterprise for redevelopment in accordance with the new land use plan. Much of the land acquired will, under a proper land use plan, be needed for parks and playgrounds. In these cases the whole cost of the land must be assumed by the local community. The same is true of land that will be used for public purposes — local public works or local public housing. The remainder will be leased or sold to private development companies, for business or residential purposes. But under the new land use plan, over-sweating of land must be forbidden, else new slums will again develop. Accordingly, for all these reasons, the new use-value of the land will usually be far less than the acquisition cost.

If one takes the average annual rental value of the 6,800,000 substandard houses in all urban communities in the United States, as disclosed in the *Housing Census of 1940,* and multiplies this by ten (in order to estimate the capital value) one arrives at a rough figure of around $1,900 per unit, or about $13 billion for the whole. Add to this the cost of nonresidential properties located in slum areas, something around $15 billion would appear to be a reasonable estimate of the total cost of buying up all the urban slums — land and buildings — in America.

If we had the courage to face this problem squarely with say a fifteen- to twenty-year plan, the program would involve an expenditure of less than $1 billion a year. For the nation as a whole this is surely a feasible financial task. The $15 billion, it must be emphasized, refers only to the acquisition cost of the land. The redevelopment program, apart from the land acquisition cost — parks, playgrounds, buildings, public and private — might come to a total of around $40 to $50 billion. Most of this construction would be financed by private enterprise. A boldly conceived program would give stimulus to construction and employment, would contribute greatly to a high level of income and would strengthen the fiscal capacity of all levels of government.

A Federal Aid Program

The land acquisition program, however, is too large a task for the cities to manage alone. Accordingly, there is a widespread opinion among those best informed that the federal government must play a leading role.[46]

Federal financial aid is needed to enable the cities and towns to purchase, or take under condemnation proceedings, whatever land is needed for urban development and redevelopment. The towns and cities are not financially able to raise the money. It is, moreover, a truly

46. The whole nation should benefit from the incomes derived from great national corporations enjoying a national market. National corporations derive their income from cities and towns all over the country, but their more well-to-do stockholders reside mainly in a few states. Accordingly the burden of urban redevelopment can only be equitably distributed by utilizing the fiscal power of the federal government.

national problem because it concerns the prosperity and well-being of the nation as a whole.

Under a program of federal aid every city would be required to make its own master plan together with specific area-project plans for redevelopment. The appropriate federal agency would thus be prepared to advance funds for land purchase up to the entire acquisition cost. The cities would not pledge their faith and credit to repay these sums. They would, however, agree to pay over to the federal government all sums derived in the future from sale or lease of the land to private redevelopment companies. The land would not be exempt from local taxes. Any return from lease or sale obtained from the redevelopment process would be paid back to the federal government.

Such a program is set forth in detail in the Thomas bill[47] which is based on the assumption that urban redevelopment will enhance the revenue-producing capacity of cities, increase employment, re-invigorate the construction industry, and raise the national income. It is believed that as the redevelopment progresses, the direct and indirect benefits from the redevelopment process will more and more justify the federal advances.

The write-down of the excess land value of slum and blighted areas, which such a program of land acquisition makes possible, will enable a private developer to use land in the central part of a city on terms of equal advantage with land in the suburbs. Commercial, industrial, and residential projects, on these terms, need not flee to the outskirts by reason of the excessive cost of the in-city land. Thus a very considerable amount of private redevelopment would be made possible by this program.

The Rehousing Problem

Nevertheless, we are compelled to face the fact that a fifteen- or twenty-year plan to get rid of slums runs smack up against the question: Where will you house the slum dwellers as slum demolition proceeds? Their incomes typically do not permit them to pay the full economic rent for a dwelling that meets minimum housing standards. What then?

There are several answers to this question. Of great importance is

47. S. 953, 78th Cong., 1st sess. (Committee Print, Dec. 10, 1943.)

the fact that a full-employment income after the war will greatly increase the number of families that can pay an economic rent. Before the war (1935–1939) some seven million families lived in substandard houses. This represented nearly one third of the total number of urban families. Indeed, one third of all families in the prewar years had a family income of under $1,000. Families with such an income could not afford to pay more than $12 to $16 per month for rent.[48] At full employment after the war, and at roughly current price levels, less than 20 per cent of families would have incomes below $1,000. That is far from a pretty picture, but it does represent progress. Of perhaps greater significance is the prospect that 25 per cent of all families might rise from below the $2,000 per annum level to above the $2,000 level. Thus, while 75 per cent of all families had an income below $2,000 in 1939, possibly only 50 per cent will be below this level in the postwar years.

We must make more progress than we have thus far made to raise the family income at the lower end of the scale. The wage differential is far too wide. The incomes in the areas of personal service, retail trade, tobacco manufacturing, textiles, clothing, leather products, lumber, furniture, motor transportation, communications, recreation and food manufacturing are unduly low in relation to other industries. The housing problem for all the people cannot satisfactorily be solved without raising incomes at the lower end of the scale.

But this problem will not easily be solved and it takes time. In the meantime, can we tolerate the persistence of slums with their cankerous and poisoning influence on our whole society?

New houses cannot be built by private enterprise within reach of the incomes of the lowest group. Yet if slum demolition is to be carried forward in say a twenty-year program, the present occupants must be rehoused. Favorable to new construction is the fact that the very process of slum clearance will tend to hold down excess vacancies. Always in the past, after some years of high residential construction, excess vacancies begin to appear, rents decline and new building construction drops off. Systematic slum clearance will help to hold vacancies down. As the middle income group move into new houses, families lower down can move one step up the housing ladder. Remodeling of old houses can play an important role. Yet there are obviously income lim-

48. The median rent paid for 6,800,000 substandard houses was $165 per year in 1939. The median family income reported was $840. See *1940 Housing Census*.

its to this upgrading process. Nevertheless, deliberate slum clearance, by preventing excessive vacancy rates, can push this development farther than automatic processes have permitted in the past.

Between the two wars we demolished obsolete houses at the rate of only 40,000 per annum. At this rate it would take us one hundred years to get rid of half of our slums without taking account of the net annual accretions to obsolete properties. A recent report of the National Housing Agency suggests a minimum demolition program of 600,000 units per year.[49] A systematic demolition program would make room for new construction.

Housing Subsidies

Yet in the final analysis, after all these measures have been taken, the fact remains that we shall have a large number of families who cannot afford the full economic rent for a dwelling, whether new or old, which measures up to minimum housing standards. If we choose to get rid of slums, if this is a program desirable or necessary from the broad standpoint of the national welfare, then these families must somehow receive a housing subsidy.

Such a subsidy, to promote the health and efficiency of the nation as a whole, can be justified no less than public funds for education. Indeed, money spent for education is largely wasted on people whose health, morals and efficiency are seriously deteriorated by housing conditions.

I am not able to see that a housing subsidy for low income families can be avoided if we choose to get rid of slums. Either a housing subsidy must be paid to private limited dividend corporations, or else we must undertake an adequate public housing program.[50]

I have talked with city officials and private real-estate men about this problem. There is, of course, divided opinion, but I have found many public-spirited citizens who are opposed to the housing subsidy to private owners. I have asked why the housing subsidy, paid to licensed and supervised private owners, might not work. In reply it is urged that public subsidy to a corporation operating for profit is not a workable

49. *Housing Needs,* National Housing Agency, Washington, November 1944.

50. I have found a few individuals, but not many, who believe that serious resentment is created by the fact that the low income groups occupy in public housing projects better homes than many self-sustaining families. In general, the better-situated people are, I believe, happy to see the slums go. Moreover, it is recognized that the lowest income groups are handicapped in so many ways that those more fortunate in income status feel no envy or resentment.

arrangement. If public support must be given, it had best be managed by a local public housing authority which does not have to mix the profit motive with public welfare. Local public housing authorities are able to appeal to very high-grade public-spirited citizens who devote their services with a high sense of public duty. It is a fact, not generally known, that in more than half of the local public housing authorities, the chairman is a high-grade, local, private real-estate operator, while a considerable proportion of the members of the board of directors are businessmen owning large urban properties. It is far from true, whatever the position of their national associations, that real-estate operators and owners are unanimously opposed to public housing.

It is probable that public housing construction ought to be planned largely as an anti-depression program. Slum clearance could be a powerful counter-cyclical device. In good years, the "seeping-up process" described above — new private housing and rehabilitated old houses — could be expected to work out pretty well. Some public housing would doubtless be necessary to take care of families displaced by slum clearance. But the bulk of public housing construction could be reserved for times when we are compelled to cope with unemployment. There is no better unemployment project than residential building. FHA housing could also be stimulated by easing the terms of lending when employment falls off.

Public housing construction might be varied from a low of 200,000 units a year to a high (if unemployment were getting really serious) of, say, 500,000 units. An average level might be 300,000 to 400,000 units per year. The capital costs could be financed, without burdening the budget, by bonds issued by the local housing authorities.

REGIONAL RESOURCE DEVELOPMENT

Aside from urban redevelopment, the fiscal capacity of local communities could be greatly strengthened in many parts of the country, and especially in the poorer sections, by a program of regional resource development. This is important no less for the towns and cities in the region than for the region as a whole. It is by now generally recognized that the Tennessee Valley Authority has fostered expansion throughout the area in which it operates. The same is true in the Columbia River Valley in the Pacific Northwest. Recently a resolution was presented to the President urging the formation of a Missouri Valley Authority.[51] The President, supporting the resolution in transmitting it to Congress, urged also the consideration of regional authorities for the Arkansas and Columbia River basins.

THE FINANCING OF EDUCATION

Local communities, both urban and rural, are burdened with the cost of financing public education. This was proper enough a hundred years ago when most wealth consisted of real estate, and taxes were collected largely from property. But this method of financing public education — a function that concerns more than any other the well-being of the nation as a whole — has become hopelessly obsolete. In a great national economy in which the great bulk of the nation's income is derived from business activity, education can no longer be financed by local property taxes without, on the one hand, seriously restricting individual opportunities for a half of the nation's children, or, on the other, without placing a seriously restrictive burden on real estate and new construction.

Many of our poorer states and localities tax their citizens more heavily in proportion to income than do the richer states. Nevertheless, the expenditures for education per pupil averaged (1939–1940) for the eight poorest states $39.44 per pupil, while the average expenditures in the eight richest states were $140.72. In some states, if all the state tax money were *all* applied to education (in addition to that now supplied by local governments), they could still not reach the average standard of the upper half of the states. If every American child is to be given minimum educational opportunities, federal funds must be forthcoming.

This is the first and most important ground for federal aid. But there is a second. Only by federal aid can the high and restrictive local property taxes be relieved. The financial problems of local communities — rural townships and counties no less than towns and cities — cannot be satisfactorily solved without federal aid. It is especially appropriate that this aid should be made for a function which is of such vital concern to the nation as a whole.

In 1939–1940 the median state expenditure per pupil was around

51. For further discussion see Alvin H. Hansen and Harvey S. Perloff, *Regional Resource Development*, National Planning Association, Pamphlet No. 16, Washington, 1942.

$85,[52] while the national average expenditure per pupil in average daily attendance was around $105.[53] Let us say that the minimum standard below which no state should be allowed to go is $80 per pupil. Suppose now that the federal government made grants-in-aid to all states, rich and poor alike, adequate to cover this minimum per pupil. That would involve an annual outlay of $2.5 billion.[54] Richer states where standards are above the minimum would, of course, finance the difference between the minimum and their higher standards. But they, as well as the poorer states, would gain relief in local property taxes, as well as increased capacity to provide more adequately for other local services.[55]

IV. A Postwar Tax Program

A high sense of social responsibility and prudence in public finance demands efficiency in government administration. True economy does not mean blind slashing of expenditures; it does mean efficient use of public funds, careful administration to eliminate waste, and thorough planning so that public expenditures may be made on useful and productive projects of a character which will increase the efficiency and well-being of our population and raise the productivity of the nation as a whole.

FEDERAL TAXATION

Four Budgetary Models

In *State and Local Finance in the National Economy* I have set forth four models of a postwar federal budget varying according to different phases of the business cycles. At the one extreme, it is assumed that a strong private investment boom is under way, with inflationary tendencies. Under these conditions federal taxes should exceed expendi-

---

52. See Alvin H. Hansen and Harvey S. Perloff, *State and Local Finance in the National Economy*, W. W. Norton, New York, 1944, pp. 18–19.

53. *Statistical Abstract 1942*, p. 134.

54. Until a really large sum like this is forthcoming, federal aid should go mainly to help minimize the gross inequalities in educational opportunities that now prevail. See Hansen and Perloff, *op. cit.*, Chap. 8.

55. Guy Greer, in the July 1944 issue of *Fortune*, has suggested that these sums be turned over to the states without any strings attached whatever, except a public accounting of the expenditures in a simplified and easily understood form. This, he argues, should go far to remove the fears of federal control of education. There is some danger, however, that this suggestion, if adopted, might lead to wasteful and inefficient administration. I am not able to see why the federal government may not set efficiency standards without controlling the content of education.

tures. At the other extreme, that of serious depression, useful and productive public expenditures, not wholly covered by taxes, should be made. Intermediate are two models, one of which provides for a balanced budget and the other for a moderate deficit. The following discussion, using somewhat modified assumptions, is based on the analysis there given.[56]

The Transition Period

Before I attempt to discuss postwar taxes, a comment is in order on taxes in the transitional period. In the transition period, wartime taxes should, I believe, in large part be retained. This applies also to the excess-profits tax. The excess-profits tax is imposed because the unusual conditions prevailing during a war result in an abnormally large volume of corporate profits. The tax is imposed on the excess of the actual income over the so-called "normal income" earned by the corporation in the period 1936–1939.[57] It is recognized that the war may cause some corporations to earn little or even to sustain actual losses during some of the war years, and in order not to penalize corporations with fluctuating income the carry-back and carry-forward of the excess-profits credit were provided.

With respect to an early repeal of the excess-profits tax, two lines of reasoning appear possible:

1. Profits and losses made in the reconversion period may be regarded as being immediately connected with the war. In other words, reconversion is really a part of the war. In this case, the excess-profits tax should be retained at least in part together with the carry-back provisions.[58]

2. Profits and losses made during the reconversion may be regarded as not directly caused by the war. If so, the excess-profits tax should be repealed, and also its carry-back provisions.

If a corporation sustains in the reconversion period an actual loss,

56. In *State and Local Finance in the National Economy* the federal aid to education was directed mainly toward raising the standard in backward states, and was accordingly smaller than that suggested here.

57. Or else the excess over a stipulated return on invested capital if the investment method is used.

58. "Carry-back" means that if profits fall below normal, the difference can be applied against excess profits in preceding years and so secure a tax refund. "Carry-forward" permits offsets against future profits. There are also carry-back and carry-forward provisions for offsetting losses under the regular corporate income tax.

such loss should be carried back and carried forward against profits of earlier and later years, respectively, in computing the ordinary corporate income tax. This much is admitted. But what about the carry-back and carry-forward provisions of the excess-profits tax? If we accepted the second line of reasoning above, the carry-back should apply only to reconversion *losses* but not to *deficiencies in normal profits* in the reconversion period. I am, however, inclined to think that it would be more equitable to retain the excess-profits tax, at a reduced rate, with its carry-back provisions (together with price control where needed) during the reconversion period. The reconversion must, I think, be regarded as a part of the war experience.

The Post-Transition Period

Addressing ourselves now to the post-transition period, it should emphatically be said that we must have a drastic reduction in taxes from the wartime level. Excess-profits taxes should be completely repealed and other tax rates should be reduced.

Apart from the pay roll taxes (social security), which are here excluded, federal taxes may broadly be classified in three categories: (a) direct personal taxes (income, estate and gift taxes), (b) corporate income taxes, and (c) excises and miscellaneous revenues.

We must first consider the relative merits of excises (selective sales taxes) on the one side, and income (corporate and individual) taxes on the other. There is, I think, growing agreement that consumption taxes are bad for business since they curtail the volume of mass purchasing power. On these grounds, general sales taxes ought to be excluded altogether under peacetime conditions. The same holds for the whole list of selective excises on all manner of products which are currently on the statute books. These have decided merit in wartime, but should be completely eliminated in peacetime.

How far we should go in reducing the excise taxes on alcoholic beverages, tobacco, and gasoline is a matter that will require much further study and should, in part, be determined by future developments. I would suggest, however, that we begin with a retention of these taxes, though with rates substantially lower than the wartime rates. Gasoline taxes ought, I think, to be reserved entirely for the states. There would remain for federal taxation alcoholic beverages and tobacco. At substantially lower rates than the present, $2 billion may be raised from these sources. Another billion may be raised from customs duties and miscellaneous revenues combined. We account thus far, then, for about $3 billion.

I have suggested that we might raise about $15 to $16 billion from income taxes (personal and corporate) and from estate and gift taxes.

Should relatively greater reliance be placed on personal income taxes or on corporate income taxes? My answer is to go relatively light on business and corporate taxation and to rely mainly upon personal income taxation. It is my view that such a tax structure will be less restrictive on private investment and business expansion than one which weighs heavily on business and corporate income.

Taxation and Risk-Taking

It cannot be denied that both corporate income taxes and the personal income tax (with graduated surtax rates) tend to restrict investment in new ventures. This unfavorable effect upon risk-taking can, however, be very materially ameliorated by the provision for loss carry-back for two years and loss carry-forward for five years. I would urge generous loss-offset provisions in order to minimize to the utmost extent the unfavorable effect of high tax rates upon risk-taking and new investment. This argument applies to taxes both on corporate and personal incomes.

The argument that income taxes discourage investment and risk-taking has appeared in technical and popular literature a number of times, but a serious analysis of it has not been made until very recently.[59] If losses cannot be offset against other income either because other income is not available or due to the absence of adequate provisions in the tax law, the investment becomes less attractive. If, however, a complete offset of losses is possible, the situation is entirely different. The yield is, of course, reduced by the tax, but so also is the possible loss.

The personal and corporation income tax law now provides for a limited carry-back and carry-forward (two years each) of business net operating losses and in addition it also provides for a five-year carry-forward of all net capital losses. The extent to which investors can utilize these provisions depends upon the availability of other income

59. See E. D. Domar and R. A. Musgrave, "The Proportional Income Taxation and Risk-Taking," *The Quarterly Journal of Economics*, May 1944, pp. 388–422.

against which losses may be offset. Here the position of various tax payers differs greatly. An established corporation or a large-scale financial investor may undertake a risky investment as a side line with the assurance that possible losses will be covered by other income derived from the main line of business. A large corporation can count on the possibility of loss offset as long as the investment in question does not exceed the income which the management is reasonably certain to derive during the period of carry-over. The present law thus provides a fair chance for loss offset to large and established business.

New businesses, small enterprises and small-scale financial investors are in a much less advantageous position. They are likely to be less diversified and are thus more apt to suffer a net loss in any one year. One venture might easily compel liquidation of the entire business. Also, new businesses are not able to offset their losses against past income because they were established only recently so that available past income is insufficient. Thus under the present law the Treasury often shares in the losses of large and established business but fails to do so for the small and new ones.

Such a discrimination is definitely undesirable. The advantages derived by the economy from the growth of new businesses and the presence of small investors are well known. While it is clear that the Treasury should share in the losses of all business alike, this objective is not easily accomplished. Extension of the carry-over periods would not suffice for the reasons indicated. To assure the possibility of loss offset, the Treasury would, in fact, have to stand ready to collect cash in case of gains and to send a check in the case of losses. This kind of approach is less radical than it may appear. Under the existing carry-back provision, the Treasury actually makes cash refunds which reimburse the taxpayer for a part of his loss.

It is not probable that surtax rates on high personal incomes can be reduced sufficiently, under modern conditions, to provide anything like the incentive to risk-taking that prevailed when income taxes were non-existent. Encouragement to risk-taking can be provided, however, even under a progressive income tax, if we allow (a) adequate loss offsets, or better yet loss sharing, and (b) tax abatement for new ventures and new physical investments. Thus in calculating taxable income, an individual might be allowed to deduct up to, say, 25 per cent of income so invested, just as one can now deduct up to 15 per cent of income for gifts to charitable or educational organizations. The per cent income thus deductible might be varied according to the requirements of the cycle.

Elimination of Double Taxation of Dividends

In addition, I would suggest that the current double taxation of dividends be eliminated. The plan which I propose is an adaptation of the British method. I doubt that we should apply the standard personal income tax rate to the corporation.[60] So low a rate on retained earnings combined with a steeply progressive individual income tax schedule would operate as a serious deterrent to the distribution of dividends. I would suggest a rate of, say, 40 per cent on the entire corporate income but with the provision that the stockholder be credited, in calculating his income tax, with his portion of the tax which the corporation has already paid on the distributed part of corporate earnings. The stockholder in calculating his income should then include "gross dividends" — the part distributed prior to the payment of the tax. The corporation would thus pay 40 per cent on the retained earnings while the stockholder would pay according to his income status on the gross (prior to taxes) distributed earnings. But there would be no double taxation on the distributed part since the tax withheld at the source by the corporations is deductible from the tax payable by the individual. Small corporations might be accorded a more favorable treatment.

A compromise, involving a partial elimination of double taxation, might be more acceptable at least at the start. On this basis the corporation might be taxed 40 per cent on the retained earnings and 20 per cent on the distributed earnings, while the stockholder would be taxed on all dividends received.

Income taxes (including the amount withheld at the source by corporations) should yield about $14 billion. This would permit a very substantial reduction from the present tax rates. Present exemptions are unduly low — $500 per individual and per member of the family. In the event that they are retained the rate applied to the first $1,000 of "taxable income" should not exceed 10 per cent, with 15 per cent in

60. The British standard rate prior to the war was far above any proposed for the United States.

the $1,000–$2,000 bracket. If the exemption is raised, the beginning rate could be higher, say 15 per cent on the first $2,000 taxable income. Beyond this bracket the rates should rise progressively to yield the total indicated. I believe, moreover, that gift and estate taxes might well be made to yield $1 billion.

With income payments of $137 billion a year, such a tax schedule would leave a disposable income for individuals after taxes of around $125 billion, far above prewar levels after correcting for price changes.

To sum up, then, direct taxes (income, death, and gift) should yield about $15 billion, including the taxes withheld by corporations; excises and miscellaneous revenues might yield about $3 billion. The main features of the program include:

1. Generous loss offsets carried back and forward in order to induce risk-taking and new investment; or even outright loss sharing

2. Major reliance on individual income tax

3. Complete elimination of excess-profits tax

4. Elimination of double taxation with a 40 per cent tax on net corporate earnings, the stockholders being credited with the part prepaid by the corporation on the distributed earnings

5. Elimination of all federal excises except alcoholic beverages, tobacco, and customs duties

Pay roll taxes might yield, assuming an expansion of the social security program, say, $5 billion. At the outset the current benefits should equal the pay roll tax receipts. In time, total benefit payments would exceed pay roll taxes, the difference being borne by the Treasury out of general revenues. Thus we should gradually move into a three-way financing of social security with employer, employee, and government contributions.[61]

STATE AND LOCAL TAXES

What about state and local taxes? These I am compelled to discuss very briefly. I would suggest that state taxes be simplified along the following lines: Complete elimination of the chaotic mess of business taxes now common among the states. State taxes would then consist of the individual income tax, corporate income tax, inheritance tax, excises on alcoholic beverages, tobacco, gasoline, and motor vehicles, and

61. For details see *State and Local Finance in the National Economy,* Chap. 12.

miscellaneous revenues. The states, taken together, would need to raise in my proposed model about $4 billion. This could be distributed as follows:

	(*In Billions of Dollars*)
Individual income tax	0.5
Corporate income tax	0.6
Death duties	0.3
Alcoholic beverages	0.4
Tobacco	0.3
Gasoline	0.9
Motor vehicles	0.4
Miscellaneous revenue	0.5
	3.9

The localities all over the country in my schedule would need to raise a little over $5 billion. This might consist of the following:

	(*In Billions of Dollars*)
Property taxes[62]	4.1
Gasoline	0.4
Motor vehicles	0.2
Miscellaneous	0.6
	5.3

The gasoline and motor vehicle taxes referred to above would be collected by the states and shared with the local communities in the manner indicated in the state and local schedules as given.

Some intergovernmental transfers would, of course, be necessary. These I cannot go into here.[63]

This is broadly the program toward which, it seems to me, we ought to work. The reform of state taxation cannot quickly or easily be achieved. The whole problem of a properly integrated tax structure, federal, state and local, is tremendously complicated and the study of it should be undertaken at an early date by a competent and broadly representative national tax commission.

62. Local property taxes could be reduced gradually below this figure if federal aid to education on the scale advocated above were adopted.
63. See Alvin H. Hansen and Harvey S. Perloff, *op. cit.*

V. Management of the Debt and Internal Stability

When all war expenditures cease we may have a public debt of around $300 billion. The magnitude of the public debt and the manner in which it is held raise two important problems: (a) will this vast public debt and the relatively high liquidity which it affords corporate and individual holders constitute an undue inflationary threat in the postwar period, or will it merely contribute to a high level of employment; (b) does the high state of liquidity incident to the ownership of public debt seriously handicap our ability to control a boom situation, should it arise?

THE HOLDERS OF THE PUBLIC DEBT

Distribution of Holdings

The ownership of government securities as of January 1945 was distributed as follows:[64]

	(In Billions of Dollars)
Government trust funds and agencies	22.0
Mutual savings banks and insurance companies	28.6
Federal reserve banks	19.0
Commercial banks	78.2
Other investors	
Marketable issues	34.4
Treasury tax and savings notes	9.9
U. S. savings bonds	40.1
	232.2

The distribution of ownership will probably be broadly similar to this by the time all war expenditures come to an end. Perhaps, in view of the large increase in savings by individuals and business, commercial bank holdings will be proportionally less than shown here.

We know that demand deposits in January 1945 were around $65 billion, of which some $40 billion were held by business concerns, about $21 billion by individuals, and $4 billion by trust funds, nonprofit associations, and foreigners. We know that currency in circulation amounted in January 1945 to about $25 billion, of which some $6 billion were in denominations of $100 or more and therefore probably were held for hoarding, tax evasion, and black market purposes.

64. *Federal Reserve Bulletin,* April 1945.

We know further that, by January 1945, currency in circulation had risen to an index of 333 (1939 = 100), while factory pay rolls had risen to an index of 330 and total income payments to 230.[65] Thus by far the largest factor accounting for the increase in currency is the increase in income and pay rolls. It is believed that part of the currency increase is due to increased service charges of banks, part to the migration of many millions of workers to new environments in which they may not easily have made banking connections. Also, as workers' and farmers' income rises, the quantity of cash carried in their pockets tends to increase faster than income. Thus a worker earning $20 a week may carry hardly any cash; while if he earns $100 a week he may carry quite a roll of bills.

The composition of the federal debt as of January 1945 was as follows:[66]

	Amount	Maturity
	(In Billions of Dollars)	
Treasury bills	16.4	3 months
Certificates of indebtedness	30.4	9–12 months
Treasury notes	23.0	3–5 years
Treasury bonds	93.4	
Nonmarketable public issues	51.7	10–12 years
Special issues	16.7	

The computed average rate of interest on the total debt was 1.92 per cent.

With these facts before us, what does it all mean with respect to the management of the debt after the war?

The first question relates to shifts that may occur in bond holdings.

Postwar Unloading of Bonds

Let us go down through the list of holders and ask the question: to what extent is each group of holders likely to wish to dispose of its government securities when peace comes?

The government trust funds (especially the unemployment and old-age trust funds) will add to or unload their holdings according to the volume of pay roll taxes compared to benefit payments. The benefit payments of the old-age trust fund (on the basis of existing legislation) are likely to remain relatively small — about $300 million per year,

---

65. *Ibid.*   66. *Treasury Bulletin*, March 1945.

while the old-age pay roll taxes at present rates amount to about $1.1 billion per year. This fund will therefore add substantially to its holdings of bonds. The unemployment trust fund, in the event of large unemployment (say 10 million) might be compelled to sell securities at the rate of $2–$3 billion per year. If, however, unemployment is low (say 2 million) the benefit payments are likely to be about $400 million per annum, while pay roll taxes may amount to about $1.4 billion per annum. It is to be hoped that the Social Security Act will be amended so as to prevent the excessive accumulation of reserves.

Savings banks and life insurance companies are not likely to be sellers of bonds. The main uncertainty relates to "other investors" — nonfinancial business concerns (corporate and unincorporated) and individuals, who hold marketable issues and United States savings bonds.

Of the $34.4 billion of marketable issue, held by "other investors" as listed above, it is not known precisely how much is held by nonfinancial business units, and how much by individuals. Probably over one half is held by business concerns. Are they likely to sell governments in order to finance postwar requirements? In view of the fact that business concerns held in January 1945 around $40 billion of demand deposits, it is likely that their accumulation of unspent depreciation funds and other reserves are largely held in the form of cash; a part, however, is held in the form of government securities.

Business postwar spending on plant, equipment and inventories will mainly be financed from these accumulated depreciation funds. Some securities will, indeed, be sold, especially in the reconversion period. But after the reconversion period is over it is not unlikely that business concerns will again be in the market for government bonds. The spending of the demand deposits need not mean any decline in total demand deposits held by business. These sums are spent, they are paid over to other business concerns who in turn deposit them, and so total demand deposits in the system as a whole will remain high. They would decline only if business concerns should pay off loans at the bank or if business should use its deposits to purchase bonds held by banks. After the reconversion period it is probable that business concerns will still hold large cash assets — larger indeed than they deem necessary. Should this be so, they may purchase bonds from the banks or pay off loans. The latter transaction would at once reduce bank deposit liabilities and, on the asset side, bank holdings of government securities.

Probably about two thirds of the United States savings bonds ($40.1 billion as listed above) are held by moderate and low income groups, and one third by the rich and well-to-do. In addition, this latter group holds perhaps one half of the marketable issues ($34.4 billion) held by "other investors." Thus say about $30–$35 billion of marketable issues and savings bonds are held by the rich and well-to-do, while about $25 billion of savings bonds are held by the middle and low income groups. What are these groups likely to do with their bonds? Will they unload or will they hold?

As to the rich and well-to-do holders, an important factor will be the trend in the securities market. The price of stocks has remained reasonably steady during the war. There has been no sharp advance in stock prices. Much the same was true in the last war. Uncertainty about the future prevails with respect to many things — wages, taxes, postwar inflation, deflation, postwar level of business activity and employment. The stock market reflects this. We do not know what the postwar period may bring. Business will more and more adjust itself to the new tax structure. We know that technical progress during and after the war, together with larger volume, will mean lower unit costs. But higher wages may largely or wholly offset this advantage. The labor situation may remain disturbing, but widespread collective bargaining, while it may mean strong pressure for higher wage rates, nevertheless substitutes certainty for uncertainty during the period of the collective contract. This means very much.

There may possibly be a tendency to shift more or less to the stock market. But the sellers of stocks will want to re-invest. After the stock market has reached a new equilibrium in relation to government securities, the latter will again be in demand. Thus any possible tendency to shift into stocks does not necessarily mean any reduced holdings of government securities by the public unless the money received from the sale of bonds is spent on new issues of corporate securities or on consumers' goods, or is held as idle cash. New issues of any considerable volume are not probable in view of the large accumulations of funds and internal savings of business during the war years. Even in the booming twenties the value of new "productive" issues (financing net additions to fixed capital) amounted to only $1.7 billion per annum.

Consider now the mass holdings of United States savings bonds. Are these likely to be cashed in large volume? I should question this very much. We know from Kuznets that the rate of savings by individuals (excluding entrepreneurs) reached an all-time high after the last war (1919–1920). Wage and salary workers are likely to add to their nest egg of savings as long as they are employed at good wages. Only in the event of a prolonged depression is any large net unloading of savings funds in prospect.

At any rate the banking system — Federal Reserve banks and commercial banks — must be prepared to act as a balancing factor, selling when the public buys and buying when the public sells. Only in this way can the market for government bonds be reasonably stabilized.

THE POSTWAR INTEREST RATE

This brings us directly to the problem of postwar policy with respect to the long-term rate of interest. If the long-term government bond market is, broadly speaking, stabilized around current levels, the long-term rate of interest will continue to be low. That the resources of the Treasury and the Federal Reserve System are adequate to maintain a stable market for government bonds cannot be doubted. By stable market is meant not a rigidly maintained price, but substantial stability. Would this be a desirable policy?

The Interest Rate as Stabilizer

Formerly it was a generally accepted doctrine that the rate of interest should be varied as a means of stabilizing the cycle. And, it is frequently asked, if terms of lending are not made severe, if credit is not restricted, reflecting itself in higher interest rates, how can an inflationary boom be prevented? May we not be confronted, some time after the war, with a situation which will compel us to raise the rate of interest, thereby forcing a decline in government bonds?

To control the cycle in the postwar years through interest rate adjustments is regarded as inadmissible by two distinct groups of economists. One holds that good monetary policy calls for holding the long-term interest rate stable at a low level; the other, while wishing to vary the interest rate if practical circumstances permitted, is nevertheless convinced that the vast holdings of government bonds by financial institutions, business, and the public generally preclude the use of this monetary weapon. Both groups view with concern the effects on the economy of a substantial fall in bond values. Both agree, on practical grounds, that this should not be allowed. The first group, however, in addition to this practical consideration, holds there is genuine merit, per se, in a low and stable interest rate, and that the alleged benefits from cyclical fluctuation of the rate of interest are not well founded.

Continued Easy Money

In the annual report of the Bank of Canada of February 10, 1944, Governor Towers stated the matter so well that I could not do better than to quote from his report. Speaking of the postwar situation, he said:

A policy aimed at higher interest rates would only become intelligible if, after war shortages are over, consumers' expenditure and capital development were to proceed at a rate which would overstrain our productive capacity. I see no prospect of such a situation arising in a form which would call for a policy of raising interest rates. Admittedly, the rate of interest is only one of many factors influencing Canada's economic position, and it is probably not as important an instrument of control as was once supposed. It remains true, however, that the prospect of unstable interest rates could make it exceedingly difficult for business to formulate long-term plans. Moreover, high borrowing costs would hamper new investment in plant, equipment, and housing, would restrict the expansion of employment, and would seriously complicate the task of government financing. There can be little doubt that the easy money policy which has been pursued since 1935 assisted in promoting recovery from the depression and facilitated the adjustments which have been required during the war period. Indication that the Bank intends to continue this easy money policy should be helpful in making plans for the future.

The Interest Rate and Boom Control

Can raising the rate of interest effectively control a speculative boom? Both on grounds of experience and general theoretical analysis, it is now widely accepted that the interest rate is a very poor instrument of control for the purpose envisaged. In a pronounced boom it is the speculative activities that ought to be clubbed down — not the ordinary run of stable industries. The former, however, make extraordinary profits. An increase in the rate of interest hits the vital industries; but affects hardly at all the high-profit speculative ventures. It is not denied that credit restriction and increasing pressure of rising interest rates can check a boom. But they do so by undermining the sound basis of prosperity and employment until the whole economy turns into a dangerous tailspin.

Once the interest rate structure has been raised sufficiently to check the boom, it is no easy matter to lower the interest rate structure in the ensuing depression, and thereby permit recovery. We have seen, during the depression of the thirties (despite an extraordinary degree of liquidity and despite low yields in the high-grade bond market), how difficult it has been to reduce the rate adequately in highly important areas such as housing and on loans in rural and small communities. The difficulty of getting the rate down, once it has been raised in the boom period, and the deterrent effect which a high rate has on recovery, present a strong argument (aside from the unstabilizing effect noted above) against the use of this device as a regulatory mechanism.

In view of what has been said above, I should incline to the view that raising the rate of interest, either (a) has very serious consequences which could not be tolerated, or (b) is not an effective way of combating temporary inflationary tendencies.

BANK CREDIT CONTROL

Consider bank credit in the postwar period as a means of controlling potential inflationary developments. It might be argued that it is not so much the rate of interest as it is the availability of credit which is important. When banks have no excess reserves, they will restrict the volume of credit available to their clients and not simply rely upon a high rate of interest to limit the quantity of credit that will be demanded. In the conditions, however, that will prevail at the end of the war, it is not likely that restriction on the availability of credit can be relied upon to control bank credit. The resources that in fact will be available to member banks will be enormous in view of their large holdings of government bonds. Before a point could be reached at which the availability of credit to bank customers could in fact be restricted, one would have to force upon the banks a perfectly terrific liquidation of their bond holdings. This action could certainly not be contemplated.

The various areas of possible bank credit control may be enumerated as follows: (a) genuine commercial loans, (b) speculative loans on the stock market, (c) consumer credit loans, (d) urban and real-estate mortgages, (e) industrial and utility bonds, and (f) government obligations.

Genuine commercial loans: It is rather unlikely that any inflationary development will spring from genuine commercial loans. We know that from 1920 on throughout the boom of the twenties, genuine commercial loans did not rise, and that in proportion to bank assets they continuously declined. There is no probability that any large resort to commercial loans is going to take place in the postwar period. Inflationary tendencies from this source are not likely to present a problem. It is true that in every inventory investment boom some increase in commercial loans occurs. It is practically a certainty, however, that when raw material prices are rising, as they do in an inventory investment boom, an increase in the rate of interest has virtually no deterrent effect. The prospective gains from a rise in the price of inventories enormously overshadows any deterrent effect inherent in an increase in the rate of interest. Other means must be found to regularize, more than we have been able to in the past, violent fluctuations in inventory accumulations. It may be that adequate inventory information may itself have a restraining effect. It may be that some tax incentive device can be found to meet this problem. Control of credit cannot do the job. It never has in the past.

Speculative loans: With respect to loans in the stock market, there are already available fairly effective controls in the margin requirements and in the powers of the Federal Reserve Board to alter these requirements. The experience of the twenties indicates that for effective regulation we must look to direct control and not to general curtailment of bank credit.

Consumer credit loans: With respect to consumer loans, I would suggest the continuation of current consumer credit controls. These controls at least ought to remain on the statute book as powers of the Federal Reserve Board. Normally, the powers would not be used, but they would and should be used when inflationary potentialities were threatening.

Real-estate investment: Here again past experience indicates that a mere rise in the rate of interest is a wholly ineffective device. The problem can be broken down mainly into the two categories of urban real estate and farm land. With respect to urban real estate, it is believed that the present powers of the Federal Housing Administration would be fairly ample to restrict the volume of new investment in housing if inflation were threatening. This could be done, without increasing the rate of interest, by raising the cash-down payment and shortening the depreciation period. It may be that the FHA should be given additional powers in this direction.

With respect to rural real estate, we have been in need, even during the war, of some measure of controlling speculation in farm land. This should be undertaken at once before the problem gets out of hand. We have learned from the last war that the most dangerous period of violent farm land speculation followed the war. It is of the utmost importance that we tackle this problem now. Various plans have been suggested which I cannot go into here.[67] Adequate control methods can be devised. The point I wish here to stress is that experience following the last war indicates very clearly that a mere increase in the rate of interest is quite ineffective as a means of controlling inflationary and highly speculative developments in farm values.

Bank investments in high-grade bonds, public and private: The value of long-term government bonds should be stabilized with a minimum of fluctuations. It may well be sound policy to prevent the long-term bond market from rising progressively. This, indeed, may involve a control of the volume of excess member bank reserves. In so far as this is true, there is indeed a problem of bank credit control. In order to maintain the value of government bonds and prevent them from falling, a high degree of liquidity in the banking system will be needed. Excess reserves should not, however, be permitted to rise to a point which would tempt banks too far into long terms, resulting in an excessive rise in the value of governments and high-grade private bonds. The Federal Reserve Board should have ample power to prevent liquidity in the banking system from rising to a point that would produce this result. There is thus the need for a control of excess reserves. What the desirable level of interest rates may be a decade or so hence, I do not pretend to know, but for the years ahead, I think we would do well to stabilize around present levels.

It has been suggested that the policy to maintain the value of government bonds would of itself progressively induce banks to move farther and farther out into long terms. The commercial banks tend to hold mainly short-term obligations. Any other policy would be undesirable

67. Mr. Eccles has suggested a special wartime capital-gains tax to be applied only to the sale of assets purchased after January 1, 1945 until such time as inflationary dangers have passed, possibly two or three years after the war. This tax would, of course, apply to securities as well as to real estate.

not only in terms of the character of bank assets but also in terms of the burden of fixed charges on the public debt.

Various means might be devised to prevent banks from moving too far out into long terms. For one thing, it is quite possible that while a postwar excess-profits tax for business in general is undesirable, such a tax on commercial banks may be desirable as a control measure. An excess-profits tax for banks would tend to keep them out of long-term bonds. With such a tax they would in general conclude that it is not worth while to move into long terms. Adequate bank earnings to meet all reasonable needs are indeed necessary; but, in view of the large holdings of bonds, it is important (in order to preserve the independence and private status of banks) not to earn excess profits.

If the interest rate on government bonds is maintained at approximately its present level, it follows that the interest rate on high-grade private bonds will continue in line with the government interest rate. This, to be sure, means that corporations can secure funds in the capital market on very favorable terms. Are there inflationary dangers in this situation? I think not. In the first place, internal sources of financing are increasingly important and the volume of new financing in the capital market is relatively small. As we have seen, it was even extraordinarily small in the good years of the twenties, amounting in the best years to less than $2 billion a year. It is true that the gross volume of new issues floated was many times this amount, but this grew out of the speculative orgy in which there was formed layer upon layer of speculative issues of holding companies and investment trusts. It was a part of the speculative picture which I have already discussed above, and which can be handled by direct methods. The danger that excessive flotation of securities in the capital markets will finance genuine new investment is negligible, I think, in view of the development of internal financing. Moreover, both theoretical analysis and practical case studies indicate that the volume of real investment made by business is but little affected by the interest rate. All manner of other considerations dominate. An increase in the interest rate is not an effective method of control.

DIRECT CONTROLS AND FISCAL POLICY

We are thus driven back fundamentally to specific measures in various areas as indicated above, and to a control of government expenditures and taxes as a means of preventing inflationary developments. With respect to the postwar restocking boom, it is admitted, I think, by everyone that we shall not be able to manage its inflationary potentialities unless we continue rationing and price controls in the areas where they are needed. Beyond this restocking boom, special controls of the character discussed above will be needed in some areas. Over and above that, the control of federal expenditures and of taxes is a powerful weapon. We must not only balance the budget but produce a budgetary surplus when inflationary tendencies develop and use that surplus to retire bonds held by the banks. It is within the framework of such controls that we must operate if we are going to manage inflationary tendencies.

Finally, wage policy is basic to economic and price stability. Wage rates should be adjusted upward from time to time as rapidly as increases in productivity permit, but no farther. Increases beyond this limit mean wage inflation. An orderly adjustment of wages in accordance with productivity but not in excess of increases in productivity is an essential part of a stabilization program.

VI. Wage Adjustment and Price Stability

This problem — extraordinarily difficult in its complexity, but inescapable — must be considered in some detail. What about the course of wage rates following the war? Some have advocated a revision of the wage stabilization formula, even while the war was in progress. Against this view, I have myself urged utmost support for adherence to the wartime wage stabilization program. I have felt that we could not safely relax this control until the war is over, because such relaxation would endanger the whole price stabilization program. Gross inequities can and have, in considerable measure, been rectified. But any substantial wartime wage revision would, I believe, be dangerous. We cannot afford to risk any threat to the internal value of our money and the wartime savings of the people while we face the inflationary pressures of peak war expenditures.

Now the war is over, however, hours will be reduced and overtime pay will be eliminated. Total pay rolls will accordingly fall. As a partial offset to the decline in the take-home pay, some adjustment of straight-time wage rates will be in order.

I shall explain presently why I believe such adjustment to be feasible and, indeed, necessary. Before I do so, however, let me stress the point that we cannot hope to achieve economic stability in the postwar unless we undertake an orderly adjustment of wage rates within the framework of a stabilization program. Should we permit a chaotic rise in wage rates now that the war is over — wage inflation — the prospects of economic stability would be very dark indeed. Wages should, indeed, be raised as rapidly as productivity permits since such increases do not necessitate any increase in general prices. Wage increases which force price increases do nobody any good, least of all the wage earner. To repeat, what is called for is an orderly adjustment of wage rates as productivity rises, within the framework of general economic and price stability.

WAGE RATES AND NATIONAL INCOME

The Total Pay Roll

Admittedly, it will not be possible to maintain the national income and pay rolls at the peak of the war effort. But there is a fairly general consensus among competent statisticians that reasonably full postwar employment would yield, at around 1942 prices, a national income of $140 billion. Now no such national income is possible unless total wages and salaries are at a balanced relation thereto. Wages and salaries in 1939–1941 constituted 62.6 per cent of the national income. In 1942–1944 they were 68.4 per cent. Applying an average of these percentages to a postwar national income of $140 billion we arrive at a wages and salaries bill of $92 billion. An analysis of the component parts of the national income in recent years suggests the following breakdown:[68]

	(In Billions of Dollars)
National income	140.0
Net corporate profits (after taxes)	10.0
Proprietors' return, interest, net rents and royalties	32.5
Payment to military personnel	2.5
Supplements to wages and salaries	3.0
Wages and salaries of civilian employees	92.0

A wages and salaries bill of around $92 billion for civilian employees, assuming a postwar national income of $140 billion, appears

68. See *Survey of Current Business,* March 1943 and February 1945.

to be reasonable. It would not be possible to maintain an income of this magnitude without a pay roll commensurate therewith.

It is therefore highly important to inquire what wages and salaries would in fact amount to assuming the continuance of the wartime scale of straight-time wage rates with no overtime. An income of $140 billion presupposes civilian employment of some 55 million workers. It is estimated that civilians employed in peacetime industries at 1943 straight-time wage rates in those industries would earn wages and salaries equal to about $80 billion. This is $8 billion short of the minimum suggested by the prewar 1939–1941 relationships, and $12 billion short of the estimated $92 billion wages and salaries based on the average ratio of wages and salaries to national income in the six-year period, 1939–1944.

Offsetting the Decline in Overtime Pay

It appears from these data that a $140 billion income could not be sustained without some increase in straight-time wage rates, as a partial offset to the decline in overtime, including penalty overtime pay. If wage rates are not adjusted upward, there would have to be a substantial fall in prices so as to permit a decline in the national income to a level commensurate with an $80 billion wages and salaries level. Any large fall in prices, however, presents serious deflationary dangers. It would be wiser to aim at substantial stability of the price level.

The pressure for higher wage rates, as a partial offset to the decline in overtime, will be very great. Even after some upward adjustment of straight-time rates is made, the take-home pay would still be substantially reduced. It will be less disturbing to the social structure to permit an orderly upward adjustment of wage rates and to maintain substantial price stability than to hold the present straight-time rates and force a deflationary adjustment of prices.

WAGE AND PRICE ADJUSTMENTS

While the adjustment of straight-time pay should in most cases be upward, in some cases wartime wage rates are out of line and a downward adjustment is indicated. Similarly, in the transition period, there will be some adjustment of prices downward,[69] while certain specific

69. In particular, agricultural prices may be expected to fall substantially below the high wartime levels.

prices, owing to the wage adjustment program, would have to rise. To reach a proper equilibrium between total wage and salary pay and a postwar full-employment income of around $140 billion, some upward adjustment in general of straight-time pay on the one side and some moderate decline in some price areas is indicated. If both adjustments are made on a moderate basis, neither should be seriously disturbing.

Increased Productivity of Labor

That straight-time wage rates can in general be adjusted upward is indicated by the changes in labor productivity which have occurred since 1939. While basic straight-time wage rates have increased about 25 per cent for all workers, and about 35 per cent for factory workers since 1939, prices have risen correspondingly — cost of living 25 per cent and wholesale prices 35 per cent. Accordingly, such increases in rates as have occurred have already been offset by price increases. Increases in productivity since 1939 would therefore permit some upward wage adjustment without necessitating further general increases in prices, or without encroaching unduly upon the profit margin.

Moreover, the reduction in unit cost, incident to much fuller utilization of plant capacity than prevailed in 1939, permits the payment of higher wage rates. This conclusion is further supported by the extraordinarily high level of corporate profits prior to taxes — $24 billion in 1943.[70] The figures were approximately the same in 1944. During the war it was appropriate for the government to take the lion's share of these profits in the form of $14 billion of corporate taxes. But in the peace, in order to increase private consumption expenditures and to offset the decline in over-all effective demand incident to the cessation of war expenditures, taxes should be reduced and wages should be increased. The workers, and not mainly the government, should share with business the surplus generated by a full-employment income. Indeed, unless they do, sustained full employment will not be possible.

Wage Adjustment With Price Stability

Let me emphasize again the importance of an orderly adjustment of wage rates as productivity rises, within the framework of economic and price stability. There is always the danger that superficial readers will

70. See *Bulletin of the Treasury Department*, May 1944.

jump at the conclusion that I have advocated indiscriminatory wage increases. This I have not done. Such action I would seriously deplore. I am firmly of the opinion that the danger to postwar inflation springs much less from the temporary shortages and the accumulated deferred demand caused by the war. The real serious threat of postwar inflation is a chaotic wage development, destructive of price and general economic stability.

It would be suicidal to engage in destructive industrial conflicts over the wage question. Wage cutting should be resisted. But equally we must have an enlightened policy against wage inflation. It is in the long-run interest of all groups, both labor and capital, to undertake an orderly adjustment of wage rates, permitting as rapid increases as technical progress makes possible. This is in the interest of employers as a group, because only by such wage adjustment can an adequate market be assured for our mass-production industries. But the upward adjustment must be limited to the requirements of economic and price stability. And this is in the interest of the entire wage-earning group, no less than for society as a whole.

Consideration might be given to the following suggestion: might it not be sound policy to establish a peacetime Office of Price Research? Such an agency would be required to report to the President and to Congress on proposed price increases, and no industry would be permitted to increase administered prices (steel, automobiles, etc.) for, say, ninety days until a full investigation had been made. Publicity, not coercion, would be relied upon for enforcement of a rational price policy — one which would promote expansion and full employment.

VII. An International Monetary and Financial Program

The conference of official delegates at Bretton Woods representing forty-four countries reached a unanimous agreement. The plans there developed involve proposals with respect to an International Monetary Fund and an International Bank for Reconstruction and Development.

These proposals were regarded as a test case. There can be little doubt that the whole world was watching to see which way the United States was going. After World War I the United States turned isolationist with respect to the League of Nations — a world political federation. This time the question is whether American policy will be isolationist on economic lines.

For a while it looked as if we were facing a crisis in international relations not unlike that high-lighted in the Lodge-Lowell debates a generation ago. But Congress approved the Bretton Woods plans.

These plans are international in scope. They promote consultation and cooperation. In the absence of international arrangements such as these, nationalistic policies tending toward economic isolation are almost certain to prevail. Such nationalistic policies are likely to express themselves in economic rivalries between blocs formed under the leadership of great nations. If cooperation on broadly international lines is not instituted, economic nationalism, isolationism, rival economic blocs, and international friction will likely be intensified.

THE FUND

The purposes and functions of the International Monetary Fund can briefly be stated. They are as follows:

1. To provide international machinery for consultation, the gathering of information, research, and the making of reports on economic conditions and developments affecting the international economic situations.

2. To provide a system of stable exchange rates with machinery for orderly adjustment of rates when necessary, thereby preventing disorderly, competitive exchange depreciation.

3. To provide a short-term line of credit, helping countries over temporary difficulties in their balance of payment position and thereby giving them time for making necessary adjustments.

Foreign Exchange Dealings

The Fund is not intended to supply foreign exchange in the ordinary case. Foreign exchange dealings will take place through private channels precisely as though there were no Fund in existence at all. In the usual case the resources of the Fund would not be used. The resources of the Fund are intended as a supplement, not a substitute for regular exchange operations. It is a second line of defense. It guarantees each member a line of credit upon which it can draw when necessary. It provides insurance against a breakdown in the international economy.

Each country is allowed to borrow at the Fund foreign exchange up to the amount of its quota, plus its gold contribution. To do so it must deposit collateral with the Fund equal to the amount borrowed over and above the original deposit with the Fund. The Fund is therefore amply protected. Moreover, the borrowing country must pay interest on the sum borrowed, the charge being higher the larger the loan and the longer it is allowed to run. It is a sensible business arrangement both for the borrower and for the Fund.

In the period following the war the Monetary Fund will provide international machinery by which the various countries can fix upon an appropriate exchange rate through an orderly process of adjustment. Through consultation and joint study between each member country and the Monetary Fund, we have reason to hope that the exchange rate structure, that will be established as a result, will provide a far better basis for international stability than would be the case if each country were quite free as after World War I to fix its exchange rate. Also, from the long-run standpoint, developments are bound to occur which will require an orderly adjustment of exchange rates. Competitive exchange depreciation can thereby be avoided.

Coercion Versus Consultation

Objection has been made to the Fund on the ground that it has no punitive disciplinary powers over its members. Those who so argue do not understand the temper of the modern world. We shall not make progress through coercive controls. No self-respecting country would join such an arrangement. We shall make progress only through consultation and mutual cooperation in the interest of all-around stability and expansion of world trade. The Fund does, however, have powers to prevent a member from abusing its privileges. It can deny access to its resources if a member is acting in a manner contrary to the purpose of the Fund. The Fund can, moreover, make reports to members about economic conditions and developments in any country which is disturbing to the general world situation.

The Fund can help members to reach an international balance without forcing upon that country a policy of deflation. It is obvious that any country can easily reach a balance in its international accounts by undertaking a rigorous deflation of income and employment to a point where imports are sharply curtailed. But such action does not promote world prosperity and world trade. It is the intent of the Fund to help countries reach a balance at a high level of production, employment, and international trade. The use of the Fund's resources affords time for adjustment. It may be that an orderly adjustment of the exchange rate is required. It may be that the country which is out of balance should undertake a program of development and diversification of its industries and agriculture. Here the Bank for Reconstruction and Development could help. Such a developmental program may make certain imports unnecessary and may create export possibilities. Thus, a new balance may be reached. Temporary borrowing at the Fund may enable a country to make such adjustment without in the meantime being forced to take uneconomic measures destructive of world prosperity and world trade.

THE BANK

The International Bank for Reconstruction and Development can greatly aid in the process of promoting fundamental international equilibrium. The Bank will be available for reconstruction in war-devastated countries and for development in the backward countries. Such reconstruction and development are basic to international monetary equilibrium. Thus the Bank reinforces the Fund.

Credit Insurance

The Bank does not supplant private international investment and private international lending. No borrowing country can use the Bank if it can float loans at reasonable rates. The Bank will, however, enable productive development projects to be undertaken in countries that could not borrow on reasonable terms without the aid of the Bank. The Bank in the typical case will insure and guarantee bonds issued in the ordinary private capital markets.

The operations of the Bank would for the most part be precisely similar to the FHA loans with which we are familiar in the United States. The borrower will pay an insurance premium (called a commission charge) into a central pool just as in the case of FHA loans. This insurance pool is a first line of defense to protect the private investor. If this central insurance pool proves inadequate, the Bank guarantees the loan.

The total volume of loans that the Bank can so guarantee may not exceed the subscribed capital of the Bank. This means in effect that the various member countries agree to underwrite loans up to the amount of their subscription to the capital of the Bank. The Bank may thus guarantee a total of $9.1 billion (the subscribed capital of the Bank).

The United States' share is $3,175,000,000. Only 10 per cent of our subscription to the Bank is to be paid in. The rest is subject to call in the event that losses are sustained.

Governments would not, under the guaranteed loan, supply the funds loaned. The funds are raised in the private capital markets from private investors. It is true that the Bank has the power to call in a maximum of 20 per cent of the subscribed capital and with these funds make direct loans. It is doubtful that this procedure will be used except in rare cases. In general, the Bank will be an underwriting institution. The funds will come from private sources, while the member countries underwrite the risk up to the extent of their subscription.

Sharing the Risk and Responsibility

Since, in fact, most of the funds will be raised in the capital markets of the United States, why shouldn't we run the institution ourselves? Why an international bank? To this there are several answers. In the first place, under the International Bank we underwrite only one third of the risk. If we ran the Bank ourselves we would have to underwrite the whole of the risk. In the second place, an international institution will tend to promote high standards of conduct and adherence to contracts. It has the same advantage as a self-governing student body. Moreover, under an international institution, it cannot be charged that the United States is playing Uncle Shylock. An international institution promotes a high sense of international responsibility and international good will.

Americans looking for outlets for their savings will find here a high-grade gilt-edge security. American exporters will benefit through the enlarged exports of equipment and machinery to the borrowing countries. And finally, the American taxpayer, as indicated above, is relieved in that other countries undertake two thirds of the risk involved. How any arrangement could be more to our national interest is difficult to see.

PROMOTING FREER TRADE

These institutions are not enough. Basic to their success, as I have repeatedly said, is a high level of income in the great industrial countries, and especially in the United States. Moreover, we must promote international arrangements to reduce restrictions on trade, remove discriminatory trade practices, and work toward a freer flow of multilateral trade. We should advance on all fronts as rapidly as possible. Each program reinforces and sustains the others. In addition to the Bretton Woods program, it is of the utmost importance to continue and extend the trade agreements program and to move forward with multilateral arrangements for the reduction of trade barriers.

Chapter 6

PUBLIC POLICIES AND POSTWAR EMPLOYMENT

Sumner H. Slichter[1]

I. The Basic Issues

With the end of the war we face the most rapid disappearance of markets in history. Within two years after the fighting against Japan, federal expenditures will drop from about $85 billion a year to $25 billion or less — an average drop of about $2.5 billion a month. Will this drop in government buying plunge the country into a severe depression? Will the enormous accumulation of needs and of record-breaking quantities of cash and other liquid assets by individuals and corporations create a demand far in excess of the capacity of industry? Or will the drop in government spending and the pent-up private demand offset each other so satisfactorily that exactly the "right" amount of employment is produced? Even if employment is satisfactory for several years after the war, will it continue to be high after deferred demand has been met? If the demand for goods is too large or too small for the capacity of industry, what, if anything, should public policy do about it?

Three Postwar Periods

The economy after the war will go through three overlapping periods. The first will be physical conversion from war production to civilian production. The "conversion" economy will be followed by a "catching-up" economy during which the demand for goods will be increased by needs and investment opportunities accumulated during the war and by the necessity of adjusting the size of the plant of the country to postwar levels of employment and income. As accumulated demands are satisfied, the third period will set in: the economy will face the test of whether it can become "self-sustaining" — whether a satisfactory level of demand can be generated from current needs and incomes and from currently developing investment opportunities. This

---

1. Lamont University Professor, Harvard University.

paper will deal mainly with the problems of the "catching-up" period and of a "self-sustaining" economy, but brief analysis of the conversion period will be necessary.

II. THE LEVEL OF EMPLOYMENT DURING CONVERSION

Conversion Unemployment

Many people believe that the physical, financial, and legal difficulties of conversion to civilian production will produce severe unemployment. In the closing months of the Japanese war about 25 per cent of the country's output, exclusive of that produced by the armed services, were war goods.[2] Although 3 million or more people will withdraw from the labor market, about 15 million servicemen and war workers will be looking for jobs within a year after fighting against Japan ceased, though not necessarily all at once.[3] The engineering difficulties

2. This estimate is based upon the man-hours required to produce war output and civilian output. The proportion of national product going into the war may be measured by the cost of the goods to the government or by the number of man-hours required to produce them, but the man-hour measure is on the whole preferable. The dollar measure overstates the physical size of the war effort. In 1944, for example, about 47 per cent of gross national output produced by non-servicemen, *measured in dollars,* was war goods and only a little more than one third measured by man-hours. Toward the end of the Japanese war over 40 per cent of the product of non-servicemen measured in dollars were war goods and about 30 per cent measured in man-hours.

The economic problems arising from the abrupt ending of the war were tempered by the revocation on May 10, 1945 of 73 orders prohibiting or limiting the production of civilian goods, including most of the "hard goods." This led many concerns to start civilian production in a small way and others to put their plans for conversion into final shape.

3. During the first year or so after the end of the Japanese war about 8.5 million men will be released from the armed services, 1.5 million from civilian government jobs, and 5 million from plants making combat munitions. Of the remaining 9 million men making war goods, perhaps half will be laid off at least temporarily.

Withdrawals from the labor market will depend partly upon the demand for labor. Unless demand is pressing, about a million persons of 65 years or over who have postponed retirement will leave the labor market within a year or two. During the war years the work force was abnormally swollen by the shifting of several million young men and women from schools and colleges into the armed services and war work. Many present soldiers and sailors will return to school for a year or two. The abnormal increase in women workers has been about 3.5 million — nearly all girls under 21 and women over 35. Women are leaving the labor market almost as fast as they are entering it. Once the efforts to induce women to accept industrial jobs are relaxed, the number of women in the labor market will substantially drop.

The withdrawal of women from the labor market will probably make the employment problem *more* rather than less difficult. The permanent addition of 2 or 3 million wives to the work force would mean that incomes and savings would be larger, but investment opportunities would be larger also. Two income earners in a family would greatly increase the proportion of families which become home buyers and would substantially reduce the average age at which couples start to buy homes.

alone of conversion are bound, in the opinion of many persons, to keep millions of workers idle for months.

In addition, conversion unemployment will be aggravated in some plants by lack of working capital due to delays in obtaining contract settlements from the government; by failure of the government to remove its equipment and supplies promptly; by failure to determine promptly who is to own or operate government-owned plants. So interdependent is modern industry that delay of one enterprise in converting will retard conversion in many other concerns.

Deflation Unemployment

Even more serious than "conversion" unemployment in the opinion of many people is likely to be "deflation" unemployment. Fear of unemployment will cause millions of employed persons to spend their money with caution. In addition, the withdrawal of people from the labor market, the reduction in working hours, and the movement of people from high-paying to low-paying jobs will cause pay rolls to drop more than the supply of goods. This will be a deflationary influence, especially because the drop in pay rolls will reduce the demand for farm products. Under these circumstances there is little chance, it is said, that private spending will rise rapidly enough to provide a satisfactory level of employment for a labor force of 60 million — say 57 million jobs.

Conversion Difficulties Not So Serious

These fears of large and prolonged conversion and deflation unemployment appear to be ill founded. One reason is that the engineering obstacles to conversion are much less formidable than is commonly supposed. Another reason is that the capacity of the civilian economy to absorb people promptly is greater than is generally realized.

Only about 6.5 million war workers were employed in plants (aircraft, ships, guns, explosives) which will make large permanent layoffs or which will have major engineering problems of conversion. The great majority of war workers were doing almost exactly the same thing during the war that they will do in time of peace.[4] Indeed, only about 10 per cent of war workers were in plants where engineering problems

---

4. Farming, railroading, iron and steel, textiles, clothing, shoe, petroleum, electric light and power, aluminum, chemicals, lumber, paper, machine tools are examples of important industries which produce virtually the same things for war use and civilian use.

of conversion will halt production for as long as four months. Even in these plants the process of conversion will produce considerable employment.

The capacity of nonwar production to provide jobs is reflected by the fact that early in 1945 there were approximately 35 million persons producing nonwar goods, as compared with 46 million in 1940. A small increase in the efficiency of nonwar industries has occurred, but wartime civilian production has been made possible mainly by an increase in the average weekly hours of from 10 to 15 per cent.[5] With a 40-hour work week about 4.5 million more workers in nonwar industries than the present number would be required merely to restore the low production levels of 1940.[6] No engineering difficulties will retard the opening of thousands of jobs in filling stations and garages now that people are able to drive their cars freely or the prompt filling of thousands of jobs now crying for people in stores, banks, hotels, restaurants, or on farms or in building-repair work.

All in all, unemployment attributable to the mere physical, financial, and legal impediments to conversion should not average more than eight weeks for each demobilized serviceman and war worker — a total of about 120 million weeks after the Japanese war. If this unemployment were all concentrated within 12 months, it would be equivalent to an average of about 2.3 million unemployed during the year.[7] If seasonal unemployment were one million and other types of frictional unemployment were 2 million, the average amount of unemployment during the first year after the war with Japan would be 5.3 million.[8] It will probably be less.

The danger of deflation unemployment also appears to be greatly exaggerated. Two facts stand out conspicuously: (a) the enormous unsatisfied needs of American consumers and business; and (b) the

5. Among 23 industries which are making substantially the same products now as before the war, the median increase in output per man-hour between 1939 and 1944 was 5.2 per cent. U. S. Bureau of Labor Statistics, *Productivity and Unit Labor Costs in Selected Manufacturing Industries, 1939–1943,* L.S. 45–3208, May 1945.

In 1940 average weekly hours in nondurable manufacturing (which may be regarded as roughly representative of nonwar industries) were 37; in 1944, about 43.1.

6. A. D. H. Kaplan, *The Liquidation of War Production,* McGraw-Hill, New York, 1944, p. 18.

7. Of the 18 million servicemen and war workers demobilized or laid off after the defeat of Japan, about 3 million may be expected to leave the labor market.

8. The *reported* amount of unemployment will greatly exceed the *actual* amount. Many persons who are leaving the labor market will call themselves unemployed in order to draw unemployment-insurance benefits.

unprecedented accumulation of purchasing power by consumers and business enterprises.

Accumulated Needs for Goods and Services

Let us first consider needs. Returning service men and women will need civilian attire of all sorts and in large quantities. Much more or less urgent repair and maintenance work has been accumulating — houses to be repainted and redecorated, heating systems and plumbing to be replaced or repaired, roofs to be reshingled, gutters to be replaced. Even dental and surgical work has accumulated. The shortages of durable consumer goods are large and pressing. At the time of Pearl Harbor, with 4 million people unemployed, Americans were driving nearly 28 million automobiles. At the end of 1944 the number was down to 23 million, and cars were leaving the road at the rate of 4,000 or more a day. By the end of 1945 the country will have 6 or 7 million fewer cars than at the time of Pearl Harbor. Most household electrical goods have not been made for civilian use since early in 1942. The accumulated need for these goods in the middle of 1945 may conservatively be put at well over twice the quantities sold in 1940.

The war has caused an abnormal increase of 1.1 million marriages during the four years ending with 1944. A high proportion of the 6.6 million couples married during this period have purchased little household equipment. The accumulated need for household goods after the war will stand at new highs. During the three years ending with 1944 families increased by 750,000 more than permanent dwelling units. When the servicemen come home, the country will experience one of the most acute housing shortages in its history.

Large and pressing needs on the part of industry have also accumulated. Enterprises not engaged in making combat munitions or closely related items have not been able to replace equipment. Over 600 articles containing iron and steel were not produced for civilian use between early in 1942 and the middle of 1945. A multitude of machines, tools, and instruments were made only in small quantities. During the same period equipment had rather hard usage and in many cases has been very poorly maintained.[9] The railroads will require

9. Multiple-shift operation has been especially hard upon machine tools and many other kinds of equipment.

large quantities of rolling stock and will need to make heavy expenditures on rails, ties, and ballast. The trucking industry will need about 2 million new trucks. In 1943, enterprises spent only $3.1 billion on durable equipment as compared with $5.4 billion in 1939, and $6.3 billion in 1937. In 1944, expenditures of private industry for equipment were $4 billion. The Department of Commerce estimated that, at the end of the war, industry would need to spend $8 billion for restoring inventories, $11 billion for deferred and current replacements, $2 billion for deferred maintenance, and $4 billion for reconversion — a total of $25 billion.[10] At constant prices this is two and one half times the business capital formation in 1940.

Accumulated Purchasing Power

Great and pressing needs for goods become demand only when backed by purchasing power. In the four years ending with 1944, individuals were compelled to save nearly $115 billion simply because their incomes were that much larger than the output of consumer goods at current prices. This is as much as they would have saved in 15 years at the 1940 rate. Over half of the savings of individuals have taken the form of liquid assets — cash, bank deposits, and government securities. Indeed, between the end of 1939 and the middle of 1944, individuals acquired substantially more liquid assets than in the previous 150 years of the Republic.[11] In addition, they cut their short-term indebtedness in half. More than two thirds of the increase in savings belong to persons with incomes of less than $5,000 a year — an income group

10. S. Morris Livingston and E. T. Weiler, "Can Business Finance the Transition?" *Survey of Current Business,* February 1944, p. 11.

11. The increase in liquid assets held by individuals between the end of 1939 and the end of 1944 was approximately as follows:

	December 31, 1939	December 31, 1944
	(In Billions of Dollars)	
Currency outside of banks	5.7	20.9
Demand deposits	9.6	21.4
Time deposits including postal savings	25.4	37.9
Government securities	5.9	34.9
Total	46.6	115.1

In the above estimates an effort has been made to exclude the holdings of unincorporated businesses. Excluded from the figure for government securities in December 1944, are securities held in individual trust accounts. These holdings exceeded $10 billion.

which saves little in time of peace.[12] Wartime savings will be supplemented by mustering-out payments to servicemen. The mustering-out payments already authorized by the federal government will be $3 billion and the states will probably add an equal amount in bonuses.

Business enterprises also have greatly increased their savings. Enterprises, both incorporated and unincorporated, have increased their holdings of cash, bank deposits, and government securities about $40 billion, or over 40 per cent, between the end of 1939 and the end of 1944.[13] In the same period nonfinancial corporations increased their net working capital from $24.6 to $45.5 billion.[14]

By the end of the war against Japan both unfilled needs and the accumulations of purchasing power were substantially greater than at the end of 1944.[15] The increase in needs and purchasing power will continue during much of the period of conversion.

The Willingness to Spend Freely

Will individuals and business concerns be willing to spend their enormous purchasing power freely during the conversion? That is the crucial question. During the four months immediately after the first World War, industrial production fell by 14 per cent and prices by less than 2 per cent, and department store sales held steady. Consumers bid

12. On this point see *Federal Reserve Bulletin,* October 1944, p. 958.

Individuals reporting annual income in excess of $5,000 each have only about one eighth of all individual incomes after taxes. Most of the increase in incomes during the war has gone to wage and salary workers and to farmers. Pay rolls and the income of farmers increased from $48.5 billion in 1939 to $124.6 billion in 1944. There has been only a small increase in dividend payments, which were $3.8 billion in 1939, and $4.5 billion in 1944. Interest payments and rents increased from $7.4 billion in 1939 to $10.6 billion in 1944.

13. *Federal Reserve Bulletin,* October 1944, pp. 953, 955, and 958.

14. Securities and Exchange Commission, *Statistical Series,* Release No. 750, May 22, 1945. Banks and insurance companies are excluded from the estimate.

15. The increase in liquid assets outside of banks and insurance companies was far greater during World War II than during the first World War. The direct participation of the United States in World War II lasted over twice as long as its participation in the first World War and war production has been a larger fraction of total production in the second war than in the preceding one.

By the middle of 1918, the increase in liquid assets outside of banks and insurance companies was nearly 31 per cent of income payments and about 45 per cent of expenditures on consumption. By the middle of 1919, the increase was nearly 53 per cent of expenditures on consumption. From the end of 1939 to the middle of 1944, the total increase in net liquid assets of individuals and nonfinancial corporations was about 60 per cent of income payments and over 75 per cent of expenditures on consumption at the rate of 1944. S. H. Slichter, *Present Savings and Postwar Markets,* McGraw-Hill, New York, 1943, p. 64.

up the cost of living by 22 per cent in a somewhat unsuccessful effort to obtain goods.[16] Prices should be better controlled after World War II, but the demand for goods should be large and brisk.

To begin with, a large part of the accumulated needs represent more or less pressing physical necessities. This is true of much of the need for clothing, particularly articles of cotton, silk and nylon, and possibly wool. The needs for repairs to residences and the needs for household goods and industrial equipment are pressing. Many additional needs (automobiles and radios, for example), though not based upon physical necessity, are more or less urgent. Significance attaches to the fact that individuals have put nearly as large a part of their wartime savings into cash and bank deposits as into government securities. This preference of many people for cash presumably marks an intention to buy goods when goods become available.

Even though many persons may be cautious about spending their money, big backlogs of orders will accumulate in many industries. Before automobile companies, for example, are fully able to turn out cars, the newspapers will announce that this, that, or the other company has orders on hand for five or six months' production. Such announcements will cause many of the unemployed to question whether their idleness is likely to last for long. They will become less cautious about spending their money. People who have been expecting to order cars, but who have not done so, will become concerned over the prospect of long delay in obtaining deliveries and will hasten to place their orders. By the time the automobile industry is ready to supply cars, it will have orders in hand for many months' production. What will be true of automobiles will be true of other durable goods.

Business enterprises also have many urgent physical needs on which managements will make expenditures, regardless of business conditions, as soon as goods and labor become available — repairs and replacements which are needed to reduce operating expenses and to remove operating difficulties. Furthermore, the war has given managements three or four years in which to accumulate new ideas and plans. Some of these ideas will be regarded as having great value in strengthening the competitive position of the enterprise. Replies to me from

16. I say "somewhat unsuccessful" because, in 1919, 23 per cent and, in 1920, nearly 22 per cent of the gross national product was devoted to gross private capital formation. In no year between 1921 and 1930 was as much as 19 per cent of the gross national product devoted to private capital formation.

159 enterprises during the summer of 1944 indicate that they expect to spend on the average during the first year after the war at least one and three-quarter times their prewar depreciation allowance.

III. BASIC ECONOMIC POLICIES DURING THE PERIOD OF CONVERSION

Public economic policy during the period of conversion should aim to hold the balance between the powerful inflationary and deflationary influences which will be simultaneously operating. It is important that the need for protection against *both* inflation and deflation be plainly recognized. To safeguard the country against deflation, the government should facilitate a quick shift from war production to civilian production, reform the tax system, extend and liberalize unemployment compensation schemes, and plan prompt expenditures on the repair and maintenance of public property. To guard against a disorderly rise in prices, the government should retain price controls and the regulation of consumer credit throughout the period of conversion and probably for a year or two longer. Management of the public debt may be used as an offset to either deflationary or inflationary influences. Let us examine these several possibilities.

SAFEGUARDS AGAINST DEFLATION

The interruption of production, due to a shift from war production to civilian production, is a deflationary influence. Consequently, every action and policy which facilitates a quick shift will be a protection against deflation.

Tax Reduction

Reform of the tax system will be an important protection against deflation because present taxes in many respects are a deterrent to enterprise. Reduction in taxes would, in addition, be a way of stimulating spending during conversion. Individuals and business concerns, finding their tax liabilities reduced, would spend part of the money accumulated for taxes, and would also spend a higher fraction of current incomes.[17] The prospect for lower taxes would encourage manage-

---

17. Taxes on business income are not marginal costs, but are shifted in the course of time because they reduce the proportion of new business opportunities which attract investment. The restraints upon the expansion of private output during the last few years

ments to make a large post-conversion output and spend more freely and promptly on replacements and on rebuilding inventories. Federal expenses during the first year after the war, however, will be so heavy that a substantial reduction in taxes would produce a continuation of the deficit in the budget. Consequently, the emphasis during the conversion period should be upon the reform of taxes rather than upon immediate general reduction of rates.

Proper attention to the difficult and complicated problems of tax reform would be facilitated if leaders of business, labor, and agriculture were jointly to work out a tax program designed to encourage the largest possible pay rolls and to submit their recommendations to Congress. Agreement among business, labor, and agriculture on a tax program is not beyond the range of practical achievement. Each of the groups is interested in the largest possible pay rolls. Consequently, the so-called "left" and "right" differences with respect to taxes are much less serious than is generally supposed. Furthermore, conferences between business, labor, and agriculture would safeguard each group against becoming committed to a particular tax program in opposition to all other tax programs. Although taxes should be drastically reformed, a high yield should be retained until the danger of a disorderly rise in prices has passed.

Liquidation of Government Bonds

As soon as civilian goods become available, a large rise must be expected in the redemption of war savings bonds and in the liquidation of government securities by nonfinancial corporations. Consequently, the government will be faced with problems of refinancing on a substantial scale. If deflationary influences are predominant, this refinancing could be handled in large part by resorting to the commercial banks, but if inflationary influences predominate, other methods should be used. These methods will be discussed below.

Extension of Unemployment Compensation

Extension and liberalization of unemployment compensation, needed in any event to promote the long-run stability of the economy, would help limit the cumulative effect of any unemployment which oc-

---

have given managements some opportunity to fix prices high enough to compensate for the government's share in income before taxes.

curred during the period of conversion. Before the war, unemployment benefits were only one tenth of pay roll losses caused by unemployment in the covered industries — partly because only about half of the unemployed in the covered industries qualified for benefits, partly because a substantial proportion of the unemployed received less than half of their average earnings in benefits, and partly because half of the unemployed exhausted their right to benefits while still unemployed. By liberalizing the eligibility requirements, raising the maximum weekly benefits, and increasing the weeks of benefit to which the unemployed are entitled, benefit payments should be raised to 25 per cent of the pay roll loss from unemployment in the covered industries.[18]

Public Works, Especially Repair and Maintenance

Some people believe that markets should be supported during the conversion period by a large program of public works.[19] Cities, states, and even the national government have very large accumulations of deferred maintenance and replacements and should be prepared to start work on repairs and replacements at short notice. Such projects will furnish precisely the sort of employment on which men can be started with little delay. Furthermore, repair and maintenance jobs will be of short duration and will release men by the time they are needed by private industry. Many communities, after four years of restricted building, will badly need new hospitals, schools, bridges, and other new construction. Such projects, however necessary for community welfare, would be poorly adapted to sustaining employment during the brief conversion period, because the peak of employment on most of them would not be reached until after the conversion period was over and after the catching-up demand had produced acute labor shortages in many localities.

SAFEGUARDS AGAINST INFLATION

The government should also be ready to prevent a disorderly rise in prices during conversion. In fact, as I have pointed out in the preceding

18. With higher premium rates, the offset to pay roll losses might be raised to one third.

19. Mr. Robert Moses, for example, who predicts a "tremendous" drop in employment after the war, proposes a $15 billion public works program over a three-year period. *The New York Times,* July 29, 1944, p. 15.

section, inflationary influences will be far stronger during conversion than deflationary influences.

Continuation of Price Control

Certainly price controls should be continued throughout the conversion period and probably for a year or two beyond. Poor administration of price controls could, of course, easily become a powerful deflationary influence. Increases in wages will probably be numerous even during the conversion period and in some cases these increases will be substantial. Unless appropriate price relief is granted, many firms will find it unprofitable to make certain parts of their line. A safe general rule for the price administration to follow is that prices should be set *a little higher* than necessary in relation to costs. Since profit margins in industry as a whole are less than five cents per dollar of sales, a price which is only slightly too high or too low makes a great difference in the profitableness of operations. A price which is slightly too high, under the visualized conditions, will be quickly corrected by competition, but a price which is too low will limit employment.[20]

Check on Demand Through Fiscal Policy

The retention of price controls will accentuate the need for other control devices, because it will increase the quantities of goods demanded. Some check on demand through fiscal policy is pretty certain to be needed. As I have stated above, the revenue needs of the government will continue large for a year or two after the war with Japan. For the first year, the federal budget is likely to be over $40 billion.[21] In

20. What people would lose by paying a price which is slightly too high they would largely recover in more employment and larger pay rolls.

21. Payments on completed war goods and terminated contracts will be about $11.5 billion. This assumes that when the war against Japan ended, business enterprises had unpaid bills from the government of about $3.5 billion (in March 1944 the amount was $3.7 billion) which will be reduced by the end of the year to $500 million; that business concerns had on hand $1.5 billion of completed product (slightly less than 10 days' production at $5 billion a month) which the government will pay for; that goods in process would on completion have a finished value of about $20 billion, and that $4 billion of this output will be completed and the remaining paid for at one fourth of the price for the completed articles.

If demobilization reduces the number of men in the armed services in a year from 11 million to 2.5 million, expenditures on compensation and subsistence at the rate of $1,500 per man would be $10.1 billion. Other operating expenses of the army and navy might be about $2 billion.

Mustering-out payments to servicemen are likely to be $3 billion, relief abroad (largely

addition, individuals will redeem a considerable volume of war savings bonds. If the deferred demand for durable consumer goods alone is roughly equal to two and one-half years' sales at the 1940 rate, or about $23 billion, redemptions of $2.5 billion war savings bonds during the year of conversion are not improbable.[22] Finally, many business concerns will finance conversion, deferred repairs and maintenance, and the restoration of inventories of civilian goods in large part by letting their short-term government securities run out.[23] This will be equivalent in some ways to a substantial deficit.

Present tax rates, which are estimated to yield about $45 billion for the fiscal year 1944–1945, are likely to yield at least $5 billion less during conversion.[24] Since estimates of both government expenditures and revenues during the conversion period are subject to wide error, and since the error may be compensating or aggravating, the estimates of the net position of the government are unreliable in the extreme. The deficit plus the money needed to meet redemptions of war savings bonds may be as high as $10 billion, especially if operations

during the first year after the war) may possibly be down to no more than one billion dollars, interest on the public debt will be about $5 billion, refunds under the loss carry-back provision of the corporate income tax about one billion dollars, the general administrative expenses of the government (including operation of the war agencies) about $3 billion, and miscellaneous outlays (including care of veterans, aid to agriculture, welfare grants, and public works) $5 billion.

The above figures make a total of $41.6 billion. Some of the estimates are highly conjectural.

22. This estimate assumes that redemptions are about as large as in 1944. Redemptions of Series E were $207 million in 1942, $848 million in 1943, and $2.4 billion in 1944. Redemptions occur mainly among new buyers and hence as sales fall off redemptions will tend to become less. Furthermore, most individuals will spend their cash before they redeem their bonds. Nevertheless, the production of several million automobiles and radios would cause large redemptions of Series E bonds.

23. Corporate holdings of government securities, according to the Securities and Exchange Commission, increased from $1.9 billion at the end of 1940 to $20.8 billion at the end of 1944. Most of this increase will eventually be liquidated.

24. If prices are well controlled, income payments to individuals may drop roughly 10 per cent during conversions. Overtime pay will drop but civilian employment will rise. There will be large mustering-out payments to veterans and a sharp rise in old-age pensions. The tax base may shrink by $9 billion and the yield of the income tax by $2 billion. The change in corporate profits depends upon several unpredictable factors such as the effect of shifts from war work to less profitable civilian lines, but if we assume that unit costs and prices have about the same relationship as before the war, corporate profits before taxes might drop from about $25 billion (the level of 1944) to well below $20 billion (they were $21.1 billion in 1943). Indeed, when one allows for conversion costs (but no appreciable inventory losses), the drop in corporate profits might be greater. At any rate a drop of $5 billion in corporate profits before taxes would reduce the yield of corporate income taxes by $3 billion.

against scattered Japanese guerrillas continue long after central resistance has ceased. More likely, however, is a small deficit or surplus — in other words, an approximate balance.

High Revenues Despite Reductions in Tax Liabilities

Fortunately, the need of business for the stimulus of tax reduction and the need of government for unusually high revenues for a year or two after the war can be easily reconciled. Two methods may be used. One is to change tax laws in ways which would increase the incentive of individuals and corporations to take risks but which would involve no immediate loss in revenue. For example, individuals might be permitted to charge capital losses after two years against general income, say, up to the point of reducing their tax liability by half.[25] Corporations might be permitted to offset losses against income for six years instead of two, as at present.[26] These changes would produce little immediate loss of revenue, and in the long run would increase revenue by making risky ventures more attractive.

A second way to stimulate employment, while meeting the revenue needs of the government, would be to authorize tax reductions to take effect when and if government expenditures over a given period (say three months) had dropped to a certain annual rate — to $35 billion and later to $25 billion. The nature of these tax reductions can be discussed more advantageously in connection with the fiscal problems of the catching-up period.

Continued Efforts to Sell Government Bonds to the People

If the demand for goods during conversion exceeds output, tax policy will need to be supplemented by efforts to sell government securities to individuals and business enterprises. The better the state of business and the more optimistic the people's mood, the larger will be the reductions of government security holdings by individuals and non-financial corporations and the greater will be their reluctance to buy additional governmental securities. A Victory issue, paying more than present war savings bonds, but redeemable only on extended notice

25. This provision could be made to apply only to losses realized two years after the passage of the tax law. Losses chargeable against general income might also be limited to $100,000 a year.

26. The present law permits tax losses to be carried back, as well as forward, over two years.

(say six months) might cause some people to increase their savings by a small amount. A special bond available only to servicemen and designed to attract their bonus money should be considered.

The most likely prospect, however, is that the year of conversion will see the government forced to sell large amounts of its securities to the commercial banks. This would place the burden of controlling prices more squarely than ever upon direct price controls — and upon the ability of business enterprises to produce large quantities of goods on short notice.

IV. Problems of the Catching-Up Period

THE NATURE OF THE CATCHING-UP PERIOD

The potential demand which will be awaiting industry after conversion will be enormous. It may be divided into two principal parts: (a) "replacement" demand, and (b) "adjustment" demand.

Replacement Demand and Adjustment Demand

Replacement demand, as the expression indicates, is the demand arising from the need to replace consumer goods and industrial equipment which wore out during the war and the need to restore depleted inventories of civilian goods. By the end of 1945, the replacement demand may be estimated at over $50 billion.[27] Adjustment demand will arise from the need of adjusting the size of the country's

---

27. The replacement demand will be composed of the following principal items:

	(In Billions of Dollars)
Durable consumer goods, equivalent to two and one-half years' output at the 1940 rate at prices 25 per cent above 1940	23.1
Nondurable consumer goods (exclusive of services) at one tenth of the purchases in 1944	6.0
Deficiency in residential construction, 750,000 dwelling units	3.5
Replacement of industrial equipment, equal to one and one-half years' purchases at the 1939 rate at 25 per cent above 1939 prices	10.3
Restoration of civilian inventories	9.0
Total	51.9

There will be a sizable deficiency in repairs to residences, industrial buildings, and public buildings and structures and also in personal services, particularly medical and dental services. Finally, there will be some replacement of industrial plant. For example, the replacement of industrial plant will probably be equivalent to industrial plant construction in 1939 at prices 25 per cent above 1939. This would come to $2 billion.

industrial plant and the quantity and quality of its housing to the much larger national incomes which will follow the war.

Adjustment demand is even more difficult to estimate than replacement demand because it is sensitive to cost-price relationships and to the outlook for profits. Over the last several generations, however, the country has maintained an investment of about $2 in factories, mines, railroads, public utilities, stores, office buildings, and inventories for every dollar of consumer goods produced each year. If consumers are spending soon after the war over $35 billion more for goods than in 1940 (in terms of 1944 dollars), the country will need to increase its industrial plant, equipment, and inventories by roughly $70 billion. Indeed, the adjustment demand may be considerably larger, because even in 1940 the country had less plant and equipment than was needed for reasonably full employment. During the previous ten years the work force had increased by six million with virtually no net additions to plant.[28] Adjustment demand for housing will also be very large. With a purchasing power of per capita incomes after taxes of 50 per cent or more above 1939, millions of people will be unwilling to put up with present housing.[29] If construction costs are not out of line with other prices, expenditures equal to one fourth or one third of the replacement cost of present housing may be warranted to adjust the quality of housing to postwar incomes.

Adjustment Demand Will Be Later and More Elastic

The replacement demand will be much less sensitive than adjustment demand to cost-price relationships, the size and trend of incomes, the outlook for profits, and the nature of public policies. Some adjustment demand will make itself felt immediately after the war. In general, however, it will be slower in appearing than the replacement demand and will be based much less upon physical necessities. Hence,

28. Despite large construction of war plants the present level of employment has been achieved only by working people nights. With 57 million people employed after the war (including 4.4 million in government civilian service and 2.5 million in the armed forces), the volume of nongovernment employment will be about 4.2 million more than in 1944. These additional people will need places to work and machines to run. In most industries they will not be content indefinitely to work nights.

29. Most of the demand for new housing comes from families receiving $2,000 a year or more. In 1939 there were approximately 10 million persons with incomes of $1,500 or more — the equivalent of about $2,000 in 1945. If income payments to individuals after the war are about $147 billion, there will be 25 million with incomes of $2,000 a year or more.

one may expect the catching-up period to go through two overlapping, but more or less distinct, phases: the "replacement" phase and the "adjustment" phase.

THE LEVEL OF EMPLOYMENT DURING THE CATCHING-UP PERIOD

The level of employment is fixed at the point where the output of goods meets the demand for goods. So long as the demand generated by a given volume of employment exceeds the output of that many workers, employment will rise.

Estimating the Output

If the work force in 1947 consists of approximately 60 million men, a satisfactory level of employment would be about 57 million.[30] At 5 per cent more hours per week than in 1940, with the efficiency of nonagricultural labor at 10 per cent above 1940, with the prices of nonagricultural finished goods at 25 per cent above 1940, and with agricultural products selling at 15 per cent below 1944, 57 million persons would produce an annual gross product of about $178 billion.[31] The demand for goods by 57 million persons early in the catching-up period may be expected to exceed $178 billion a year. Let us analyze this demand.

30. These figures are monthly averages. The seasonal highs and lows would be more than a million above and below the monthly average.

31. This amount is derived as follows:

	(*In Billions of Dollars*)
Armed forces	2.8
Interest on public debt	6.0
Nonagricultural civilian output	156.9
Agricultural output	12.2
Total	177.9

Hours are estimated at 5 per cent above 1940 because this is the maximum increase which is possible without incurring considerable penalty overtime. The estimate of 10 per cent above 1940 in the output per hour of nonagricultural labor is less than the normal gain. If the estimates of the Bureau of Labor Statistics for nonwar industries are approximately correct (see footnote 5), it is a gain of about 5 per cent above 1944. The immediate effect of war seems to be to retard the increase in industrial efficiency. The assumed output for nonagricultural civilian employees in 1947 at prices 25 per cent above 1940 is $3,464 per worker as against $2,399 in 1940. Agricultural employment is assumed to rise from a monthly average of 8.1 million in 1944 to the same level as in 1940 — namely, 9.2 million. In the case of agriculture, the rise in the number employed is assumed to be offset by a drop in hours worked per week, so that the physical product remains the same as in 1944.

Estimating the Demand

Local and state governments would take about $10 billion of the gross national product and the national government about $19 billion. This would leave $149 billion of output available for individuals, business concerns, and foreign customers. If the national product were $178 billion, income payments to individuals would be about $147 billion.[32] After payment of personal income taxes, individuals would have about $134 billion to spend on consumer goods or to save.[33] How much would they spend on consumption?

After an upheaval so disturbing to living habits as the war, a projection of prewar consumption patterns cannot be expected to yield accurate estimates of expenditures.[34] During the last sixty years, however,

32. This estimate is based upon the following assumptions:

	(In Billions of Dollars)
Gross national product	178
Less business taxes	18
Less business reserves	10
Add social security, relief, and transfer payments	7
Less corporate undivided profits	6
Less contributions to social security funds	4
Income payments to individuals	147

Business taxes during the early part of the catching-up period are likely to be high. Nevertheless, deductions for losses may bring them below the figure assumed which is almost 33 per cent below 1944. Business reserves are assumed to be the same as in 1944 and undivided corporate profits slightly above 1944. Social security and relief payments, though somewhat larger than most estimates which I have seen, may even be larger than I have assumed. Many people who leave the labor market will draw unemployment compensation. Payments to veterans will be large. The rise in old-age insurance payments is particularly difficult to forecast. If employment opportunities are good, retirements will be postponed and pension payments will be kept down. After the old-age insurance tax is increased, contributions to social security funds will be more than $4 billion.

33. This presupposes fairly stiff federal personal income taxes — yielding about $11 billion (as against $17 billion at the present high rates). State income taxes are assumed to yield about $2 billion. It is assumed that total federal taxes (business plus personal) will exceed federal expenditures for goods and services (i.e., excluding $3 billion transfer payments) by $2 billion and that local and state governments will spend for goods $1 billion more than their incomes.

34. Among the changes which may cause a much larger or smaller fraction of incomes to be spent on consumption after the war than before are:

1. The distribution of income may be substantially different.

2. Income tax payments after the war will be roughly three times as large as prewar. About two thirds of them will be made by persons receiving $5,000 a year or more — the income classes who before the war did two thirds or more of the saving. A rise in income payments from $70.8 billion (about $93 billion in prices of 1944) to $147 billion would increase the income payments to persons receiving $5,000 a year or more from $18 billion (in 1944 prices) to about $38 billion and income after taxes from about $14.9 bil-

despite great changes in commodities and modes of living and the great rise in real incomes, the proportion of income devoted to con· sumption has remained surprisingly steady — showing a slight tendency to increase.[35] During most of the last twenty years, except years of depression, about 89 per cent of disposable income has been spent for consumption.[36] Were this stability of spending pattern to continue after the war, the expenditure of about $119 billion for consumption goods would accompany a disposable income of $134 billion.

Let us check this figure by recent experience. In 1944, when people had incomes of $137.5 billion after paying their personal taxes, individuals spent $90.9 billion on nondurable goods and services. Over one tenth of the adult population were in the armed services and were being fed, clothed, housed, and given medical attention by the government. If beefsteaks, milk, butter, cheese, fuel oil, gasoline, tires, cigarettes, cigars, candy, silk, nylon, film, Pullman space, and hotel accommodations had been readily available, if people had had time to take vacations, if they had not been buying war savings bonds as a patriotic duty, and if 8.5 million (out of 11 million) servicemen had been civilians buying their own food, clothing, shelter, and medical services, would not the civilian demand for nondurable goods have been at least 15 per cent more than it actually was? At this rate of

---

lion (in 1944 prices) in 1939 to about $28 billion in postwar. From this increase of about $13.1 billion will come most of the increase above prewar in individual saving.

3. The disposition of individuals to save may be affected by the huge amount of saving that has occurred during the war. Habits of saving acquired during the war may persist after the war. More likely, however, the large accumulation of savings during the war may make people ready to spend their incomes more freely.

4. The disposition to save depends partly upon expectations concerning the future. Optimistic expectations (belief that one's income will rise or that tax rates will fall) encourage spending. Pessimistic expectations (belief that one's income over the long run will fall, that tax burdens will rise, or any other fears for the future) encourage saving. Between 1922 and 1929, when individual incomes were rising, the proportion of incomes saved had a slight tendency to decline — largely because the optimism generated by rising incomes discouraged saving. The level of saving after the war will depend upon whether individuals are optimistic or pessimistic about their future incomes.

5. The war, and developments stimulated by the war, are changing living habits. There has been an enormous extension of vacations with pay and revolutionary changes in transportation. As a result, expenditures on vacations may be greatly increased. The number of persons eligible for old-age insurance on retirement has greatly increased, and the time when their pensions will be payable will be much closer in 1947 than it was in 1940.

35. S. S. Kuznets, "Capital Formation, 1879–1938," University of Pennsylvania Bicentennial Conference, *Studies in Economics and Industrial Relations,* p. 70.

36. C. Warburton, "Monetary Expansion and the Inflationary Gap," *The American Economic Review,* Vol. 34, June 1944, pp. 305 and 307.

spending, a demand for about $101.8 billion of nondurable goods and services would accompany an income of $134 billion after taxes. On durable goods (automobiles, refrigerators, radios, oil burners, household utensils, garden tools, cameras, and other articles expected to last more than a year) consumers spend in good years about 10 per cent of their incomes after taxes. This would indicate a demand of about $13.4 billion. Total expenditures on consumer goods after the war would be $115.2 billion, close to the estimate in the preceding paragraph. Let us use this lower of the two estimates.

Allowing for Deferred Demand

Allowance must be made for the deferred demand that has accumulated during the war. Let us assume, in order to be conservative, that *no* deferred demand for nondurable goods has accumulated — though large needs for clothing, repairs, and many forms of services have been piling up. The deferred demand for durable goods by the end of 1945 may be put at two and a half times the quantities sold in 1940, or about $23.1 billion. Actually it will probably be considerably larger — particularly if substantial bonuses are paid to servicemen. If the catching-up demand for durable goods were spread over three years, it would average $7.7 billion a year, and it may exceed $10 billion for a year or two.

Individuals buy new housing as well as consumers' goods. Despite the acute housing shortage, building will be retarded in the early years after the war by the disposition of many prospective home buyers to await clarification of postwar trends. Let us assume that residential building will be no greater in physical volume than in 1940, or about $3 billion at 1944 prices.

What quantities of goods will business demand? The normal demand for plant and equipment in a fairly good year is about 9 or 10 per cent of the gross national product.[37] With the large amounts of deferred maintenance the proportion would probably be higher than in 1929, when 12.1 per cent of gross national product went into plant and equipment. Let us assume, to be conservative, that business ex-

---

37. The portion of gross national product spent on business plant and equipment in selected recent years was: 1923, 10.1 per cent; 1925, 10.2 per cent; 1926, 10.8 per cent; 1929, 12.1 per cent; 1936, 8.2 per cent; 1937, 9.5 per cent; 1939, 8 per cent; 1942, 9.2 per cent.

penditures on plant and equipment are only 10 per cent of gross national product, or $17.8 billion. Restoration of inventories will take about $3 billion a year for two or three years. The great needs of the rest of the world, the destruction of productive capacity in many countries, the large foreign balances in the United States, and large foreign holdings of gold will cause the export of goods from this country to exceed imports, at least for several years after the war, by $3 billion a year or more — considerably less than at the end of the first World War.[38]

All of this adds up to a total demand for goods by the governments (national, state, and local) of $29 billion a year, by consumers (including residential building) of $125.9 billion, and by business and foreigners of $23.8 billion, or a grand total of $178.7. This is slightly more than $178 billion, the estimated output of 57 million men working 5 per cent more hours and at 10 per cent greater efficiency than in 1940. Evidently, the demand for goods during the early part of the catching-up period is likely to test the capacity of American industry.

PRICE MOVEMENTS DURING THE CATCHING-UP PERIOD

Important postwar changes in the *structure* of prices now appear to be virtually certain. The prices of farm products have risen nearly 100 per cent since 1939; raw materials, 60 per cent; finished goods, 25 per cent. Prices of farm products will fall.[39] Unions, after several years of restraint during the war, will press for higher wages. The rise in wage rates will limit the drop in pay rolls and thus help to limit the drop in agricultural prices.[40] The reduction in working hours and loss of take-

38. The figure of $3 billion would not include goods purchased by our government and given or loaned to other countries.

39. Although the prices of farm products are likely to be lower by 1948 than in 1944, they will be substantially above prewar. Cash receipts from farm marketings in recent years have fluctuated between 10 and 14 per cent of the incomes of individuals after taxes. This proportion has obtained regardless of whether the total national income was large or small and regardless of whether the prices of food were high or low. If cash receipts from farm marketings are 12 per cent of a disposable income of $134 billion, they will be $16.1 billion in comparison with $19.9 billion in 1944. Output of farm products in years of normal weather will be 20 to 25 per cent larger than in prewar years. If most other prices remain at approximately the levels of 1945, if the government does not seriously interfere and if there is no important new foreign competition, prices of farm products during the early catching-up period will be about 15 per cent below the levels of early 1945.

40. The drop in government pay rolls will be considerably more than the drop in pri-

home pay will stimulate the demands of unions and the strong market for labor will enable unions to enforce increases.[41] Labor efficiency, which has gained little during the war, may be expected to rise rapidly.[42] Nevertheless, a substantial rise in wage rates will probably mean some increase in the prices of many finished goods. Among the prices paid by the ultimate consumer, rents, which have advanced little, will rise substantially, and many foods and many articles of apparel will drop.

Increase in Prices: Moderate or Rapid?

Although important changes in the structure of prices are in prospect, rapid changes in the general level of prices will probably be avoided. Serious weaknesses in prices might develop were an "air pocket" in demand to occur between the replacement and the adjustment phases of the catching-up period. This possibility will be discussed later. On the other hand, the deferred demand for consumer durable goods may become quite impatient. Servicemen will spend their mustering-out pay and state bonuses promptly. The acute housing shortage may cause the demand for residential building to develop more rapidly than I have assumed. Foreign balances in this country and gold holdings are enormous and a large part of them may become impatient demand. If a great demand for commercial and industrial construction occurs while the replacement demand for consumer goods is still large and before industrial efficiency or productive capacity have been substantially increased, prices may be difficult to control. Bank de-

---

vate pay rolls because there will be an increase in nongovernment employment. At wage rates 10 per cent above 1944 and with 38 million nongovernment employees and 6.9 million government employees (including 2.5 million men in the armed services) I estimate that nongovernment pay rolls will be about $84.5 billion and government pay rolls about $13 billion compared with $88.4 billion and $24 billion respectively in 1944. This estimate is crude and is not based upon detailed assumptions concerning distribution of the work force. Often overlooked is the fact that nongovernmental employees shortly after the war will be about 10 per cent more numerous than in 1944.

41. Are wage increases likely to reduce the demand for labor and goods by encroaching upon profits or are they likely to bring about offsetting increases in prices? Whether wage increases are inflationary or deflationary depends upon circumstances. In times when a large part of the demand for capital goods is sensitive to the prospect of profits, a rise in costs may have a deflationary effect. An important peculiarity of the "replacement" phase of the catching-up period will be the abnormally large demand for both capital goods and consumer goods which will be relatively insensitive to prices.

42. Although *realized* gains in labor efficiency during the war have been small, the *potential* gains have been appreciable. Many improvements in methods have been developed and much valuable experience has been acquired.

posits are likely to rise substantially — the result of liquidation of government securities by individuals and nonfinancial corporations and the sale of refunding issues to commercial banks. The turnover of bank deposits in 1944 was about 11 per cent below 1939. When consumers have more leisure to spend their money, when they are able to buy the kind of goods they desire, when they anticipate tax reductions, when the fear of postwar depression has evaporated, when restrictions on the purchase of materials by business and on production are removed, one must expect the turnover of money to rise. The expansion of deposits and the rise in turnover could easily cause trouble.[43]

Despite the possibility of a too-rapid advance in prices during the catching-up period, I believe that any rise will, on the whole, be moderate and orderly. The public has shown greater willingness to hold large quantities of cash than most people would have predicted. People also seem to be developing an unwillingness to reach for goods at high prices. Considerable buying will be deferred after the war in expectation that goods embodying important improvements will soon be available. Finally, business will be far better prepared than after the first World War to raise its efficiency and to increase its capacity.

THE POSSIBLE "AIR POCKET" BETWEEN REPLACEMENT AND ADJUSTMENT PHASES

Much of the large replacement demand will be met within a very short period. Replacements of clothing, and most deferred repair work, and restoration of inventories will probably be completed within two or three years. Foreign buying will probably also drop substantially about the same time.

If the replacement demand generates enough adjustment demand, particularly building construction, to offset the drop in replacements, the shift from the replacement phase to the adjustment phase of the catching-up economy will be smoothly accomplished. If the replacement demand, however, is crowded into too short a period and produces a substantial rise in prices but fails to generate very much adjustment demand, the economy may experience a sort of air pocket in demand and a severe, though possibly short, depression.

43. With the turnover of deposits as high as 1939 and physical production 60 per cent above 1939, prices would be about 20 per cent above 1944. Were the rise to occur rapidly, it would touch off speculative buying.

V. PUBLIC ECONOMIC POLICIES DURING THE CATCHING-UP PERIOD

What public policies are indicated by the economic prospects during the catching-up period? What should the government do about prices, taxes, management of the debt, the possibility of an air pocket in demand? What should it do to facilitate the smooth transition from the catching-up economy to a self-supporting economy?

PROBLEMS OF PRICE POLICY DURING THE CATCHING-UP PERIOD

Continued Price Control

The prospect that the huge catching-up demand will tax the capacity of industry indicates the need of keeping wartime price controls for a year or two or longer after the conversion period. Possibly industry will increase output and cut costs so rapidly that these controls will be unnecessary, but they should be available if needed. The public, it is true, may refuse to tolerate the retention of wartime rationing and price controls. It is difficult, however, in 1945 to determine just what the public will tolerate in 1947. When consumers become vividly aware of the huge deferred demand for goods, particularly durable goods, continuation of price controls may receive strong support.

War Surpluses, Export Control, Credit Control

Direct price controls may be supplemented by other methods. There will be government-owned surpluses to be sold. The commercially usable surpluses, however, will be small in relation to consumer demand. Informal controls may be established over the expenditure in the United States of the enormous foreign-held balances of exchange and gold.[44] Although a few countries will lack dollar exchange, the world as a whole for several years will have too much for the capacity of American industry. Machine tools, which will be in great demand for a limited period, could be supplied by the United States in huge quantities, but foreign purchases of automobiles and other consumer goods will have to be restricted for a year or two. Loans should be made sparingly to countries which need capital. The United States should encourage imports by consenting to moderate undervaluations of foreign currencies in relation to the long-run competing power of the foreign country.

---

44. Canada, Sweden, Switzerland and Australia will, of course, undoubtedly get their share of the business in finished goods.

"Regulation W," restricting credits to consumers, should be given a statutory basis and continued, with minor modifications, but it cannot be counted upon to restrict substantially the demand for consumer durable goods. People will be too well able to buy without borrowing. The huge holdings of government securities by the commercial banks plus the undertaking of the Reserve Banks to support the price of government securities presents new and different problems of credit control. An expansion of business could easily lead the banks to increase their reserves (and their loans and investments) by selling government securities in large amounts. Such action could not be tolerated. In order to give the Reserve System more adequate control over increases in demand deposits, the Board of Governors should be given wider authority to fix the reserves required of member banks.[45] Most important of all, fiscal policy and management of the debt will need to contribute to the implementation of price policy. The use of these devices during the catching-up period will be discussed presently.

The avoidance of a disorderly rise in prices of finished goods during the catching-up period may require that the government postpone well-meant plans for stimulating business through public construction. After three or four years of restricted building, the several governments will have large construction needs — some of them urgent. Nevertheless during the replacement phase of the catching-up period, the local, state, and national governments should exercise foresight and ingenuity to keep public construction to a minimum.

Limiting the Drop in Prices of Farm Products

No less important than avoiding a disorderly rise in the prices of finished goods early in the catching-up period will be the prevention of a disorderly drop in farm prices about two or three years after the end of the war. As I have pointed out, the avoidance of a substantial drop in farm prices requires a considerable rise in wage rates. If wage rates are gradually increased about 20 per cent during the first several years after the war, pay rolls will be well above $112 billion by the time that deficiencies in food stocks have been made up. This would

45. With business enterprises as liquid as they will be after the war, credit controls, even at the best, will have only limited effect upon the demand for goods. The net increase in the working capital of corporations between 1939 and the middle of 1944 was nearly four times the current volume of commercial loans by national banks to corporations.

prevent a substantial drop in the prices of farm products (see footnote 39). Rapid technological progress, however, will be needed to prevent increases in wage rates from forcing large advances in the prices of nonagricultural products. Since the government has undertaken to support the prices of many farm products at 90 per cent of parity for two or three years after the end of the war (and since serious weakness in farm prices would create a demand for an extension of the guarantee), it is important that the rise in wages does not produce substantial increases in nonagricultural prices. This can be avoided only by rapid technological progress.

TAX POLICY DURING THE CATCHING-UP PERIOD

Some people believe that the government should guard against possible general weakness in prices by operating at a deficit during the catching-up period. The secular growth in production and incomes, it is said, would gradually raise the yield of taxes until a balanced budget is ultimately achieved.

Federal Expenditures and Tax Revenues

The sponsors of budget deficits during the catching-up period point out that very stiff tax rates will be necessary to balance the large postwar budget. The normal postwar budget of the government will be at least $20 billion a year — over three times the amount raised by federal taxes in 1939.[46] During the early years of the catching-up period federal expenditures will be substantially above the postwar normal — by several billion dollars a year or more.[47]

---

46. Estimates of the postwar budget vary with assumptions. It seems realistic to assume a large army and navy and substantial payments on social welfare. Such assumptions yield the following results:

	(*In Billions of Dollars*)
General administrative expense	2
Army and navy	6
Interest on public debt	6
Social welfare and continuing service to veterans (exclusive of social insurance)	3
Miscellaneous subsidies and other items	3
	20

This estimate is probably too low rather than too high. Furthermore, federal expenditures will probably not reach the normal postwar level until four or five years after the war.

47. After the first World War the federal budget did not reach the approximate postwar normal until the fiscal year 1921–1922.

The tax rates necessary to produce this amount will be very stiff. Indeed, a yield of $11 billion from the federal personal income tax (about half the budget) at income payments of about $147 billion a year, would require that a man with two dependents pay about 33 per cent on income immediately above $15,000, about 40 per cent on income immediately above $20,000, and 50 per cent on income immediately above $75,000.[48] These tax rates would have to be supplemented by stiff taxes upon corporate incomes and substantial excise taxes.

Income tax rates of such height would greatly limit the willingness of the well-to-do, who do most of the saving, to embark upon risky ventures. When venture capital does not go to work, large amounts of security-seeking capital remain uninvested, because security-seeking capital requires the cushion of protection which venture capital gives. In view of the stiff tax rates needed to balance the budget during the catching-up period, would not the country be wise to incur a deficit until the rise in national income, by increasing the yield in taxes, brings about a balanced budget?

Budget Deficits?

The answer to this question, in my judgment, is "No." The catching-up period, with its heavy replacement and adjustment demand will be unusually favorable to employment. Consequently, a tax system which prevented high employment during this period would not permit it a few years after the replacement and investment demand have been met. The *kind* of taxes affects the volume of employment no less than does the *level* of taxes. Furthermore the tax system is extraordinarily bad. Consequently reform of taxes has great promise of making possible both high employment and a balanced budget.

Reform of the Tax System

How should the tax system be reformed? There are three principal ways of making a living: (a) working for others, (b) lending one's

48. The rates will vary, of course, with the size of exemptions and the steepness of the progression. The above figures assume exemptions of $500 for each income recipient and each dependent, as in the 1944 act. These exemptions would exclude from the tax base somewhat more than half of the income received by individuals. The rate which is most important in determining the effect of taxes upon employment is the *marginal* rate of taxation — that is, the fraction of any increment of income going to the government. Keeping exemptions low is a way of keeping the average rate of taxes high, while keeping down the marginal rate of taxation.

capital, (c) becoming the owner or part owner of a business. The busi-ness owner may be a self-employed operator of his own business, or he may be a stockholder in a huge corporation. Regardless of whether the business owner uses only his own labor and his own capital or whether he hires labor and capital, he makes his living (or part of it) by putting men and capital to work. A tax system, in order to yield large revenues without limiting employment, should be designed to make business ownership attractive. It should encourage people to make all or part of their living either by self-employment or by becoming owners or part owners of business concerns; it should encourage enterprises to im-prove and enlarge their plants and equipment; it should foster inno-vation, pioneering, and new enterprises; it should help the community produce resourceful and adventurous men who are willing to risk large losses in the hope of achieving large gains.

By these tests the present tax system is very bad indeed. It penal-izes heavily the creation of jobs because much of the income derived from giving jobs (the distributed part of corporate profits) is taxed at far higher rates than income derived from holding jobs or lending capital. Pioneering, innovation, and expansion are discouraged be-cause the government takes a large share of the gains and allows only a meager offset to losses. This reduces the attractiveness of risky invest-ments relative to safe investments. The income from business owner-ship is especially uncertain and income from new concerns is even more uncertain than income from established concerns. Consequently the present tax system encourages men to avoid business ownership and in particular it stacks the cards against new concerns. Especially unfortu-nate is the fact that the larger a man's income the less attractive under present tax laws are risky ventures in relation to safe ones. The shun-ning of risks by the well-to-do is revealed by the fact that the propor-tion of total dividends going to persons with net incomes of over $50,000 dropped from nearly 40 per cent in 1925 to 25 per cent in 1939 — although this drop to some extent represents the transfer of securi-ties to wives and children.

Restrictive Effects of Taxes Mitigated Through Shifting

Is the tax system, however, really as bad as it seems? If the volume of enterprise is restricted by taxes, are not the supply of goods and the demand for labor and loan capital also limited? Do not the prices paid by consumers, therefore, gradually rise relative to wages and interest rates (or wages and interest rates fall relative to prices) so that the taxes on enterprise are gradually shifted to consumers, employees, and lenders of capital? After the tax has been so shifted, it no longer limits enterprise.

Taxes on corporations are in the long run probably fairly completely shifted, at least in unregulated industries where nearly all production is carried on by corporations. For that reason too much attention has probably been paid to the effect of the corporation tax upon employment. Nevertheless, the shifting of the tax occurs only slowly and painfully, because the tax does not directly affect marginal costs. It produces a new price structure by reducing the attractiveness of investment opportunities and thus temporarily limiting investment and temporarily producing unemployment. Certainly the enormous increase in corporate taxes during the last thirteen years has not been completely shifted.

The progressive tax upon individual incomes is shifted much less completely than the tax upon corporate incomes — in fact, for the most part, the personal income tax is probably not shifted at all. The progressive income tax means that the net yield on an investment varies for each income recipient. Under our tax rates the variation is wide. The relationship between prices and costs may never change sufficiently to offset the high marginal rates paid by large income recipients. As a result, stiff progressive income taxes may permanently tax out of existence for many savers large numbers of risky investment opportunities and thus may lower the level of employment at which the economy reaches equilibrium.

Six Important Changes in the Tax System

The tax system may be reformed to encourage enterprise and raise employment by the following steps:

1. Repeal the excess-profits tax. This tax virtually deprives many enterprises of an incentive to do more business than they did in 1939, and in particular handicaps new concerns which need to increase their capital out of earnings. The tax should remain for at least a year after the war in order to capture war profits and should be repealed in two steps in order to avoid stimulating unhealthy speculation in securities. Without delay, however, the income exempt from the excess-profits tax should be raised from $10,000 to $50,000. A larger exemption is particularly important to new enterprises.

2. Permit business losses to be carried forward six years as an offset against income from business, corporate and noncorporate. This provision would be particularly helpful in encouraging men to back new enterprises, but it would also stimulate innovations and experiments of all sorts.

3. Permit long-term capital losses to be deducted against personal income up to the point of reducing tax liability by half or not more than $100,000, as I suggested in Section III. This provision would also be important in making capital available to new enterprises.

4. Reduce the corporate income tax to slightly above the prewar level — say 20 per cent. The full rate should not apply to corporate incomes below $50,000 a year. The reduction to 20 per cent should be spread over four or five years, but should be authorized in advance to permit the expectation of decreases to stimulate employment. Since the price structure has probably become fairly well adjusted to the prewar corporate tax, it is not imperative that corporation taxes be reduced below 20 per cent. Exemption of corporate incomes up to $50,000 from the full tax is desirable to compensate small enterprises for their special difficulties in raising capital.

5. Tax incomes from self-employment or from dividends at substantially lower rates than from salaries or interest. The differential in surtax rates need not extend below $10,000 a year. It is important, however, to make business ownership and especially risky ventures attractive to persons who pay high surtaxes. High surtax rates on salaries and on income derived from interest do no particular harm to employment. Hence, it would be wasteful to reduce taxes on all parts of large incomes in order to make business ownership and risk-taking attractive to the well-to-do. Reductions in taxes on personal incomes should be spread over several years, but authorized in advance.

6. Tax the proportion of income invested in new plant or equipment or invested in new equity issues used for financing new plant or equipment at less than the standard surtax rates.[49]

Effects of Taxes on Saving and Investment

The proposed reforms would give the country a tax system which would raise the demand for labor by giving strong encouragement to people to derive incomes from making jobs. More specifically the proposed reforms would increase the attractiveness of starting new business enterprises and would make the savings of the well-to-do an important source of adventurous capital — as they should be.

Many people believe that surtaxes should vary only with the size of income, not with sources or uses of income. This policy would greatly increase the difficulty of getting surtaxes on personal incomes low enough to induce the well-to-do to assume their share of business risks.

49. The simplest way to handle this provision administratively would be to require taxpayers to pay the standard tax, but to permit them to apply for an abatement.

Liberal offsets to losses would help, but might not be sufficient because men who take long chances usually expect to win rather than to lose. Nevertheless, if the corporate income tax were kept quite high (say at 40 per cent with lower taxes on corporate incomes of less than $50,000 a year), the revenue needs of the government might be met with sur-taxes on large incomes low enough not seriously to impede risk-taking. During the catching-up period the corporate tax would probably be shifted in most lines of industry rather promptly to consumers.

Some people believe that employment would be stimulated more ef-fectively by keeping corporation taxes high (say at 40 per cent) and raising the exemptions in the personal income tax and reducing cer-tain excise taxes which fall largely on small income recipients. This reasoning assumes that the corporation tax falls on corporations, which means on the stockholders. As many stockholders are savers, higher corporate income taxes, together with a higher exemption on personal incomes and lower excise taxes, would mean that the demand for goods by the government would be financed to some extent by reducing the saving of individuals rather than by reducing their consumption. As a result the consumption function would be more favorable to employ-ment.

The above reasoning is defective because it overlooks the fact that a tax on corporations, until shifted, reduces investment opportunities and, after it has been shifted, falls largely upon consumers of products made by corporations. During the catching-up period the corporate income tax in most industries would be shifted rather promptly. Con-sequently, the proposal simply amounts to the suggestion that con-sumers of products produced mainly by corporations be subjected to a special tax burden in order to relieve other consumers of paying an ex-cise tax. It is not significant from the standpoint of total employment.

How far the community should go in reducing the yield of taxes dur-ing the catching-up period obviously depends upon how far it is willing to go in reforming taxes to encourage job-making and risk-taking. If the reforms are thorough, rates will need to be high enough to yield a large surplus — especially during the catching-up period. The opti-mism engendered by reforms in taxes would stimulate individuals to buy goods and enterprises to expand and improve their plants. This in turn would increase the liquidation of government securities. The re-

sulting need for a budget surplus is discussed below in connection with
the problem of managing the public debt.

THE MANAGEMENT OF THE PUBLIC DEBT

Demand for Bond Redemption

If war finance ends with individuals holding some $60 billion of government securities and nonfinancial corporations $30 billion, as seems
likely, liquidation by individuals will probably run about $2 billion a
year and by nonfinancial corporations about $4 to $7 billion. As I have
pointed out above, the more prosperous the economy and the more
optimistic people's mood, the larger will be the liquidation of government securities.

During prosperous years it will be desirable for the government
to meet part of its refinancing needs by selling its securities to individuals and nonfinancial corporations. This will prevent liquidation
by individuals and corporations from producing an inflationary effect
and will build up future demand for consumer goods.

During the catching-up period, however, large sales of government
securities to individuals and nonfinancial corporations will not be easily
accomplished. People who have saved far more than usual for three or
four years and have postponed purchasing many things will not be in a
mood to buy government securities instead of goods.[50]

Some government securities will be sold to government trust funds
(especially if the old-age pension tax is raised, as it should be), to savings banks, and to insurance companies. The free funds of savings
banks and insurance companies, however, will be largely needed to
help meet the demands of new concerns for capital, of some old concerns for working capital, and of a multitude of people for mortgage
money. It is important to note that the large redemption of government
securities to make first payments on homes will create an enormous demand for mortgage money by persons who would not otherwise have
demanded it. In the main, therefore, the refinancing needs of the government during the catching-up period will have to be met either by
the commercial banks or by a budget surplus.

---

50. Many pay roll deduction plans, perhaps most of them, will be kept in effect. They
are a convenient way of saving and, for that reason, are attractive to many workers.

Refinancing or Budget Surplus?

Refinancing through commercial banks would, of course, mean an expansion of demand deposits. Indeed a substantial increase of demand deposits ($15 billion and probably much more) in the first five years after the war is to be expected. If the reform of taxes is feeble and half-hearted and if public policies continue to be hostile to enterprise, considerable refinancing through the commercial banks may be needed in order to stimulate the economy. On the other hand, if the government does a good job of reforming taxes and of encouraging business, if commercial loans are expanding, and if the velocity of circulation of money is rising, a substantial increase in demand deposits as a result of the shift of government securities into the banks would make the prevention of a too-rapid rise in prices difficult in the extreme. Let me repeat, the more thoroughly taxes are reformed to encourage enterprise, the larger will be the budget surplus needed.

THE PROBLEM OF AN AIR POCKET IN DEMAND

Both the government and business should be prepared to prevent an air pocket in demand from developing between the replacement and adjustment phases of the catching-up period and to mitigate its effects in case it does occur.

Spreading the Replacement Demand

Whatever helps to prevent a disorderly and speculative rise in prices, reduces the danger of an air pocket. If the rise in prices is controlled, replacement buying will be spread over more years than if consumer purchasing power were largely absorbed by a rapid advance in prices. The longer the replacement phase of the catching-up period, the less is the danger that the various replacement demands will terminate so closely together as to produce a precipitous drop in total demand. Fortunately the large demand for automobiles will give support to business — indeed, in the first decade after the war domestic purchases of passenger cars are likely to be well over fifty million.

Adjustment Demand Depends on Taxes and Building Costs

The extent to which the replacement demand generates adjustment demand will depend (a) upon the reform of taxes and (b) upon building costs. The reform of taxes should occur early in the catching-up period in order that business concerns may have a clear basis for long-term planning. The large number of men who have learned the building trades in the shipyards during the war and the brisk competition which promises to prevail between raw materials and methods of construction after the war may prevent building costs from rising above other prices. Nevertheless, trade unions, employers, and the government should be alert to the danger of a rise in building costs limiting the expansion of construction.

To mitigate the effects of an air pocket in demand, should one occur, the economy should be well provided with arrangements to limit the contraction in private spending and to offset its effects. Discussion of such arrangements can advantageously be postponed to Section XI which will deal in general terms with the problem of limiting fluctuations in economic activity.

VI. The Prospects for Employment in a Self-Supporting Economy

The duration of the catching-up period cannot be predicted. Were the propensity to consume to rise after the war, a decade might be required before the plant of industry, the supply of durable consumer goods, and the quality of housing had become fairly well adjusted to postwar incomes. A slowly rising propensity to consume would greatly facilitate a smooth transition from the catching-up economy to a self-sustaining economy. Sooner or later, however, the economy will lose the support of the catching-up demand. Then it will face the test of whether currently developing consumer needs and investment opportunities will provide "full" or virtually full employment.

SAVING

Estimating the Propensity to Save

Many people believe that a satisfactory level of employment will not be possible after the catching-up demand has been met. They construct models showing large amounts of savings at high levels of income and ask where the investment opportunities to absorb these savings will be found. Some attempts to estimate savings at high postwar incomes assume that individuals with given real incomes will have substantially the same propensity to save after replacement demand has been met as did persons with the same incomes before the war.

This procedure is faulty in two respects. It overlooks the fact that a general rise (or fall) in incomes itself affects the propensity to save. In addition, it ignores the changes in living habits which occur during the passage of time. Between 1880 and 1940, for example, the propensity to consume rose fast enough to produce a slight decline in the proportion of saving to total income — although per capita real income in the meantime increased well over twofold.[51]

Possibly the propensity to consume will continue to rise fast enough to produce a slow drop in proportion of savings to total income. The many new ways of spending money make this likely. Possibly business enterprises will succeed in considerably reducing the disposition to save among the well-to-do. Possibly influences associated with the war may cause a sharp drop in thriftiness, as the first World War did in Britain. In 1908 about 12.2 per cent of the national income was saved; in 1913, about 13 per cent; in 1929, about 7.2 per cent, and in 1935, about 6.9 per cent.[52] Or possibly the war may engender saving habits which produce a sharp rise in savings. No one knows. The safest assumption is that the proportion of individual incomes saved will continue to remain about the same — namely, 11 per cent of incomes after taxes. If this assumption is true, the level of employment after the catching-up period is likely to be satisfactory.

The Sum of Individual and Corporate Savings

The shift to a self-sustaining economy will probably occur between 1950 and 1955. By 1953, the work force will be about 63 million. If employment is 60 million and efficiency has moderately increased, gross national product, in 1944 prices, would be about $215 billion, disposable income approximately $168 billion, and individual savings about $18.5 billion a year.[53]

To these must be added corporate savings. Corporate sales (with

51. Among the many conditions which affect the proportion of national income saved are: changes in commodities available for consumption (the automobile, for example); changes in working hours and the spread of vacations; changes in the proportion of self-employed (this group seems particularly disposed to save); changes in the proportion of city population to total population (city dwellers are less thrifty than rural dwellers); changes in the proportion of retired persons who are living on their savings.

52. Colin Clark, *National Income and Outlay*, Macmillan, Toronto, 1937, pp. 185–270.

53. An increase of 15 per cent in output per capita over 1948 is assumed.

60 million persons employed) would be approximately $270 billion at 1944 prices. In order to sustain a high level of employment, corporate profits need to be about 5 per cent of sales.[54] The cyclical fluctuations in corporate savings are large, varying from 40 per cent of profits in the prosperous twenties to considerably less than nothing during the depression of the thirties. In the long run corporate savings depend upon needs. If venture capital is obtainable from individuals on reasonable terms, perhaps one fifth of corporate profits on the average, or $2.7 billion a year, might be saved. If depreciation allowances by 1950 are running $11 billion a year, the contribution of business enterprises to gross savings would be about $13.7 billion.[55] The total volume of investment-seeking funds would be $32.2 billion.

INVESTMENT

The volume of attractive investment opportunities after the catching-up period will depend upon many unforeseeable conditions: tax policy, other public policies, labor relations, international relations, and the rate of technological discovery.

Estimating the Investment Demand

A demand for only $32.2 billion of investment-seeking funds a year, however, would mean a considerable drop in investment opportunities relative to the period 1880 to 1930. During this time gross capital formation was 18.7 per cent of gross national product. There was little variation in this ratio from decade to decade.[56] If this ratio were maintained, gross capital formation of $40.2 billion would accompany a gross national product of $215 billion. Possibly $2 billion of this capital formation might be financed out of taxes. On the other hand, figures on gross capital formation do not include all items which are

54. In the twenties corporate profits were over 6 per cent of sales; in 1937 and 1939, the best prewar years, less than 4 per cent. There is, of course, a large spread between different enterprises and also between different industries.

55. Part of depreciation allowances consists of gross savings of unincorporated enterprises.

56. S. S. Kuznets, "Capital Formation, 1879–1938," University of Pennsylvania Bicentennial Conference, *Studies in Economics and Industrial Relations*, p. 70. Gross national income undoubtedly depends upon gross capital formation more than gross capital formation depends upon gross national income. The experience since 1879 indicates how opportunities for capital formation may be expected to grow if conditions are reasonably favorable.

financed out of investment-seeking funds — part of the cost of investigating investment opportunities and of marketing new security issues. These items are nearly large enough to offset the financing of some capital formation out of taxes. Hence, if investment opportunities were about as attractive as during the period 1880 to 1930 a demand for about $40 billion of investment-seeking funds would accompany a gross national product of $215 billion.

Replacement and Expansion

What demand for investment-seeking funds might reasonably be expected? Replacements may be expected to absorb the depreciation allowances of $11 billion a year. Industrial capital per worker (including inventories), which will be about $4,500 by 1953, has been growing during the last fifty or sixty years at more than 2 per cent a year. To maintain this rate of increase would require about $5.4 billion of investment-seeking funds each year. The number of workers will grow by about 550,000 a year. To provide each additional worker with $4,500 of capital will require $2.4 billion a year.

The demand for housing will be very large by past standards because the market for new houses is almost entirely among families with an income of $2,000 a year or more. In good years the housing industry, with all its faults, has obtained from 10 to 12 cents out of every dollar after taxes received by persons with incomes of $2,000 a year or more. An attractive product marketed with reasonable skill should attract about 8 cents out of every dollar after taxes received by persons with $2,000 a year or more. If disposable incomes are $171 billion, the incomes after taxes of persons receiving $2,000 a year or more will be $134 billion or more, indicating a housing market of $10.7 billion.

Clubs, churches, and private schools would absorb half a billion more, and another billion would be required to finance the sale of new security issues, to pay part of the cost of investigating investment opportunities, and to pay reorganization expenses which are charged to capital. The state and local governments may be expected to absorb from $1 to $3 billion a year.

Even if the demand for investment-seeking funds is less in relation to incomes than it was during the late nineteenth century, it should average, with employment at about 60 million and conditions moderately favorable, about $32 to $34 billion a year. This demand for investment-seeking funds may never be achieved or it may be greatly exceeded. It is conservative, however, when tested by experience. Certainly it is not more than millions of businessmen might develop in a vigorous competition to excel and to offer consumers more for less money.

VII. The Responsibility of the Government for Employment

Suppose that after the catching-up period the economy fails to provide a satisfactory level of employment, except possibly in a few boom years. Let us assume that the level about which employment fluctuates is 3 million, or even more, below a satisfactory level. This is not a remote possibility, and the nation should be prepared for it. What can and should be done to *assure* that after the catching-up period employment is high and stable?

GUARANTEE VERSUS ENCOURAGEMENT

Proposals for Government Guarantee of Employment

Many people believe that the government in some way should "guarantee" or "underwrite" prosperity or a high level of employment. Recently a special supplement of *Fortune* suggested:

> We propose that the government should underwrite permanent prosperity; that it be established government policy, whether Republican or Democratic, to maintain reasonably full employment in the United States. . . . We believe the government should set a minimum and a minimum reasonably close to full capacity below which employment should never be permitted to fall.[57]

A similar proposal was made by Chester Bowles, head of the Office of Price Administration, in a speech to the Detroit Economic Club in April 1944. He said:

> The essential role of Government in our economic future . . . must be to underwrite a high level of business activity and thereby to release the full energies of all our people under the democratic free-enterprise system.

A subcommittee of the Senate Committee on Military Affairs has prepared a bill entitled "Full Employment Act of 1945" which declares

57. "The United States in a New World," III: The Domestic Economy, Supplement to *Fortune*, December 1942, p. 7.

that "all Americans able to work and seeking work have the right to useful, remunerative, regular, and full-time employment, and it is the policy of the United States to assure the existence at all times of sufficient employment opportunities to enable all Americans who have finished their schooling and who do not have full-time housekeeping responsibilities freely to exercise this right."[58]

The President, according to the bill, is required to transmit to Congress at each regular session a "national production and employment budget" which shall set forth (a) the estimated expenditure by private enterprisers, consumers, and government required to assure a full-employment volume of production, and (b) the estimated actual volume of expenditure by consumers, private enterprisers, and government during the ensuing fiscal year. If the prospective investment and other expenditure are less than required for "full" employment, the President shall set forth a program for encouraging larger nonfederal investment and other expenditure. If the expected increase in nonfederal investment and other expenditure is deemed insufficient to provide full employment, "the President shall transmit to Congress a general program for such federal investment and expenditure as will be sufficient to bring the aggregate volume of investment and expenditure . . . up to the level required to assure a full-employment volume of production."[59]

The Government Must Provide Incentives

Let us grant that the "government," because of the scope and nature of its authority, has a great and distinctive responsibility for the level of employment. More than any other organization in the community the government is able to assume responsibility for incentives — to see that individuals, enterprises, trade unions, and trade associations have incentives to behave in ways that produce a high and stable level of employment.[60]

---

58. 79th Cong., 1st sess., S–380, Sec. 2(b).

59. *Ibid.*, Sec. 3(c).

The British Government in its White Paper on Employment Policy issued in 1944 states that "The Government accept as one of their primary aims and responsibilities the maintenance of a high and stable level of employment after the war."

60. The ethical system of the community, of course, provides incentives. It is always under construction. Millions of people contribute their bit to the process of constant change and some private organizations, such as educational institutions and churches, may at times exercise considerable influence. The government, however, has control over incentives which no other organization possesses.

If too few people try to make a living or part of a living by putting men and loan capital to work, the government is in a position to make business ownership more attractive. If the volume of investment opportunities is insufficient, the government can do something about it. If individuals and business enterprises show an excessive disposition to save, the government is in a position to discourage saving. If consumers and business concerns accentuate the fluctuations in employment by going into and out of debt at the wrong time, the government can provide incentives for a different timing.

In contrast, consider the position of the individual, the enterprise, the trade union. They are too small to consider the effect of their actions and policies upon the general situation. They cannot afford to behave in a certain way simply because such behavior would be favorable to employment. A man might raise the general level of employment in the community by becoming an adventurer and starting a business of his own, but no one would assert that it is his *duty* to start a business if he prefers to be a job holder. Likewise, business concerns and trade unions must be expected to pursue their self-interests (and indeed to have the "right" to pursue their self-interests) regardless of the effect upon employment, so long as they conform with the law and with the ethical codes of the community.[61]

METHODS OF FULFILLING A GUARANTEE

Does it follow from the government's distinctive responsibility for employment that it should "guarantee" or "underwrite" the level of employment? "Guarantee" and "underwrite" are strong words and raise fundamental questions which have received little attention. For example, a government guarantee presupposes that the conditions which determine the volume of employment are well known and that these conditions are pretty much within the control of the government. Are either of these assumptions true? Could the government make good on a guarantee without regimenting the economy?

Two Principal Types of Unemployment

The proposal that the government "guarantee" employment is invariably made by persons who believe that the volume of employment

---

61. The capacity of a community to control conduct by developing new ethical rules as new conditions and problems arise is a good measure of the level of its civilization.

is always sensitive to the amount of spending and that increases in spending produce more or less proportionate increases in employment. This is true only up to a certain point and under certain conditions. Unemployment may be divided into two principal types: (a) unemployment caused by various imperfections in markets; and (b) unemployment caused by an excessive propensity to save or a deficiency of enterprise. The first type of unemployment may be called "market imperfection" unemployment, or, to use a shorter, though less descriptive, term, "structural" unemployment. The second type of unemployment may be called "deficiency of enterprise" unemployment.

Structural Unemployment

Structural unemployment may be attributable to:

1. *Distortions in the price structure.* Some goods which are elastic in demand are persistently overpriced. Businessmen in setting prices on goods take account of both margins and prospective volume. As margins are more definite than expected changes in volume, they are likely to have an undue effect upon price-making decisions — that is, goods are likely to be priced too high for the maximum profit and, of course, for the maximum employment.

2. *Distortions in the wage structure.* Some communities or industries, by reason of their high wages, attract and hold more men than can obtain steady work. The building trades, the garment trades, and the coal industry are examples.

3. *Seasonal fluctuations in demand.* Many of the seasonally unemployed remain on the employer's pay roll without drawing pay. They retain their check numbers; they keep their locker in the shop with their work clothes in it; and they expect to be called back to work.

4. *Frictions in the labor market.* There are always persons looking for jobs who have not yet found a job which suits them; also persons who do not move to the places where jobs are to be found.

5. *Abnormally low efficiency, reliability, or adaptability.* All sorts and conditions of men seek jobs. Most of these men are industrious, honest, reliable, reasonably intelligent, and able to get on with other people. Some people who seek jobs, however, have very low intelligence or very limited mechanical ability or are lazy, unreliable, dishonest or unable to get on amicably with their associates. As one would expect from the wide dispersion of human abilities, the least employable 5 per cent of the work force is far less employable than the other 95 per cent and obtains work only when the need for labor is great or when temporary help is desired on a simple and easily supervised job.

Spending May Not Help

Structural unemployment is not sensitive to the volume of spending.

The unemployed men in a declining New England textile town or in the anthracite coal region are not readily put to work by spending money on dams and flood control in the Missouri Valley. The amount of structural unemployment in time of peace is likely to vary from 3 to 5 million. If one reviews the employment record in the United States since 1920, one finds that most of the unemployment in most years has consisted of types which are little affected by changes in the volume of spending.[62] A guarantee of employment or opportunities for employment would presuppose that the government either was ready to make direct and well-focused attacks upon structural unemployment or was willing to exclude structural unemployment from its guarantee.

The conditions which determine the volume of private spending are only partly within the control of the government. Indeed, drops in private spending may be large, sudden, and quite unpredictable. Consequently, there is no assurance that the government will be able to spend soon enough and on a large enough scale to maintain employment in the face of rapid drops in private spending. Lack-of-enterprise unemployment is sensitive to changes in the volume of spending up to a certain point, but beyond this point increases in spending have more effect upon prices than upon employment. The sensitiveness of employment to changes in the volume of spending will be discussed in the next section. Increases in spending may have a very limited effect upon the number of jobs.

The government should not base a guarantee of employment or of opportunities for employment upon the simple assumptions (a) that public spending can be increased fast enough to offset any drop in private spending, or (b) that lack-of-enterprise unemployment can be easily eliminated by more spending.

Guaranteed Employment in a Free Society?

Would a government guarantee of employment require a high degree of regimentation, a great central management of the economy? At what occupations, in what places, at what rates of pay would the

62. The amount of structural unemployment is difficult to estimate but it is probably fairly large. Certainly an increase of one per cent in employment, or 500,000, might be expected from better pricing. Another 500,000 of unemployment is probably attributable to distortions in the wage structure. Seasonal unemployment probably averages a million and frictional unemployment 500,000. If the least efficient 5 per cent of the work force has an unemployment rate of 50 per cent, they contribute one million to the volume of unemployment.

government guarantee employment? Men could not expect to have their employment guaranteed lighting gas street lights or shoeing horses. It would plainly be better for the government to guarantee *opportunities* to work rather than to guarantee a given number of jobs. Opportunities for employment, however, depend upon the wage structure, upon the policies of trade unions, and upon the results of collective bargaining. Wages may rise so fast in response to increases in the demand for labor that little increase in employment would occur. Consequently, every proposed wage change or change in working conditions which might affect the demand for labor would require government approval. In other words, employment guarantees, even if in terms of opportunities rather than jobs, would necessitate a high degree of central management in the economy.

The conclusion of this analysis is that much unemployment is not sensitive to changes in the volume of spending; that many of the conditions which determine the volume of private spending are beyond the control of the government, particularly in the short run; that the government can scarcely hope to spend fast enough or on a large enough scale to offset all decreases in private spending; that increases in spending may have more effect upon prices than upon the man-hours of employment; and that even an attempt to guarantee employment opportunities rather than a given volume of employment would involve considerable policing of the wage scale and the operation of collective bargaining. Consequently, it would seem sensible to recognize that in a free society some unemployment is inevitable, and to develop arrangements for compensating it and for preventing drops in employment from producing too-large drops in private incomes.

VIII. How May the Government Encourage Employment?

Although the government would be wise to avoid guaranteeing a given number of jobs, it cannot avoid responsibility for incentives and for endeavoring to stimulate industry whenever the volume of employment is unsatisfactory. The action of the government must depend upon which kind of unemployment it is attacking. Reducing frictional unemployment is a matter mainly of improving sources of information about jobs and arrangements for placing men; reducing seasonal unemployment is a matter of giving industries incentives to stabilize production. Removal of price distortion unemployment requires better-informed pricing policies by business concerns. Removal of wage distortion unemployment is beyond the control of the government unless it is willing to formulate and enforce a national wage policy.

Most discussions of how the government might reduce unemployment relate to lack-of-enterprise unemployment — that is, the unemployment which arises from a propensity to save which is too high in relation to investment opportunities. Furthermore, most discussions of how the government might increase employment begin and end with the proposal of deficit financing. As a matter of fact there are several steps which the government might take. Among them are:

1. Removing specific obstacles to the expansion of production
2. Providing specific incentives for employers to hire more persons
3. Creating specific incentives for individuals and enterprises to spend rather than to save
4. Supplementing private spending with public spending
5. Changing the relationship between saving and investment opportunities by tax policy

Let us examine these possibilities.

REMOVING OBSTACLES TO THE EXPANSION OF PRODUCTION

Obstacles to the expansion of production take many forms. Taxes designed to discourage the consumption of certain articles, such as the tax on oleomargarine, slightly limit total employment because production is partly determined by the richness of the choice open to consumers. Many laws and regulations limit the volume of investment opportunities because they impede the replacement of old processes or products with new. Examples are obsolete building ordinances and restrictions on technological change in trade-union agreements. Monopolies may restrict employment either by narrowing the consumer's range of choice or by reducing investment opportunities in particular industries. Up to a point, however, monopoly may increase investment opportunities by giving innovators a better prospect of gaining from their inventions.[63] Removing impediments to production is the logical first step for the government to take in seeking to increase employment.[64]

---

63. In other words, there is an optimum degree of monopoly from the standpoint of maximizing investment opportunity and employment. Patents illustrate the point. The present law protects the holder for seventeen years. This period of protection undoubtedly stimulates more invention than would a period of either six years or one hundred years.

64. Some obstacles to production, such as obsolete local building codes, are beyond the

PROVIDING INCENTIVES FOR EMPLOYING MORE WORKERS

Various incentives for employers to hire more workers have been suggested, for example a bonus or a tax rebate for every new employee hired and retained for a given period. This sounds like a simple and businesslike proposal. Nevertheless, there are formidable objections to it.

Much expansion of employment comes from causes beyond the control of management. Hence, the rewards would go in large measure to concerns which would have increased employment anyway. The rewards would also in the main go to the successful enterprises. Hence, concentration in industry would be subsidized, and the successful concerns would be enabled to encroach faster than ever upon the less successful. Problems of cyclical control would be introduced. The rewards would stimulate the expansion of employment during booms and might make booms become disorderly. During periods of contraction probably few firms would attempt to earn them. Consequently, the subsidy would do least good when it would be most needed.[65]

PROVIDING INCENTIVES TO SPEND RATHER THAN TO SAVE

Since some unemployment is produced by an excessive propensity to save, why not penalize saving by taxing the proportion of incomes saved at higher rates than the proportion of incomes consumed? The small income recipient who needs to save could be protected by making the differential tax on savings apply only above a given amount — say savings in excess of $5,000 or $10,000 a year.

Would the government tax severely the savings of a man who has recently had heavy losses and who is attempting to rebuild his fortune? If so, the net stimulating effect of the plan would be small, because the heavy tax on savings would tremendously accentuate the desire to conserve. Some of these difficulties might be avoided by a generous loss

---

control of the federal government, which is the logical body to assume general responsibility for employment. Nevertheless, many localities could increase their employment by modernizing their building codes and reducing the burden of taxation upon real estate.

65. The subsidy might be given to all firms which make a better employment record than their direct competitors, regardless of whether their employment rose or fell. The principle is simple, but its administration would be impracticable because the competitors of any given enterprise are not easily identified. Many enterprises are in a dozen or more industries.

carry-over and by not counting repayment of debts up to a certain amount a year as savings. At the best, however, the administrative complications of the scheme would be great.

SUPPLEMENTING PRIVATE SPENDING WITH PUBLIC SPENDING

If public spending were to produce a net increase in demand, it would have to be financed by a deficit. If the economy is not self-supporting, the budget would show more and larger deficits than surpluses and the public debt would be growing. How useful would a more or less perpetual deficit be in maintaining a high level of employment?

Attacking Results Instead of Causes

Some persons have advocated that there be a deficit whenever employment is below a satisfactory level. The analysis in the preceding section shows that this would be unwise. Deficits are not useful in reducing structural unemployment. How useful are they in reducing unemployment caused by a deficiency of enterprise — or by an excessive propensity to save?

To begin with, one should note that deficit spending *as such* is an attack upon results rather than upon causes. This is the most important criticism to be made of the policy. No great and difficult problem can be solved simply by attacking its results. Except in special situations, such as in periods of recession, deficit spending does not remove the impediments to private spending; in fact, it may underwrite their retention.[66] It does not materially alter the amount of enterprise in the community and it does not directly alter the propensity to save.[67]

Deficit spending, it is true, might be devoted largely to projects which increase private investment opportunities — the TVA, roads, airfields, irrigation projects, scientific research are examples. This would greatly strengthen the case for deficit spending. Some advocates of government spending, however, have questioned whether it is prefer-

66. Critical situations may arise in which government spending helps to remove excessive surpluses or prevent deterioration in the credit of private concerns or in improving the credit of private concerns. In most instances, however, the pump-priming effect of government deficits is small.

67. The policy of government spending, it is true, might lead people to expect steadier incomes. Greater stability of incomes would reduce the risks of business and, to that extent, would increase investment opportunities. Furthermore, the expectation of steadier incomes might reduce slightly the propensity to save among persons with small incomes. These effects, though useful, cannot be regarded as very large.

able to spend deficits on public works rather than on relief.[68] Most of the deficits in the United States between 1933 and 1939 were spent in ways which did not permanently increase employment opportunities in private industry.[69] Much discussion has been devoted to the needed quantity of government spending, but little attention has been given to its quality.[70]

Effects Divided Between Prices and Employment

Deficit spending (or any other kind of spending) affects prices as well as the volume of production and employment. The price effects of deficit spending have been little explored and ignorance of them makes the efficacy of deficits difficult to appraise.

In the first place, it is well known that some prices are more responsive than others to changes in the volume of spending. Consequently, changes in the volume of spending produce changes in the price structure. These changes in the price structure in turn affect the volume of spending. Expansions and contractions in spending have a way of producing turning points. A variety of conditions produce these turning points, but one of them is probably the changing structure of prices itself.[71]

In the second place, deficit spending (or any other kind of spending) may raise prices in general as well as increase employment. How the effect of deficits is divided between prices and employment depends upon conditions. A considerable rise in prices may occur even when unemployment is large, as is shown by the rise in prices between 1933 and 1937 or between 1939 and 1942. Between 1933 and 1937 an in-

---

68. See Paul A. Samuelson, "Fiscal Policy and Income Determination," *The Quarterly Journal of Economics,* Vol. 56, August 1942, pp. 599–601.

69. If deficits had created investment opportunities in private industry on a substantial scale, recovery in the United States would have been much more rapid and would have been accompanied by a rising turnover of bank deposits.

70. It has been suggested that deficit spending be used to "stabilize" the construction industry. The advisability of this policy depends upon conditions and upon what is meant by "stabilize." If the dovetailing of deficit spending on construction with private spending on construction so raises annual earnings of workers in the construction industry that hourly rates (and hence construction costs) are kept lower than they otherwise would be, the policy is a wise one. On the other hand, the attempt to stabilize the construction industry might keep wages up in the face of a long-run drop in the demand for construction. Under these circumstances the attempt to stabilize the industry would prevent needed long-term adjustments in the price structure.

71. An examination of some of these theoretical issues will be found in a paper by Hans Staehle, "Relative Prices and Postwar Markets for Animal Food Products," *The Quarterly Journal of Economics,* Vol. 59, February 1945, pp. 237–79.

crease of 61 per cent in expenditures for the end product of industry (exclusive of pay rolls of the armed services and interest on the public debt) produced only 20.1 per cent increase in man-hours of civilian employment. Private spending is more likely than public spending to increase employment and less likely to increase prices because part of an increase in private spending is usually devoted to increasing the capacity of industry to supply the kind of goods which consumers demand. Public spending, while it may increase the demand for goods, does not usually have much effect upon the capacity of industry to produce food, clothing, fuel, and shelter.

As the capacity of industry is approached, any increase in spending (whether financed by deficits or otherwise) produces greater and greater increases in prices and smaller and smaller increases in employment — a result of the fact that the last capacity put into operation is high-cost capacity. Between 1939 and 1944 an increase of 108 per cent in expenditures on the end product produced only a 37.6 per cent increase in man-hours of civilian employment.[72] Even the huge increase of over $50 billion in expenditures on the end product between 1940 and 1942 reduced unemployment only from 7.3 to 2.4 million. In 1944 an expenditure of about $180 billion (exclusive of compensation of the armed services and interest on the public debt) was required to give employment to about 51 million civilian workers — or $3.6 billion for each million man-years of employment. Between 1942 and 1944, an increase of about $40 billion in expenditures on the end product of industry raised employment only by the equivalent of 2.5 million civilian workers, or about $16 billion for each million man-years of additional employment, or an increase of 30 per cent in expenditures on end product to raise employment by 5 per cent.[73]

The Disadvantages of Large Deficits

If deficits are good, why raise *any* money by taxation? Why not finance *all* public expenditures by deficits? Raising *some* money by taxation implies that there is an optimum size of deficit. What determines

72. The increase in weekly working hours in manufacturing is assumed to be representative of all industry.

73. The actual number of people employed outside of the armed services dropped from 52.1 million in 1942 to 51.9 million in 1944. Weekly hours of work, however, seem to have increased. In manufacturing they increased from 42.8 to 45.2. The increase of weekly hours in manufacturing during this period may be regarded as representative of industry as a whole.

this? Can deficits become too large and too continuous? Do they ever lose their efficacy in stimulating employment?

Taxation is an orderly and controllable way of limiting the consumption of some people and enterprises so that resources may be devoted to the use of the government. Taxation has the weakness that it does not enable the government to be supported by idle resources, in case idle resources are available. Deficits may be too large (a) because, if financed directly out of current savings, they raise interest rates and limit employment, (b) because, if financed by credit expansion, they raise prices and thus constitute a form of taxation which does not permit the distribution of the burden to be controlled with precision, or (c) because, by creating expectations of tax increases, they limit the amount of "purely private" employment, that is the amount of employment that would be provided out of private incomes after taxes have been paid and with the budget balanced.[74] One or more of these disadvantages of deficits may become important before all idle resources have gone to work.

Deficits and the Fear of Higher Taxes

If deficits could be counted upon to raise taxable incomes in proportion to the increase which they produce in the expenses of government, deficits would never arouse fears of higher taxes. Unfortunately, however, deficits may produce only small increases in the national income and hence, in taxable incomes. The effect of deficits upon the national income depends upon the quality of government spending. There is reason to believe that deficit spending is less effective than most private investment in raising the national income — a result of the poor qual-

74. For purposes of this discussion, it is convenient to classify employment into the following four classes:

1. "Purely private" employment as defined above — namely, the amount of employment that would be provided from the expenditure of private individual and corporate incomes after taxes and with the budget balanced

2. The employment provided by the expenditures of the government under a balanced budget

3. Employment directly provided by the government either in the public service or in private industry by deficit spending

4. Employment provided in private industry by the indirect results of deficit spending

When deficits arouse expectations of tax increases they are likely to diminish the first type of employment. The increases in the third and fourth type will, up to a certain point, offset the decrease in the first type.

ity of deficit spending. Deficits, of course, increase service charges on the public debt. Probably more important, however, are the permanent new operating expenses of government which are created when deficits are spent for new purposes or new public works. If the expenses of government attributable directly or indirectly to deficits rise faster than revenues, deficits are likely to arouse expectations of tax increases.[75]

Taxes may be so low that even expectations of substantial increases have no effect (or only negligible effects) upon employment. For many years federal expenditures in the United States have been growing far faster than the national income: six times as fast between 1913 and 1939. Even as late as 1929, however, the federal government took less than 5 per cent of income payments to individuals. Eventually taxes may become so high that the expectation of further increases materially reduces the amount of "purely private" employment.

Taxes have already reached the level in the United States where purely private employment is extremely sensitive to the prospect of increases. Consequently, deficits large enough to arouse expectations of tax increases are likely to produce little net gain in employment. Uncertainty concerning the future of taxes is itself a deterrent to long-range planning and hence to the increase in purely private employment. Consequently if deficits had to grow cumulatively unless taxes were increased, the community would be wise promptly to raise taxes sufficiently to prevent the expenses of government from rising faster than revenues.

When deficit financing requires that tax rates be increased to prevent the deficit from growing cumulatively, its effect upon purely private employment will depend upon the kind of taxes which are increased or are expected to be increased. If the community is strongly committed to avoiding taxes on incomes derived from putting men and capital to work, the unfavorable effects of deficit financing upon purely private employment will be limited to the reductions which higher taxes make in disposable income. On the other hand, if the community meets the rising cost of government largely by heavier taxes on incomes derived from creating employment, the unfavorable effects of the policy of deficit spending upon purely private employment will largely or

---

75. The expenses of the government may rise faster than taxable income without creating the expectation of tax increases provided the system of taxation is a progressive one.

completely offset the rise in "publicly induced" private employment.[76] The disappointing success of deficits in stimulating employment during the thirties is partly attributable to the practice of the community in meeting needs for more revenue by higher taxes on corporations, on dividends, and on large incomes from which venture capital comes. Deficits were interpreted to mean larger future burdens for job makers.

Deficit Spending Versus Tax Reductions

Whether deficit spending causes the expenses of the government to rise faster than revenues will depend partly upon whether private industry is expanding rapidly or slowly. The more "mature" and stagnant the economy, the greater is the danger that deficits will make stagnation worse by causing government expenses to grow faster than revenues and thus limiting the increase in purely private employment. In other words, the more serious the impediments to expansion of purely private employment, the more important becomes a direct attack upon the impediments, and the less satisfactory becomes the policy of offsetting the impediments rather than removing them.

The expectation of tax reductions is itself stimulating to employment, especially if taxes are already high and if there is reasonable expectation that a substantial part of tax reductions will apply to business profits.[77] Certainly a firm intention by the government to reduce taxes over a period of years after the war would be a strong encouragement to employment and would be worth many billions of dollars in larger pay rolls. Except in a rapidly expanding economy large and frequent deficits would be incompatible with the expectation of tax reductions over an extended period. Consequently, the efficacy of deficits as a way of increasing employment must be balanced against the efficacy of tax reductions. A point is eventually reached where taxes are so high and the desire for reduction in taxes on the part of job makers and con-

76. Heavier taxes upon employment reduce purely private employment (a) by diminishing the amount of disposable income at any given level of employment, and (b) by reducing the amount of employment which it is advantageous for private industry to provide under any given set of cost-price relationships. The first unfavorable effect upon purely private employment is offset by the rise in government-financed employment. Our concern is with the second effect of heavier taxes upon purely private employment because this is a net effect.

77. Individuals would undoubtedly be stimulated to spend more freely by expectations of tax reductions, but the effect upon personal spending would probably be less than the effect upon business spending.

sumers so strong that employment would receive more stimulus from a policy of reducing taxes than from a policy of more or less perpetual deficits.

This point has probably been passed by a considerable margin, because the government is taking half or more of any increase in the type of incomes which produce most investment-seeking funds. Consequently, as soon after the war as practicable, the policy of reducing taxes should be substituted for the policy of deficit financing. Deficits should be limited to years of recession and should be small enough to permit both some reduction in taxes and, over longer periods, some reduction in public debt. The people of the country would be wise to set a goal for their servants in government — namely, that, in the absence of extraordinary military needs, expenditures be reduced to about 10 per cent of the net national income by 1970. Since the national income will be rising, the tax burden could be reduced to 10 per cent by 1970 through holding federal expenditures to $25 billion a year or slightly less.

CHANGING THE SAVING-INVESTMENT RELATION THROUGH TAX POLICY

If unemployment is caused by an excessive propensity to save (or an insufficient supply of enterprise), why not limit savings by stiff progressive income taxes? Unfortunately, higher marginal taxes cannot cure the problem of excessive savings.

Less Saving But More Investment Opportunities

An excessive propensity to save is always associated with a shortage of risk-taking capital relative to security-seeking capital. I have pointed out in Section V that higher marginal rates of taxation would reduce the relative attractiveness of risky ventures and raise the relative attractiveness of secure investments, particularly to the well-to-do. Hence, most of whatever savings the taxpayers had left after taxes would be added to the supplies of security-seeking funds. Since the supply of venture-seeking funds would be reduced, the surplus of security-seeking funds would in most cases be greater than before the increase in taxes.

Tax policy, however, may easily be used to control the relationship between the propensity to save and the volume of investment opportunities. This may be done by two sets of surtaxes, as suggested in Section V — a stiff surtax on general income (mostly salaries and interest) and a lower surtax on incomes derived from self-employment and dividends and on that part of incomes devoted to expanding plant and equipment. By this simple device the government can produce opposite effects upon the propensity to save and the volume of attractive investment opportunities. If the propensity to save is excessive in relation to investment opportunities, the spread should be increased between the surtax on general income and the surtax on income derived from self-employment and from dividends, and on that part of income which is invested in new plant and equipment.

It would be unwise, however, to attempt to use this device to compensate for the temporary cyclical shifts in the attractiveness of investment opportunities. Other devices (discussed in Section XI) should be used to limit the cyclical movements of employment. The spread in surtax rates should be set on the basis of estimates of the long-run relationship between the propensity to save and the volume of investment opportunities.

Differential Surtax Rates Versus Deficit Spending

A spread in surtax rates, of course, would be no more a panacea for unemployment than deficit spending is a panacea. It would simply help to prevent the type of unemployment attributable to a deficiency of enterprise. It would have the important advantage of mitigating the uneconomic effects of progressive income taxes upon employment. The progressive income tax was introduced on the grounds of equity and without regard to its effect upon the demand for labor. Implicit in the progressive income tax is the assumption that the community suffers from no "lack-of-enterprise" unemployment. High marginal rates, as I have pointed out in Section V, greatly reduce the marginal efficiency of capital for the well-to-do and thus tax out of existence billions of dollars of investment opportunities and reduce the demand for labor. Hence, the progressive income tax is in a sense regressive: it imposes a heavy burden upon the workers who must sell their labor at a lower price or who are not able to sell their labor at all. Differential surtax rates would not prevent the community from taking whatever fraction of the incomes of the well-to-do that it wished to take. They would simply permit this appropriation to occur without disastrous effects upon the marginal efficiency of capital and upon the demand for labor.

Differential surtaxes seem to be superior to deficit financing as a device for meeting the problem of long-run or chronic deficiency of enterprise — should such a problem exist after the catching-up period. Deficit financing, however, is superior to a spread in surtaxes as a device for limiting cyclical unemployment. During the early phases of recession, no device may stimulate much private investment because enterprises find it advantageous to await developments before making long-term commitments. Under such circumstances deficit spending by government is a convenient offset to the drop in private spending. For meeting a chronic deficiency of enterprise, however, differential surtaxes have several advantages over deficit financing:

1. The danger of the corruption of political life associated with large public expenditures is greatly reduced.
2. The danger of discouraging enterprise through expectations of tax increases is avoided. No long-run increase in public debt is necessary.
3. A high level of employment is made compatible with reduction in the public debt and with the stimulating effects produced by the expectation of a lower tax burden from the debt.
4. The stimulus of a differential in surtaxes upon private business is likely to be more effective than the stimulus of public spending. This is not to say that public spending, if wisely planned, may not open up important new private investment opportunities. A special incentive for people to make a living by business ownership, however, does something which public spending does not ordinarily do. It increases the number of ambitious and resourceful men in the community — men who start businesses, who launch innovations and experiments. It makes for more vigorous competition between new enterprises and old enterprises, new methods and old methods, new products and old products. And since the volume of discovery depends partly upon the vigor with which men strive to excel, it increases the rate of technological change and the amount of investment opportunities. Carefully planned public spending may, to a limited extent, produce these same results, but when spending is for spending's sake, it is likely to encourage men to look to the government for aid and support rather than to rely upon themselves.

IX. The Responsibility of Labor and Business for Employment

Should not labor and business, as well as the government, assume responsibility for the general level of employment? Does the unique control of the government over incentives mean that business and labor need not concern themselves with employment?

The government in a democracy is not separate and apart from the people; it is simply one of many organizations through which people act collectively. Its policies should originate in large part from outside the elected and hired personnel of government. This is important, partly because people outside government are best able to know how industry would be affected by proposed policies and partly because people inside government tend to become unduly committed to the support of existing policies.

Individual Units Versus National Organizations

The individual trade union and the individual business concern are, of course, too small to assume much responsibility for employment. Both labor and business have nation-wide organizations — the American Federation of Labor, the Congress of Industrial Organizations, and the United States Chamber of Commerce — which are big enough to concern themselves with the general level of employment. These organizations may appropriately attempt to influence the policies of government, of trade unions, and of individual business enterprises in the interest of more employment and greater demand for labor.

The federations of labor, e.g., should have the responsibility of protecting the total volume of employment opportunities from being narrowed by the policies or actions of any given union. The federations of unions have an interest in a well-balanced wage structure, in contrast with the interests of certain strong unions which may push the wages of their members too high for the good of labor as a whole. Wage rates in residential building, an important outlet for investment-seeking funds, may be so high as substantially to limit employment throughout the economy. The federations of labor have an interest in a high rate of investment, whereas certain unions may find it to their own interest to impede the adoption of improved equipment or new methods.

Likewise, the Chamber of Commerce of the United States is broad enough in its membership to represent the common interest which all enterprises have in a high level of employment. Business as a whole, no less than labor, has an interest in a well-balanced wage structure and in conditions which are favorable to innovation and experimentation; yet the makers of certain products may seek to preserve obsolete building codes or to fight the introduction of a new competing product — glass milk bottles versus paper milk bottles.

Business as a whole has an interest in an abundant supply of adventurous capital, capital willing to risk big losses on the chance of making big gains, capital willing to back able young businessmen who would like to start new enterprises. This is the kind of capital which has been pretty much taxed out of existence since 1932. Business as a whole has an interest in the lending policies of commercial banks and in the willingness of commercial banks to make risky loans at commensurate rates of interest. Recent developments in bank examination and the great depression have made banking supercautious. Business as a whole has an interest in developing a compromise between the bad banking of the nineteenth century and the supercautious banking of the present. Business as a whole has an interest in an up-to-date investment banking industry. The industry grew up when finding supplies of capital was a greater problem than finding investment opportunities. Consequently, the investment banking industry, through its traditions and personnel, is better equipped to sell securities than to find investment opportunities. And it is better prepared to sell bonds to large buyers than sell equity issues in moderate amounts to persons in the middle income brackets. Finally, business as a whole, no less than labor, has an interest in public policies which affect the level of employment.

The Interests of Labor and Business as a Whole

Are labor and business likely to develop organizations which effectively represent the interests which most enterprises and most trade unions have in common? The process is likely to take time. The American labor movement, for example, has been built on the principle of autonomy. Each national union is left free to run its own affairs with little or no interference from either the American Federation of Labor or the Congress of Industrial Organizations. Only in fields where the national unions do not make their own individual policies and where the several unions have common interests, such as taxes, do the federations make policies for labor as a whole. Consequently, the interests of plumbers, carpenters, or steelworkers are better represented than the interests which all workers have in common. Essentially the same situation exists in the business world. The United States Chamber of Commerce has not yet developed into a strong corrective for the particularism of enterprises and trade associations in different industries.

X. A Broad Attack Upon a Possible Chronic Deficiency of Enterprise

If the country, after the catching-up period, is confronted with a chronic deficiency of enterprise, the attack upon the problem should be broad and should be designed to reach the fundamental determinants of the supply of enterprise. Certainly no form of fiscal policy, be it deficit spending or differential surtax rates, should be relied upon as a panacea.

Investment Opportunities Not Given, But Created

Although it is formally correct to describe a chronic deficiency of enterprise in terms of the relationship between investment opportunities and the propensity to save, this statement of the problem is unrealistic. Investment opportunities do not simply exist, and their number cannot be taken as given. It is a major defect in much modern economic analysis that it takes the volume of investment opportunities as given and does not explore their determinants. A visitor from Mars who read Keynes' *General Theory,* or indeed much other recent economic analysis, would conclude that the businessman is merely a person who puts additional increments of capital to work until the marginal efficiency of capital equals the rate of interest.

The businessman, in actual fact, is not simply an equator of marginal returns. Both investment opportunities and opportunities to raise the marginal propensity to consume must be discovered or created. They are discovered or created by imaginative and original men and by hard and skillful work. They are exploited by adventurous investors who are willing to risk large losses in order to make large gains. The volume and quality of investment opportunities, therefore, depend in large part upon (a) the number and quality of business managers and their technical assistants, and (b) the number of enterprising investors — the men who are willing to back enterprising managers.

The number and quality of managers, of their technical assistants, and of adventurous investors are not fixed and unalterable. Even before the war, industry was grievously understaffed in the field of investment analysis — a carry-over of the days when investment opportunities sought the capitalist, not the capitalist the investment opportunity. By "investment analysis" is meant, not the superficial statistical analysis of the securities of seasoned concerns, but the exploration of new investment opportunities. Most insurance companies, for example, are not staffed to do a thorough job of investment research, to look into many small situations where the security may be good, though not generally known to be good. An eastern company with assets of $700 million has had a staff of only five investment analysts, not all of them full time.

Adventure or Security: the Basic Philosophy

Particularly do the number and quality of managers and adventurous investors depend upon facilities which the community possesses for developing men of originality, boldness, and leadership. These depend fundamentally upon the scale of values in the community and upon the philosophy which it teaches its young men. Any community must, of course, seek a balance between conformity and pioneering, security and adventure. There must be enough desire for adventure to match the desire for security, enough willingness to gain an income by job-making to absorb the people who wish to be employees.

A community which goes too far in teaching its young men to conform rather than to pioneer, to be followers rather than leaders, to seek careers in old businesses rather than in new businesses, will have an inadequate supply of enterprise and will suffer from an excessive propensity to save. Fundamentally, the demand for labor and the volume of employment are determined by the philosophy of the community. This is why a community which suffers from a deficiency of enterprise should not be content with attacking the problem through such superficial instruments as fiscal policy. The problem requires that the community examine its scale of values and its institutions for the purpose of determining whether values, institutions, and policies should not be modified to make business ownership more attractive as a source of income. Responsibility for meeting the problem must be shared by all value-making organizations in the community — educational institutions, churches, business organizations, and trade unions.

XI. Combining Stability and a High Level of Employment

Although the long-run level of the propensity to consume, of the flow of investment opportunities, and of the preference for cash can be controlled within wide limits, short-run changes in the attractiveness of investment opportunities and in the preference for cash cannot be controlled. Can lack-of-enterprise unemployment, therefore, be entirely prevented? This problem has received little consideration. In order to keep employment stable at a level which permits only structural unemployment, enterprise would need to be stimulated so vigorously and savings discouraged so drastically that temporary dips in the flow of investment opportunities would still leave the demand for investment-seeking funds in excess of the supply. The backlog of unexploited investment opportunities might fluctuate in amount, but the actual volume of investment would not fluctuate. Increases in consumption could not be counted upon to offset declines in the actual volume of investment. On the contrary, declines in investment would produce some decline in consumption.

CYCLICAL EXPANSION AND ITS CONTROL

Would not an economy such as I have described have to be highly regimented in order to be stable? At operation high enough to eliminate all but structural unemployment, the supply of most commodities would be far less elastic than now and the cost function for additional production from existing plant (above-capacity operation) would presumably be sharply rising.[78] In fact, the costs of additional output would rise sharply even before capacity operation had been reached. Under these conditions could price movements be permitted to control the allocation of resources? Would competition for resources easily touch off an upward spiral of prices? Would wage increases have to be limited to the capacity of the economy to provide additional consumer goods? Would investment-seeking funds have to be rationed? In short, would an economy with enough investment opportunities to avert deficiency-of-enterprise unemployment require controls of raw materials, prices, wages, consumption, and investment similar to wartime controls?

78. The cost function would not be vertical because capacity operation is defined in terms of a normal work week.

Fiscal Policy to Control Booms

Only experience can answer these questions. Even if direct controls similar to wartime regulations can be avoided, strong indirect controls will be needed. The expansion of commercial credit or of consumer credit cannot be permitted to aggravate difficulties at times when demand for goods threatened to exceed the capacity of industry. Some help could be obtained from fiscal policy. It has been proposed that taxes be set so as to balance the budget at a "satisfactory" level of employment — say, at a level where unemployment would be only of the structural types.[79] Budget surpluses, it is said, would limit expansion of demand above this point and deficits would limit contraction of demand below it.[80]

Budget surpluses would be far from a completely satisfactory or effective instrument of price control. In the first place, they have the important disadvantage of being nonselective. The need for restraint does not appear in all industries at the same time. Demand is always cropping out at new points and is outrunning capacity in some industries while other industries still have idle men and equipment. Speculative accumulation of inventories occurs (as in 1937) long before full employment has been reached. The more closely to capacity the economy operates, the more important becomes mobility in the work force. In the second place, it would not be practicable to take by taxation *all* additional income generated by demand in excess of the output of industry at a "satisfactory" level of employment. In fact, it would probably be impossible to take more than one third of any increment of income payments to individuals without repressing enterprise unduly.

The government might ease markets somewhat by making temporary cuts in its own expenditures — deferring some maintenance, replacements, and public construction. Such action, of course, could not be counted upon to give relief where it would be most useful in limiting the rise in prices.

79. This use of the word "satisfactory" does not mean that the community should be resigned to accept structural unemployment as inevitable.

80. The government would be wise to balance the budget at slightly below a "satisfactory" level of employment. The budget surplus might be devoted to retiring either part of the debt held by the public or part of the debt held by the banks. Each year individuals and corporations would be converting part of their holdings of government securities into cash for the purpose of buying goods. Retirement of this part of the debt would not be deflationary. As capacity operation was approached and as the surplus increased, the government would retire a larger and larger part of the debt held by banks.

Particularly important in an economy which aims to operate at a "satisfactory" level of employment would be encouragement to industry (a) to retire equipment after a few years of use so that standby capacity consists of fairly up-to-date and low-cost apparatus, and (b) to increase capacity promptly as demand for goods grows. The cost of additional output would then rise less sharply as a "satisfactory" level of employment was approached.[81] An incentive for industry to use up-to-date equipment for standby capacity could be provided by tax policy — by allowing enterprises to write off new equipment in less than the actual life. The whole policy of encouraging enterprise would involve, among other things, providing the conditions which lead business to expand capacity promptly as demand for goods grows.

The Need for Comprehensive Controls

Suppose that the policy of stimulating enterprise so vigorously that there is no unemployment except structural unemployment leads to some rise in prices as a satisfactory level of employment is approached. Might not a slow rise in prices be useful in keeping the demand for goods adjusted to the capacity of industry and thus avoiding the need for elaborate and burdensome controls? The rise in prices would increase profits, and hence business savings. Would not the simultaneous increase of business savings and profits lead to an expansion in the capacity of industry which would limit the rise in prices?

The answer to this question is not necessarily "Yes." Expansion of productive capacity helps, of course, to hold down prices — that is one reason why an increase in private spending is more likely to raise employment and less likely to increase prices than an increase in public spending. Nevertheless, the optimism generated by expanding incomes may lead individuals to reduce the proportion of their incomes saved. Furthermore, expanding incomes may lead to an increase in consumer demand financed by credit. Finally, larger purchases of equipment and plant would raise pay rolls in the capital goods industries and thus increase the demand for consumer goods before they increase the capacity of industry. As the capacity of industry is approached, the supply of consumer goods could easily fall behind demand. Strong resistance of consumers to substantial increases in prices, a firm refusal to

81. The plant and equipment capacity of industry is usually greater than the labor capacity — that is, industry as a whole has more equipment than the labor force could operate simultaneously.

pay very much more than previous prices, would be the best control, but no one could count on it.[82] Consequently, the complete elimination of nonstructural unemployment would probably require either (a) that industry be encouraged to maintain at all times substantial amounts of low-cost standby capacity or, (b) that the government enforce more elaborate regulation of materials, production, prices, and wages than the community would tolerate in time of peace.

Lower Employment May Be Preferable

Rather than risk comprehensive controls over economic activities, the community may prefer that demand fluctuate, not around a level of only structural unemployment, but slightly below this level. The lower the level of demand, however, which the community endeavors to maintain, the more important become arrangements to halt or to offset contractions in employment.

THE CONTROL OF CYCLICAL CONTRACTION

Unemployment Compensation

Cyclical contraction of employment may be limited to some extent by developing unemployment compensation schemes into more effective arrangements for offsetting drops in pay rolls. I have suggested that approximately one fourth of the pay roll loss in covered industries might be compensated.

Budget Deficits

Fiscal policy may be useful in limiting contraction of employment. On this subject there is need for clarification of thinking. Thus, two recent writers assert that by budget deficits the government can provide "at all times active purchasing power that stands in reasonably stable proportion to the potential supply of goods, in order to prevent too drastic fluctuation in prices."[83] Deficits may be created by:

1. A drop in revenues with no change in tax rates and no change in expenditures

82. A rise in interest rates does not appear to be effective in limiting consumption when employment and pay rolls are increasing because when people take a more and more optimistic view of the future, their propensity to consume rises. The rise in interest rates would limit investment. In so far as investments were financed by plowed-back profits, however, the higher interest rates would have little effect.

83. Beardsley Ruml and H. Chr. Sonne, *Fiscal and Monetary Policy*, National Planning Association, Pamphlet No. 35, p. 6.

2. Reduction in tax rates with no increase in expenditures
3. An increase in expenditures with no change in tax rates
4. Both a reduction in tax rates and an increase in expenditures

If nothing is done about expenditures or tax rates, a depression will bring a deficit to a budget previously in balance simply by reducing the yield of taxes. Such a deficit simply keeps the budget neutral with respect to nongovernment expenditures. The government avoids depressing private spending, but it does not increase its demand for goods and no changes are introduced in tax rates to stimulate business managers to make larger and bolder production plans. Consequently, the deficit gives no one an incentive to increase expenditures.

Reduced Taxes

The effect of a deficit which is increased by cuts in taxes would depend partly upon which taxes were lowered. Evidence is lacking on whether a reduction in taxes on business profits would assist recovery more than a reduction on taxes on consumption or on personal incomes. Too much must not be expected from the reduction of either type of transfers to the government provided the reductions were expected to last only a short time — say two or three years. The principal effect of reductions in taxes would be to assist business enterprises or individuals to pay their debts and to strengthen their cash position. Both of these results, however, may be useful in paving the way for a revival of spending.

Temporary reductions in taxes, however, must not be expected to have much effect upon long-range planning by business concerns or long-term commitments by individuals. Furthermore, the efficacy of tax reductions would be pretty completely destroyed if uncertainty arose as to whether the revenue needs of the government would eventually be met (a) by restoring old taxes, or (b) by imposing new taxes. Certainty is itself an important favorable condition. Consequently, taxes should not be reduced in order to increase the deficit without, at the same time, authorizing a definite schedule of higher taxes to become effective after a satisfactory level of employment has been attained.

Increased Spending

If the deficit were deliberately increased by expanding government expenditures while keeping tax rates unchanged, new incomes would be directly created. These incomes might materially help absorb inventories and accelerate the repayment of indebtedness, thereby reducing the pressure upon prices and helping to prevent the development of unfavorable cost-price relationships. If some of the increased expenditures were regarded as permanent, expectations of increases in taxes might be created. Such expectations would retard recovery and undo much of the good of the deficit in retarding contraction.

Should a deficit be increased by simultaneously raising expenditures and reducing tax rates? This procedure might be regarded as evidence of financial irresponsibility and as presaging almost anything in future fiscal policies. Such an interpretation of the deficit would discourage forward planning and raise the preference for cash, accelerate the depression, and retard recovery.[84] Perhaps governments will never be willing or able to commit themselves to long-term fiscal policies. Nevertheless, if governments eventually realize that the effectiveness of fiscal controls depends upon long-run stability in fiscal policy, possibly they will become scrupulous in accepting the commitments which previous administrations have made — and also careful to avoid creating expectations which future administrations cannot meet.

Incentives for Stabilized Replacement Expenditures

Perhaps the most promising step which might be taken to limit cyclical contractions of employment would be to provide business with a strong incentive to stabilize expenditures on replacements. These outlays are very large — about two thirds of all purchases of equipment and much larger than all outlay by the national, state, and local governments upon public works. Unfortunately, expenditures on replacements fluctuate violently.[85] An inducement to budget these replace-

---

84. Even if the simultaneous increase in expenditures and reduction in tax rates were interpreted as *eventually* meaning inflation, its immediate effect would be to raise the preference for cash. Business managers who fear a possible inflation do not immediately buy commodities. They avoid tying funds up in specialized equipment and build up cash balances with the intention of converting these balances quickly into commodities as soon as prices show signs of rising. Consequently, the expectations of possible inflation (in the not immediate future) are deflationary.

85. Definite information on the amount of fluctuation in expenditures for replacements is lacking because expenditures for expansion and expenditures for replacement cannot be easily and accurately separated year by year. Expenditures for producers' durable goods (exclusive of construction) in 1926 dollars fluctuated from $3.5 billion in 1921 to $6.9 billion in 1929, $5.4 billion in 1932, and $7.4 billion in 1937. Harold Barger, *Outlay and Income in the United States, 1921–1938*, p. 50. Wholesale prices of manufactured goods were used to make a rough correction for changes in the price level.

ments at a steady rate more or less independently of business conditions could easily be given by offering a substantial abatement in the corporate or personal income tax to any enterprise which, during the preceding five-year period, spent *all* of its depreciation allowance for new plant and equipment and which in no year of the five spent less than a given proportion of its depreciation allowance (say 80 per cent) for plant and equipment.

XII. The Management of the Public Debt

When war expenditures cease, the federal debt will probably be about $300 billion. Commercial banks will own about one third of it; savings banks or insurance companies, one sixth; government trust funds and local public bodies, one eighth; nonfinancial corporations, one sixth to one fifth; individuals, one fifth. Interest charges on the debt will be nearly 4 per cent of income payments to individuals.[86] The huge debt will be a new economic condition of great importance. How will it affect the operation of the economy? Will it help or hinder the maintenance of a high level of employment? Will it make for stability or instability? Can it be repaid? Should it be repaid? Can management of the debt be useful in stabilizing the economy?

HOW THE DEBT MAY AFFECT EMPLOYMENT

The effect of the debt upon employment will depend upon how the volume of spending is affected (a) by the mere ownership of government securities and (b) by large transference of incomes from taxpayers to the owners of government securities.

Bondholders' Propensity to Consume

The effect of the ownership of the debt upon spending habits would have been more favorable to employment had the Treasury succeeded in selling more government securities to individuals. Less than half of the enormous savings of individuals has gone into government securities. Nevertheless, individuals at the end of the war hold about $60 billion of government securities.[87]

86. Interest on the British public debt after the Napoleonic wars is estimated at nearly 8 per cent of the national income and after the first World War at 7 per cent.

87. At the end of 1944, approximately 85 million Americans owned $45 billion of government securities. Eight out of 13 persons owned government bonds and 27 million persons were buying war bonds each month.

Most of these holdings represent an abnormal increase in accumulated savings. Ownership of government securities will tend to encourage people to increase the proportion of their current incomes which they spend on consumers' goods or on buying a house. Likewise, as I have pointed out, individuals, even after the catching-up period, will convert government securities into goods.[88] Both of these processes will help keep up a high level of employment.

Taxpayers and Interest Recipients

The effect of interest payments on the debt upon employment will depend upon who pays the taxes to meet the interest and who receives the interest. To the extent that interest charges on the debt require heavy taxation of enterprise, the debt will limit employment. Consequently, the debt is one of several reasons why drastic and sensible reform of taxes after the war is necessary.

The more widely distributed the debt, the smaller the problems which will be created by the payment of interest. Interest payments to nonfinancial corporations are not likely to be large after the catching-up period. In any event, they will not create a problem unless public policies or other conditions discourage enterprises from rapidly spending their incomes. Some people believe that interest payments to the well-to-do will be deflationary. If attractive investment opportunities are abundant, interest payments to the well-to-do will create no problem.

Some people are also concerned about the possible deflationary effect of interest payments on the debt held by the commercial banks. Part of the incomes of commercial banks goes to operating expenses and to dividends. If the banks are enterprising in putting their resources to work, interest payments to them will not be deflationary.[89] The large holdings of the public debt by commercial banks make imperative the development of more enterprise in banking. Again it be-

88. By the end of the catching-up period nonfinancial corporations will have converted most of their government securities into goods.

89. Although some banks are much more enterprising than others, the system of bank examination has been quite effective in depressing enterprise among the commercial banks and in fostering the idea that no risky loans should be made. Obviously risky loans should be made provided the rate of interest compensates for the risk. Sometimes it is said that concerns of doubtful credit standing cannot afford to pay high rates of interest. Often it is more advantageous for the concern to pay a high rate of interest than to go without additional working capital.

comes clear that the large debt increases the need for making the entire community more enterprising.

REPAYMENT OF THE DEBT

Should the debt be repaid? Can it be repaid without preventing a satisfactory level of employment? Gradual repayment would be desirable (a) partly because it would help prepare the country for the possibility of a third World War, and (b) partly because it would help create the expectation of a declining tax burden.

Determined as everyone is that the barbarism of war shall cease, this cannot be counted upon to happen. Preparedness for war will reduce the likelihood of war, and reduction of the debt would be part of preparation. The expectation of a declining tax burden would be an important stimulus to enterprise — increasing the demand for labor and helping to maintain high employment.

Budget Surplus and Debt Redemption in Good Years

Repayment of the debt will be facilitated by redemptions because redemptions will tend to raise incomes and thus to raise the yield of taxes. Repayment of securities redeemed by individuals will simply offset the inflationary effect of the redemptions. The best opportunity to repay part of the debt will occur during the catching-up period, when liquidation of government securities by individuals and nonfinancial corporations will be unusually large. Good opportunity to repay the debt will continue long after the catching-up period — for redemptions by individuals will continue for many years. Indeed, much residential construction during the next twenty years will be financed by redeeming or selling government securities.

The reduction of the debt will be concentrated in good years. Indeed, in bad years the federal budget may be expected to show a deficit. Furthermore, as I have pointed out several times, redemptions will be greater in good years than in bad. This will introduce a new and important problem because shifts from government securities into goods will be equivalent in some respects to a deficit in the budget — a deficit which rises as business improves and falls as business gets worse. Hence, the maintenance of stability will require that the federal budget show a substantial surplus in good years and a wider cyclical fluctuation in tax yield than would be necessary if bond redemptions did not fluctuate or if redemptions were larger in bad years than in good.

In other words, high tax revenues will be necessary to avert the necessity of financing the large redemptions in good years by resort to the commercial banks — which, of course, would make redemptions produce an increase in bank deposits at exactly the wrong time. High taxes, as I have pointed out, are not incompatible with high employment, but the stiffer the rates, the more important become tax reforms designed to encourage job-making.

XIII. Some Conclusions

The foregoing analysis suggests a number of conclusions:

1. The volume of conversion unemployment is likely to be much less than most people fear. With wise public policies conversion should be accomplished smoothly and quickly.

2. The demand for goods during the catching-up period is likely to require substantial increases in industrial efficiency — especially if the tax system is reformed to encourage people to make part of their living by becoming job-givers.

3. Although most controls over materials and production should now be promptly removed, controls of prices should probably be kept for a year or two. Even if not used, they should be available.

4. Although taxes should be reformed to increase the attractiveness of job-giving, a high yield of taxes sufficient to produce a substantial budget surplus should probably be maintained during the catching-up period. The greater the disposition of individuals and corporations to convert government securities into cash, the higher the tax rates which the government should keep in effect.

5. Many changes may be made in taxes to stimulate business without reducing the yield of taxes. Indeed, if taxes are reformed to make job-giving more attractive than job-holding, there is no reason why a very high yield of taxes should not be compatible with a very high level of employment.

6. Some taxes which may appeal to people on the ground of fairness, such as a stiff progressive income tax, may be bad for employment. Consequently, the community must compromise between taxes which are good for employment and taxes which are fair according to prevailing standards of justice.

7. The work of determining the country's tax program should not be left solely to Congress. A joint tax program should be worked out by representatives of business, labor, and agriculture and submitted as a joint recommendation by them to Congress.

8. No one knows whether the country, after the catching-up period, will have difficulty in maintaining a satisfactory level of employment. There is no reason, however, to assume that precisely the right amount of employment will automatically be produced. The country, therefore, should be prepared either to prevent an excessive demand from producing a disorderly rise in prices or to stimulate a larger volume of employment.

9. Although many people fear that the propensity to save in the long run is likely to be too high for the volume of investment opportunities, these forecasts may prove wide of the mark. The propensity to save has been falling for some time, and the war and conditions created by the war are likely to make it fall even more.

10. The efficacy of spending, whether private or public, as a method of reducing unemployment has been greatly exaggerated. The several types of structural unemployment are not sensitive to changes in the volume of spending and need to be attacked by selective and especially designed methods.

11. The effectiveness of private or public spending in increasing employment depends upon the slope of the cost function. As the capacity of industry is approached, costs rise sharply and increased private and public spending becomes less and less effective in increasing employment. If a high level of employment is to be maintained, the zone in which the cost function has only a slow rise to its slope needs to be broadened. Information concerning the relation of cost-keeping to pricing is fragmentary and unsatisfactory. Managements may load too large a share of overhead cost on output produced with stand-by capacity.

12. Public spending is more limited in its capacity to increase employment than private spending because after a certain point it arouses expectations of tax increases.

13. Taxes at present rates are so high that the prospect of gradual reduction would probably stimulate employment more than would the prospect of more or less continuous deficits.

14. Tax reforms offer good opportunity to control the long-run relationship between the propensity to save and the volume of investment opportunities. Consequently, it should be unnecessary to use deficit financing to supplement private spending except on a limited scale during periods of depression. Tax reform has important advantages over deficit financing as a device for dealing with an excessive propensity to save.

15. If chronic deficiency-of-enterprise unemployment exists after the catching-up period, it should be attacked by broader methods than deficit spending or tax reforms. The institutions and policies of the community should be altered to make business ownership more attractive and to give stronger encouragement to young executives in established concerns to become business starters and to men of means to back new concerns. In the last analysis the amount of enterprise and the demand for labor depend upon the philosophy of the community and its scale of values. A country in which everyone wished security would inevitably have too many job-seekers and too few job-givers.

16. No community has ever become great by simply seeking security. Nations are made great by adventurous pioneers who gain satisfaction from life by trying new things. Of late years the United States has made a fetish of security. Regardless of whether the country, after the catching-up period, has sufficient employment, it should diminish the extreme emphasis placed upon security.

17. Stimulation of enterprise sufficient to eliminate all nonstructural unemployment would probably require more elaborate controls of materials, production, wages, and prices than the community would tolerate.

18. The small proportion of the federal debt held by individuals will increase the difficulties of managing the postwar debt. That part of the debt redeemed by individuals or liquidated by nonfinancial corporations will be converted into goods. Consequently, repayment of this part of the debt will not be deflationary.

19. The debt held by the commercial banks will present difficult problems. The conditions which make repayment of part of the debt held by commercial banks desirable will also increase the disposition of individuals and nonfinancial corporations to convert government securities into goods. Thus the government may need a very substantial

surplus in order to redeem part of the debt held by the commercial banks.

20. Whether the payment of interest on the debt to the commercial banks is deflationary or not will depend upon how much enterprise the banks show in putting their money to work.

Chapter 7

FREE ENTERPRISE AND FULL EMPLOYMENT

John H. Williams[1]

I. THE PROBLEMS AND THEIR MAGNITUDE

I agreed to take part in this symposium with considerable misgiving, and did so on the understanding that I would not be expected to present an economic program for the postwar period but could discuss some of the basic ideas and issues involved. The fundamental problem is how to achieve a high, stable, and growing level of production, income, and employment. It is a problem not primarily of the transition from war to peace but of the long-run operation of our economy under normal peacetime conditions.

Domestic and International Factors

The problem has domestic and international aspects so intertwined that there is little point in trying to say which is the more important. As the literature developed in the interwar period, there was much emphasis upon the conflict that appeared to be involved — for example, in the discussion of the gold standard — between internal and external economic stability. The development of monetary, and later of fiscal, policy was largely on lines of the "closed economy" analysis and away from the ideal of an internationally interdependent world which had characterized nineteenth-century economics. This still seems to me one of the basic issues. But there is probably by now a large measure of agreement on the following propositions. High production and employment within countries should be sought by methods that do not operate at the expense of other countries but are mutually helpful. Economic stability in the leading countries, and particularly in the United States, is a necessary condition of world stability. Economic stability in this country will have to depend primarily upon the domestic policies pursued.

1. Nathaniel Ropes Professor of Political Economy, Harvard University; Vice President, Federal Reserve Bank of New York.

337

How much domestic outweigh international factors, so far as this country is concerned, is indicated, for example, by the fact that our export surplus in 1919, when it was abnormally large, amounted to $4 billion. Our total current account surplus in 1919, including the invisible items, was only $1.5 billion, while the domestic income-increasing expenditures — for durable consumer goods, inventory accumulation, equipment, and construction — were about $22.5 billion. Comparable figures for a postwar year this time would be an export surplus of over $7 billion and domestic income-increasing expenditures of about $42 billion. It seems obvious from such figures that our chief concern must be with domestic policy and that on this will mainly depend international stability as well.

Production and Employment Before and During the War

The problem of production and employment in the postwar period must be viewed against the background of the war and the experience preceding it. The mass unemployment of the thirties had no precedent. The significant circumstance is not that unemployment grew from about 3 million in 1929, which is generally regarded as consistent with full employment, to almost 14 million in 1932–1933 at the bottom of our deepest depression, but the fact that in the recovery that followed, which was undoubtedly one of the largest recoveries in our history, mass unemployment persisted. By 1939 we had reached and surpassed the gross national product of 1929, though we were still somewhat below it on a per capita basis. But the number of unemployed in that year was 10.4 million, and it was not until 1941, when the stimulus of the war and of our defense program was already pronounced, that unemployment fell below 8 million, for the first time since 1930.

Then came our entry into the war, which affected powerfully both production and employment. Twelve million workers were taken into the armed forces and nearly 2.5 million into the federal war agencies, at the same time that production was expanded far beyond any level previously reached. That this could be done without a national service act was one of the surprises of the war. On the labor side, we have taken up the slack, reducing unemployment to under a million, have lengthened hours from 37.6 a week in 1939 to 45 hours, and have expanded the labor force by some 5 to 6 million persons who would not normally be employed. On the side of production, the explanation is less clear.

One reason for the great expansion of output is undoubtedly the greater concentration in mass production industries which wartime production has made necessary. Whether it is also due to increased efficiency over comparable peacetime production is a debated question.

War Production and Civilian Production

The postwar problem would be simpler if we had increased war production by reducing civilian output, assuming that could be done without serious inflation. The problem would then have been the comparatively simple one of conversion of equal magnitudes. If, for example, starting with our gross national product of $89 billion in 1939, we had reduced civilian production to, say, $45 billion and war production had comprised the other $44 billion, the postwar problem would be to restore peacetime consumption and investment to their original dimensions.

But actually our war production has been piled on top of the highest level of consumption in our history. All estimates of the gross national product that I have seen agree upon this point, though they vary considerably in others. According to the Department of Commerce estimates, the gross national product has increased (in 1943 prices) from $110 billion in 1939 to $195.7 billion in 1944; consumer expenditures have increased from $76.7 billion in 1939 to $96.1 billion in 1944.[2]

Such high consumption in wartime has been made possible in part by the virtual elimination of private capital formation, which declined from $13.5 billion in 1939 to $1.8 billion in 1944; but it has been due much more to the rise in government expenditures from $19.9 billion in 1939 to $97.9 billion in 1944, including $90.5 billion of federal expenditure, of which $85 billion was war outlay. The war expenditure did not of course create consumer goods, but it created high consumer incomes and the expansion of total production under this stimulus gave us high consumption as well as the great output of military goods and services.

Our problem is how we are to shrink war outlay from some $80 to

2. All estimates have been converted to the 1943 and not the 1944 price level because most of the widely used estimates of postwar gross national product are in 1943 prices. It should be emphasized that the index of cost of living used to convert prices to the 1943 basis is only a very imperfect measure of price changes relevant for an estimate of gross national product. It is used because no price index better suited for this purpose is readily available. The cost-of-living index increased from 1943 to 1944 only 1.5 per cent.

$90 billion a year to perhaps $6 billion under normal peacetime conditions and fill up the gap sufficiently to avoid large unemployment. But these figures do not of themselves give the dimensions of the problem. We do not need to fill up the entire gap. The labor force will shrink as the process of replacement of those drawn into the armed forces by persons not normally employed is reversed; and the return to a normal work week will reduce output, and the expenditure necessary to sustain it, consistently with high employment.

On the other hand, we must allow for the normal growth of population and labor force, and there is the particularly thorny question of what allowance to make for increased productivity, the growth in output per worker. In the background of the postwar employment problem, moreover, lies the fact that in the thirties increased productive efficiency resulted more in unemployment than it did in expansion of output. That was, indeed, the great economic problem, new in our experience, of the prewar period.

Another important aspect of the problem is that at wartime levels of national income we generated much more money income than we spent. Liquid assets of individuals and businesses in the form of currency, demand and time deposits, and United States government securities amounted to $193.6 billion by the end of 1944; holdings of such assets have increased $111.5 billion during the past three years.[3] One of the chief questions is how under normal conditions money incomes will be divided between spending and saving. This is a different question from that of the temporary effects of wartime savings in the transition period.

Postwar Full Production and Employment

The central question around which discussion of the postwar problem has revolved is the quantitative relation between production and employment. What will be the size of the labor force, what volume and composition of production will be required to provide jobs for it, and what kinds and amounts of expenditure, private and public, will this production involve?

The estimates that have been made by various government and private agencies show a large measure of agreement. Based on Depart-

3. See "Liquid Asset Holdings of Individuals and Businesses," *Federal Reserve Bulletin*, June 1945, p. 532.

ment of Commerce data, they are grouped closely around a gross national product for a normal postwar year (1947 is frequently taken) of
$170 billion (1943 prices) and a net national income of $140 billion,
estimated to provide employment for 56 million, leaving 2 million normally unemployed.[4]

According to these estimates, the gap to be filled will be very large.
With the gross national product running at the end of 1944 at an annual rate of about $200 billion, the decrease must not exceed $30 billion, and if we make comparison with the year 1943, the year whose
price level is projected and which was certainly a year of full employment and probably the year of greatest strain on the labor force, the
reduction can be only $15 billion, or 8 per cent. All of these studies
agree that if we should return to the 1939 level of national income,
which was the highest to that time, we should have unemployment of
15 to 20 million.

Much of the planning and program-making by nongovernmental
organizations and individuals has been geared to these estimates.
These, for example, are the figures taken as its goal by the Committee
for Economic Development. They underlie the Committee's tax program[5] and also that prepared for the National Planning Association
by Beardsley Ruml and H. Christian Sonne.[6] Some private estimates

4. Gross national product is the total money value of all goods and services produced
by private individuals, business, and government. The national income is a narrower concept, representing income payments to individuals plus net corporate saving. As computed statistically, the gross national product equals the national income plus capital replacement and business taxes.

See the Department of Commerce study by S. Morris Livingston, *Markets After the
War*, March 1943, and also his "Postwar Manpower and Its Capacity to Produce," *Survey of Current Business*, April 1943; also "Jobs After the War," by E. A. Goldenweiser
and E. E. Hagen in the *Federal Reserve Bulletin*, May 1944; and see also "Transition to
Peace: Business in A. D. 194Q," *Fortune*, January 1944.

In these estimates, the total postwar labor force is taken at about 60 million (compared
with 55 million in 1939), and it is assumed that 2 million will remain in the armed forces.

The year 1947 may prove to be too early for a normal year, but perhaps no special importance should be attached to the year taken; figures for some later year taken as normal
should vary proportionately, except as further specific developments are expected, such as
a stepping-up of the increase in productivity, etc. E. E. Hagen and N. B. Kirkpatrick,
"The National Output in 1950," *The American Economic Review*, September 1944, estimate a gross national product in 1950 (at 1944 prices) of $195 billion and a national in-
come of $165 billion.

5. *A Postwar Federal Tax Plan for High Employment* proposed by the Research Committee for the Committee for Economic Development, August 1944.

6. *Fiscal and Monetary Policy*, a pamphlet prepared at the request of the Business Committee of the National Planning Association, June 1944.

have been lower. The national income assumed as the basis for the Twin Cities Postwar Tax Plan[7] is $120 billion (1942 prices), and the assumption made by W. L. Crum in his discussion of the postwar federal budget is that national income will average $115–$125 billion (1942 prices) in the decade 1946–1956.[8] These, however, so far as I know, are informal estimates, and the only detailed analysis I have yet seen which takes issue with the official estimates is that by Joseph Mayer of the Brookings Institution, who estimates that full-employment national income in 1947 (at 1943 prices) will be $123 billion.[9]

Estimates of Productivity

Attempts to estimate the ratio of output to employment involve elements of judgment and conjecture. The official data on gross national product and net national income are estimates of monetary expenditures and do not tell us anything directly about the physical volume of production and its relation to employment. By correcting for changes in price level between one period and another we can get a fair approximation, but this must assume that there are no marked changes in price relationships or in the composition of production, as between, for example, agriculture, industry, and trade, or in the distribution of the labor force; or else allowances must be made for the changes that have occurred. In projecting production trends into the future, the problem is, of course, more difficult and the results less certain.

All such difficulties are greatly magnified when we are comparing war and peacetime conditions, for war, however well managed, represents a convulsion of the whole economy. Especially difficult to estimate as between war and peace conditions are changes in productivity, the volume of output per worker. For the war industries there is really no basis of comparison, and one is forced to fall back upon a judgment.

7. *Postwar Taxes,* The Twin Cities Research Bureau, St. Paul, Minnesota, June 1944. This estimate would be $127 billion in 1943 prices.

8. See John W. Welcker, "The Federal Budget: A Challenge to Businessmen," *Harvard Business Review,* Summer Number 1944. In terms of 1943 prices, this figure would be $122–$133.5 billion.

9. *Postwar National Income: Its Probable Magnitude,* October 1944. See also an article by Rufus S. Tucker, "Projections of National Income," *The Conference Board Business Record,* December 1944—January 1945, in which various recent estimates of postwar gross national product and related magnitudes are analyzed and compared. Tucker himself estimates that under conditions of full employment, postwar gross national product might be in the neighborhood of $125 billion of 1943 purchasing power.

This is a particularly difficult circumstance when, as now, war outlay constituted some 40 to 45 per cent of the gross national product. Simon Kuznets in his study, *National Product, War and Prewar,* indicates his preference for the assumption that the relative efficiency in war production has been 20 per cent below that of the most nearly comparable peacetime industries,[10] and on this assumption estimates that national income and gross national product increased about 50 per cent from 1939 to the first half of 1943, as against an increase in the Department of Commerce estimate for the same period of 75 per cent.[11]

The Growth of Productivity

It is often said that the challenge of the postwar period is that the war has revealed a hitherto undreamed-of capacity to produce. If we can produce so much in war why not in peace, with due allowance for voluntary leisure; and must we not do so if all who need jobs are to have them?

The force of this question is not much weakened by these differences in the estimates of wartime production. Even Kuznets' estimate still leaves the rise of output unique in our history, particularly when we consider that it has been placed on top of the already high level of out-

10. As I have said, the gross national product is an estimate of money expenditure rather than of physical output. Thus any increase in costs, such as overtime pay, increases the national "product" relative to the physical volume of output. To make a true comparison between war and prewar production, one would need to have comparable prices, wage rates, and other costs. I agree with Kuznets that under war conditions when costs are not a decisive consideration and there is pressure to get the most output in the least time, despite the drain of experienced man power and management into the armed services, money expenditure is likely to rise relative to production, and that this rise is not revealed by our available price data. Against this, however, is to be put the fact that for the economy as a whole there is a greater concentration during war in mass production industries where productivity is highest.

11. Simon Kuznets, *National Product, War and Prewar,* Occasional Paper No. 17, National Bureau of Economic Research, New York, February 1944. He compares his estimate also with a rise in the Federal Reserve Board index of industrial production of 114 per cent in the same period, the difference being "due partly to a difference in coverage and partly to a different treatment of productivity of factors in the war industries." See also a study by Geoffrey Moore, *Production of Industrial Materials in World Wars I and II,* Occasional Paper No. 18, National Bureau of Economic Research, New York, March 1944, which estimates a rise in total output of industrial materials from 1939 to 1942 of 35 per cent, as against a rise in the Federal Reserve Board index of 68 per cent for the same period.

For discussion of Kuznets' analysis see "Some Comments on Professor Kuznets' Study" by Milton Gilbert, Hans Staehle, and W. S. Woytinsky, and a "Reply" by Simon Kuznets, *The Review of Economic Statistics,* August 1944.

put in 1939.[12] It is, however, a matter of real importance to determine to what extent programs for the postwar period are based upon wartime phenomena which may be inaccurately measured, or upon wartime relationships without due allowance for changes that will occur under peace conditions, or upon developments which are likely to have only temporary, rather than long-run, effects.

The estimates I have cited of postwar national product and employment are projections of a prewar year (usually 1940), based on a normal work week, and with allowances for the growth of population, the rise of prices, and a cumulative annual rate of increase in productivity. Thus in a sense they skip the war. If there is any serious error arising out of faulty measurement of wartime changes, it would most probably be in the correction for prices, since 1943 prices are assumed and these involve the difficulties I have mentioned.

An error might arise, too, from the implicit assumption that the postwar composition of production and employment will be not dissimilar from that before the war. The factor most responsible for the high postwar estimates is the assumed rate of increase of productivity. The rate of growth of productivity used by the Department of Commerce is 2.5 per cent per year compounded, based on the period 1929–1941.[13] In computing the prewar rate of advance, it might be better to leave out years beyond 1939; and in applying it to the postwar period, we should consider carefully the range of application.[14] Perhaps allowance should

12. In Kuznets' view the rate of increase in our national product during the war period is not so unusual as most estimates have indicated. With the wartime rise of 50 per cent, he compares a rise from 1933 to 1937 of 45 per cent in national income and 37 per cent in gross national product. This comparison, however, as he points out, disregards the phase of the business cycle. The rise in the thirties was from a year of very deep depression, whereas the wartime rise was from a year of high activity by prewar standards. To attain a rise of ". . . as much as 50 per cent during somewhat less than four years from such a relatively high base is an achievement unique in the historical course of our national economy during recent decades." *Op. cit.,* p. 26.

13. S. Morris Livingston, "Postwar Manpower and Its Capacity to Produce," *Survey of Current Business,* April 1943. In their projections from 1940 to 1947 Goldenweiser and Hagen (*op. cit.*) take half this rate of increase to allow for retardation in the application of wartime technical advances to peacetime production.

14. Solomon Fabricant, *The Relation Between Factory Employment and Output Since 1899,* Occasional Paper No. 4, National Bureau of Economic Research, New York, December 1941, shows an average gain in output per man-hour in manufacturing industries from 1899 to 1941 of 2.9 per cent compounded.

According to recent studies of the National Bureau of Economic Research, during the last forty years the average annual percentage increase of per capita output has been 1.7 per cent in agriculture and in public utilities (including transportation) as well as in

be made also, as Goldenweiser and Hagen have done, for delay in applying wartime technical advances to peacetime production, but this seems mainly a question of what year to take as a normal peacetime year; it might suggest 1950 rather than 1947.

My own guess is that the postwar period, at least in the manufacturing industries, will be characterized by a rate of technological advance at least as high as that which characterized the interwar period. It will be surprising if the war does not provide a powerful impetus, for war jolts us out of familiar ways of doing things and forces upon us new methods and techniques. This is not inconsistent with Kuznets' view that efficiency in war industries has been below that of the most nearly comparable prewar industries.

In attacking the problem of postwar employment, we must have as clear a conception as possible of our goal. I shall assume that the order of magnitude is more or less what the official estimates say it is. I doubt, however, the wisdom of formulating economic programs so dependent on precision forecasting that even moderate errors can seriously impair the recommendations made. And, above all, we must not mistake the measurement of the problem, absorbing as that is, for its solution.

II. Fiscal Policy and Budget Deficits

Since the great depression the most widely discussed cure for unemployment has been fiscal policy. It has come to have much the same prominence as central bank policy had in the twenties. It has been the history of major ideas about economic policy that there is a warming-up period followed by a cooling-off period, and we have yet to look at fiscal policy in adequate historical perspective.

The Rise of Fiscal Policy

It is sometimes said that economists know how to prevent or cure unemployment by fiscal means and that the main trouble has been that

---

manufacturing; it has been higher (2.6 per cent) in mining. These percentages refer to output per employee and not to output per man-hour, as does Fabricant's percentage. However, there are good reasons to believe that average hours worked in mining or in public utilities decreased not less than in manufacturing. Finally, it must be kept in mind that Fabricant's estimate of 2.9 per cent covers wage earners only and not all persons engaged in manufacturing whereas the percentages given above refer to *total* employment (including salaried employees), which might be a better measure of productivity because of the long-run increase in clerical and similar jobs connected with the production process.

they have not had their chance.[15] It will perhaps help our perspective to recognize that what we call "compensatory" fiscal policy was a product of the depression, to which economists turned only after the monetary policies on which they had mainly relied to fight the depression had failed, although they were carried to unprecedented lengths.

Since the depression, theories about fiscal policy have gone through three fairly distinct phases and are still, in my opinion, in process of seeking reasonably firm ground on which to stand. We seem always — and the same was true earlier of central bank policy — to be a step behind, the turns in our thinking following the turns in events, rather than the other way around. And yet it is undoubtedly true that fiscal policy will have an indispensable role in any well-rounded program for the postwar period.

Three Phases of Fiscal Policy

The early "pump-priming" phase of fiscal theory assumed that, apart from business cycle fluctuations, the economy could sustain itself at full employment. It called for a cyclically unbalanced budget, with deficits in depression and surpluses in boom periods. Though the nature of the reasoning may have somewhat shifted, there is now wide agreement, I think, on the desirability and necessity, at least for major economic fluctuations, of a cyclically unbalanced budget. But the severity of the depression, and particularly the recurrence of depression in 1937–1938 at a time when the federal budget came momentarily into balance, led to a growing preoccupation with long-run contractive tendencies toward oversaving and underinvestment which were much discussed in this country under the name of "mature economy."[16]

The word "compensatory" came to be used in a second sense. Deficits would be needed not only to compensate for depression, with offset-

15. Cf. Walter Lippmann, *New York Herald Tribune*, November 26, 1942: "Since 1920 men have discovered the principle of prosperity. This discovery is much the most important advance in human knowledge in modern times. It is the discovery that government can by the proper use of public funds create a condition of full employment for all its people. Heaven help the administration which refuses to apply this knowledge in the post-war world." See also his more recent statements in the *New York Herald Tribune*, September 7 and September 23, 1944.

Cf. "The Domestic Economy," *Fortune*, Supplement, December 1942, p. 7: "We propose that the government should underwrite permanent prosperity."

16. The reasoning stemmed mainly from "Keynesian economics," and especially from Lord Keynes' book, *The General Theory of Employment, Interest and Money*, Harcourt, Brace, New York, 1936.

ting surpluses during booms (though the possibility of boom became for many as remote as that of depression in the late twenties), but also to compensate for the long-run contractive tendencies. This opened a prospect of an indefinitely expanding public debt and started a controversy about the economics of public debt which has been continuing ever since. My own view was that on this reasoning the debt charges would be a growing fraction of national income, and in the process the system of private capitalism would disappear.[17]

The war has given the discussion a new turn. With a federal debt in prospect within a brief time of perhaps $300 billion, the debt takes on a new importance. In a few years we have acquired a debt to which deficits of the size of those of the thirties would have carried us only after two or three generations. This has brought a new sense of urgency into our efforts to think through the economic and political implications of a large public debt and to determine our attitude toward its further growth. Deficit spending has not been discarded as an instrument of postwar full-employment policy; but, apart from the short-run cyclical aspect, it has been less emphasized. In its place has come a new emphasis on "developmental" public expenditure, not financed necessarily by deficits, and a much increased interest in the possibilities of using taxation as a compensatory fiscal device.[18]

Postwar Budget Deficits

The preponderant view now seems to be that postwar deficits will be small or merely cyclical. The CED tax plan for high employment says of the budget: "The Committee is convinced that the fifteen years of uninterrupted federal deficits should be brought to an end after the war."[19] It calls for a surplus and debt retirement at a national income of $140 billion. The Ruml-Sonne tax plan contemplates a balanced budget at this level of income.[20]

Alvin Hansen has presented models of postwar national income in accordance with which the budget would be balanced at $140 billion, but he regards as more probable, on the average, a national income of $135 billion, with an annual deficit of $3 billion. This would involve a

17. See my *Postwar Monetary Plans and Other Essays,* Chap. 4, Alfred A. Knopf, New York, 2d ed., 1945.
18. The use of taxation as a tool of compensatory policy was in the literature of fiscal theory before the war, but with an emphasis secondary to that on deficits.
19. *Op. cit.,* p. 23.   20. *Op. cit.,* p. 9.

gradual growth in the public debt, though with surpluses in booms as well as deficits in depressions. But with a growth in national income of "3 per cent per annum, due partly to an increase in labor force and partly to increasing per worker productivity . . . the ratio of the debt to income would, on this model, continuously fall."[21]

The new developments in the discussion of fiscal policy do not adequately explain the reduced emphasis on deficits. The main explanation lies in the assumption of a new set of facts. The models[22] prepared to illustrate the composition of postwar national product, breaking it down into the categories of consumption, investment, and public spending, are not simple projections of the prewar composition but are based upon estimates of what might be regarded as "reasonable" amounts in each category. This is a method which permits of considerable latitude. The larger the amounts estimated for private expenditures, the smaller will be the gap to be filled in by public expenditures. It is an interesting question how much such models are affected by the mathematical necessities of the case. The postwar national income envisaged as essential for full employment is only slightly less than the present wartime level, and of a wholly different order of magnitude from the actual prewar level. The wartime national product, moreover, has in it some $80 billion a year of military expenditure and involves a deficit of some $50 billion a year.

The difference between such figures and any practicable program of peacetime public expenditures is so large that there is an understandable tendency to assume as large figures for consumption and private capital formation as can reasonably be devised. I have no quarrel with these estimates when stated as goals that we must try to reach. But the models can do no more than indicate the general order of magnitude of the problem. So much of the discussion has revolved around these purely static *tableaux économiques* that the point should be emphasized that, helpful as they undoubtedly are as a first approach to the problem, they are in no sense a solution.[23]

21. Alvin H. Hansen and Harvey S. Perloff, *State and Local Finance in the National Economy*, W. W. Norton, New York, 1944, Chap. 11, p. 240.

22. See besides Hansen's models referred to above, H. Christian Sonne, *A Preview of National Budgets for Full Employment, Model T,* National Planning Association, Washington, June 1944. See also *National Budgets for Full Employment,* NPA, Pamphlets Nos. 43 and 44, April 1945.

23. I do not mean to imply that their authors necessarily think they are solutions. I

Stabilization Versus Expansion of National Income

Probably the chief question to be asked about fiscal policy is whether, like the monetary policy out of which it developed, it is not more useful as an instrument for stabilizing national income at a given level than for lifting it to a new high order of magnitude.[24] When it was a question of compensating for short-run differences between saving and investment in a full-employment national income of, say, $80 billion, roughly that of 1929, the deficits contemplated were temporary and comparatively small.[25] But the problem as it was posed in the late thirties was far more serious, for not only was the deficit spending to be permanent to compensate for the assumed long-run contractive tendencies in private spending, but it was to be applied to a national income which by reason of the strong tendency toward technological advance would have to expand continuously in order to provide full employment.

Thus the problem assumed ever larger proportions. It is small wonder that the advocates of deficits were saying in the late thirties and the early war years that the trouble with deficit spending was its small size — it should have been $10 to $15 billion a year rather than $3 or $4 billion — and were pointing to the wartime expansion of output and the accompanying deficits as proof of what could be accomplished.[26] If now we expect that the budget will be balanced, or nearly

grant, too, that to the extent the estimates for each of the three broad categories of consumption, capital formation, and public expenditure are broken down into their parts they provide not only a general goal but a number of more specific goals which may help in planning postwar output and employment. But the more detailed the estimates, the greater is the likelihood of error. As I said earlier, projections of the gross national product involve assumptions, stated or implicit, about future price relationships and the pattern of production and employment. The more we break down the gross product into pieces, the more hazardous such assumptions become. I have this kind of reservation about Morris Livingston's attempts to break down the postwar national product, industry by industry; *Markets After the War,* Department of Commerce, Washington, March 1943.

24. This would not, of course, rule out public expenditures to assist in further growth.

25. Prior to the thirties, net investment was roughly 12 per cent of national income; see Simon Kuznets, "Capital Formation, 1879–1938," *Studies in Economics and Industrial Relations,* University of Pennsylvania Press, Philadelphia, 1941.

26. Cf. J. M. Keynes, "The United States and the Keynes Plan," *The New Republic,* July 29, 1940. He refers to the failure of the deficit spending to produce "anything like full employment in the United States," and ascribes the failure to the "gigantic powers of production" of a modern industrial state. "Coupled with institutional factors which tend to encourage accumulation and retard the growth of consumption when incomes increase, this means that an unprecedented output has to be reached before a state of full employ-

balanced, in the postwar period and that the wartime level of national income will be nevertheless maintained or only slightly lowered, we must be counting heavily upon other measures, or else — as has happened before — merely projecting a prevailing state of mind.[27]

III. The Responsibility of the Government

However it is to be achieved, the maintenance of high employment is being accepted as the basic economic responsibility after the war by both government and business. The discussion of methods here and in England has covered a wide area and revealed a great diversity of viewpoints. Through it all have run the two fundamental questions. How much is it a problem of mitigating cyclical fluctuations, and how much one of creating continuous expansion? How far and in what ways must government intervene?

The British White Paper on Employment

In England, in the widely heralded White Paper on Employment Policy, issued on May 26, 1944, the government has officially accepted responsibility for maintaining employment. But apart from the transition from war to peace the White Paper treats the problem as mainly one of cyclical unemployment and directs its recommendations mainly toward offsetting variations in private investment by public works; and, as a second line of attack, stabilizing consumption through cyclical variation of social insurance contributions.

The question of the budget is treated cautiously in the White Paper. Though there is no need, the Paper holds, to adhere to a strict balance, "none of the main proposals contained in this Paper involves deliberate planning for a deficit in years of subnormal activity." It insists that the principle of long-run balance of the budget cannot be abandoned; "the Government will have equally in mind the need to main-

---

ment can be approached. The full industrial and agricultural capacity of the United States may well exceed 1929 by as much as, or even more than, 1929 exceeded 1914. . . . The conclusion is that at all recent times investment (and public) expenditure has been on a scale which was hopelessly inadequate to the problem. . . . It appears to be politically impossible for a capitalistic democracy to organize expenditure on the scale necessary to make the grand experiment which would prove my case . . . except in war conditions."

27. See Note (p. 391) on "Financing Postwar Full Employment by Means of Deficits," prepared by George Garvy at my suggestion.

tain the national income, and the need for a policy of budgetary equilibrium such as will maintain the confidence in the future which is necessary for a healthy and enterprising industry."[28]

The Beveridge Program

Many people, even in this country where opposition to government intervention is greater than in England, would not regard this as a very bold program, even for its limited purpose. In contrast, Sir William Beveridge in his report on *Full Employment in a Free Society*[29] poses the problem as that of planning for continuous expansion. He presents a program that would include:

Abolition of want by social security and children's allowances . . . ; collective outlay to secure good houses, good food, fuel and other necessaries at stable prices for all; . . . regulation of private investment by a national (governmental) investment board . . . ; extension of the public sector of industry . . . ; a new type of budget based on the datum of man-power and designed to ensure year by year total outlay sufficient to set up demand for the whole productive resources of the country; control of the location of industry . . . ; organised mobility of labour . . . ; controlled marketing of primary products, so as to stabilise overseas demand . . . ; and international trade arrangements based on acceptance of three fundamental conditions of multilateral trade: full employment, balancing of international accounts and stability of economic policy.[30]

Sir William holds that "the time calls for total war against unemployment and other social evils, not for a war with inhibitions." Whatever one's view of his specific proposals, they show the scope and gravity of the problem as seen by one of the most distinguished British economists. His reference to war is significant. It is only in war that we get really full utilization of resources, and his question, which is widely asked also in this country, is: if we can do it in war why not in peace? The answer suggested is that we can if we are willing to use war methods, and Sir William's own program is in considerable part an adaptation of war methods to peace.

28. Cmd. 6527, published in the United States by permission of the Controller of H. M. Stationery Office by the Macmillan Company, pp. 24, 26.
29. Allen and Unwin, London, 1944, published in the United States by W. W. Norton, New York, 1945. See also Sir William Beveridge's analysis of the White Paper, just mentioned, "The Government's Employment Policy," *The Economic Journal*, June–September 1944.
30. *The Economic Journal*, June–September 1944, p. 174.

The Costs in Terms of Freedom

But this raises the question of costs in terms of other values. Many would question whether Sir William's proposals can properly be called an employment program "in a free society." It seems true, though so far the world's experience has been confined mostly to war and preparation for war, that in a state-controlled society, with planned and rationed production and consumption and a state-directed labor force, there would be a fuller utilization of resources than there could ever be in a free society. The question is how far we could move in that direction and still preserve our political liberties and the economic freedoms of choice which are the essence of our way of life. The problem, to be sure, is always one of compromise. We have long ceased to have, and probably no one really wants, a laissez-faire system. But Sir William Beveridge's program, while stopping far short of a completely regimented society, suggests it sufficiently as the road along which his kind of planning would progress (he speaks of it as only a beginning) to put it in the category of last or late resort, so far as this country is concerned, after we have experimented further with a war on unemployment "with inhibitions."

Two questions about our kind of economic system impress me as having a special bearing on our problem. The first is that, whatever its faults, ours has been in terms of productivity a highly progressive society. That, indeed, is the largest aspect of our postwar problem of employment; it is because the rate of increase of productivity per worker has been so high, and will probably continue to be, that we face the need of greatly expanding our postwar output beyond the prewar level. Whether some other economic system would be as efficient, apart from the special stimuli of war, we do not know. The Russian experiment as yet is not comparable because it is being applied to a country at a lower stage of development and with a different institutional framework. If efficiency is the test, there is a strong presumption in favor of retaining and improving what we have instead of striking out in new directions.

The second question is whether our kind of economic system does not have to operate on the basis of slacks — slacks in materials, in plant and equipment, and in employment. This is for me a much more bothersome question. It has been estimated that even in boom periods under peace conditions we do not get much above 80 per cent of full capacity operation. Though this is probably an exaggeration it illustrates the problem. Failure to utilize resources fully, including labor, is often referred to as a sign of waste. But full utilization is not easy to define. The task of the producer in our kind of system is to produce at lowest possible cost, and his use of resources, including labor, is governed by this fact. As his output expands he faces anew, at each step in the process, the question whether to use more or better machines, whether to use machines instead of man power, and whether to use new techniques which are both capital- and labor-saving. In such a system, under conditions of rapid progress, there is bound to be a surplus of both men and resources, continuously being reabsorbed through expansion of output but recreated through further advances in productivity. Of course, we do in war, when we are straining to get the most output in the shortest time, and under conditions when ordinary cost considerations do not count, get full utilization of resources by totalitarian methods. But this is not a usable answer in time of peace.[31]

What Should We Strive For?

There are some who hold that technical progress and high real income are not our main objectives, and that if we have to choose between high income and high employment we had better choose the latter. But we do not want to choose, if we can help it, between less efficient production, providing jobs for all at low real income, and more efficient production, throwing increasing numbers of workers on to relief rolls and into make-work jobs. Yet for me this is the most perplexing aspect of the subject. One effect it has is to make me want to be careful how we define the postwar problem. The goal can be stated as that of providing high employment or that of preventing high unemployment. The first is the better, but the second is probably the safer form of statement.

The year 1941 has been much referred to as a model year which showed us what we can do and must strive for. Under the stimulus of the war and our defense program but without as yet much wartime control, we reached a level of national income substantially beyond any previously reached. By any previous standard it was a year of highest prosperity. But it was also a year of 6 million unemployed. The con-

31. See again my *Postwar Monetary Plans and Other Essays*, Chap. 4, "Deficit Spending," pp. 78–81.

trast between prewar unemployment and wartime full employment has made us as a nation acutely conscious of the issue. In the political campaign of 1944 the promise made by both sides was "jobs for all." Unless people have short memories, a postwar year as good as 1941, after due allowance for growth, will fail to satisfy. How much better we shall be able to do, and at the same time live up to the other campaign promises to sustain democracy and restore free enterprise, will be interesting to watch.[32]

IV. The Transition from War to Peace

I have taken considerable space to describe the dimensions of the problem and the limitations within which we propose to attack it. To sum up, our problem is how to raise the gross national product from $110 billion (1943 prices) in 1939 to a full-employment level that will need to be about $170 billion by 1947 and to increase by about 3 per cent a year thereafter. Actually, of course, we shall not go at it in this way. We shall start from our wartime level of about $200 billion and try to come through the period of transition to peace with a national product only moderately below this level. In the process we must absorb a decline of some $80 billion a year of military expenditure. This we are proposing to do by methods consistent with free enterprise and democracy, and with a balanced, or only moderately underbalanced, budget.

Retaining the High-Employment Level

Much of the current discussion seems aimed at how to keep postwar full employment, once achieved, rather than at how to get it. Many of the plans for revising the tax structure and social security, for example, are based on the assumption of a full-employment national income. This does not lessen their importance or suggest that the discussion should be deferred. The processes of getting and keeping high employment cannot be separated but must interact upon each other.

To the question how we are to bridge the transition from war to peace in the first two or three years after the war, retaining high employment, and thus have a favorable opportunity for creating the con-

32. I am not sure whether I have made it clear in the text that insistence on a really full utilization of resources would require in peace, as it has in wartime, the use of direct controls. See my *Postwar Monetary Plans and Other Essays,* Chap. 3, pp. 56–57.

ditions and putting into effect the policies necessary for its longer-run continuance, I can see no better answer than that we must treat the transition as an extension of the war emergency. We must be prepared to use whatever combination of private and public spending — including large deficits if necessary — the circumstances may require. But if, after the transition period, the private economy cannot sustain itself without substantial deficits, our efforts to solve the problem within the limits set will have failed and we shall find ourselves in a longer process of transition toward some other kind of state than the free private-enterprise system we have heretofore known.

Reconversion to Civilian Production

The reduction of military expenditures will represent the greatest loss of market in our history. How successfully private expenditure can fill the gap during the transition period is a much-debated question. The favorable circumstances will be the accumulation of deferred civilian expenditures, coupled with the large wartime savings. If the war had ended in two widely separated stages it would have helped greatly.

Morris Livingston has made a detailed analysis of the magnitude of the changes in expenditures, production, and employment during the interval between the end of the European war and the end of the Pacific war.[33] Assuming that the production of combat munitions would be cut by one third, he estimated that 4 million out of the 15 million workers then engaged in war production would be released, and that 2 million may be released from the armed forces. Somewhat more than half of the 6 million could be absorbed by a one-third reduction of the increase in the work week since 1940, by voluntary withdrawals from the labor force, and a rise of a million in the minimum labor float, now much below normal, leaving somewhat less than 3 million to be absorbed into civilian employment. This would be an addition of about one tenth to the 25 million already so employed. Apart from the technical problems involved in the release and conversion of plant, equipment and materials, the offsetting of this comparatively moderate contraction of war output through the expansion of civilian output to fill deferred demands should not present a major problem.

It is not my purpose in this paper to discuss the technical aspects of

33. S. Morris Livingston, "Magnitude of Transition from War Production," *Survey of Current Business,* Department of Commerce, August 1944.

reconversion. But it should be noted that, to the extent that these may involve delays, there will be need for public expenditure in addition to whatever may be required by the strictly economic dimensions of the problem. To the extent that private war savings are absorbed by un-employment due to such delays, they cannot be counted on to finance deferred demands for goods. But, with good planning, reconversion to peace ought to present fewer difficulties than conversion to war. There is the fundamental difference that the latter involves a sharp and pronounced expansion of output encountering scarcities and bottle-necks at every turn, whereas reconversion to peace, even though high employment is maintained, will be a process of contracting output and relaxing pressure on supply. Even though the contraction must be held to moderate proportions the reconversion should be a faster and a sim-pler process. This view seems borne out by the announcements from the War Production Board and the Office of War Management that re-conversion will be effected to the fullest possible extent by a process of decontrol.[34]

The Reduction of Government Expenditures

According to the Department of Commerce analysis just referred to, even the moderate contraction in numbers employed and in working hours in the period before the Pacific war ended would reduce total wage and salary income by $10 billion. But this decline seemed insuffi-cient to retard or offset the essential deferred expenditures of business, the demands of consumers for durable goods not now available, and

34. In making this comparison between conversion to war and reconversion to peace I do not wish to minimize the difficulties involved in the latter process. It seems clear now that the official statements made in September 1944 were premature and unduly optimis-tic. The duration of the European war and, still more, the interval between the ending of the wars in Europe and in the Pacific were overestimated. To be sure, a longer interval between the end of fighting in the two theatres of war would have simplified the problems of reconversion and decontrol. Because the end of fighting on both fronts was but a few months apart the interval was a much shorter one than had been anticipated. Experience seems to indicate that, at all stages between the end of the fighting part of the war and the end of the transition to normal peace conditions, the problem of control will remain im-portant and the relaxation of controls will have to be worked out progressively in the light of conditions. Though it is true, as I have said, that for the economy as a whole re-conversion to peace will be a process of contracting output, which should make it a sim-pler process than that of conversion to war, there will almost certainly be the following difficulty. The expansion of civilian production will have to be both large and rapid, and this process may well involve scarcities in production facilities and bottlenecks in supplies similar to those encountered in the expansion of wartime production. The relation of these two problems to production, price, and credit controls and to rationing is a subject too large for consideration here.

postponed public works. When, however, the full contraction of war expenditures occurs, the decline of incomes will be much greater. In the above analysis it was assumed that the federal government would still be spending not less than $60 billion a year for war purposes. But with the war over, military expenditures will drop to perhaps $6 billion a year. From the 1944 level of about $100 billion, total government expenditures will drop to perhaps $30 billion. Even allowing for the estimated drop in the full-employment gross national product from $200 billion in 1944–1945 to $170 billion in 1947 (but rising by 3 per cent a year thereafter), the net gap to be filled is $40 billion a year.

We face two questions. How far will deferred civilian demands go toward filling up this gap? What is to take the place of the deferred demand once the process of restocking has been completed? In answering these questions it is not permissible, as seems sometimes to be done, to say that with a full-employment national income we shall have consumption, investment, and public expenditures of full-employment magnitudes, and then lay on top the deferred demands and the savings accumulated in the war. This way we could indeed raise the specter of inflation. We must face the questions as I put them. Otherwise we assume away the problem.

Deferred Civilian Demand

Intensive analysis of the deferred demand has been undertaken both by government agencies and privately. Since other contributors to this volume have in the past, and presumably in this book as well, gone into the matter much more thoroughly than I, my comment can be brief.

Undoubtedly, for a short period this accumulated demand could be of large proportions. It has been estimated that the deferred demand for consumer durable goods should amount to $4.4 billion a year for four years.[35] Probably a much larger item will be postponed private capital formation. Now almost nil, gross private capital formation averaged $13 billion a year from 1936 through 1941. Not only should it revive, but because of accumulated replacement needs, postponed expansion, replenishment of inventories of civilian goods and the cost of reconversion it should for a time substantially exceed the prewar volume. There should be also a substantial backlog of demand for housing. There have been estimates that residential construction after the

35. Sumner H. Slichter, "Jobs After the War," *The Atlantic Monthly,* October 1944.

war might amount to one to one and a quarter million units a year, requiring a $5 billion volume of expenditure. These estimates are very high by any previous standards but could well prove true in the aftermath of a war, with its greatly increased marriage rate and greatly reduced residential construction.

In calculations of this kind there is usually added to our own civilian demands accumulated during the war the export surplus representing the needs of foreign countries for rehabilitation and reconstruction; the need for further development abroad would probably come at a later stage. In 1919 our export surplus was about $4 billion and a corresponding surplus this time would have to amount to nearly twice as much. But in regarding the export surplus as an offset to declining war expenditure we must bear in mind that our lend-lease exports are running (1944) at the rate of $11.5 billion a year and our total exports, $14.3 billion a year. To make the same relative contribution to national product, postwar exports would have to be at least three times their prewar magnitude.

If we look at the figures of wartime saving, estimated at about $107 billion in the past three years — of which about $65 billion represents saving by individuals (including their holdings of government securities) [36] — without asking for what it might be spent, the possibility of filling the gap looks even brighter. But what will happen to these savings is problematical. Very likely the savers will hold on to a large fraction, though no one knows how much; and perhaps the better lead is to stick to estimating the needs (besides unemployment) for which some portion might reasonably be spent. To the point often made that the very existence of these savings will make people more willing to spend their current incomes I will return later in another connection, but it does not help us here unless we first explain how adequate current income is to be created.

Continuing Growth of Demand

Whether these deferred demands, large as they are, will prove large enough to fill the gap left by the reduction of military expenditures seems to me doubtful. In any case, they will not do so for long. Beyond

36. "The Wartime Expansion of Liquid Assets," *Federal Reserve Bulletin,* October 1944.

will lie the question what to rely on when the catching-up process is at an end. To some degree from the start we must depend on growth of new demand, and on this increasingly we must rely as we come out of the transition into normal long-run peace conditions. While growth of demand is being fostered through combined business and governmental policy, public expenditure may have to play an important role. But I conclude again that if after the transition has been passed we find ourselves compelled to fall back upon substantial deficits — and not merely on a cyclically unbalanced budget, with perhaps a modest average deficit to assist in further growth — we shall have failed to achieve our objective within the limits we have set.

V. THE LONG-RUN PROBLEM

This brings us to the long-run problem. I do not approach it with great confidence. Most of the programs and analyses I have seen seem unduly optimistic. The fact that the war has ended in two stages and that we shall have large deferred demands are certainly favorable factors, but they are temporary factors, and cannot disguise the fact that the long-run problem is one of unprecedented proportions.

How Many Jobs Are Needed?

I have pictured the problem as a net drop of $40 billion below the requirements of a full-employment national income. Put in human terms, the end of the war will involve the shifting of 15 million war workers and 9 million from the armed forces into civilian employment or into unemployment. A number of attempts have been made to work out in some detail the reabsorption of workers. In order to achieve full employment with a normal labor force and a peacetime pattern of employment, consumption, and private capital formation, a total of about 13 million workers (9 million to be demobilized from the armed forces and 4 million net to be released from industries now devoted to war production) would have to be provided with employment or withdrawn from the labor market. Some of this total would be taken up by reducing hours to a normal work week and by retirement of women, young people, and old people now abnormally employed. By allowing for absorption into agricultural employment (probably too high already for normal peacetime needs), and into trade and service industries — and a minimum labor float of 2 to 3 million — the problem has been worked down in some of the analyses to a question whether construction, which employed a half million workers before the war, could employ two and a half million. This would involve expenditure of $15 billion a year on construction. Assuming $5 billion on residential housing (a high figure as I have already indicated) and perhaps $2 or $3 billion on business construction (probably also a high figure in view of the large volume of wartime construction, much of which may be convertible to peacetime uses) such an annual construction program would involve $7 or $8 billion a year of public works.[37]

But underneath all such calculations lies the fact that a full-employment national income has already been assumed. Like the models I referred to earlier, they are helpful in breaking down the dimensions of the problem and giving a general indication of the goals to be sought. But they do not of themselves throw light upon the processes whereby such goals are to be reached.

Three Main Courses Toward the Goal

The fundamental question is whether we must have a grand plan, with comprehensive government control, or whether, given the short breathing spell of the two-stage war termination and the deferred demands — and such temporary budget deficits as may be required — we can work out an answer consistent with the form and the spirit of the free-enterprise system. As the problem is often put in this country, if business does not succeed government must. To this might be added the question, if business and government combined do not succeed by free-enterprise methods, how far shall we be driven upon some other course — whether that suggested by Sir William Beveridge or some other? As I said earlier, the answer depends in part upon our general scheme of values, political and social as well as economic.

There seem to be three main courses open: (a) the adoption of fiscal and monetary policies to stabilize income and employment, and in so far as possible to expand them, but subject to the qualification that large public expenditure, and especially large deficits, will gradually transform our economic system into some kind of public economy; (b) non-

37. See Alvin H. Hansen, "Wanted: 10 Million Jobs," *The Atlantic Monthly*, February 1943.

fiscal policies, both business and governmental, to make the private economy function more effectively within itself and respond more promptly to forces making for expansion; and (c) the development of new wants, new products, and new processes. We shall need to rely heavily on all three.

Is Consumption Merely a Passive Factor?

At the core of the problem are the relationships among consumption, investment, and public spending. In much of the monetary literature of the interwar period consumption was regarded as the passive factor and investment as the factor responsible both for short-period fluctuations of national income and for long-term growth. The role of budgetary deficits was to compensate for variations in investment. The British White Paper on Employment Policy runs mainly in these terms, though, as I have said, it treats budgetary deficits very cautiously.

Even from the short-run standpoint this approach leaves something lacking. The view that consumption is the passive factor ignores the fact that expenditure on consumer durable goods shows quite as wide a range of cyclical fluctuation as expenditure on producer goods. The business cycle is not so much a cycle of investment as a cycle of durable goods, both producers' and consumers'. It is the postponability of the expenditure rather than the character of the goods that seems principally to matter, and since the first war the turns in expenditure on consumer durable goods have led the way into booms and depressions quite as often as those on producer goods. When we consider that since World War I the volume of expenditure on the two types of goods has been of about the same magnitude, it seems doubtful whether there is any more to be said for a policy of stabilizing investment than for a policy of stabilizing consumption of durable goods. Both seem necessary.

The Growth of Consumption

But our postwar problem is more a problem of growth than of stability, and from this standpoint especially the concept of consumption, as propped up by and dependent upon the volume of investment, must be re-examined. All the estimates I have cited agree that consumption must expand by at least 40 per cent by 1947, and correspondingly more thereafter, beyond the level of 1939. To what extent must this great rise in consumption, amounting to at least $30 billion, be brought about by policies designed to expand investment and/or public expenditure, and to what extent must consumption be made to stand on its own feet? No doubt we shall need to do both, but it is important to see that there is a fundamental difference in the two approaches.

The view that consumption must be dependent upon investment, or on public spending as a substitute, will always, I believe, leave us subject to the basic worry that the objects of expenditure may not be enough. Thus, before the war, we worried about declining opportunities for investment. When we look at the postwar period we find it difficult, apart from the purely temporary deferred demands for capital goods, to picture a volume of new investment much beyond $10 or $12 billion a year. In 1939 it was roughly half that. It then becomes a short and fairly obvious step to the view that we must look to public investment as the way out — both to encourage private investment and to take its place.

I have no quarrel with this kind of policy, except to raise the question of its adequacy. The desire to avoid spending merely for spending's sake seems now to be general. One of the most difficult questions about public works has always been whether it would be possible to assemble enough worthy projects to provide an adequate prop for a national income which, by reason of the strong tendency toward technological advance, needs to be ever larger to furnish adequate employment. Probably, as the necessity unfolds, we shall do a better job in this regard than ever previously. But the more public spending our program requires, the more we shall need to scrutinize the objects of expenditure. The broad and general view that we can afford whatever we can produce, and that the one thing we cannot afford is unemployment, covers leaf-raking and building causeways to the moon as well as economically desirable expenditure.

What I feel inclined to question is the adequacy of the whole approach. Consumption is roughly eight parts of national income; investment, or a budgetary deficit to take its place, is the other part. If we hope to bring about a great expansion of postwar national income compared with prewar, we shall have to attack consumption more directly. Private investment and public expenditure, important though they are, cannot be more than stepping stones to the final goal. The growth of national income depends only secondarily upon "income creation" by either private investment or public expenditure and primarily upon the price-cost relationships at work throughout the whole economic structure.

Flexibility of Prices and Incomes

Fiscal and monetary theory has been developed largely on the basis of an assumption of price rigidity as a *force majeure*. It is based on the view that if the price system is not responsive to economic changes we can compensate for its defects. For short-period fluctuations this is often a helpful approach, but when the problem assumes large proportions, as in our present case, we are forced to dig down deeper and remove the defects, if only for the reason that the task of "compensation" becomes unmanageably large. What seems needed, more fundamentally than fiscal policies, is to make our economy more responsive and adaptable within itself.

Much attention needs to be given to the question of how the benefits of increasing productivity can be diffused more rapidly through the economic system by downward adjustments of prices and upward adjustments of incomes. If this interflow of income between production and consumption could be made more effective, there would be less need for reliance on public spending and, indeed, even on investment itself. My own view of an advancing economy is one that relies more and more on better technique and organization to increase its output, and more and more upon a rapid diffusion of the benefits through price reductions and income increases to expand consumption correspondingly.

Investment and Price Reduction

In the economic literature investment has been treated chiefly in two senses: the income-increasing sense, which is its role in Keynesian economics, and the cost-reducing sense, in which the earlier economists regarded it. For the problem of growth and progress there can be little question that the second is much the more fundamental function. From the long-run standpoint, investment is significant not primarily because of the money income and the employment provided by the capital goods industries themselves but because of the fact that by producing consumer goods in more efficient and therefore cheaper ways it releases consumer income for expenditure on other goods and services, and by increasing productivity per worker makes possible upward adjustments of incomes and increased voluntary leisure.

This has been the heart of the productive process under the free-enterprise system. In a task of the present magnitude it seems inescapable that we shall be forced to rely upon making it work rather than upon compensating for its failures. Indeed I think it can be demonstrated that if investment (or public spending) does not have these cost-reducing effects it can never rise beyond being a kind of perpetual pump-priming device, needing always to be renewed and always on a larger scale.[38]

Once the emphasis is shifted to this aspect of the investment process, it becomes just another step to recognize that investment is only one way to reduce prices and raise incomes. In a modern highly capitalistic society capital replacement tends steadily to increase relative to new investment, and the question of growth and progress becomes increasingly how to improve equipment and technique through the replacement of old capital. How far this process has gone in England has been shown by Colin Clark.[39] The yearly additions to British home capital have declined since 1875. Clark's figures on net investment as a percentage of national income show a decline from 12.2 per cent in 1907 to 8.1 per cent in 1924, 7.2 per cent in 1929, and 6.9 per cent in 1935. His conclusion is:

I believe the facts have destroyed the view up till now generally prevalent, that the rate of economic growth was primarily dependent upon the rate at which capital could be accumulated. The very rapid expansion at the present time [before the war] is taking place at a time of heavily diminishing capital accumulation. What is more remarkable, practically none of the capital which is being saved is being put into productive industry proper.

Kuznets has shown that in this country in 1919–1935 replacement constituted 68 per cent (1929 prices) and new investment 32 per cent of the yearly average volume of gross capital formation.[40] Leaving out public agencies, his figures were 81 per cent replacement and 19 per cent net capital formation.

38. See William Fellner, "The Technological Argument of the Stagnation Thesis," *The Quarterly Journal of Economics*, August 1941.
39. *National Income and Outlay*, Macmillan, New York, 1938, p. 270.
40. *National Income and Capital Formation, 1919–1935*, National Bureau of Economic Research, New York, 1937, p. 49 and Table 14. In a later analysis covering the longer period, 1919–1938, Kuznets found that net investment was 33 per cent of gross capital formation. See his "Capital Formation, 1879–1938," *op. cit.*, Table 2, p. 60.

Price Reduction and Saving

The main objection that is made to this way of achieving economic progress is that it does not absorb saving. Outlets for saving through investment are reduced and, at the same time through the cost-reducing effects of new technique, consumer wants are satisfied with less expenditure and saving is increased.

I discussed earlier the relation of technological progress to unemployment. We have here apparently its counterpart in terms of money income. The more directly and cheaply we seek to satisfy our wants, the more we defeat ourselves by throwing money income out of use. By insisting sufficiently on the intractability of the propensity to save we might persuade ourselves that the higher the cost and the greater the roundaboutness of production, the fuller would be employment both for labor and for income. The alternative, from this point of view, would be to have the government absorb an increasing portion of the community's money income and spend it on make-work jobs, in order to offset the efficiency of the private-enterprise system. Efficient public expenditure might only re-create the problem by again satisfying wants too cheaply and with too little labor.

I have never been convinced of the reality of the tendency toward oversaving which has been the chief preoccupation of monetary theory for the past decade.[41] Most of the prewar estimates of saving were estimates of real investment, and prove only that, as might be expected, changes in national income have been accompanied by changes in investment. How much of income took the form of idle saving, and to what extent investment may have exceeded or fallen short of saving through accompanying changes in bank credit are aspects of the question usually not covered by the analysis. What the estimates seem to indicate, for this country, is a constant long-run relation between income, investment, and consumption since as far back as 1880.[42]

In other words, while national income has risen greatly over this period, standards of living have risen correspondingly, and the great bulk of income has gone into consumption. Saving, at least as measured by real investment, has remained a constant fraction of income. In England, on the other hand, according to Colin Clark's data previously cited, saving has been a diminishing fraction of a growing national in-

41. See my *Postwar Monetary Plans and Other Essays,* Chap. 4.
42. Simon Kuznets, "Capital Formation, 1879–1938," *op. cit.,* p. 69.

come for at least the last generation. Samuelson's analysis of the American data yields the striking conclusion that consumers in the aggregate spent virtually all their increases in money income and that any additional saving accompanying rising income almost wholly took the form of business saving.[43]

The Rate of Saving in the Future

For the postwar period concern about the possible depressing effect of saving is heightened by our wartime experience. At the war level of national product we were generating much more income than we spent.[44] One explanation offered is that living standards lag markedly behind income, so that the temporary effect, at least, of a large and sudden rise in national income is a great increase of saving. On these grounds some economists have predicted that in the postwar period, even if for a while we spend enough, publicly and privately, to generate a national income of $140 billion, the effects will soon be dissipated by saving. Consumers and business concerns will fail to spend their current incomes.[45] This view is heightened by projections of prewar studies of consumer expenditure[46] which indicate that at a national income level of $140 to $150 billion we might save as much as $30 billion a year.

My guess is that these fears will turn out to be exaggerated. One point, referred to earlier, is that the very fact of accumulated wartime saving may make people more willing after the war to spend their current incomes. But a much more important point is that wartime saving would have been much less if there had been consumer durable goods available to spend it on. In the twenties, the last period of sharply rising national income, there was no evidence that consumption lagged

43. See Alvin H. Hansen, *Fiscal Policy and Business Cycles*, W. W. Norton, New York, 1941, Chap. 11, Appendix, pp. 250–60 by Paul A. Samuelson.

Samuelson's analysis is based on Kuznets' data (1919–1935). For consumers he finds a marginal propensity to consume of 0.97, and for business enterprises a marginal propensity to save of 0.49. "This [business saving] accounts for most of the leakages incident upon net investment: as far as these data go, the leakages incident upon household savings are much smaller and possibly negative" (p. 257). In his conclusion (p. 260) he again emphasizes "the very sensitive relation of consumption to aggregate income payments."

44. See "The Wartime Expansion of Liquid Assets," *Federal Reserve Bulletin*, October 1944.

45. See Gunnar Myrdal, "Is American Business Deluding Itself?" *The Atlantic Monthly*, November 1944.

46. National Resources Planning Board, *Consumer Expenditures in the United States*, 1939; and see also *Family Expenditures in the United States*, 1941.

markedly behind income, and expenditures on consumer durable goods, including automobiles and residential housing, expanded faster and relatively more than either total income or investment. Consumer durable goods are quite as much an outlet for saving as investment, and when we take them both together the assumption underlying modern monetary theory, that income tends to run to waste in idle saving, seems far less plausible.

VI. A High-Consumption Economy

In attacking consumption directly, our best hope is to develop new consumer wants and goods to satisfy them, especially the durable goods the demand for which, in response to efficient production as reflected in prices, is highly elastic.

Lessons from the Automobile Industry

The chief generator of national income in our time has been the automobile. It seems important to note, too, that the growth process to which the automobile gave rise does not lend itself to the conception of consumption as the "passive factor" induced and propped up by investment. From modest beginnings, first a circus curiosity, then a luxury, and finally a necessity, the demand for which has reached down into lower and lower income brackets, the automobile has generated both consumption and investment on an ever widening scale. And the accompanying growth of consumer credit shows that it has not failed to make inroads on saving.

The history of its successive price reductions, improvements in quality of product, and advancing wage rates, all accompanied by an ever widening market, mark the automobile industry as the model on which to build our future growth in a far more realistic sense than the models of national income setting forth the proportions of consumption, investment, and public spending which I earlier discussed. If we could repeat this experience with any combination of new and improved products after the war, it would probably be our best means of achieving a high-employment level of national income and consumption.

Similar Possibilities, Especially in Housing

The war has produced or improved further a number of such products. The helicopter, food-freezing in homes, air conditioning on a national scale, nation-wide television networks are some of the things we talk about. But perhaps the chief opportunity on a scale comparable with the automobile would be in housing, if we could impart to it some of the enterprise and ingenuity which have characterized the automobile industry. Here is a market at least equally as large and one that should be equally as attractive as an outlet for saving. In the past we seem to have approached it primarily from the standpoint of public expenditure — how much public housing or public assistance to private housing may be needed as an offset to oversaving. But the characteristic free-enterprise method of solving the problem would be to provide housing, as we have provided automobiles, of a quality and at prices which the community felt it could afford and could not do without.

This does not imply that there will not always be an important area for public housing, but it does suggest that one of our greatest needs in preparing for the postwar period is a thorough exploration of the conditions in the construction industry. No industry, as all analyses agree, is more essential to expansion of national income and employment, and no industry today is more characterized by primitive methods, high costs, and monopolistic and racketeering elements. I heartily agree with Beardsley Ruml's proposal that we should have a national commission to study the construction industry.[47]

New Products and More of the Old

It is sometimes objected that new products replace old ones. This is often the case, but any implication that consumption does not grow on balance is abundantly disproved by the history of consumer durable goods in our own time, and the reason obviously is that new products have generated new income.

On the other hand, we must not conclude that consumers' purchases can be increased only if new products are created. This would imply that the existing needs are fully satisfied. According to prewar studies of consumer expenditures, in 1935–1936, 54.9 per cent of all American families (all those earning less than $1,250) and 60.7 per cent of single individuals (all those earning less than $1,000) *dissaved* in order to cover their current living expenses. These estimates strongly suggest that in order to develop a vigorously expanding high-consumption

47. Beardsley Ruml, "A Postwar National Fiscal Program," *The New Republic*, February 28, 1944.

economy, governmental and business policies should be directed toward modifying the distribution of national income. This is the logical and necessary counterpart of the tendency toward technological advance which, as I said earlier, is the chief explanation of the high estimates of postwar full-employment national income. It points to wage policies, profits, social security, and taxation as areas especially in need of study if we are to accomplish our objective.

A High-Wage Economy

A high-consumption economy, i.e., an economy with a high level of income but no excessive saving, should be a high-wage, low-profit economy. Wartime changes have substantially modified in this direction the prewar distribution of income, and in reconverting to peace our aim should be to see how much of this shift it is desirable and feasible to retain. Labor will surely now want to retain its pay envelope, despite reduction of hours and loss of overtime rates. Such demands could easily be excessive, but we should recognize that it is easier to achieve a high-consumption economy by holding to a tolerable minimum reduction in wage rates from the present level than it would be under peace conditions to raise them from the prewar level.

The great difficulty about raising wage rates as a means of raising national income is the conflict between wages as income and wages as cost. What happens when there is a large and sudden peacetime rise of wage rates was shown in 1937. The rise of wage rates in the first half of 1937 was probably the greatest in our history in so short a period, apart from war. The result was a sharp decline in profits. This, along with the rise of prices and the wave of forward buying (which in turn were related to the uncertainties growing out of wage-rate increases, wage disputes, and fears of strikes) had more to do, I have believed, with the renewal of depression in that year than the temporary balancing of the budget. Broadly speaking, wage-rate increases must follow rather than precede advances in productivity and output. But once achieved, as now in war, they must be held so far as possible.

High Wages Versus Planned Spending

To the maintenance of a high-wage structure I would subordinate the role of public expenditure or any type of what I have called the propping-up method of sustaining consumption. By this I do not mean to deny the importance, even in the longer run, of public expenditure. There will undoubtedly be a growing need for expenditure that can be undertaken only by the community as a whole. I am sympathetic to public expenditure to promote higher standards of health, education, and security. By such means we can help to put a floor under consumption and at the same time increase the productivity and general well-being of our people.

I am sympathetic also to the private planning of expenditure, such as that advocated by the Committee for Economic Development. By breaking down the problem, community by community and industry by industry, we should be able to accomplish much toward providing a shelf of private as well as public works[48] to help sustain production and employment through the transition period. But all this, important as it is, is either temporary or secondary. To the long-run problem we need a more analytical approach. If one may use such a figure of speech, we need an approach that runs more in terms of the biology of the organism of the private-enterprise system — what essentially gives it life and makes it grow? So long as the "compensatory" approach is kept secondary to this, and is not built up into a device to make the free-enterprise system tolerate more comfortably its organic diseases, it can be a most helpful and necessary secondary method of attack.

A Low-Profit Economy

I have suggested that a high-consumption economy should be not only a high-wage but a low-profit economy. This is a particularly difficult aspect of our problem. We must not lose sight of the fact that ours is a profit-seeking economy. Profit has been the mainspring of change, both in regard to long-run growth and short-run fluctuations.

Profits fluctuate much more than any other type of income. The history of corporate profits in the interwar period was one of large and

48. While it is possible and desirable for individual industries and communities to look ahead and plan for, and thus hasten, their necessary and foreseeable capital improvements, on the analogy of the public-works shelf, this seems to me an approach of limited and temporary possibilities. To plan for long-run industrial growth by this method encounters the difficulty, probably inherent in the free-enterprise system as against the state-controlled economy, that we cannot foresee changes in price relationships and in the pattern of production and employment which in a growing economy, particularly following a war, are bound to be great. I expressed earlier my skepticism about the suggestion (see S. Morris Livingston, *Markets After the War*) that businessmen should break down the postwar projection of national income and employment by individual industries and have each one undertake to do its share.

rising profits from 1922 to 1929, large net losses in the depression and slow recovery thereafter. Not until 1941 did corporate profits before taxes surpass the peak of 1929. One of the most debated questions in the thirties was whether the rate of profits was not too low in relation to the volume of business to induce adequate investment and expansion. The sharp setback in profits caused by the increases in wage rates in 1937, the new social security contributions by employers, and the depression of 1937–1938 lent support to this view. But in 1940, when the national income for the first time exceeded that of 1929 on a per capita basis, corporate profits before taxes were about equal to those of 1929, and in 1941 they were nearly double.[49]

Surveying the whole experience, we must ask whether profits were not too high in the twenties as well as too low in the thirties. Profits are both cause and effect of business-cycle fluctuations. A rise in profits which feeds on itself cyclically results in losses later on. Lower and more stable profits would not necessarily mean lower average profits over the period of the business cycle. A lower rate of profits in a more stable economy would be preferable, even from the standpoint of business itself, if it did not impair long-run growth.

The most outstanding fact about the interwar experience was the marked stability of the long-run relation between the level of profits and the volume of national income. In 1940–1941 there was a substantial identity of the profit-income relation with that of the late twenties. But in marked contrast was the change in unemployment. There were 5 to 6 million more unemployed in the later period of high national income than in the earlier one. The growth of both income and profits in 1940–1941 was in response to external stimuli. Rising national income, under the stimulus of the war and our defense expenditures, generated profits which, if they had not been increasingly absorbed through taxation, would have been inordinately high.

There is a strong presumption that income must increase relative to profits. If the free-enterprise system is to grow from within itself, the rise of profits in response to increasing productivity, new methods, and new investment must be passed on rapidly in the form of higher wage rates and lower prices. Only in this way can the expansion of national income be made a self-continuing process, rather than one that needs

49. See Dwight B. Yntema, "Corporate Profits and National Income," *Survey of Current Business,* September 1944.

increasingly to be propped up by public spending. How to absorb profits into higher wages and lower prices in a steady and orderly manner which business can tolerate without deflationary setbacks or the impairment of investment is the central problem.

Profits and Business Savings

One major question involved is the relation of profit to saving. No aspect of the savings problem has been more discussed than that of business savings. Much data and analysis have been developed, especially in connection with the Congressional hearings in 1939 by the Temporary National Economic Committee. The relation of profit to saving stands out strikingly. In 1929, for example, a year of high national income, profit, though only 10 per cent of income, was 46 per cent of saving.[50] But 1929 was a year of high investment, and all that such figures by themselves indicate is that capital expansion was to a large extent financed internally rather than through the securities market. The chief complaint of the thirties was that business savings tended to remain idle. It was supported by the contention that improved machinery and technique were financed out of depreciation funds rather than from profits.

There was, I think, much truth in this view, though it should not necessarily imply criticism of corporation practice. Under conditions of rapid technological advance, the high rate of obsolescence involved requires large replacement funds. But it does mean, as I indicated earlier in reviewing British experience, that in a highly advanced industrial economy, replacement becomes increasingly important relative to new investment, and in consequence the outlets for saving out of current income, whether from profits or from other forms of income, are increasingly reduced.

Reasoning of this sort was responsible for the short-lived undistributed profits tax of 1936. The tax came at a time when business profits were already being undermined by unduly large and rapid wage increases and were about to face a new depression. It represented also a mechanical approach to the problem, emphasizing graduated penalty rate provisions and making inadequate allowance for small and new enterprises. It proved highly effective in forcing distribution of profits

---

50. See Moses Abramovitz, "Savings and Investment: Profits vs. Prosperity?" *The American Economic Review*, Supplement, June 1942, p. 65.

through sustained and increased dividends at a time of diminishing profits. In 1937 business dissaved a billion dollars at the very time when, because of wage increases, social security contributions and renewed depression, idle business saving had for the time being ceased to be a problem.

But for the postwar period the question remains one of paramount importance. The central question regarding profits is whether we must tax them away and redistribute them, with due regard for new enterprises and for risk-taking investment in old enterprises, or whether, if business were not taxed, it would itself pass on the benefits of increasing productivity to the consumers in higher wage rates and lower prices.

VII. TAXATION

This brings us to the problem of postwar taxation. There has been, I think, a tendency to oversimplify the subject. Public finance, taking revenue and expenditure together, can theoretically restrict or promote the flow of national income or have a neutral effect. But we have to recognize at the outset that taxation, of almost any sort, tends to be restrictive, and if our objective is to have a balanced, or a nearly balanced, budget, this is a hard fact to reckon with.

The Restrictive Effects of Taxation

That is especially true when we have to think in terms of a postwar federal budget which has been variously estimated at from $18 to $25 billion. No doubt we should like to have a tax structure which would promote consumption and investment (particularly of venture capital), encourage new and small enterprises, raise wages and lower prices, and discourage idle saving. But this is asking much of an instrument whose basic tendency is to be restrictive. We have yet to discover how effective taxation can be as a tool of compensatory fiscal policy. But the very size of the postwar budget indicates that the subject must be put high on the agenda of postwar policy.

It has been estimated that, assuming the repeal of the excess-profits tax, our present federal tax structure and tax rates, at a national income level of $140 billion, would yield about $31 billion. Our problem is how much we can reduce the tax burden, and in the process reshape it so as to minimize its restrictive effects on the growth of national income and employment.

Many of the tax plans now being discussed seem to me to exaggerate the amount of tax reduction that will be possible and therefore the amount of freedom we shall have in revising the tax structure. If we could assume, for example, the widely used estimate of $18 billion of postwar federal revenue (exclusive of social security taxes), we could go a long way in reducing excise taxes and corporation income taxes, and could rely relatively much more than at present on the individual income tax, which students of taxation have long regarded as the ideal form of tax. But even a budget of $18 billion, if it were to be financed exclusively or mainly by the individual income tax, would require a tax with a very broad base, low exemptions, a high normal rate, and a steeply progressive schedule of surtax rates. This would meet objection from those who hold that such a broad application of the income tax to low incomes restricts consumption, and from those who hold that unduly steep progression impairs investment.

In a subject about which as yet we really know very little, all generalizations are dangerous, but it seems a cardinal principle of taxation that the amount of emphasis that can be placed on any one kind of tax depends upon the amount of revenue to be raised. If the revenue required is large enough, a simple one-tax structure begins to defeat itself by the restrictions it imposes on the flow of income, and we have to spread out into other kinds of taxes, even though in themselves they may be less desirable. The higher the burden of taxation, the stronger the presumption becomes that to have a balanced tax system we must use different kinds of taxes.

Federal Postwar Expenditures and Taxes

Whether federal postwar taxation can be held down to some such figure as $18 billion will depend on the expenditures and upon the attitude we adopt toward balancing the budget. As I have indicated, there seems now to be a strong drift toward balancing the budget at full employment, with only modest departures either way, as between those who feel that at full employment we should be able to effect some debt reduction and those who feel that, while the budget should be balanced at full employment, it is more reasonable to expect that even in fairly prosperous years we shall fall short of this objective and require a modest deficit.

My own feeling is that federal expenditure of $18 billion a year is an underestimate. Such an estimate is usually arrived at by dividing expenditures into three roughly equal parts — military, interest charges, and other. Postwar military expenditures are particularly hard to estimate, and expenditures for veterans, if history is any guide, are likely to be a large and growing item in the budget. Public foreign investment and relief will probably also be substantial. It seems difficult also to picture a typical postwar year without considerable expenditure for public works, even if our planning for high employment meets with substantial success. We should think of public-works expenditure not only from the viewpoint of "income-creating" deficits but also from that of socially desirable and necessary expenditure (not necessarily financed by deficits), the kind of spending that the community needs to do collectively.

All in all, my guess is that federal expenditures are more likely to amount to $20 to $25 billion a year than anything under that. If this estimate turned out to be more nearly correct, we should then have either to modify our attitude toward deficits or to raise more revenue. If we raise the estimate of revenue the simplicity apparent in some of the postwar tax plans disappears. Whether or not the individual income tax could provide most of the revenue for an $18 billion budget, it certainly could not supply some additional billions without pinching severely either on the lower end of the scale where consumption is restricted or on the upper income brackets where investment is impaired. This is the kind of awkwardness that such a restrictive instrument as taxation inevitably presents as the amount of revenue required increases.

Taxation to Restrict Saving

The preoccupation of fiscal theorists with taxation as a compensatory device has been with the absorption of idle saving. Whereas deficit spending is supposed to offset such saving by creating new income, taxation is regarded as a device for absorbing the saving and restoring it to the income stream. Granted that taxation is restrictive, if we could use it to restrict idle saving without impairing either consumption or investment we could improve the flow of income.

If under conditions of high taxation a country were shifting from a system of indirect taxes to a system of direct taxes, consumption could be greatly relieved and saving much reduced. But a number of studies have indicated that, when a country has already a large and progressive income tax, the possibilities of further absorption of saving through the income tax are not great, while the danger of restricting consumption or investment is likely to increase more than in proportion to the yield.

The reason is that the great bulk of national income is in the lower and middle income brackets, so that to get a high yield these are the brackets that must be taxed. Thus, under the 1944 rate schedule well over one third of the total yield comes from taxpayers with net incomes of under $3,000 and only one third from incomes above $10,000. One effect that recognition of these facts should have is to make us realize that public expenditure offers no easy road to expansion of national income if it carries a presumption, as I think inevitably it must, that as expenditures increase the tax burden will increase, whether proportionally or not.[51]

The Corporation Income Tax

In recent tax proposals the chief subject of discussion and controversy has been the corporation income tax. A rather striking change has occurred from the insistence in the late thirties on taxing corporate profits, especially undistributed profits, in order to absorb idle business sav-

51. See Abram Bergson, "The Incidence of An Income Tax on Savings," *The Quarterly Journal of Economics*, Vol. 56, February 1942; and Gerhard Colm, "Full Employment Through Tax Policy," *Social Research*, November 1940. See also R. A. Musgrave in an article soon to be published in *The Quarterly Journal of Economics*. The conclusion that progression of the income tax cannot be relied upon to secure a drastic reduction in savings checks with conclusions reached by an unpublished study of the National Resources Planning Board (*Wartime Planning for Continuing Full Employment*, Interim Report by Full Employment Stabilization Unit, August 1942).

Musgrave has estimated that in an income tax yielding $16 billion a shift from a flat rate schedule of 30 per cent to the most progressive schedule possible (which would leave nobody with a net income after exemptions of over $2,300) would increase the incidence of the tax on savings by only about $3 billion.

Some calculations by Moses Abramovitz ("Savings and Investment: Profits vs. Prosperity?" *The American Economic Review*, Supplement, June 1942, p. 80), based on the estimates of tax burdens and savings by income groups presented by Colm and Tarasov (*Who Pays the Taxes?*, Monograph No. 3, TNEC hearings) indicate that "a truly enormous shift of taxes from the relatively poor to the relatively rich would be required to effect a substantial reduction of savings." In the fiscal year 1939, the year to which the Colm-Tarasov figures refer, he estimates that "a 30 per cent reduction of the amounts people desire to save (aggregate income being constant) would have involved the extinction of all taxes on the incomes of families earning less than $2,000 a year and the distribution of this burden among higher income groups. The groups so relieved of taxation contributed in 1939 no less than 45 per cent of total tax revenues. Moreover, since the taxes on the lower income groups are levied mainly by states and local governments, what is involved is nothing less than the stupendous task of local rather than national fiscal reform."

ings to the present emphasis on the desirability of relieving corporations from taxation.

The case for relief from corporate taxation is usually put on two main grounds: first, that the tax absorbs funds which would otherwise go into higher wages and lower prices, that it is in effect a tax on consumption; and, second, that it absorbs funds which would otherwise go into investment. It ought to be pointed out that the first of these grounds rests on the view that the tax is shifted, and the second on the view that it is not. In the past, economic theorists have mainly, though not unanimously, emphasized the second view, but there is probably no subject on which we need more light. One of the chief difficulties is that we have not yet had much experience, under peace conditions, with a high level of taxation.

Very likely the corporate income tax is both shifted and not shifted, depending on the circumstances. But it seems to me doubtful that, to the extent the tax is not shifted, investment would be impaired by a moderate tax rate. On the other hand, even if part of the tax is shifted, the interwar behavior of profits does not suggest that this is a very sure or rapid process, and it seems by no means clear that reduction of the corporate income tax would be the best way to sustain consumption as against the reduction of excise taxes and of the individual income tax on the lower income brackets. As I have said, when the aggregate amount of possible tax reduction is limited, we are forced to think in terms of the comparative merits of reducing different kinds of taxes.

One of the chief arguments for greatly reducing, if not virtually eliminating, corporate income taxation has been that at present we tax corporate income twice, once against the corporation and again in the hands of the dividend receiver. This seems to me a valid argument, not because of the double taxation involved (we have many forms of double taxation) but because we are discriminating against equity financing as compared with fixed indebtedness and thereby impairing both stability and growth of national income.

Taxation of Undistributed Profits

But this leaves the question of what to do about undistributed profits, which last year were about half the total. I have already reviewed the prewar discussion of undistributed profits as a main source of saving. Various suggestions have been made as to how the undistributed portion of corporate income could be reached by a tax on the stock-holders. But this, even if it could be done, and I have not yet seen a sug-gestion that sounds practicable, would not meet the point about taxing idle corporate saving. The conclusion seems warranted that if distrib-uted profits are to be exempted or substantially relieved from taxa-tion, a fairly high rate of taxation of undistributed profits must be re-tained.

But this is the most puzzling aspect of the subject. We must bear in mind that financing out of undistributed profit is an important source of new investment. The view often expressed that business should be compelled to face the test of the security market when it contemplates expansion overlooks the fact that for new and small businesses this is often not a practical possibility,[52] and even for larger companies with widely fluctuating earnings may be unwise if the financing involves an increase of indebtedness.

A tax policy which virtually forced the distribution of earnings to stockholders regardless of circumstances and left to business manage-ment little discretion regarding its reserves against possible future losses or its methods of financing future expansion would surely be too mechanical. It could have a paralyzing effect upon the attitude of busi-ness both toward new investment (or any sort of innovation involving risk-taking) and toward the policy of wage increases and price reduc-tions so essential to a progressive system of free enterprise. I therefore find it hard to say whether a heavy tax on undistributed profits with little or no tax on distributed profits or a more moderate tax on total profits would be the better compromise toward achieving the not easily disentangled aims of forcing idle business savings into use, on the one hand, and encouraging business enterprise and initiative, on the other, as a means of expanding national income and employment.

But in any case such a low over-all rate as the 16 to 20 per cent tax recommended by the Committee for Economic Development or the 5 per cent franchise tax (plus 16 per cent normal tax) proposed in the Ruml-Sonne plan seems unrealistic, at least on any other basis than that federal expenditures will be as low as these plans assume.

There is one further important distinction between the amount of

52. See especially the studies by J. Keith Butters and John Lintner, *Effect of Federal Taxes on Growing Enterprises:* Study No. 1, The Lockheed Aircraft Corporation, April 1944; Study No. 2, Polaroid Corporation, November 1944, Research Division, Graduate School of Business Administration, Harvard University.

corporate income taxation and the way it is applied. I entirely agree with the suggestion made in many of the current tax plans that the corporate income tax should include liberal provisions for averaging income over a period of years by carrying losses forward and back.[53] To encourage risky investment, the application of the averaging principle to irregular personal incomes also deserves careful study.

The Order of Tax Reductions

Surveying our postwar tax problem as a whole, we are brought back to the question of how much tax reduction will be possible, and this as I have said will depend upon the volume of expenditures and our attitude toward deficits. Assuming that under the present law the tax yield (exclusive of the excess-profits tax) would at a national income of $140 billion be about $31 billion, we must consider the rival claims of different kinds of taxes for reduction and work out some system of priorities. A reduction of about $6 billion could be effected by cutting in half the excise taxes ($2.6 billion), repealing the 3 per cent normal rate personal income tax ($3 billion), and repealing the capital stock and declared value excess-profits tax ($350 million). Most of the current tax plans put these reductions high on the list.[54]

If we could reduce the federal budget by another $5 billion to $20 billion, perhaps the next logical claimants for reduction would be a cut in the first bracket surtax rate under the personal income tax from 20 per cent to 15 per cent, which would effect a reduction of $2.8 billion, and exclusion of dividends from the corporate tax base, which with a 40 per cent corporate tax rate would mean a reduction of $2.2 billion. Alternatively, a cut of the over-all corporate income tax rate to 30 per cent would give a reduction of $1.55 billion. Other schedules of possible tax reduction could be worked out, but this one will serve to illustrate how limited are the possibilities so long as we assume that the federal tax yield must be $20 billion or more, rather than some sub-

53. See J. Keith Butters, "Discriminatory Effects of the Annual Computation of the Corporation Income Tax," *The Quarterly Journal of Economics,* Vol. 54, November 1939.

To encourage rapid technological advance, we should also permit adequate deductions for depreciation and obsolescence.

54. A conspicuous exception is the Twin Cities tax plan (*Postwar Taxes,* The Twin Cities Research Bureau, St. Paul, Minnesota, June 1944), which favors both high consumption taxes and high corporation taxes in order to reduce the progression of the individual income tax, in keeping with its view that large personal incomes are the chief source of venture capital. It ought to be said, however, that this plan calls for a substantially higher total revenue than the other plans I have mentioned.

stantially smaller amount. I would hesitate to put the relief of corporate income from taxation ahead of any of the other reductions I have mentioned.

Taxation and Fiscal Policy

The results of this brief survey of the tax problem are depressing. We are dealing, as I have said, with a restrictive instrument. Granted the importance of having the best tax system we can devise, the point to emphasize is that, inescapably, it will be a burdensome system. When we add in state and local taxes, the total burden will be some $30 billion or more, or between a quarter and a fifth of a full-employment national income.

Against the tax burden we should, of course, put the possible expansive effects of different kinds of public expenditure. Without denying that with the right combination of expenditure and revenue we might achieve some net expansive effects, it does seem true that the economists have scarcely begun to analyze the problem in this way. Instead (because of their preoccupation with the oversaving theory) they have been regarding public expenditure and taxation as alternative methods of correcting the flow of income. My own view is that unless we frankly accept budgetary deficits as the means of income expansion, an approach of which I have long been skeptical and from which there seems now to be a general desire to back away, we are forced to work primarily in other directions than fiscal policy to develop a satisfactory theory and policy of the growth of income and employment in a free-enterprise system.

This brings me back to a view I expressed in an earlier section of this paper: that fiscal policy is a better instrument for business cycle stability than for growth. A policy of cyclically unbalanced budget combined with tax reductions in depression and tax increases during booms could probably accomplish much to stabilize national income, if such a policy is politically and administratively feasible. For business cycle purposes, it would be desirable to have a sufficiently simplified tax structure so that with few changes in the rate schedules up or down we could effect the desired changes in the revenue and in the budgetary deficit or surplus. It does, however, seem an oversimplification to suppose that we could fix once and for all upon rates that would automatically produce the results desired as the national income fluctuates.

Finally, for the reasons I have given, it seems to me an oversimplification to suppose that we can get away from a mixed tax system including the individual income tax, the corporation income tax, and excise taxes. With a need for revenue as large as seems to be in prospect the mixed tax system probably offers the best assurance of a balanced system resting as lightly as possible on consumption and investment.

VIII. Money and Banking

Our postwar problem of income and employment is many sided. I have been trying to discuss the core of the problem rather than to make a comprehensive survey. There are many aspects which, for want of space or knowledge, I must omit. But two sets of questions seem to me hardly less central to our whole attack upon the problem than those I have discussed. One is monetary and banking policy, and the other our relations with the outside world. Both deserve fuller treatment than my remaining space permits.

Changes in Central and Commercial Banking

Taking the war and the interwar periods together, there have been revolutionary changes in both central and commercial banking. These changes have stemmed chiefly from the growth of the public debt. The commercial banks have become mainly dependent for assets and for earnings upon the public debt, and in the process central bank policy as an instrument of control of economic fluctuations has been largely supplanted by fiscal policy. The larger the public debt becomes and the more of it the banks hold, the less feasible it becomes to exercise a general monetary control.

Monetary policy in the past has worked mainly through the effect of central bank control over reserves and deposits upon the rate of interest, which in turn was supposed to influence investment and employment. In the early thirties monetary and fiscal policy were regarded by economists as complementary. If the problem had remained that of business cycle control, on the assumption of a budget balanced for the cycle as a whole, a combination of general monetary control affecting interest rates and the money supply, with fiscal policies working through deficits and surpluses to affect the volume of expenditures, might have offered possibilities of more effective stabilization of national income and employment than we had ever previously attained.

Perhaps a moderate and gradual long-run growth of the public debt, if the debt were held mainly by nonbank investors, would not have interfered seriously with this kind of control policy. But when the debt is large and the bank share of it substantial, stability of interest rates becomes increasingly essential and general monetary control has to give way to a policy of "maintaining orderly market conditions" for government securities.

These changes in the character of central and commercial banking, already apparent in the later thirties, have gone much further under the necessities of wartime financing. The maintenance of orderly war market conditions developed into a conscious maintenance of a fixed pattern of interest rates, stabilized at a level lower than ever before in the history of this or any other country. To fight wartime inflation earlier economists would have put monetary controls first, fiscal controls second, and direct controls last, but in World War II the emphasis was precisely reversed. This was a striking but a correct and necessary change; it occurred in all the countries at war.

In wartime the banking system should provide an assured market of last resort for Treasury financing, and the only kind of control appropriate is through limiting the banks' participation to what is necessary (after adequate effort is made to finance government expenditures through taxation and borrowing from nonbank sources) and limiting the rate of interest on securities sold to banks to prevent undue bank earnings at the government's expense. In the early part of the war much concern was felt over the fact that our Treasury was borrowing more from the banks than from the public, but in the last two years this tendency was progressively corrected.

Inflation and Deflation After the War

Looking to the postwar period, we face the facts that the federal debt will be large, some $300 billion, that the banks have acquired about a third of it, and that in the process total deposits and currency have had a huge growth — from about $61 billion in June 1939 to about $151 billion in December 1944. There may well be a further large increase in the banks' government security holdings and hence in the money supply after the war. It depends (apart from further budgetary deficits) on whether the public will want to liquidate its securities to buy consumer goods and to what extent business will liquidate securities, and also borrow from the banks, to finance reconversion and capital expansion.

Those who anticipate an inflationary rise of prices in the transition period stress these possible monetary changes. Such a development could occur in the interval of reconversion while civilian goods are still scarce. This indicates the need not only of speedy and orderly reconversion but of retention of wartime controls until such a danger is passed. But I am much more impressed by the longer-run deflationary possibilities arising out of the abundance of raw materials and man power and the great drop in war expenditures. I have long believed that the quantity of money, by itself, has a permissive rather than a positive effect on prices and production, and our whole experience since 1929 has seemed to show that the relation is much looser than almost anyone had previously supposed.

The Prospects of Monetary Control

I can see no prospect of revival of a general monetary control in the postwar period. This is not merely, or perhaps even mainly, a question of the vulnerability of the banking system to a rise in interest rates. In the last two war years the banks pursued a prudent policy regarding the maturities of their security holdings; their holdings of maturities beyond ten years have not increased and nearly two thirds of their holdings mature or are callable within five years. This does not mean, however, that a rise in interest rates would not find the banks very sensitive and might not precipitate a wave of government security selling by banks, as happened in 1937 in response to the raising of reserve requirements.[55] But the larger fact, I think, is that as the debt increases the whole economy becomes vulnerable to any substantial change in interest rates and the public and the Treasury, as well as the banks, develop a strong vested interest in stability of rates.

How much room there may be for other types of monetary control is problematical. With the great decline in excess reserves that has occurred during the war there might be some room for monetary control through variations in the shorter rates of interest. But the logical alternative, if a general monetary control is no longer feasible, is more direct controls, such as those we now have over the stock market use

55. To stabilize bank holdings of government securities, the device of a government bond reserve against deposits has been suggested by Lawrence Seltzer and others.

of credit and consumer credit. Both of these, I think, should be permanently retained and some other possibilities, such as control over urban housing and farm mortgage credit, carefully explored.

But this kind of monetary control has, I am inclined to think, a limited range of application; it seems best suited to control of the use of credit in organized markets providing a standardized collateral for loans. I doubt, for example, whether it would be an effective method of control over business inventories, which have been one of the chief elements of business cycle fluctuations. There is also the question how far we want to go in this direction. The rationing of credit for specific purposes does not go so far as the rationing of private spending or even as Sir William Beveridge's suggestion of public direction and control of private investment, but it is not unlike in kind and raises similar questions about the meaning of a "free society."

The Future of Commercial Banking

The public debt and the banks' holdings of it raise important questions also about the future of the commercial banking system. Though interest rates have been low, bank earnings have become abnormally high because of the great volume of financing. Meanwhile the great growth of deposits has produced a marked decline in the ratio of capital to deposit liabilities. This puts an increasing premium on comparatively riskless bank lending and investment, such as government securities. It is the kind of process which feeds upon itself. It could raise the question whether banking should become a public function, or at least the question of how much its services in holding the public debt should cost the Treasury.

Interest will be one of the chief items in the postwar budget, amounting perhaps to a fourth or more of federal expenditures. There have been already a number of proposals for reducing the interest on the part of the debt held by banks. My own view is that the amount of interest that could be saved by any reasonable proposal would not be great, and that steps taken in this direction could arouse fears in the rest of the community about the goodness of the government's promises to pay. For the future of the banking system, as well as for stability and growth of the economy, what is most to be desired is that we should get more and more of the debt into private hands and free the banks to take a larger share in serving the credit and investment needs of private enterprise.

IX. INTERNATIONAL TRADE

In concluding this paper I can comment only briefly on the international aspects of our postwar problem. As I have said, national income and employment will have to depend primarily upon domestic policies and conditions. But our economic and financial relations with other countries will have an important secondary influence upon our own market, and may well be the decisive factor in determining whether and when international economic stability can be achieved.

The Foreign Demand for American Exports

The international and the domestic sides of the problem raise some similar questions. The cessation of lend-lease now the war has ended will be the foreign trade counterpart of the reduction of military expenditures here at home and, like the latter, will raise the question of how the gap is to be filled under peacetime conditions. In answering the question we shall again have to distinguish between the period of transition from war to peace and the longer-run conditions.

Undoubtedly in the years immediately after the war the foreign demand for American exports will be large. We can foresee something of its character. There will probably be important amounts of lend-lease goods in process of production which could serve civilian needs abroad if satisfactory arrangements, possibly through the Export-Import Bank, could be made for long-term financing. There will also be the supplies to be financed by the United Nations Relief and Rehabilitation Administration, to which the United States is contributing $1.35 billion. There will be demands for goods to assist in reconstruction, as distinct from relief. It seems very desirable, in our own interest, to define reconstruction broadly and even generously, as meaning, for example, that the capacity of foreign countries to produce and export should be restored as rapidly as possible and with as much emphasis as is prudently feasible upon external aid rather than at the expense of the internal standard of living, which has been so greatly depressed in many countries. There will be also, as here at home, large deferred demands for consumer durable goods. Besides all these, there will be demands from the young and from the less developed older countries for capital goods to assist in development of their resources.

The Financing of the Exports

Without pretending to be exhaustive, I have said enough about the foreign demand to suggest that it will be large. How large it will be will depend to a great extent on the financing. To a greater degree than seems generally realized foreign demands for our goods can be financed by the importing countries themselves. The war has greatly increased the gold and foreign exchange resources of many countries. Canada has come out of the war a creditor country; and for the other countries of the British Empire the main problem will be the status of their accumulated balances in London.[56] The Latin American countries now have large gold and dollar balances; their short-run problem will be how to refrain from overspending. In Europe, the neutrals — Sweden, Switzerland, Spain, and Portugal — have all increased their foreign exchange resources, and Holland, Belgium, and France still have large reserves of gold.

All in all, there is at present some $20 billion of gold and dollars owned by foreign countries, as compared with about $5 billion at the end of World War I and $7 or $8 billion in 1929. This widespread increase in exchange resources is the result of the wartime foreign expenditures by this country and England, combined with the lack of goods on which the balances could be spent. It represents the international counterpart of the wartime savings and deferred demands which have accumulated here at home, and bears the same kind of relation to our postwar problem.

Undoubtedly, however, there will be important demands for recon-

56. It is perhaps inaccurate to describe these balances (which amounted to $12 billion at the end of 1944) as frozen. They will be available for spending in England, or within the sterling area, but presumably on a time schedule related to the development of British capacity to export. By means of a dollar credit to England they could be made available for spending anywhere in the world, but this may not be thought to suit the British interest so well as the more direct means these balances afford of developing British export trade, even though exports to liquidate these balances represent payment of a debt rather than any new benefit to the hard-pressed British economy. The existence of these balances suggests also that England may have important bargaining advantages, and these may have a significant bearing on such questions as the development of the sterling area, imperial preferences, and the development of trade along bilateral versus multilateral lines. Obviously the balances will require the maintenance of exchange control for some years to come. There is not room for discussion of these problems in this paper.

struction and development which will have to be financed by foreign investment, and the capital will have to come primarily from the United States. Our experiences after the last war indicated that foreign investments misdirected are worse than none at all. We greatly need to develop improved standards and procedures and to differentiate more carefully between the kinds of expenditure which should be financed at home by the borrowing country and those which should be financed with foreign funds. There is a tendency, I think, to exaggerate both the amount of capital that could effectively be spent abroad and the speed with which the expansive effects upon our own economy could be generated.

The Bank for Reconstruction and Development

There is a widespread belief, born largely of our unfortunate experiences in the twenties, that foreign investment of private capital will involve some kind of insurance. It was from this point of view that I first came to recognize the desirability of the Bank for Reconstruction and Development proposed at Bretton Woods.

The Bank agreement faces up squarely to the fact that the bulk of the lending would have to be done by the creditor countries, and mainly by the United States. The capital of the Bank would serve mainly as a contingent guarantee fund to guarantee issues marketed either by the Bank itself (its own debentures) or by other public or private agencies. To have the insurance take an international form would have many advantages. Besides the fact that it is equitable that all countries should share in the risk, it opens up the possibility of developing, through the collective action of borrowers and lenders, the standards and procedures of sound investment to which I have referred. The Bank, according to its provisions, would avoid the practice of "tied loans," would require written reports by its own committees on loan projects, would control the loan expenditures and confine loans, with rare exceptions, to the financing of capital goods actually needed from abroad. In these and other ways it could serve as an agency for continuous international consultation and cooperation.

Exports and Employment

My special interest in this section is in the contribution that American foreign trade and investment can make to the solution of our postwar problem of employment. This contribution will be through the export surplus.

Despite what I have said about the large foreign demands, especially in the transition period, it will be a mistake, I think, to count very heavily upon the export surplus to fill up the gap that will be left by the cessation of war expenditures. There is, first, the point I mentioned earlier, that even though postwar foreign demand is large it will have to be very large indeed to make the same relative contribution to national income and employment as is now being made by lend-lease exports. There is the further consideration that in the future, if we wish to see a proper balance restored in the world, we must increasingly emphasize imports. We have seen the evil consequences of a mechanical propping-up of our economy by one-sided trade involving either a draining from the rest of the world of its monetary resources or a foreign "investment" which does not eventuate in a flow of goods from the borrowing countries. We have seen also the conflict generated at home when, as a consequence of large-scale foreign investment, we have to face up to the logic of the process and ask ourselves which industries and which workers are to meet the competition of the foreign goods that are the only means whereby in the end the investment can be justified.

The propping-up of our national income and employment through the export surplus represents the same kind of mechanical approach to national income and employment which I discussed in connection with budgetary deficits. I favor the development of international trade through the freer flow of goods and capital on the same grounds as I have argued for the revitalizing of the private-enterprise system here at home. They are the logical counterparts of each other. But this view emphasizes the volume of trade as a whole, and the cost-reducing effects that can be achieved through a better utilization of the world's resources, and not the export surplus, which suggests instead a desire to get leverage for our own employment at the expense of the outside world.

Domestic Policy and International Stability

It should help our perspective to recognize that this country produces almost half of the world's manufactures and uses more than half of the world's raw materials. It follows from this fact that the solution of our own problem of employment must be predominantly domestic.[57] It follows also that the greatest contribution we can make toward international economic stability will be to solve our problem domestically and to maintain a high, stable, and growing level of production, income, and employment. Under these conditions we would need large amounts of foreign goods and could most readily afford to take the lead in reducing barriers to the international flow of goods and capital.

It seems no exaggeration to say that not only will postwar international economic and monetary stability be primarily dependent upon the success of American domestic economic policy but the character of the program we adopt and the success we have with it may go far toward determining what kind of economic and political system will prevail in the world. In the postwar world we shall find the nations strung out at various points along the way between the private-enterprise economy and some sort of state-controlled economic system. Perhaps our most important new problem in international trade and financial relations will be the question of how countries so different in economic and political character can work out mutually beneficial relations.

Will it be possible under such heterogeneous conditions to restore the system of multilateral trade which is the logical counterpart of the free-enterprise national economy or will the balance swing the other way? It would be rash to attempt an answer to this question, but it does seem clear that the greatest contribution we can make toward the preservation of our kind of economic system, both here and elsewhere in the world, will be through the achievement of high national income and employment by methods directed primarily toward making the private-enterprise economy function more effectively.[58]

57. As I indicated earlier, after the last war (1919–1920) the export surplus, though abnormally large, represented only about one seventh, and domestic factors about six sevenths, of the aggregate of income-increasing expenditures.

58. In planning this paper originally, I had hoped to have a section on postwar planning for international monetary and economic cooperation, and in particular, to analyze the Bretton Woods proposals for an International Monetary Fund and a Bank for Reconstruction and Development. These proposals, ever since the publication of the original plans in April 1943, have been a leading preoccupation of mine. But I concluded finally that an adequate treatment of them would require an expansion of my paper well beyond the space allotted or an undue compression of the domestic questions which seem to me of primary importance in a discussion of our own problem of postwar production and employment. Except, therefore, for the brief reference to the Bank in relation to postwar foreign investment, I have omitted the subject altogether.

I have had reservations about the Monetary Fund. Some of these have been technical in character. But the largest question, in my mind, has been whether it was best to approach the problem in terms of a general international monetary organization, as the Fund agreement proposes, or to begin with the major countries whose currencies are the chief means of international payment and whose policies and circumstances will have a predominant effect upon the character of postwar international trade and currency relations. From the outset I felt that the key to the question whether we shall be able to restore multilateral trade and a system of reasonably free and stable exchanges lies in finding a solution of England's special problems. Whether this is done with or without the Monetary Fund, or before or after adoption of the Bretton Woods proposals, it still seems to me the central question. Perhaps the chief dangers in the Monetary Fund approach are that we may fail to appreciate the fact that the success of the Fund will have to depend primarily on what is done, outside the Fund, toward solving England's special problems and that we may regard adoption of the Fund as in itself a solution of those problems.

For a statement of my views see my *Postwar Monetary Plans and Other Essays,* 2d ed., 1945, and also a more recent paper, which deals particularly with the British problem, "The Bretton Woods Agreements," *Proceedings of the Academy of Political Science,* May 1945.

FINANCING POSTWAR FULL EMPLOYMENT BY
MEANS OF DEFICITS

In an attempt to get some idea of how large postwar full-employment deficits might be on the basis of prewar reasoning, the following table has been prepared. It projects the 1939 figures to 1947.

HYPOTHETICAL DEFICIT SPENDING IN 1939 AND 1947 ON
ASSUMPTION OF FULL EMPLOYMENT
(*In Billions of 1943 Dollars*)

	1939		1947	
	Actual	At Full Employment	At 1939 Employment Levels	At Full Employment
Available for private use:	*90.2*	*102.9*	*99.2*	*118.8*
Consumers' expenditures	76.7	88.6	84.2	102.3
Gross capital formation	13.5	14.3	15.0	16.5
Government expenditures (federal, state, and local):	*19.7*	*33.8*	*28.0*	*49.3*
Interest on Federal debt	1.0	1.0	5.5	5.5
Income-creating expenditures	5.0[a]	18.4	5.5	26.0
All other expenditures	13.7	14.4	17.0	17.8
Gross national product	*109.9*	*136.7*	*127.2*	*168.1*
Business taxes	12.9	15.5	13.0	16.0
Capital charges	9.2	10.6	8.0	9.0
National income	*87.8*	*110.6*	*106.2*	*143.1*

a. Total federal expenditure for work relief and CCC (2.1 billion) plus half of the expenditure for public works (2.1 billion) and aid to agriculture (1.5 billion). This estimated total income-creating expenditure is equal to the federal budget deficit.

* This Note (see page 350) was prepared at my request by George Garvy, Research Department, Federal Reserve Bank of New York. — *John H. Williams*

Estimates of gross product "at full employment" involve first assumptions as to the size and distribution of the labor force. It is assumed that in both 1939 and 1947 full employment would be consistent with the existence of a "frictional unemployment" of 2 million persons; the strength of the armed forces in 1947 is placed at 2 million.

It is assumed that at full employment the number of workers would have been 52.6 million in 1939 and that it will be 55 million in 1947; and that at full employment in 1939, the number of persons engaged in agriculture, government work, and domestic service would have been the same as the number actually employed in 1939. No change is expected between 1939 and 1947 at "full employment" in agricultural and domestic employment; an increase of 10 per cent is anticipated for civilian government employment. The remaining industries will absorb 2 million additional workers.

In order to estimate gross national product exclusive of interest on public debt at full employment, gross output per person employed was estimated for major industry groups from Department of Commerce data for 1939. It was assumed that no increase in productivity would take place in either government or domestic service; for agriculture the total increase in output per worker employed between 1939 and 1947 was estimated at 20 per cent. All other industries were split into two groups; the first includes all mechanical industries like manufacturing, mining, construction, transportation and public utilities. For this group the cumulative increase of output per person employed was placed at 2.5 per cent per annum. This implies that technical progress made during the war will be applied in 1947 to civilian industries at a scale sufficiently large to warrant the assumption that, on the whole, past productivity trends have been effective throughout the whole eight-year period. For all other industries (service, trade, etc.), which in 1947 are expected to employ, as in 1939, about half of all persons in this group, an annual increase in productivity of only 0.5 per cent is anticipated. This is admittedly a conservative view, but it has been deemed preferable to err on the low side. Since underemployment due to short hours existed in 1939, gross output for both groups was raised 2 per cent as compared with actual figures. In 1947, the additional 1.6 million soldiers and sailors are expected to add to gross output $1,250 each. Finally, interest on federal debt ($1 billion in 1939 and $5.5 billion in 1947) was added.

It is estimated on the basis of the above assumptions that at full employment in 1939 our economy would have produced a gross national output of $136.7 billion (in 1943 prices); the corresponding figure for 1947 would be $168.1 billion. For the hypothetical case that in 1947 employment remains at the 1939 level it was assumed that gross national product would be larger than in 1939 due to increase in productivity.

To estimate the amount of income-creating government expenditures needed to fill the gap between the potential gross national product at full employment and gross product at 1939 employment levels (and its projection into 1947) an instantaneous multiplier of two was used for illustrative purposes. Income-creating expenditures of government were increased in the two estimates at full-employment level by half of the amount of the gap, the largest part of the other half being allocated to consumers' expenditures; regular expenditures of government as well as gross capital formation were increased only moderately.

In order to derive, from the figures for gross national product, estimates of national income, business taxes and capital depreciation were estimated on the basis of past relationships. To facilitate comparisons between the two years, estimates of gross national product and national income in 1939 were converted to the 1943 price level by using the cost-of-living index of the BLS.

The cost of achieving full employment through federal deficit financing is estimated roughly in the following table:

(*In Billions of 1943 Dollars*)

| | 1939 | | 1947 | |
| | | | At the 1939 | |
	Actual	At Full Employment	Employ-ment Ratio	At Full Employment
Government expenditures	11.1	24.9	18.0	38.9
Government revenue	6.1	7.7	13.0	17.6
Budget deficit	5.0	17.2	5.0	21.3

It has been assumed here that the entire burden of obtaining full employment through deficit spending would be borne by the federal government. Column one gives the actual figures for 1939. It has been assumed that at full employment revenue would increase in the same proportion as national income. Expenditures in column two have been estimated by adding the estimated increase in income-creating expenditures and half of the increase in "all other" government expenditures (the other half is credited to state and local governments and balanced by their increased receipts under full employment) to actual expenditures in 1939. A similar procedure was applied for 1947. For conditions paralleling those of 1939 it was assumed that revenue would fall short of expenditures estimated at a minimum figure of $18 billion by an amount corresponding to the 1939 deficit.

Chapter 8

SUMMARY AND ANALYSIS

Fritz Machlup[1]

I. Economic Objectives

FULL EMPLOYMENT

Effective slogans sometimes develop into social objectives. If they are well along in this development they may quickly gain general acceptance simply because objectors run the risk of being regarded as unsocial, as opposed to the public interest. If you are asked "Do you agree that we should have full employment?" you just cannot answer "No." The courageous may answer with a qualified nod: "Yes, but . . ." And the politic one will give an unqualified assent, resting on a mental reservation to the effect that full employment does not mean what the words say but has a special "scientific" meaning, known to the initiated; a meaning which would allow very substantial unemployment to exist under the condition of "full employment."

The universal acceptance of "full employment" as a social objective has frequently been misused in that a certain, very specific economic policy was called by its advocates *the* "full employment policy," with the obvious implication that no other policy was designed to attain full employment. "Are you in favor of full employment policy?" thus became a hard question to answer. If you knew that "full employment" had been appropriated as the trade-mark of the specific policy which you refused to endorse, you could not answer in the affirmative — and had branded yourself as a cold-hearted opponent of full employment.

These unfair tricks with the term full employment have raised the question as to whether we had not better avoid the expression altogether. Some scholars do try to stay away from it; others use it, but are careful in stating its meaning and in avoiding its spurious use as designation of a specific policy.

---

1. Goodyear Professor of Economics, University of Buffalo; Acting Managing Editor, *The American Economic Review*.

How Full Is Full Employment?

Williams states early in his essay, speaking of the prosperity year 1929, that 3 million unemployed "is generally regarded as consistent with full employment" (p. 338). He further reminds us of the fact that 1941, which "by any previous standard . . . was a year of highest prosperity," was "a year of 6 million unemployed" (p. 353). And he is not too optimistic concerning our ability to do much better than that in time of peace.

Anderson mentions that unemployment of "one or two per cent of the population" was ordinarily "regarded as a matter of course, when allowance is made for seasonal unemployment, for sickness, and for men shifting from one job to another, and for that rather considerable part of the population which was unwilling to work all the time and which preferred roving around" (p. 11). Periods like the present, when persons are temporarily drawn into the labor force who work only as long as the unusually large demand for labor lasts, are characterized as periods with "negative unemployment."

Clark also states that "at the height of the war effort we had over-employment equivalent to more than ten million workers, including overtime" (p. 75). The various normal types of seasonal and frictional unemployment he includes in his concept of the "float" of unemployed. For "a long-run peacetime normal" of this float "three million does not seem too large, as a tentative first approximation." Certain unavoidable fluctuations "will raise the average" and, moreover, "the normal 'float' in this country during the postwar transition will be larger" because "an economy which is in the midst of far-reaching shifts and readjustments actually needs a larger unemployed 'float' " (p. 76). Clark calls it "a really high level of employment" if "unemployment were approximately stabilized at a 'float' averaging not more than three to four million" (p. 116). He admits that "it is misleading to call this 'full employment'," but finds that the term is "probably too generally accepted to be dislodged" (p. 76).

Hansen does not warn us explicitly concerning the meaning of full employment, probably assuming that readers will remember the warnings he has expressed in some of his other writings on the subject.[2] The

2. E.g., in his pamphlet *After the War — Full Employment*, published by the National Resources Planning Board, 1943, p. 3. In a long footnote, Hansen states that shifts of labor

amount of unemployment which he would consider compatible with a state of full employment can be derived from his national income computations (p. 257). His postwar full-employment national income of $140 billion contains $92 billion as wages and salaries of 55 million workers in civilian employment. The $2.5 billion which constitute "payment to military personnel" may be assumed to go to approximately 2 million men. This would mean 57 million men employed and another 3 million unemployed if, as most computers do, he reckons with a work force of 60 million.

Ellis is quite explicit on the matter. He assumes that, with a labor force of about 60 million, frictional unemployment of 2 million must be allowed for (p. 132).

Slichter is the only one of our six authors who avoids using the term full employment. He speaks instead of a "satisfactory level of employment." Assuming a work force of approximately 60 million, a "satisfactory level of employment" would be about 57 million. Slichter divides unemployment into two principal types: "lack-of-enterprise unemployment" and structural or "market-imperfection unemployment" (p. 306). Their causes as well as their cures are different. If society does not choose to attack the market imperfections it will have to be satisfied in peacetime with from three to five million unemployed, this being the approximate amount of structural unemployment (p. 307).

Full Employment, at What Cost?

Full attainment of all social objectives in a world of limited resources is impossible because some goals are in conflict with others. Awareness of the fact that we must choose among alternatives leads most social scientists to qualify their endorsement of any particular social objective. Do we want full employment? "Yes, but not at all cost." We want other things too and wish to ponder their relative importance and the extent to which we might have to forego their attainment. In the words of Clark, "unconditional 'musts', settled in advance without investigating what they are going to cost, are likely to prove an expensive luxury" (pp. 72–73).

---

between industries and regions must necessarily occur in an expanding economy, and that the unemployment connected with such shifts, as well as seasonal unemployment, is compatible with "full employment."

CONFLICTING ECONOMIC GOALS

It is often assumed that the objectives "full employment," "highest national income," "stability," and "growth" are all perfectly compatible with one another. There is, however, serious doubt about it — particularly whether it is possible to combine full employment with the highest possible real income of the community, and whether stability is consistent with the greatest possible growth of productivity.

Choosing Among Alternatives

Can anything be said about the preference of our society for the particular goals, about the probable choice that would be made among them, if they can only be attained alternatively?

Clearly, no absolute preferences can be established. We cannot choose between "more employment" and "more income" without knowing how much we have to forego of the one in order to secure more of the other. We might decide in favor of full employment if it costs us only two or three per cent of the highest achievable income; but we might choose to put up with a certain amount of unemployment if this were a condition for reaching a substantially higher national income.

Likewise, most of us would be willing to accept some degree of instability if it were inevitable in the process of accomplishing a substantial improvement in productivity. On the other hand, if even slight progress were bound up with violent fluctuations in employment and income we might find that it was not worth the trouble.

In comparing the desirability of "more income" with that of "stable income," much will depend on the temperament of the person who makes a decision. Do you prefer a stable 90, or fluctuations from 75 to 125 yielding an average of 100? If, at these terms, you are inclined toward stability, how would you choose between a stable 90 and an average of 100 resulting from fluctuations between 80 and 120?

Considering the wide range of temperaments of those who are called upon to make choices of this sort (in their writings or, worse still, in the policy-making bodies of a democratic society) ; and considering the impossibility of getting any reliable estimates of the actual cost of stability in terms of progress, or of the cost of progress in terms of stability, unanimity would be surprising. Many of the differences of opinion among economists are of this kind and are then mistaken by a bewildered public for real differences in the fundamentals of economics.

Employment, Efficiency, Stability, Progress

Not every economist accepts the reasoning on the basis of which the existence of conflicts among the various goals is asserted. Hansen, for example, regards "stability, full employment and a rising standard of living" (p. 206) as a triad of objectives, to be aimed at simultaneously by one and the same policy. In particular, "an ever growing, expanding economy is both a goal in itself and a necessary condition for the achievement of full employment" (p. 226).

Of course, this does not mean that maximum stability, maximum employment, and maximum growth can all go together. That stability, employment, and growth are joint products of one policy is not inconsistent with the theory that they go together up to a point and, beyond it, become alternatives.

Williams, inquiring into the relationship between full employment and growth, poses the question whether a rapidly progressing economic system "does not have to operate on the basis of slacks — slacks in materials, in plant and equipment, and in employment" (p. 352). And he concludes that continuous efforts to produce at lowest possible cost and to exploit "new techniques which are both capital- and labor-saving" are liable to throw men and other resources out of use at each step in the process. Thus, "under conditions of rapid progress, there is bound to be a surplus of both men and resources," a surplus which is continuously being reabsorbed through expansion of output but recreated through further advances in productivity (p. 353). Highest efficiency and increasing efficiency are bound up with the existence of unemployment.

Williams is perplexed by the unfortunate choice "between less efficient production, providing jobs for all at low real income, and more efficient production, throwing increasing numbers of workers on to relief rolls and into make-work jobs." He decides against full employment as an objective, and restates the goal "as that of providing high employment or that of preventing high unemployment" (p. 353).

Anderson warns against accepting permanent full employment as an unconditional objective. Unemployment, to him, is a symptom of some economic disorder. Its causes must be attacked; to strike at the symptom "is a superficial and a dangerous procedure. There must be temporary unemployment, there must be reaction, readjustment and liquidation. The reaction and the unemployment themselves may easily facilitate the prompt readjustment" (p. 15).

Clark affirms that "there are some kinds of unemployment which are actually useful, or are inseparable from useful changes or processes." In other words, the constant adjustments which are necessary for the sake of efficiency and the changes which are needed in the interest of progress make some unemployment indispensable, and "an indiscriminate demand for complete removal is not helpful" (p. 74).

Slichter discusses the conflict between stability and full (or "satisfactory level" of) employment. He states that the control of inflationary expansion becomes too difficult if the satisfactory level of employment is approached; and that, for this reason, it might be preferable to stabilize employment somewhat below that level (p. 327).[3]

EQUALITY AND LIBERTY

Conflict may exist not only among economic objectives but also between economic objectives and fundamental social values. Most explicit as to such values is Ellis, who begins his essay with professing his creed as "liberal, individualist, equalitarian, and internationalist" (p. 126). According to his own definitions of these "basic objectives," they imply (a) "reliance upon a competitive price system as against political authority for the largest part of economic control"; (b) "emphasis upon individual 'rights' or liberty as against the negation of such liberties in an omnipotent state"; (c) "advocacy of a degree of equality of income" which would be attained if incomes from inherited wealth were minimized but differences in efficiency, skill and daring were fully expressed in differential compensations; and (d) "abandonment of all efforts directed toward . . . insulation" (with a qualification regarding immigration).

3. Slichter shows here a conflict of three objectives: We may have both stability and full employment if we accept regimentation. We may avoid both regimentation and fluctuations if we accept less than full employment — and, of course, the full employment which is meant here is already much less than full employment in any more literal sense.

Clark also refers to the possibility that "if we are going to spend our way to full employment and do not want to suffer from endless inflation, we shall be forced to maintain ceiling controls over wages and prices as a permanent peacetime measure" (p. 114).

These objectives, telescoped into a rough sketch, would make up an economy with competitive free enterprise, with little government intervention except as needed for maintaining the competitive mechanism, high inheritance and gift taxes, and free trade. These are his ideals; but he makes compromises whenever conflicts arise among these and with other objectives. But Ellis is convinced that these objectives are not in conflict with the goal of "full employment" provided it is achieved "through exploiting and extending the advantages of a competitive price system" (p. 132) ; and he views the goals "high level of income," "expanding level of income" and "stable level of income" in harmony with the basic objectives.

Income Distribution

When Ellis introduces himself as an "equalitarian" he does not mean to advocate absolute equality of income. Apart from certain Utopian socialists and highly idealistic social reformers, few economists have favored absolute income equality. The main reason for the acceptance of inequality of income has been the recognition that total productivity would be drastically reduced if different productive contributions were not to receive their reward through differential compensations. Soviet Russia has officially recognized this fact and rejected any attempts to "level" individual incomes at the present stage of her economic development.[4]

Another reason was advanced, in days bygone, for accepting gross inequalities of income. It was said that capital formation depended on the amount of saving, and that the willingness and ability to save depended largely on an income distribution which allowed a small part of the population to receive a disproportionally large share of the national income. It was added that this inequality in fact worked to the benefit of the underprivileged low income group. The rapid growth of productivity made possible by the capital formation, which in turn was the result of the income inequality, permitted a continuous and substantial increase of the low incomes — much more substantial than a reapportionment of total income into equal shares could yield.

This argument, it is contended, has lost its validity, and its exact opposite is now advanced. If capital formation in this country is no

4. See Joseph Stalin, *The New Russian Policy,* John Day, New York, 1931. In Stalin's language the "socialistic" stage maintains income differentials, which are supposed to disappear only in the ultimate, "communist" stage.

longer held back by any shortage in the supply of savings, if the propensity to save is not too low but rather too high in relation to the available opportunities for private investment, then greater equality of income is wanted. The premise of the old argument, that greater inequality increases the willingness and ability to save, is fully retained. But, if less rather than more thriftiness is now wanted, inequality is attacked as harmful — quite apart from any claims of fairness or social justice.

This argument for greater equality of income is not an ultimate objective but is subservient to the objectives of high levels of employment and income. It is from this point of view that Hansen demands "better income distribution," higher wages, progressive income taxation (p. 218). For the same reasons Williams hopes for a "high-wage, low-profit economy" (p. 370): Profits are a rich source of savings, wages are more fully spent on consumption; a "high-consumption" economy would not suffer from excessive saving and the unemployment that goes with it.

More Equality, an End in Itself

Ellis advocates a greater degree of income equality not as a means to an end, not in order to reduce the economy's propensity to save; to him, "a more equal sharing is an end in itself." To achieve it he proposes "a whole gamut of measures," the most radical of which are "confiscatory death duties." Only the less drastic kind of inequality which results from differential compensation for different productive services is to be maintained; though perhaps this too may be slightly reduced through fuller "equality of opportunity through free public education and through a general relaxing of monopoly restriction" (p. 134).

Slichter recognizes a conflict between ideas of fairness or equality and the goal of a high employment level. He believes that a stiff progressive income tax, appealing to many "on the ground of fairness," is probably "bad for employment" because it is apt to reduce investment more than saving. "Consequently, the community must compromise between taxes which are good for employment and taxes which are fair" (p. 333).

Against Regimentation

All six contributors emphatically reject personal government and totalitarian control, although not all of them are equally eloquent on this subject. Conflicts between any economic objectives and the fundamental goal of political liberty give rise to great concern and the general presumption is to resolve them in favor of liberty.

In the opinion of Ellis, the need for economic stability does make necessary a large measure of government control (p. 128), but a type of control which is impersonal and not selective (in the sense of discriminatory, p. 146). Any other type of governmental control of "planning," recommended by Ellis only for the transition period, must be "so constituted as gradually to attenuate itself, in place of propagating itself and approaching collectivism" (p. 197). His program is to "secure high standards of living and high levels of employment under the economic governance of a competitive price system and not of the subjective judgments of planners and of other less benevolent tyrants" (p. 196).

Anderson states the position most pungently. "When government undertakes to coordinate economic life, there is required a central plan and a central brain." In time of war, objectives are definite and "a good deal can be done in the way of intelligent coordination and control." But in peacetime, with the multitude of alternative objectives, "the government is hopelessly clumsy and ineffective" (p. 28). "Totalitarian economic planning under a dictator with unimpeded powers, who also possessed clear objectives and superhuman intelligence, might make a consistent economic plan. Our democracy could not" (p. 36). "Effective economic planning would have to be preceded by complete centralization of our government. Democracy, local self-government, and individual rights protected by the courts would have to be done away with. The reconstitution of Germany's government under Hitler points the way — for those who wish to pursue it" (p. 29).

Slichter certainly does not wish to pursue it. His sentiment becomes clear from his selection of recommended economic policies. If a program appears to be linked with regimentation, Slichter discards it in favor of alternatives which can work without central management. Indeed, the basic philosophy of all his prescriptions is the use of "incentive methods."

According to Slichter, the government may and should "assume responsibility for incentives — to see that individuals, enterprises, trade unions, and trade associations have incentives to behave in ways that produce" the desired results (p. 304). If the government is saddled with responsibilities beyond the provision of effective incentives, this might necessitate "a high degree of regimentation, a great central management of the economy" (p. 307). In a conflict between the objective "Satisfactory Employment Level" and the objective "Avoidance of Regimentation," Slichter suggests that "the community may prefer" a lower employment level to more employment with more regimentation.

Clark, discussing "Goals and Standards," states: "If the country sets for itself a rigorous standard of completely full employment . . . and if this is an absolute and unconditional 'must', the only system which can meet this test will be an outright collectivistic economy, and probably one of the centrally administered type" (p. 72). While Clark does not exactly say that he would not like such a system, he does proceed to write a whole essay on the possibilities of "high-level employment, as stable as it can be made" in a private-enterprise economy (p. 76). He has stated elsewhere that he rejects a socialistic answer, on the ground that its compatibility with personal and political freedom is highly doubtful.[5]

A Free or a Planned Society?

Williams also prefers a "free society." To be sure, "probably no one really wants a laissez-faire system,"[6] but he is opposed not merely to a "completely regimented society" but also to any kind of planning which may tend to progress toward it (p. 352). He clearly sees the conflict between the goals "freedom" and "full employment" when he states that "insistence on a really full utilization of resources would require in peace, as it has in wartime, the use of direct controls" (p. 354 n). Solutions of our economic problems should employ only "methods consistent with free enterprise and democracy" (p. 354). Williams does not in this essay come out with any strong and direct statements in favor of "the system of private capitalism," but his position can be inferred from the fact that he fears and condemns continuous deficit financing and a rising debt burden partly because he believes

5. See "The Relation of Government to the Economy of the Future," *Journal of Political Economy,* Vol. 49, December 1941, pp. 799–802.

6. Ellis likewise is anxious to show that laissez faire is not identical with liberalism, because the latter, relying on a competitive price system, calls for state action against monopolistic forces (p. 127).

that the system of private capitalism would disappear in the process (p. 347).

Although Hansen emphasizes the need for government planning (p. 212), his essay abounds with statements on possible ways to encourage private investment and to "enlarge opportunities for private enterprise" (p. 211). If he stresses, more than any of the other participants in the symposium, the desirability of a very extensive public investment program, he wishes to make sure that "the government would not enter the general production field at all. That would be the job of private enterprise" (p. 212).

His plea for "planning" is not for the sort of thing which others so strongly oppose as "central management" of the economy. Hansen wants merely a planning of public projects, of tax adjustments, of the budget. Nobody can object to the most careful planning of fiscal and other governmental policies — even if the specific plans which are proposed are the subject of bitter controversy. It is another matter that the fiscal policies recommended by Hansen may have consequences which, according to Ellis and Williams, involve the danger of a drift toward a socialist or fascist system (pp. 138, 360). Hansen does neither wish nor believe that his recommendations actually have any such implications. Indeed, he has often expressed his belief that his methods were designed to preserve the free-enterprise system and to avert any revolutionary changes.

II. Economic Problems

SIZING UP THE EMPLOYMENT PROBLEM

Before the end of the war, 63 million persons were employed. Of these, 52 million were in civilian occupations and 11 million in the armed forces. Some of them will not want employment now that the war is over; on the other hand, persons who are now of school age will seek employment. On balance the labor force should be about 60 million.[7]

From Wartime to Postwar Figures

The federal government has been spending at an annual rate of $100 billion. Two or three years after the war, federal government expendi-

7. Ellis, p. 132; Hansen, p. 258; Slichter, p. 268; Williams, p. 392.

tures may have been cut to between $20 billion and $30 billion. This is a rather rapid disappearance of effective demand for goods and services. Will it not cause terrific unemployment?

The cut will probably not be at one stroke. Government expenditures can decline only gradually because of settlements of contract terminations, mustering-out pay, etc.[8] This will alleviate the problem,[9] for if the first reductions of governmental buying are by and large made up through increased civilian buying, the gap created by further reductions of government expenditures will be less overwhelming.

Another alleviation will come from a shortening of working hours, at least to the prewar level. The reduction in potential supply of output resulting from the shortening of the labor week, and the withdrawals from the labor force, though partly offset by increased productivity, will appreciably mitigate the shock caused by the reduction in effective demand. The reduction in potential gross national product is estimated at some $30 billion; hence, the reduction in "supply" will take care of $30 billion of the cut in total demand.[10] With the demand for goods and services reduced by some $75 billion a year, a "gap" of $45 billion will remain to be filled by increased consumption and investment. If the "gap" is not completely filled, unemployment will follow.

Hansen, Williams, Slichter and Ellis discuss measures designed to fill the gap. Anderson is not concerned with calculating or filling the gap, but with the restoration of economic equilibrium, especially through readjustments in cost-price relations which, in his opinion, could avoid or cure any unemployment that would result from the reduced demand. Ellis accepts this position for the long run, but not for the immediate transition period. Clark is skeptical concerning the success of either of these approaches if they are undertaken by themselves rather than in combination. He speaks of the "spending" and the "response" as "the energizing and the enabling conditions," respectively

8. Slichter expects that a year after the end of the Japanese war federal expenditures will still be over $40 billion (p. 277).

9. For other alleviating factors see Williams, pp. 355–57.

10. Williams, p. 357. In view of the prospective return of soldiers to the labor market it may seem peculiar to speak of a shrinking in the labor force. The reason lies in the fact that the 11 million persons in military service are now counted as employed and as producers of services which constitute a part of the gross national product. Hence, their discharge is not an addition to the labor force.

(p. 83), and analyzes the problems of effective demand as well as those of effective response.

From Prewar to Postwar Figures

The formulation of the problem as one of transition from actual wartime to desired postwar figures is regularly supplemented or preceded by a formulation which compares the prewar situation, either 1939 or 1941, with that expected to prevail or desired to prevail after the war.

Actual employment in 1939 was 45 million. If 57 million people (out of a labor force of 60 million) are to find employment after the war, an increase by 12 million, or almost 27 per cent, over the 1939 employment must be achieved.[11] Productivity per worker has certainly increased since 1939. By how much is anybody's guess: the estimates vary between 10 and 20 per cent.[12]

The effect of increased employment and increased productivity is expressed in the comparison between the actual gross national product of 1939 and the potential gross national product of 1947. Since prices are now higher than they were in 1939, for the purposes of the comparison we must first translate the national product of 1939 from the actual $88.6 billion at 1939 prices into an equivalent $110 billion at 1943 prices.[13] With this gross national product of $110 billion we then compare the potential 1947 gross national product of $165 billion or $180 billion.[14] The rise would be $55 billion or $70 billion, i.e., 50 to 63.6 per cent. This is a big increase. Will there be enough demand for it?

THE DEMAND FOR THE NATIONAL PRODUCT

The gross national product is composed of (a) what is purchased by the people as consumers, (b) what is purchased by businessmen when they invest in capital goods (plant, equipment, inventory) and (c) what is purchased by governments.[15]

11. Williams (p. 392) puts 2 million men into the postwar army and thus looks for only 55 million civilian jobs; also Anderson (p. 9) speaks of only 55 or 56 million employed.

12. Ellis, p. 133; Williams, p. 392.   13. Williams, p. 391.

14. Slichter (p. 282) has $178 billion; Hansen (p. 219) and Williams (p. 391) have $170 and $168 billion, respectively, and Ellis (p. 132) has $180 billion.

15. This scheme is a bit rough and calls for a few comments. First of all, it seems to exclude the things which are not purchased at all but which people are making for their own use. This is simply corrected by treating them as if they had been purchased by the

The three basic categories of effective demand are then (a) consumers' expenditures, (b) gross business investment,[16] and (c) government expenditures. The problem that chiefly occupies the minds of most economists speculating about postwar employment is whether the three items, without undesired boosts of government expenditures, will add up to an amount sufficient to secure the desired level of employment.

The Right Demand Called Forth by the Right Prices

This type of reasoning is rejected by Anderson. He does not ask whether a sufficient amount of purchasing power stands ready to demand all the things which could be produced at full employment. He asks instead whether relationships between prices, costs and profits, and the proportions of the industries, are sufficiently adjusted or adjustable to permit an equilibrium at full employment (pp. 13, 29). When the demand for labor falls, a reduced price of labor can still

---

makers themselves. Then there are the outlays for construction of residential buildings, outlays which some put under the heading of durable consumers' goods, others of capital goods. Private persons build homes for themselves and business firms build homes for rent; thus the aspects of consumers' demand and capital investment are both present and it does not really matter under which heading the outlays are entered.

There is, furthermore, the export surplus, which might be dealt with as an entirely separate item, e.g., as "what is purchased here by foreign countries in excess of what is imported from abroad." In order to have fewer main headings most writers treat the export surplus as a part of the investment item. After all, an export surplus can exist only if loans are made to foreign countries, that is to say, if somebody "invests in foreign assets" or if gold is imported, that is, if somebody (usually the Monetary Authority) "invests in newly imported gold."

Finally, among the purchases of the government is always the "abstinence" of government bondholders, paid for as "interest on the public debt." These payments are included in the gross national product. (Interest payments by business firms are included in the gross national product since they enter into the value of the things produced: the product of industry is divided among wages, rents, interest, taxes and profits. It would be inconsistent, in the computation of the gross national product, to include the services of industrial bond and stock holders, but to exclude the services of government bondholders.) Likewise, the costs of maintaining the army are included as purchases of services by the government, and these military services are a part of the national product. On the other hand, if the government pays relief or any sort of compensation for which no service was rendered, the expenditures are treated as "transfer payments" and not as any part of the national product. It should be clear that this purely statistical part of the national product as the abstinence of government bondholders does not raise any problems of finding an adequate effective demand for it and, thus, of securing employment of available resources.

16. The acquisition of a new machine constitutes effective demand no matter whether it is a replacement for an outworn piece of equipment or whether it is "new" investment. The question of "net investment" is relevant for the calculation of the net national income rather than of the gross national product.

secure employment for everybody who seeks it at the lowered equilibrium wage (p. 22).

Anderson's thesis does not mean that the disappearance of the demand for labor now exerted by the war expenditures of the government will have to be absorbed solely through wage reductions. Consumers' expenditures are going to be higher; and, in particular, business investment may assume large proportions when enterprise is no longer restrained and intimidated by ill-conceived government policies. How much business investment would be forthcoming if government interferences with free markets were removed, Anderson does not say; he stays away from all arithmetical guesswork and forecasting. His solution relies chiefly on a system of prices that "tell the truth," on "functional prices" which call forth all the demand that it takes to clear the supply (p. 29).

Hansen, Slichter, Williams, Clark and Ellis do not place such full reliance on a flexible system of functional prices. Ellis comes nearest to it, but he does not accept it for the immediate postwar period. Although he believes in "economic expansion through competitive markets,"[17] he finds that the removal of governmental restraints and monopolistic restrictions requires a number of institutional changes. It takes "basic reforms to realize a genuinely competitive economy" (p. 140). It takes time to achieve such reforms and, even if we began introducing them without delay, we must resort to direct supports to "total spending" (p. 134) "until the effects of these basic reforms begin to be felt" (p. 136).

A most careful analysis of the significance of the "cost-price structure" for the functioning of the economy and for the attainment of a high and stable level of employment is contained in Clark's essay. He rejects the theory that "the behavior of prices and wages" can "cure either cyclical or chronic depression," but he concedes that a proper behavior "may be necessary to a cure of underemployment, though not by itself sufficient" (p. 102). He rejects the idea of attaining full employment through a general wage and price deflation (pp. 99, 101), but he concedes that the relative wage structure "may create a problem of employability" (p. 112), a situation in which certain groups of labor are "priced out of the market" (p. 113).

The importance of "cost-price relationships," and the need for a

17. Ellis, p. 126, the title of his essay.

more responsive and adjustable price structure are not denied by Hansen, Slichter and Williams. Indeed, Williams holds that the future growth of national income will largely depend on adjustments of prices and incomes (p. 363). Nevertheless, the emphasis is different and an aversion against "deflationary" solutions and against downward adjustment of wage rates is inherent in the reasoning of these authors. The adequacy of total effective demand remains their central theme, although their methods of securing it differ.

Total Demand: A Rosy Picture

"Given" the desired level of employment and the assumed average productivity, the total demand to which the three expenditure items of consumers, business and government "should" add up follows. The figures which many economists put on paper for the three items are, in the words of Williams, "not simple projections of the prewar composition" of the national product but are based upon "estimates of what might be regarded as 'reasonable' amounts in each category" (p. 348). The figures reproduced in the following pages refer to the gross national product in "1947," that is, in the first year assumed to be without governmental war expenditures. The gross national product and the amounts in each category are calculated at 1943 prices.

Ellis cites the estimates made by Goldenweiser and Hagen.[18] Their figure for the gross national product, originally $170 billion, was later revised[19] to $180 billion. Slichter computes a figure of $178 billion for the gross national product at the "satisfactory" level of employment. His estimate of total demand is $178.7 billion, which means that according to Slichter's estimates there will remain a slight excess demand to cope with (pp. 282–86). This is his set of figures:

18. E. A. Goldenweiser and Everett E. Hagen, "Jobs after the War," *Federal Reserve Bulletin,* May 1944, pp. 424–31. These estimates are as follows:

(In Billions of Dollars)

Consumers' expenditures (excluding housing)		113
Gross investment		27
Plant and equipment	15	
Inventories	3	
Residential construction	7	
Export surplus	2	
Government expenditures (federal, state and local)		30
		——
Demand for gross national product		170

19. See Ellis, p. 132, n. 11.

	(In Billions of Dollars)	
Consumers' expenditures		125.9
Nondurable goods	101.8	
Durable goods (including housing), current	13.4	
Durable goods (including housing), deferred	10.7	
Gross investment		23.8
Plant and equipment	17.8	
Inventories	3	
Export surplus	3	
Government expenditures (federal, state and local)		29.0
Demand for gross national product		178.7

In this scheme (as in the one by Goldenweiser and Hagen) it is assumed that the government expenditures are fully covered by tax revenues; budgets are balanced.

Total Demand: A Gray Picture

Some of Hansen's figures are very similar to, if not the same as, those given by Goldenweiser and Hagen, but Hansen presents them for a different purpose: not as estimates of an expected outcome but rather as standards which one may hope to reach but not to maintain (p. 224). Hansen discusses the estimates at different places of his essay, without adding them up. Putting them together in the usual scheme, we find that they add up to only $164 billion, or $6 billion less than the $170 billion which Hansen assumes to be the size of the gross national product at full employment:

	(In Billions of Dollars)	
Consumers' expenditures[20] (excluding residential construction)		112
Gross investment		27 (or less)
Plant and equipment	15 (or less)	
Inventories	1	
Residential construction ⎱	11 (unlikely)	
Export surplus ⎰		
Government expenditures (federal, state and local)[21]		25 (or more)
Demand for gross national product		164

20. Hansen estimates disposable income at $125 billion and individual savings at $13 billion (p. 220). Consumers' expenditures, therefore, must be $112 billion.

21. Hansen presents a federal budget with total expenditures of $28 billion, which in-

As to the estimates of private gross investment, Hansen raises serious doubts (a) that a volume of investment in plant and equipment of $15 billion can be "maintained year in and year out without creating vast excess capacities," and (b) that housing and foreign loans can absorb $11 billion year after year (p. 224). On account of probable deficiencies in these items, Hansen thinks that as much as $6 billion of savings, which cannot find their regular outlet in private investment, may have to be absorbed by government borrowing, financing public works (in addition to $5 billion already included in the normal expenditures of the federal government). A part of the potential excess savings may be absorbed by additional private investment for which opportunities are opened up by "developmental" public undertakings (p. 225). Deficit financing would not be needed every year but only in those years in which the gross investment figures of the "model" cannot be attained.

In Slichter's set of estimates the three groups of expenditures add up to a demand large enough to buy the full-employment product. In Hansen's set, they fall slightly short of it and are expected to go even that far only if government expenditures can be readily expanded to make up for any slack in business investment.

Total Demand: A Dark Picture

Williams reminds us that advocates of "compensatory spending" have often explained the unsatisfactory results of deficit financing during the thirties by the "smallness" of the deficits. These "inadequate" deficits were $3 billion or $4 billion instead of the $10 billion or $15 billion which, according to some writers, might have been "adequate" (p. 349). Williams is now surprised to find that we are offered the prospect of postwar full employment with balanced budgets. What makes these authors believe that consumption and business investment after the war will be high enough to make governmental deficit spending unnecessary as an offset to excess saving?

Williams suspects that, in arriving at the high estimates of postwar demand with balanced budgets, one might be "merely projecting a prevailing state of mind" (p. 350). And he proceeds to show what a

---

clude $12 billion transfer payments, such as social security and veterans' benefits (p. 214). Income-creating federal expenditures are, therefore, $16 billion. The expenditures of the states are $3.9 billion, and those of the localities are $5.3 billion (p. 245). The three together are $25.2 billion.

set of figures would look like if we projected Keynesian "prewar reasoning" to the year 1947.

There was considerable unemployment in 1939, in spite of a budget
deficit of $4 billion. It was said that full employment could have been
achieved in 1939 if the government had expanded its income-creating
expenditures and had incurred a deficit of $14.8 billion.[22] Starting from
actual 1939 figures, then tuning them to the higher level of government spending, and finally projecting them to 1947, with the larger
labor force and increased productivity (p. 392), Williams arrives at
the following set:

	(In Billions of Dollars)
Consumers' expenditures	102.3
Gross investment	16.5
Government expenditures (federal, state, local)	49.3
Demand for gross national product	168.1

In this projection of prewar reasoning and prewar figures, full employment is achieved only with government expenditures of almost
$50 billion, of which, according to a separate calculation (p. 393),
$21.3 billion are raised by borrowing. A deficit of that size in a "nor-
mal" peacetime year would be considered intolerable by all members
of our panel of economists.

Williams does not present this ghastly set of figures as a prediction;
his intention is merely to show the amount of deficit spending which a
literal application of the prewar Keynesian reasoning would require.
The figures serve also the purpose of demonstrating that things may
look very different from the results of the various "reasonable" computations and that we must not make any programs which depend on the
correctness of our mathematical models (pp. 345, 348).

Clark does not publicly participate in the "game of estimating how
big the national income will have to be and how much we shall have
to spend on consumption and capital outlays . . . in order to give
everybody a job." If he has at all indulged in this "popular indoor
sport," it must have been in privacy, for he presents no figures and tells
the reader to "use any of the available estimates he likes; they all alike

22. An "instantaneous multiplier" of 2 was used in the calculation. Accordingly, an
increase of government expenditures by $11 billion would have raised gross national prod-
uct by $22 billion.

call for a great deal more income than the country has ever produced before in peacetime" (p. 77).

Consumers' Expenditures — After Taxes

In the above models of postwar demand we saw variations in the figures for consumers' expenditures from $102 billion to $126 billion. Since the latter figure included outlays for residential construction, which are not included in the lower estimates, the real differences are not quite so large as they seem. But we should be well aware that all estimates of future consumers' demand are tenuous.

An estimate of consumers' expenditures for some future year does not require merely that we know approximately (a) the size of the national income and (b) the people's "propensity to consume," but (c) we must also know the disposable income which they will keep after paying direct taxes. As to the people's inclination to save or to consume, out of a given disposable income, one can hardly make predictions with any degree of confidence: one cannot rely on the continuance of the (allegedly) "observed" habits of the past, particularly in a postwar climate in which so much will depend on unpredictable occurrences — facts or rumors — and the ensuing psychological "disturbances." It is perhaps still more difficult to predict the mood of Congress in writing future Internal Revenue Acts. Yet unless we know the taxes to be paid out of a given income, we cannot possibly know what the disposable income will be.[23]

These difficulties are mentioned here not in order to deprecate the estimates presented by our authors. These estimates are not predictions. The authors who put down a figure for consumers' expenditures in 1947 do not know what the taxes will actually be in that year, but they are making assumptions about a reasonable tax structure and on that basis compute the tax receipts of the government and the disposable income of the people. The results are not supposed to foretell the future, but to give an idea about possibilities and about orders of magnitudes.

23. To be exact, the following procedure is necessary for the calculation of the disposable income: From the gross national income we have to deduct (a) the corporate income taxes, (b) excise taxes, (c) other (state or local) business taxes, (d) contributions to social insurance funds, (e) depreciation, depletion, etc., (f) undivided profits, (g) personal income taxes (federal and state) ; and then we must add the so-called "transfer payments of the government." Cf. Arthur Smithies, "Forecasting Postwar Demand," *Econometrica*, Vol. 13, January 1945, p. 3.

SAVING AND INVESTING

All estimates of consumers' expenditures imply, of course, estimates of the volume of saving. The difficulty with such estimates is that past experience is no reliable basis for predicting future performance — even if circumstances were not much different and income levels were the same. Can past experience be useful as a basis of estimates for the future if the circumstances are drastically changed through the abnormal events of several war years, and if the income level is to be 50 per cent higher than before? Even if we know how much people saved when their total incomes were between $70 billion and $100 billion, can we tell how much they will save when their incomes are around $140 billion?

How Much Will People Save?

The chances for reasonable estimates are not as bad as it might seem. While total incomes in the past were so much lower than what we hope they will be in the future, they did include a full range of different income brackets. Thus, the statisticians were able to "observe" the saving habits of those who made $2,000, $5,000, $10,000, $100,000 a year. An increase in the national income means that some people who had been in the $1,000 bracket will have climbed to the $2,000 bracket, some of those who had made $4,000 will be making $5,000 and so on. If the newcomers to a higher income level could be assumed to live, on the average, just as the average of the old householders on that income level had lived, the statistician would have little trouble presenting an exact computation of total savings. But may he dare make that easy assumption?

In Slichter's opinion, a projection of prewar patterns of saving and consuming into the postwar years cannot yield accurate estimates (pp. 283, 300). The propensity to save is not constant. Between 1880 and 1940 it sank fast enough to cause "a slight decline in the proportion of saving to total income," although real income in the same time "increased well over twofold." After the war the propensity to save may continue its decline; yet, for all we know, it may instead rise sharply because of the saving habits engendered during the war (p. 300). When he considers the latter possibility, Slichter thinks only of the years after the completion of the "catching-up period" with its heavy purchases to meet long-deferred demand. For he has little doubt about the emergence of brisk buying to make up for involuntary abstinence during the war years, and he believes that this catching-up may last several years — anything between two or three years (p. 289) and a decade (p. 298).

Hansen is inclined to predict a strengthening of the propensity to save even for the first few years immediately following the war. Consumption standards do not quickly catch up with new levels of income and, moreover, people may view the future with uncertainty and thus be rather conservative in their spending. To raise consumption and lower saving through deliberate governmental measures seems desirable to Hansen, but these measures "will at best operate slowly and gradually" (p. 219).

Clark is more optimistic on this point. To "undertake to change the amounts that consumers will spend out of a given income" seems to him to be one "of the most promising lines of effort" (p. 95). The "volume of consumption from a given income is something that can be influenced, and is one of the most logical and promising areas in which to work" (p. 97).

Williams shares neither the belief in "the intractability of the propensity to save" (p. 365) nor the "exaggerated" fears of inordinately high postwar savings (p. 366). He cites the marked reduction of the ratio of savings to income which took place in England during the three decades prior to this war (pp. 364, 365), and also certain tendencies in the United States pointing in the same direction.

The chief point, however, which Williams makes against the oversaving theories is that it is fallacious to consider consumption as a "passive" factor, entirely dependent on income and thus indirectly on investment (pp. 361, 367). Consumption can be attacked "directly" (p. 362), especially through the development of "new consumer wants and goods to satisfy them" and through the adoption of a low-price policy (p. 367). According to Williams, the history of the automobile has taught us a lesson which we should not forget: consumption can be "generated" and can make notable "inroads on saving." He sees similar possibilities in a number of industrial developments: the helicopter, food freezing and air conditioning in homes, television, and, above all, cheaper and better houses (pp. 367–68).

The Saving-Investment Problem

Hansen is not reassured by the possibilities of lifting the "consumption function." In his opinion, "however much we may strive to raise consumption, an inescapable problem will remain to find adequate investment outlets for the people's savings. Yet if we do not do so, we cannot maintain full employment" (p. 225).

His point is that at the desired high income levels people would want to save much more than enterprising businessmen would be able to use for investment in new plants and equipment. This theory of "oversaving" was often formulated in the simple words "saving exceeds investment"; but many modern economists reject this simple formulation.[24] To accord with their more sophisticated formulation we have to say that "at the full-employment income the propensity to save is excessive in relation to the available private investment opportunities."

It is well worth while to reflect a little on the nature of this statement, especially on its purely hypothetical character. Its primary purpose is the explanation of unemployment. It does not say, however, that there are not sufficient private investment opportunities to absorb all that the people care to save at the *actual* level of income. It is altogether an "if" proposition. It says that *if* incomes were as high as they would be under full employment, people *would* want to save so much more than the amounts for which businessmen could find profitable investments, that incomes and employment would have to fall again and the economy would quickly return to the state of unemployment.

If this proposition were false it might conceivably be found out; but if it should be true, it could never be verified. For, regrettably, the full employment which is supposed to bring forth the high level of saving in the face of insufficient opportunities for private investment, could for that very reason never exist. But for all we know its nonexistence may just as well be due to reasons other than oversaving.

The oversaving thesis, even if not verifiable, may yet be very plausible. Of its two parts, the high saving propensity and the low invest-

24. It is all a matter of definitions. If saving is defined as the unconsumed part of income (Saving = Income minus Consumption) and income is defined as the sum of consumption and investment (Income = Consumption plus Investment) then, logically, saving is *identical* with investment and can never exceed it. The expression "saving exceeds investment" can be used if saving is defined as the portion of the income of the *preceding* pay period which is not spent for consumption or if "intended saving" and "realized saving" are distinguished.

ment incentive, the former has much more acceptable factual support. The existence of certain saving habits is demonstrable through observation in the past, and their projection into the future, though not reliable, may still be permissible if we do not intend to get more than approximate results. The prediction of inadequate investment incentives, however, is of a different character. It has not been possible to discern any definite "investment habits" functionally associated with measurable variables such as income levels, income changes or profit rates.[25] Are statements about future investment opportunities or investment incentives then merely "hunches" or are they supported by good evidence?

Investment Opportunities and Technical Progress

Hansen believes that there is sufficient evidence to warrant pessimistic statements about "the probable volume of profitable investment outlets" (p. 220). His analysis of the replacement demand and expansion demand for capital leads him to the pronouncement that "the volume of gross capital formation which is economically feasible depends upon [national] income considered both with respect to its level and its growth, as determined by the rate of technical progress and the growth of population" (p. 221).

This statement sounds more deterministic than it is upon closer inspection. Level and growth of national income are not made the ultimate determinants of private gross capital formation, since income growth is recognized as dependent in part upon technical progress. Thus, to arrive at pessimistic conclusions concerning investment is to imply that the prognosis concerning technical progress is not too good — at least not good enough to offset the reduced prospects associated with the other elements of growth: increases in population and natural resources.

Other views on future developments in technology and on the investment opportunities opened up through technological innovation are more optimistic. Anderson recalls the "great spurt" in the utilization of new technological ideas that came soon after the last war, and

25. A high correlation between total profits and national gross product, with the former series leading by six months, was shown and explained as the effect of profits upon investments, and investments upon gross product and income, by Stanley Lebergott, "Forecasting the National Product," *American Economic Review,* Vol. 35, No. 1, March 1945, pp. 59–80.

he believes "that the future holds a similar promise of a new great spurt of technological improvement" (p. 17). His optimism in this respect is tempered only by a fear of labor-union resistance to new technology.

"We cannot foretell the future course of technology, but the present scene is bright with promise," remarks Ellis. He regards the arguments supporting the "technological stagnation thesis" as inconclusive. He points to technological unemployment and increased business risks as possible results of technical progress, and holds that "it would be difficult to assert whether technological progress in the future will aid or impede the flow of investment under private enterprise" (p. 130). Here is a peculiar difference of opinion: Ellis, while optimistic as to the emergence of new technological developments, is not necessarily optimistic as to their effects upon profitable investment. Hansen, on the other hand, does not expect much by way of technological revolutions, but implied in his general thesis on capital formation is the assumption that any progress that does occur will, like any other growth factor, increase investment opportunities.

Technology, Replacement and New Investment

Hansen's general thesis as to the dependence of investment demand on the growth of income is somewhat qualified by his statement that depreciation reserves and maintenance expenditures of industrial firms are not only "adequate to maintain productive capacity but even to increase it on a substantial scale" (p. 222). If better machines are developed but are installed in mere replacement of the worn-out ones, then this part of technical progress will fail to open up opportunities for new investment. Hence, an unquestionable growth of productivity and income would occur without any new capital formation.

The same point is made also by Williams. He remarks that "the question of growth and progress becomes increasingly how to improve equipment and technique through the replacement of old capital" (p. 364) and that "this way of achieving economic progress" does not absorb saving (p. 365). If improved machinery can be "financed out of depreciation funds rather than from profits" the "outlets for saving out of current income" are reduced. Rapid technological advance does not repair this situation because "the high rate of obsolescence involved requires large replacement funds" (p. 372), which are then available for the financing of the improvements. It is in another phase of technical progress that Williams seems to see relief from these pessimistic conclusions: the development of new products, and reductions in costs and prices of products with elastic consumers' demand, may bring about the new investment demands which are usually associated with technological progress (pp. 367–69).

Institutional Obstacles to Private Investment

Clark warns of the dangers "of going on the assumption that the vigorous and pioneering type of private investment is incurably a thing of the past" and of "laying burdens on business (or failing to remove them) which would make sure that the spirit of vigorous, pioneering investment will not revive" (p. 81).

Giving business investment "the stimulus of an open field" (p. 94) by "removing deterrents as far as possible" (p. 93) seems to have definite possibilities, according to Clark. Ellis, Slichter and Anderson are unanimous in stressing the existence and possibility of removing impediments to expanded production and investment. In the words of Ellis, "it deserves explicit emphasis that the greater the role which is assigned to the institutional obstacles, the more rational is the policy which concentrates upon increasing investment" (p. 131). And indeed this is the policy which he endorses. In the scheme of Slichter, "removing impediments to production is the logical first step for the government to take in seeking to increase employment" and investment (p. 309). And in the eyes of Anderson, the removal or relaxation of "restraints and inhibitions which government itself in recent years has placed upon capital, business enterprise, and labor" (p. 9) will be all that is needed to set things right.

In Clark's opinion, "the most tangible obstacle [to private investment] lies in the tax system, and here reform is definitely in order" (p. 93). Another and "perhaps one of the really important deterrents is intangible," namely the "atmosphere or 'climate' of hostility and faultfinding which may detract" from the human rewards of business success (p. 94).

Ellis lists as the chief obstacles "monopolistic restriction, taxes which bear upon enterprise, obstacles to the free international movement of goods and capital, unjustifiably high interest rates in certain areas, and the discouragement to investment from the recurrence of depressions" (p. 131).

Slichter likewise states that "monopolies may restrict employment either by narrowing the consumers' range of choice or reducing investment opportunities in particular industries."[26] He also explains that certain taxes may become impediments to production, employment and investment; in particular, he shows how the high marginal rates of income taxation "reduce the relative attractiveness of risky ventures" (p. 317). Furthermore, "many laws and regulations limit the volume of investment opportunities because they impede the replacement of old processes or products with new. Examples are obsolete building ordinances and restrictions on technological change in trade-union agreements" (p. 309).

Union resistance to technological change is also one of the restraints singled out by Anderson (p. 17). He proposes that in planning our general policies we give full attention to this serious threat to progress and investment. But the bulk of the many restraints mentioned by Anderson are "wholly a matter of governmental policy" (p. 31). The unequal degrees of competition in industry are not held to be serious obstacles (p. 32). His list of obstacles includes "the strangling of the international movement of goods" through high trade barriers, which prevent foreign investment; the undermining of "financial confidence" through monetary policy; the manipulations of the labor market through the labor legislation of the New Deal; the closing of "the accustomed outlets for funds in American industry" through the Securities and Exchange regulations; the imposition of tax rates so high "that industrial investment by men of substantial means became hazardous in the extreme, and in the case of very large fortunes, almost impossible" (pp. 36–37).

The Inducement to Invest

Even if Anderson, Slichter and Ellis may differ in the measure of importance which they assign to specific kinds of restraints, they are in

26. Slichter qualifies this statement by adding: "Up to a point, however, monopoly may increase investment opportunities by giving innovators a better prospect of gaining from their inventions" (p. 309).

agreement about the strategic role of institutional obstacles to private investment and employment-giving enterprise.

Public policies, taxation in particular, according to Anderson, have "paralyzed the economic activity of many of the most productive brains of the country, turning men of great ability and economic knowledge and large investing power into timid men." To this Anderson adds: "We must set such men to work again, and we must set their capital to work again in risk-taking, dynamic activities" (p. 53). In the same vein, Slichter says: "Investment opportunities do not simply exist, and their number cannot be taken as given." They are "discovered or created by imaginative and original men and by hard and skillful work. They are exploited by adventurous investors who are willing to risk large losses in order to make large gains" (p. 322).

PROFITS, TAXES AND INVESTMENT

All the contributors seem to agree that our tax system impedes investment. The direct impact of taxes is, of course, upon consumption and upon saving, since every dollar which is paid as tax would otherwise have been spent or saved. It is generally assumed that taxes on low incomes are more restrictive of consumption and taxes on high incomes more restrictive of saving. At the same time, taxes have various direct and indirect effects upon investment, the strongest of which is probably due to the reduction of the prospective gains from enterprise. Taxes on business enterprises, such as the corporate income tax and the excess-profits tax, take a big cut off any profit; and the individual income tax takes another cut. What is left for the investor may be too little to make risk-taking worth while.

Investment Incentives Minus Taxes

Business losses are deductible from taxable income, and certain provisions in the tax laws make it possible to deduct losses incurred during one year from net income earned during other years. Hence one might think that taxation reduces the risk of losses just as much as it reduces the chance of gains — leaving the net incentive to invest unaltered. This is not so, for several reasons. That the tax rate effective for additional income due to a large profit — because of the higher bracket — is higher than the rate effective for the loss deduction may be only a minor qualification. That the provisions for carrying losses back or forward into prosperous years are limited to periods which may be too brief to allow full deduction, is probably more important. The really significant point is that for new ventures undertaken by new firms there are no "previous" years to which losses could be carried back and there may be no future years to which losses could be carried forward. Hence, in these cases taxes reduce only the potential profit; the potential loss is unaltered, because there is no income from which it could be deducted. An additional factor affecting the investment incentive is probably that to most venturous men "moderate risk — modest gain" propositions are not as attractive as the "high stake — high gain" propositions which would be possible without the vanishing-magic of the tax system.

All six authors refer to the restrictive effects of our tax system upon the propensity to bear risks. Ellis argues that certain business taxes penalize "venture capital" (p. 173) and that "a progressive income tax tends to have a discouraging effect on new ventures. It may reduce the compensation for investment in such enterprises below an adequate level, at least in those cases in which the returns before taxes are barely large enough to compensate for the higher risks involved" (p. 175).

Clark likewise holds that "one of the things that is most needed is a tax system which does not unduly discriminate against the taking of risks" (p. 109).

Although Williams warns that in this difficult field "all generalizations are dangerous," he finds it safe enough to assume that corporation taxes tend to restrict investment and that "unduly steep progression" of the individual income tax "impairs investment" (p. 374).

Some strong statements of Anderson on the tax question have already been quoted. His essay offers a generous assortment of indictments of the present tax system. Of the excess-profits tax he states that it reduces "the lure of large profits" which is needed if businesses are to expand (p. 52). Of the high personal income tax rates in the upper brackets he says that they "paralyze all initiative on the part of men who would be extremely alert and dynamic and useful in the economic life of the country if the taxes were lower" (p. 53).

According to Slichter, the present tax system "penalizes heavily the creation of jobs because much of the income derived from giving jobs . . . is taxed at far higher rates than income derived from holding jobs or lending capital. Pioneering, innovation, and expansion are discouraged because the government takes a large share of the gains and allows only a meager offset to losses" (p. 293). High marginal surtax rates in the individual income tax "greatly reduce the marginal efficiency of capital for the well-to-do and thus tax out of existence billions of dollars of investment opportunities and reduce the demand for labor" (p. 318).

Hansen apparently shares such views: "It cannot be denied," he states, "that both corporate income taxes and the personal income tax (with graduated surtax rates) tend to restrict investment in new ventures." And he suggests measures to ameliorate "this unfavorable effect upon risk-taking" (p. 241).

Tax Shifting and the Profitability of Investment

The recognition that taxes have an effect upon the volume of profitable investment does not necessarily contradict Hansen's thesis that investment opportunities are related to the level and growth of the national income. This relationship is only a broad and general one and need not rule out the existence of other influences, especially over short periods. The effect of taxation is often claimed to be merely temporary. Rather than the tax rates, it may be the *changes* in tax rates which affect the volume of profitable investment, and this effect, it is often held, exhausts itself after some time.

An explanation of such a view may be found in the theory that income taxes can in the long run be shifted forward to consumers and backward to "factors of production" (including labor). According to this theory, higher income taxes, through reduced investment and reduced long-run output, eventually cause product prices to be higher and factor prices (including wages) to be lower so that the profitability of investment in the long run is not altered. Contrariwise, a reduction of income taxes eventually results, according to this theory of shifting, in lower product prices and higher factor prices so that the profitability of investment is only temporarily increased by the tax reductions.

Hansen does not advance this theory. But it happens that Williams makes certain positive statements about the possibility of shifting the corporate income tax (p. 377) and Slichter states that "taxes on corporations are in the long run probably fairly completely shifted, at least in unregulated industries where nearly all production is carried on by corporations" (p. 294). In any event, whatever shifting occurs is a matter of the long run. And, if the effect of reducing taxes on enterprise really exhausts itself through shifting, it should be emphasized that it is only increased investment, increased employment and increased production which, by causing lower product prices and higher factor prices, would gradually wear down the enhanced profitability of enterprise. Thus, even if all taxes are assumed to be shiftable, one may conclude that tax measures can secure a substantial increase in the volume of *new* profitable investment at least for some time, and, through increased capital *replacement,* a permanent increase in the volume of gross investment.

Innovation, Taxation and Monopolistic Devices

The theory that the stimulus for new investment and enterprise — afforded by reduced taxes on profits and on incomes from profit — tends to wear out, would have more force if technology and wants were "stationary," that is, if techniques and tastes never changed. The increased returns to enterprisers might all be transformed in time (through increased demand for labor, increased supply of products, and the operation of the mechanism of competition) into benefits to consumers and workers, with no permanently increased residuum left to the enterprisers — provided products and techniques did not change over time. The argument does not hold for profits from innovations, that is from ventures with novel products and novel techniques.

The pioneer knows that others will come after him if his ventures meet with success. The innovator reckons with the eventual emergence of competitors. But he is satisfied that he is a jump ahead of the others; all he needs is the expectation of making enough money while he is in the lead. The speedy appearance of competitors is among the risks with which the innovator counts. If the gain which he can make in the meantime is sufficiently attractive he will go ahead. And this attractiveness depends, among other things, on the tax system.

Slichter points out that innovators may be more willing to undertake new ventures if their lead can be secured through patents and other monopolistic devices (p. 309).[27] Unfortunately, schemes to foster in-

27. This view was most forcefully presented by Joseph A. Schumpeter, *Capitalism, Socialism and Democracy,* Harper, New York, 1942, pp. 101–05.

vestment by "leaders" through restricting investment by "followers" are beset with the danger that investment on balance is more restricted than encouraged through this protection of the pioneer from his potential competitors. Instead of erecting barriers to competition in order to increase the pioneer's prospective gain, it is probably simpler and safer to increase it by letting him keep more of it — that is, by not taxing it away.

The greater the slice the government takes from the returns to venture capital, the more necessary does it become to "bribe" capital into new ventures by permitting monopolistic devices to fence off any competing investments. The result is an artificial plugging of outlets for masses of investible funds in order to channel a small portion of them into well-protected "investment opportunities." If innovators were permitted to keep more of their gains they would be attracted to new ventures despite the probability that "the gravy" would soon be gone, owing to the unrestricted stream of competing investments which would follow them into the new fields. The smaller the taxes cutting into profits and into incomes from profit, the more worth while will it be to take risks, including the risks of unrestricted competition.

Reductions of taxes on enterprise thus may contribute to the creation of additional opportunities for private investment on at least three scores: ventures in new products or new processes become more attractive; increased investment in existing lines becomes profitable; and the pressure for the use of monopolistic devices against new investment is weakened and the pressure for their removal strengthened.

Taxation, Saving and Investment

The case for reduced taxes on corporate profits and on individual incomes from profits is not as clear, however, as it might appear on the basis of the above arguments. Lower taxes on income from enterprise may achieve the desired increase of the inducement to invest, but they will also produce an increase in the ability to save. Will the saving-investment problem of a "mature" economy be alleviated through tax reductions? Will the effects upon investment be stronger than upon saving?

The answers of all six contributors seem to be unanimously affirmative, since they all favor certain reductions in taxes on business income. Clark goes right to the heart of the problem when he says: "Very heavy taxes on the high brackets not only cut into savings, but also reduce the incentive to venturing capital in business undertakings. To be effective, the taxes must stop short of the point at which the second effect would neutralize the first" (p. 91). The present structure of tax rates is probably above "the point at which the rich man is discouraged by the high rates," that is, above the point at which "he shrinks his capital outlays by one dollar or more for every dollar that is added to total spendings because the poor man has more money to spend than he had" before the tax structure was made more progressive (p. 96).

Slichter also states that "stiff progressive income taxes" cannot "cure the problem of excessive saving." He explains that "an excessive propensity to save is always associated with a shortage of risk-taking capital relative to security-seeking capital" and that "higher marginal rates of taxation would reduce the relative attractiveness of risky ventures and raise the relative attractiveness of secure investments." He concludes that "since the supply of venture-seeking funds would be reduced, the surplus of security-seeking funds would in most cases be greater" under stiffer progression (p. 317).

Since one can never be certain as to whether a reduction of taxes will increase the inducement to invest more than the propensity to save, one might prefer to play safe and adopt a system of differential tax rates under which the total tax bill on high incomes can be maintained in spite of a lighter tax burden on income from enterprise. Slichter proposes such a tax system. It would have two sets of surtaxes: "a stiff surtax on general income (mostly salaries and interest) and a lower surtax on incomes derived from self-employment and dividends and on that part of incomes devoted to expanding plant and equipment" (p. 318). This scheme is intended to restore the attractiveness of enterprise and new investment, thus reversing the tendencies of the last decades.

PROFITS AND WAGES

"Profit has been the mainspring of change, both in regard to long-run growth and short-run fluctuations," says Williams (p. 370). "The heart of the problem is business profits," says Anderson (p. 17), and "it is profit income that is crucial in determining the ups and downs of business" (p. 20). Clark speaks of a minimum, or lower limit, of profit in our economy: "the amount necessary to afford sufficient incentive to invest" (p. 108).

The Strategic Role of Profit

The other essays in this symposium may not contain any equally direct references to the importance of profit in the working of our economic system; but that their authors recognize the strategic role of profit is apparent from their position in the discussion of taxation. Ellis, Hansen and Slichter, no less than the others, show concern about the undue encroachment of taxes upon profits. The six authors seem to be unanimous as to the desirability of rescuing the profit incentive from being driven out by taxation.

The unanimity concerning the effects of tax rates might lead the reader to expect similar unanimity concerning the effects of wage rates. Yet we find the house divided on certain parts of the wage question.

Nobody, of course, would ever doubt the desirability of "high wages," and everybody would admit that wage rates can be boosted "too high" under given circumstances, causing difficulties either in the form of unemployment or in the form of inflation or both. But where does "too high" begin? Differences of opinion on this point may be a matter of practical judgment or of basic economic theory. Economists with the same basic ideas on the economics of wage levels and wage structures may differ in their diagnosis of the surrounding circumstances; and, conceivably, economists with widely differing ideas on the significant principles may agree as to what would be appropriate under the actual conditions.

The chief difficulty, in the words of Williams, lies in the "conflict between wages as income and wages as cost" (p. 369). And, as Clark says, "offhand conclusions are frequently drawn, based entirely on one or the other side of this two-sided aspect" (p. 99). Some call for higher wages, contending that this will help employment because of the increased income and increased effective demand. "This ignores the fact that wages are also costs," says Clark. Others call for lower wages, contending that this will help employment because of the reduced cost of production. This emphasis on wages as costs "ignores the fact that they are also purchasing power" (p. 99).

An increase in wage rates will certainly increase cost;[28] whether it will increase or decrease total money income, and whether, if it in-

---

28. Both average cost and marginal cost are increased through an increase in wage rates; i.e., at any given volume of output, unit costs will be higher than before the wage rate increase.

creases income, the resulting increase in effective demand for goods and services will affect business activity more strongly than the cost increase, are open questions. Increased labor costs reduce profit; increased demand and sales increase profit. Will profit, on balance, be reduced or increased when wage rates are raised? And, if profit is in fact reduced, what will be the repercussions on investments, on employment?

Too High Wage Rates May Reduce Profit and Employment

Anderson stresses the effects of wages as cost and minimizes the effects of wages as "purchasing power" or effective demand. "It is in the relation of prices to costs, of course, that the central problem of profits is found. And labor costs are a major factor in total costs" (p. 17). He shows that the share of labor in the national income is so large and the share of profit income so small that a sudden increase in the former at the expense of the latter can bring about "a great disorder and force a great business reaction. . . . Relatively small variations in the great factor, labor income, can make tremendous variations in the minor factor, profit income" (p. 20). And he discusses the crisis of 1937, among other similar experiences, as an illustration or "test" of the adverse effects which "a sharp and drastic rise in wages and in labor costs" may have upon profits, business activity, and employment (p. 25).

Williams refers to the same experience as an illustration of "what happens when there is a large and sudden peacetime rise of wage rates. . . . The result was a sharp decline in profits" (p. 369). This was probably among the chief causes of the "renewal of depression" in 1937. Business profits were "undermined by unduly large and rapid wage increases" (p. 372).

When Ellis discusses the question "as to how far wages can be advanced, by collective bargaining or otherwise, without producing unemployment," he thinks of both the structure (i.e., the relative wage rates as between different industries or locations) and the general level of wages. As to structure, he mentions the necessity of "downward adjustments" of excessively high wage rates in particular industries (p. 182). As to the general wage level, he fears that the presence of monopoly profits in industry may be taken as justification for increased pressure for higher wages, and that such "advances in wages may be attained only at the cost of lessened employment" (p. 183). Ellis warns that a "forcing of wages above the economic value of the work" acts as "a direct tax on employment" and may result in "chronic unemployment and investment stagnation" (p. 184).

According to Clark, "the structure of relative wages may be more important than the general level of wages in determining whether industry" can furnish sufficient employment opportunities (p. 111). Certain socially desirable wage increases "might be an obstacle to employment" (p. 77) and "the obstructive effect" of certain monopolistic wages is "a highly practical matter" (p. 103). Minimum-wage standards "may create a problem of employability" possibly so serious that "instead of increasing the total amount of pay going to these lower-paid workers, the effect might conceivably be to reduce it" (p. 112). And as relative wage structures "become noncompetitive, the altered differentials are likely to make it harder for particular groups of workers to find employment, and may in effect price some of them out of the market" (p. 113). To the advocates of high wages as a means of expansion Clark replies "that it is inherently possible that some wages might be high enough to be obstacles to expansion of production from the cost side" (p. 99).

Slichter mentions "distortions in the wage structure" among the causes of structural unemployment. "Some communities or industries, by reason of their high wages, attract and hold more men than can obtain steady work. The building trades, the garment trades, and the coal industry are examples" (p. 306). Slichter — like Clark — places major emphasis on the wage structure. "Opportunities for employment," he states, ". . . depend upon the wage structure, upon the policies of trade unions, and upon the results of collective bargaining" (p. 308). But he does refer to the general wage level when he asks: "Are wage increases likely to reduce the demand for labor and goods by encroaching upon profits or are they likely to bring about offsetting increases in prices? Whether wage increases are inflationary or deflationary depends upon circumstances. In times when a large part of the demand for capital goods is sensitive to the prospect of profits, a rise in costs may have a deflationary effect." Replacement demand, however, is "relatively insensitive to prices" and, therefore, inflationary effects of wage increases after the war are deemed to be more probable (p. 287, n. 41).

Hansen, likewise, does not fear unemployment but only price inflation as the result of excessive wage increases after the war. Increases beyond the limit set by increased productivity "mean wage inflation" (p. 256). "Wage increases which force price increases do nobody any good, least of all the wage earner" (p. 257). "The real serious threat of postwar inflation is a chaotic wage development, destructive of price and general economic stability" (p. 260).

Too Low Wage Rates May Reduce Demand and Employment

Hansen's occasional warnings against too high wage rates are interspersed in a discussion which is essentially a warning against too low wage rates. "Wage cutting," or even a failure of achieving upward adjustments of wage rates, may involve "serious deflationary dangers" (p. 258). In order to sustain a certain national income, a "wages and salaries bill" commensurate with that income must be secured. Since that pay roll — at least $92 billion — cannot be secured at current wage rates, wage rates must be "adjusted upward." A "proper equilibrium" between pay roll and "full-employment income" must be maintained, or full employment cannot be sustained. Wage increases are needed "in order to increase private consumption expenditures" and to assure "an adequate market" for our industries (pp. 258–59).

Slichter sees in low wage rates the danger of an inadequate market for farm products. He expects that in the postwar transition period the labor unions will be able to "enforce" increases in wages sufficient to "limit the drop in agricultural prices" (p. 286). He anticipates that the rise in wage rates will cause "some increase in the prices of many finished goods" (p. 287), but he believes that the rise "will, on the whole, be moderate and orderly" (p. 288). "If wage rates are gradually increased about 20 per cent during the first several years after the war, pay rolls will be well above $120 billion by the time that deficiencies in food stocks have been made up. . . . Rapid technological progress, however, will be needed to prevent increases in wage rates from forcing large advances in the prices of nonagricultural products" (pp. 290–91). But the wage increases are needed to support the demand for agricultural products.

While Clark does not support any increase-wages-to-increase-demand schemes, he sees in wage-reduction schemes the danger of demand reductions. He doubts that "a general deflation of wages and prices" is a remedy for underemployment (p. 101), because "falling prices lead to inventory losses, and tend toward a niggardly policy of hand-to-mouth buying. Moreover, the prices and wages are not merely the costs which buyers must pay; they constitute also the incomes out of which the buying must be done" (p. 99). The low-price policy which is so important for a high level of employment should not be based on drastic wage deflations but on "low profit margins" and "low profit rates" (pp. 106–07).

Williams' hope for "a vigorously expanding high-consumption economy" rests partly on a modified distribution of income: he calls for "a high-wage, low-profit economy" (pp. 368–69).[29] Lower but more stable profits, according to Williams, would be preferable "even from the standpoint of business" (p. 371). The changed distribution of income, through reduced profits and increased wages, should result in reduced saving and increased consumption. Yet, Williams' advocacy of the "maintenance of a high wage structure" does not mean a blanket endorsement of the policy of "raising wage rates as a means of raising national income" (p. 369). His main concern is the distribution of the benefits of advances in productivity. He demands that these benefits be passed on to the consumers in higher wage rates as well as in lower prices (p. 373).

Wage Rates Rising With Productivity

"Broadly speaking," says Williams, "wage rate increases must follow rather than precede advances in productivity and output" (p. 369). "The way to bring about rising wages," says Anderson, "is to have a steady growth in the volume of capital, outrunning the increase in population, and rapid technological progress" (p. 21). "With a general improvement in techniques or management, a good case can be made," says Ellis, "for permitting the gain to accrue to labor by a combination of approximately stabilizing the prices of consumers' goods and permitting money wages to rise parallel to the average increase in efficiency" (p. 183). "Increases in productivity," says Hansen, ". . . permit some upward wage adjustments without necessitating further general increases in prices, or without encroaching unduly

---

29. Williams' program for high wages does not, however, include wage increases immediately after the war. He merely suggests that "reductions in wage rates from the present level" should be held "to a tolerable minimum" (p. 369).

upon the profit margin. . . . It is in the long-run interest of all groups, both labor and capital, to undertake an orderly adjustment of wage rates, permitting as rapid increases as technical progress makes possible" (pp. 259–60). "The reducing of production costs through increased productivity is pretty universally regarded as the unquestionably sound way to finance wage increases," says Clark (p. 118).

This sounds like a more than ordinary measure of agreement among economists of otherwise different schools of thought. The theme that wages should rise with technical productivity is intoned by this quintet of voices almost in unison. Yet some minor differences are noticeable upon closer examination. Anderson does not state how much of the total increase in productivity, which results from increased capital and advanced technology, should go to labor in the form of higher wage rates. Williams proposes that the benefits of increased productivity be distributed only in part through higher wage rates, the rest being passed on to the consumer through lower product prices. Ellis and Hansen prefer to maintain stable price levels in the face of increased outputs and to have all the increase in average productivity translated into higher wage rates. And Clark, without stating any preferences, confines himself to analyzing some of the difficulties involved in these schemes.

An increase in wage rates, if it is to be also an increase in the total pay roll, must be accompanied by an enlargement of the money flow. This is not always recognized. Williams, for example, after mentioning "how the benefits of increasing productivity can be diffused more rapidly through the economic system by downward adjustments of prices and upward adjustments of incomes," goes on to the following statement: "If this interflow of income between production and consumption could be made more effective, there would be less need for reliance on public spending and, indeed, even on investment itself" (p. 363). This does not altogether jibe. "Upward adjustments of incomes" must mean *money* incomes — or they would not have to be mentioned separately besides the downward adjustment of prices. Higher money incomes must mean increased effective money circulation, which in turn *presupposes* more aggregate investment or public spending.

Ellis is quite explicit concerning the necessity of "a combination of wage and monetary policies" (p. 183) even if he does not specify just what sort of monetary policies will have to be followed. Hansen does specify them by stating: "Investment each year must in fact exceed the savings made out of 'disposable' income in Robertson's sense, in order to make possible a rise in income commensurate with rising productivity. This excess of investment would normally be financed by an increase in bank credit, which in a growing society must occur in order to provide sufficient circulation media to transact the ever growing volume of trade at stable prices and in addition to provide sufficient money (currency and demand deposits) to ensure the necessary degree of liquidity required to maintain a low rate of interest" (p. 225 n).

To put it in other words, the new money (currency or bank deposits) needed to pay the increased incomes will have to be "created" through borrowing from the commercial banking system, or it may be money "reactivated" through the use (dishoarding) of existing idle funds. This dishoarding and borrowing will have to be done by private industry, financing some of its investments, or (failing a sufficient private investment demand) by the government, financing some of its budget deficit. To make it possible for wages to increase together with productivity, that is, to secure an increase in total money incomes, a larger volume of investment or public spending is needed than merely for maintaining a given wage level and given income flow.

Higher Wage Rates Where Techniques Improve

Advocacy of a program of raising wage rates at the *pace* at which technical productivity advances is invariably bound up in popular thinking with the dangerous misunderstanding that wage rates ought to be raised at the *place* at which the progress occurs. For example, if technological improvements are made in the automobile industry and in coal mining, permitting higher output per worker (or, that is, lower cost per unit of output), many people take it for granted that increased wage rates for the automobile workers and coal miners are in order. Union leaders, as a matter of fact, take the program as a justification for higher wage demands in the very industries in which the technological innovations have taken place. The result is a gross distortion of the wage structure, which may cause chronic "structural" unemployment in the industries concerned. Business leaders take the program as a danger to the returns of the investments undertaken to introduce technical innovations. The result is increased reluctance to invest, which aggravates the chronic unemployment in the whole economy.

This behavior of union leaders and business leaders, harmful as it is, is undoubtedly sensible from their points of view. Union leaders are always watchful as to the best opportunities for successful pressure for wage concessions. They know that firms or industries which have recently improved their profit position through the introduction of economies will more easily give in to the wage demands of their workers. Business leaders, on the other hand, learn quickly that the squeeze will be on as soon as their new undertakings prove successful. The risk of provoking higher wage demands will then be included among all the other risks of new investment, and will thus increase the obstacles to investment.

From the point of view of the whole economy, an increase in wage rates in precisely those industries in which the need for labor is diminished, owing to increased output per worker, is absolutely perverse. If a given or even increased output can be produced by a smaller number of workers, the "natural" reaction on a "perfect market" would be a reduction of wage rates, guiding the displaced workers into other fields of production.[30] If this wage reduction is precluded and even a wage increase is put in force, which prevents the laborsaving innovations from permitting reductions in the production costs and selling prices of the products in question, the mechanism for the reabsorption of the released labor is stalled and chronic unemployment ensues.

But this is not all. If the same type and quality of labor is employed in the industry in which the technological improvement has occurred and in other industries in which no such progress has taken place, and if in the former industry a wage increase is put in force, a wage differential is created which tends to *attract* more workers to the very industry which has just reduced its work force. One of two things will then happen. Either artificial barriers to the mobility of labor are erected, keeping workers out of the industry which pays higher wages. Or the unions get the higher wage rates adopted everywhere and thus cause

30. Except in cases of exceptionally high elasticities of demand for the particular product. To some it appears anything but "natural" that an increase in average physical productivity of labor should result in lower money wage rates. Yet, if technical improvements increase the efficiency of, say, coal so that less is needed for given outputs, a fall in the price of coal is generally regarded as a matter of course.

cost increases in industries where there are no offsetting economies, with the result that employment will be reduced also in these industries.

Equal Average Rise of Wages and Productivity

Ellis is anxious to avoid such misunderstandings of the wage increase thesis and the dangerous consequences of its misapplication. He warns against "restrictive devices" of labor unions and insists that "the wage which 'clears the market' with free entry for qualified applicants in each classification is the socially justifiable wage" (p. 185). The wage rate which clears the market is defined as the wage which "absorbs the supply of laborers offering to work at that wage" (p. 184). Ellis makes it clear that "the workers employed in the firms or industries where efficiency has advanced are not to be the favored beneficiaries of the progress in the technical arts, but all-round wage increases commensurate with the average growth of productivity in the economy and supported by appropriate monetary policy should ensure the widest possible distribution of the additional real income" (p. 183).

If the average growth of productivity is a certain percentage a year, the thought of Ellis and Hansen is that wage rates should rise by the same percentage *on the average*. Since a wage boost in an industry in which no economies have occurred would encroach upon profits and cause unemployment, monetary policy is called in to "support" the wage increase through expanding the buying power of the people; that is to say, a general increase in effective demand must be engineered, large enough to permit a rise in selling prices as compensation for the higher cost. On the other hand, product prices would fall in industries where technological improvements allow economies beyond the average percentage. The resulting average change in prices is supposed to be zero, with the average increase in output equal to the average increase in money incomes.

In reality, the scheme can hardly work that smoothly. It does not include control measures to limit wage demands of unions or wage concessions of industry. (Nor does it include control measures to ensure cuts in prices where technological improvements allow economies beyond the average.) If there were provisions to the effect that the annual average wage increase in the economy should be "commensurate with the average growth of productivity," efficient trade unions would be in a continuous race for the biggest share in the increment of the national product. The earlier and the bigger the raise which a union could obtain, the less would be left for others; probably nothing would be left for the weaker unions or the unorganized part of labor.

On the other hand, if increases in productivity were passed on not through wage increases but through reduced product prices, no scramble for disproportionate shares would arise and the increased output would be distributed as equitably as the existing wage structure permitted. The objection that the existing wage structure is not a fair one can be easily answered by pointing to the fact that the same bargaining strength and monopolistic militancy which has created the present wage structure is likely to be effective in the campaign for further wage boosts and thus to aggravate any existing bias and inequity. The benefits of technological progress cannot possibly be distributed as smoothly through bargaining for higher wage rates as would be possible through lower product prices, automatically reduced through the mechanism of really competitive markets. The difficulty with this program is that we cannot rely in all industries on the effectiveness of the degree of competition that exists; monopolistic industries may resist price reductions commensurate with the reductions of production cost.

This discussion, admittedly, is largely academic. Most union members, correctly or mistakenly, regard the ability to obtain wage raises as the raison d'être of trade unionism. As Clark says, "union leaders are under pressure to produce a gain for their membership every now and then, to earn their salaries and to justify the union dues and overhead" (p. 117). Hence, a scheme which takes account of continued campaigns for higher wages is surely more realistic than a scheme which assumes that the labor leaders will be satisfied with stable money wages of gradually rising purchasing power. Since the unions cannot claim reductions in commodity prices as their victories, and since labor unions have become part and parcel of a liberal-democratic society, it will be politic to grant them, in the form of increased money wage rates, the successes necessary for their survival. But it is equally important for their survival, and that of a liberal-democratic society, that they learn to practice moderation. The growth of all-round productivity might opportunely be used as the standard and upper limit of their drive for higher wage rates. Wage boosts in excess of the growth of productivity may have destructive consequences. Wage increascs in step with productivity can be made compatible with the functioning of the economic system.

Wage Increases and Aggregate Spending

Many people raise the question as to why authors who agree that a reduction of business profits through *taxes* will act as an obstacle to investment should not agree that a reduction of business profits through *wages* will do the same. According to some, increased wage outlays would be even more discouraging to enterprisers than increased tax outlays, because business taxes, by and large, have to be paid only if there are profits whereas wages have to be paid before the enterprise can be sure that it will make any profit at all. An argument on the other side is that higher wage payments will help business because of increased sales to wage earners.

If increased wage receipts mean increased spending by wage earners, do not increased tax receipts mean increased government spending? Anderson seems to think so. He remarks that the "government itself is a good spender, and government employees are good spenders" (p. 54). Hansen, on the other hand, proposes that after the war, in order to maintain effective demand, "taxes should be reduced and wages should be increased" (p. 259). Obviously, if a switch of business outlays from taxes to wages is to contribute to total demand, it must be assumed that reduced taxes will not affect government spending. Hansen's proposal is, therefore, clearly based on the assumption that government expenditures are not dependent upon government revenues.[31]

Hansen's proposal rests also on the assumption that increased wage rates will be accompanied by increased total pay rolls, which implies that the demand for labor is inelastic. This is still a question on which

---

31. This illustrates how easy it is to exaggerate differences of opinion among economists. That governments spend all their tax revenues is usually a perfectly safe assumption. Economists accustomed to reasoning in terms of balanced budgets have regularly assumed that higher tax revenues mean higher government expenditures, and lower tax revenues mean lower government expenditures. Economists who are used to reason in terms of budget deficits take government expenditures as given and independent of tax revenues. Hence, they no longer assume that the funds raised by taxation are re-spent by the government; since the government spends anyway, taxes or no taxes, the spending is analytically separated from the taxing. The result is confusing to many: for, while wage income gives rise to workers' expenditures, tax income does not give rise to government expenditures.

there is difference of judgment and insufficient analysis to resolve the differences.

Elastic or Inelastic Demand for Labor?

According to Anderson, "the demand for labor is highly elastic, increasing sharply with a moderate decline in wages, and falling off sharply with a moderate rise in wages, other things equal." "Employment falls off sharply" and the total take-home wages are reduced when "in a given state of demand" wage rates are pushed up (p. 20). Anderson cites good authority for this view. As a matter of fact, a large majority of economists hold it — except that many believe that the qualification "in a given state of demand" deprives it of much of its force because the demand is likely to be changed by the change in wage rates.

Some of the differences of opinion on the elasticity of the demand for labor are due to the fact that writers do not make it clear how much time they assume to elapse, and what types of repercussions they assume to take place, between the change in wage rates and the change in employment. Among the more important repercussions are: (a) changes in the immediate expectations of businessmen as to their markets; (b) changes in actual expenditures for consumption — in particular, changes in the rate at which income recipients will save under the impact of changed money incomes and, perhaps, changed commodity prices; (c) changes in investment plans by businessmen under the impact of changed production costs, demand and liquidity. In view of these and other possible repercussions it becomes clear why generalizations are anything but safe and why, according to Slichter, the effects of increased wage rates may be "inflationary or deflationary," depending upon circumstances (p. 287).

In time of war, when war materiel must be produced no matter at what cost, and when the government and banking system create any amount of money that may be needed to finance the cost, the demand for labor is absolutely inelastic. Increased wage rates can then be only inflationary. In peacetime, if government purchases are relatively insignificant and employment is largely a matter of business decisions, the conditions are very different. Much will depend on "timing" and "psychology."

For the postwar transition period Hansen, as we have seen, expects that wage increases beyond a certain point would be inflationary or, in other words, that the money demand for labor would be inelastic. Slichter gives reasons for holding the same view: he believes that replacement demand is "relatively insensitive to prices" (p. 287). Anderson does not think so and expects an elastic labor demand in the transition period, with "terrific unemployment" if wage rates are not reduced, but not very great reductions in wage rates needed to avoid it (p. 22).

Postwar Wage Adjustments

The situation concerning wage level and wage structure in the postwar transition period is very confused and it is difficult to say what types of adjustment would be most conducive to the maintenance of employment.

There is the call for a downward adjustment of the wage level which, according to Anderson, should reduce the cost of labor in response to the reduced demand for labor for war production (p. 22). There is, on the other hand, the call for an upward adjustment of the wage rate level which, according to Hansen and Slichter, is needed to support effective demand, preventing a decline in the wage bill due to the loss of overtime payments (pp. 258, 287).

There is the impatience of union leaders who, according to Slichter, "after several years of restraint during the war, will press for higher wages" (p. 286). There is, on the other hand, the dilemma that continued stability of the cost of living may not be possible unless certain wage rates recede from their elevated wartime level; this might be necessary to permit certain goods which have not been produced for several years again to be made and sold at the old prices which figure in the present cost-of-living index.

The reductions in take-home wages may be drastic in many areas. The length of the working week will be reduced; not only do fewer hours mean proportionately smaller weekly earnings, but the loss of overtime will also reduce average earnings per hour. In addition, shifts from highly paid war jobs to relatively poorly paid positions in civilian manufacturing and service industries will cause a substantial diminution of the wage bill.

It would be useless to demand that hourly wage rates be raised in order to compensate for shorter hours and loss of overtime, because many of the industries in which hours of work are shortened will also release part of their working force. Should the wage rates, for example, in the shipyards be increased just at the time when large numbers of workers are laid off? The workers laid off in the shipyards may go back to the lumber yards or paper mills or gasoline stations, where the prevailing rates of pay are far below the rates paid in the shipyards. That the lumber yards, paper mills and gasoline stations adjust their wages to the high level of earnings in war industries would be well-nigh impossible: it might mean wage rate boosts up to 100 per cent or more. And, of course, any substantial increases in wage rates in civilian industries would ruin the chances of keeping prices from rising way above their present level.

Under these circumstances one can hardly hope for the "right" adjustments in wage level and wage structure, that is to say, for adjustments most conducive to a high and stable level of employment under a stable, or only slightly increased, price level. Wages may be too high from the point of view of labor cost and too low from the point of view of effective demand; and rising labor cost and falling effective demand are of course the worst possible regimen for the maintenance of employment. In such a dilemma the recourse to public loan expenditures as the "easiest" remedy for unemployment will be all but a matter of course. Constant recourse, however, to government spending as a "regular" full-employment policy may have very significant repercussions upon wage policies. Before we analyze what the contributors have to say about these repercussions, we shall examine the discussion of fiscal policy and public investment programs.

FISCAL POLICY

The three major variables of fiscal policy are government expenditures, government revenues, and net government borrowing. The quantitative and qualitative decisions concerning all three variables, that is to say, the answers to questions as to "how much" and "in what form," may have an important bearing on total economic activity.

Three Variables

It goes without saying that the quantitative answers concerning any two of the three variables by and large determine the third. For example, once the amounts of expenditures and revenues are fixed, there is little leeway concerning the amount of net borrowing (that is, no more leeway than is permitted by changes in the size of the government's cash balances). The problems of the magnitude of public spending and the size of the budget deficit are regarded by many as the most crucial of all postwar problems.

The importance of qualitative decisions is fully recognized by all the contributors, especially as to expenditures and revenues. What are the fields in which government spending would be complementary rather than competitive, encouraging rather than discouraging, to business spending? What forms of taxation, what structure of tax rates, would be least restrictive of business spending and consumers' spending? What are the effects of the public debt, what forms of its liquidation and what changes in its character (e.g., as to the interest rate) would reduce any disturbing or impeding effects to a minimum?

The prescription of fiscal policy as a "cure for unemployment" came into prominence only in the thirties. Much heated controversy has taken place since. For several years many advocates as well as critics have looked upon permanent deficit financing as the essence, instead of merely one type, of fiscal policy. The deficit, however, is only one variable in the equation and, indeed, it may become zero and still leave much scope for fiscal policy as a (positive or negative) employment-making factor. Fiscal policy in this wider sense is at present one of the "hottest" issues among economists.

Three Objectives

The first objective of fiscal policy, conservatively conceived, was to provide for the most necessary services which government must produce, beginning with police and court functions and ending with road construction and flood control. A more progressive extension may include slum clearance and similar projects too big or too risky for private enterprise but definitely worth while if the nation can afford them.

As long as this objective — raising the money needed for desirable services — is not linked with any other purpose, government revenues will be adjusted to the magnitude as well as to the time of the public expenditures. The only other inherent policy aim will be to have the tax system so constructed as to satisfy certain rules of economy, equity, productivity and what not.

To mitigate cyclical fluctuations of the economy has become a second objective of fiscal policy. In its more conservative conception, the policy would operate solely through anticyclical timing, without changing the amounts of expenditures and tax revenues over the whole cycle. By collecting taxes chiefly during the expansion phase of the cycle and scheduling all postponable expenditures during the contraction phase, a stabilizing influence may be exercised upon economic activity. The government's budget would show deficits in some years, surpluses in others, but would be balanced over longer periods — say, ten years. Expenditures would still be limited to projects deemed worth while in themselves, not only for their effects on employment.

Some more "progressive" proponents of an anticyclical fiscal policy are more liberal on the expenditure side and advocate resorting during depressions to government projects which would be left undone if it were not for the need of employment. Others are more lenient on the side of tax-raising. They would not insist that depression deficits be completely made up during more prosperous years and would allow the budget to show moderate deficits over longer periods.

In progressing from mere timing procedures to the abolition of the two quantitative limitations — (a) to allow no expenditures beyond those undertaken for their own sake; (b) to allow no long-run deficits — "anticyclical" fiscal policy grows in scope and eventually becomes geared to a third, still more ambitious, objective: to ensure full employment at all times.

Hansen, for example, believes that "the adoption by government of a compensatory and developmental fiscal program" is required if a stable and high level of income and employment is to be maintained (p. 206) — not merely as a "temporary expedient" but for "continuous adjustment" of aggregate spending (pp. 207–08). While four other participants besides Hansen favor anticyclical fiscal policy, they do not share his belief in the efficacy of fiscal policy as a major instrument in a long-run full-employment program; some of them, indeed, strongly reject it.

Three Methods

Neither Hansen's advocacy of fiscal policy as instrument of the ambitious full-employment objective nor the objections raised by the other contributors in this volume deal directly with certain recent refinements of the quantitative theory of fiscal policy.[32] "Fiscal policy," as was said

32. Oxford Institute of Statistics, *The Economics of Full Employment,* Oxford, 1944; Sir William H. Beveridge, *Full Employment in a Free Society,* London, 1944; New York, 1945; Henry C. Wallich, "Income Generating Effects of a Balanced Budget," *Quarterly*

before, must not be identified simply with "increasing public spending" and "deficit financing." It is not a one-way policy; in fact, it presents a choice of several methods of raising effective demand — or of lowering it if inflation should threaten.

Three principal methods of fiscal policy for raising total income can be distinguished, according to Hansen and other recent writers on the subject. Basic to the theory is, of course, the assumption that, starting from a state of underemployment, an increase in effective demand would not be largely absorbed by higher wages and higher prices, but would instead call forth the desired increase in employment and production. The three principal methods are: (a) reducing the tax rates without reducing expenditures, thus increasing the deficit; (b) increasing expenditures without increasing the tax rates, thereby increasing the deficit; (c) increasing expenditures and increasing also the tax rates enough to raise sufficient revenue for the expenditures.

The income-creating effects of the first two methods are more obvious than that of the third. That an equal increase of expenditures and revenue should generate additional effective demand has been seriously questioned. Slichter, for example, states categorically: "If public spending were to produce a net increase in demand, it would have to be financed by a deficit" (p. 311). Hansen's point is that every dollar which the government spends for goods or services[33] adds directly (i.e., without considering any re-spending by the recipients) one full dollar to effective demand, whereas one dollar collected by the government as a tax may reduce effective demand directly by less than a dollar (without considering the reduction of re-spending by the persons whose income was cut owing to the taxpayer's reduced purchases).

This proposition is true on the assumption that the added tax takes from the taxpayer some money that he would otherwise have saved,

Journal of Economics, Vol. 59, November 1944; Arthur Smithies, "Forecasting Postwar Demand," *Econometrica,* Vol. 13, 1945; Leonid Hurwicz, "Discussion," *ibid.;* Arthur Smithies, "Full Employment in a Free Society," *American Economic Review,* Vol. 35, 1945; Richard A. Musgrave, "Alternative Budget Policies for Full Employment," *ibid.;* Alvin H. Hansen, "Three Methods of Expansion through Fiscal Policy," *ibid.* The exposition in the text follows largely the presentation by Hansen in the last-mentioned paper.

33. "Real expenditures" of the government are usually distinguished from mere "transfer expenditures." The former constitute directly a demand for currently produced goods and services, while the latter do not. Examples of transfer payments are: unemployment benefits, relief, bonuses for veterans, old-age benefits. They furnish "income payments" without being part of "national income" or gross national product. The expenditures referred to above in the text are real expenditures.

and on the further assumption that despite the higher taxes business investments do not decline, or decline less than the saving. On the basis of these assumptions, the tax will reduce consumption as well as saving. To the extent that the taxes cut into saving, the tax-financed expenditures of the government will increase effective demand. To the extent that the taxes cut into private consumption expenditures, the tax-financed expenditures will merely shift demand from the private to the public domain. Since tax-financed public outlays ordinarily *shift* demand ever so much more than *create* demand, it will take a very large increase in government spending to achieve "full employment" through fiscal policy with a balanced budget. (And if private investment should not stay unchanged but decline — as it may in consequence of the higher tax rates — the increase in government spending and taxing would have to be still greater in order to produce the desired net increase in employment.)

The other two principal methods of fiscal policy operate with deficits. A given size of the deficit will create less demand by the tax-reduction method than by the expenditure-raising method. Indeed, Hansen says that "taken by itself alone, tax reduction would be relatively ineffective," and that it should be used merely to "reinforce the effect of increased public expenditures" (p. 208). The reason for the greater effectiveness of spending is easily understood. Every dollar of additional loan-financed expenditures of the government is a net addition to effective demand. One dollar of tax reduction, however, does not add one full dollar to effective demand (without considering respending) because the relieved taxpayer may save some of it, and only the part which he spends becomes demand. (Again it is assumed that private investment is not increased in consequence of the tax reduction.) If a given amount of additional income or employment had to be created by one of the two methods, the necessary tax reduction would be much larger than the alternatively required increase in loan expenditures.[34]

34. The increase of private saving resulting from the tax reduction would, in equilibrium, be applied to the financing of the budget deficit — unless there was also an increase in private investment ensuing from the tax reduction. The increase in incomes achieved by the loan-expenditure methods would likewise raise saving (not directly but in the process of re-spending the primary income) which would in equilibrium finance the loan issues of the government, but it would also (on the basis of given tax rates) raise tax revenues to some extent, which would contribute to the smaller dimension of the eventual deficit.

Slichter presents a short analysis of four different methods of creating a budget deficit (pp. 327 ff). Two of these methods are identical with those discussed above. Slichter's analysis includes the effects of tax reductions upon business investment. The analysis becomes thereby more realistic; it also loses the deceptive "precision" which the simpler assumption of constant private investment makes possible.

A Schematic Presentation

It may be helpful to illustrate the chief differences between the "three methods of achieving full employment through fiscal policy" in the following scheme of (arbitrarily chosen) figures. Assume government expenditures and tax revenues to be balanced at $18 billion; a state of underemployment exists and it is decided to cure it through increasing effective demand by way of fiscal policy.

	Situation 0	Method I	Method II	Method III
Expenditures	18	18	25	38
Taxes	18	8	20	38
	—	—	—	—
Deficit	0	10	5	0

Method I leaves expenditures unchanged but reduces tax rates. The increased disposable income results in increased consumers' spending. Tax revenues at the lower rates are decreased by $10 billion, making for a budget deficit of that amount.

Method II leaves the tax rates unchanged but increases government expenditures by $7 billion. Besides the increased public spending there is increased consumers' spending out of the increased incomes. Because of the rise in incomes, tax payments increase by $2 billion, resulting in a budget deficit of $5 billion.

Method III increases government expenditures by $20 billion and raises tax rates enough to get the same amount in additional taxes out of the increased incomes. Consumers' spending (and saving) is not allowed to increase because taxes absorb so large a part of the income. The increase in national income takes only the form of government projects; the budget is balanced.[35]

This very crude way of presenting a rather sophisticated theory will,

35. If private investment increased, saving and consumption could also rise; and the increase in national income would be distributed over consumption, investment, and tax-financed government projects.

I hope, be pardoned by its advocates. But it must be doubted that a fuller exposition, especially an exposition of the exact mechanisms which are supposed to be operative in the quantitative theory of fiscal policy, would be really worth while in view of the arbitrary assumptions on which the theory is based. For example, while it assumes that we know the changes in saving and consumption which would follow upon changes in taxation or government expenditures, nothing is done concerning induced changes in private investment. As long as we do not know what the effects upon investment would be, the assumption of "private investment remaining unchanged" is probably the best way out. But it severely reduces the value of the whole theory. A tax reduction may encourage private investment; so may an increase in consumers' demand. A larger budget deficit, on the other hand, may under existing business psychology discourage investment. What changes in the inducement to invest may be expected, on balance, if reduced taxes are linked with higher deficits, or if increased demand is linked with increased taxation, is anybody's guess.

Choosing Among the Three Methods

Those who object most strongly to government expenditures for things not really worth while for themselves and done only to create employment, should prefer the first method. It provides for a minimum of public spending and leaves the overwhelming portion of total effective demand to the private sphere: consumption and business investment. The drawback of this method is that it involves the largest budget deficit, the largest annual increase in the public debt.

Those who object most strongly to deficit spending and to increases in the public debt, should prefer the third method. It provides for a balanced budget and thus keeps the debt from growing. The drawback of this method is that it involves the highest amount of government expenditures, large parts of which undoubtedly are for things which the people would not want to "buy" if they were given a choice. Thus the nation would be spending a large portion of its income for things it does not really want; public spending would assume such an important part of aggregate spending that the character of the economy as one of free enterprise would soon be lost.

Those who object to both the large rise of the debt and the large encroachment of the public sector of the economy upon free consumers' choice, are in a predicament. If they feared the two developments equally and saw no other ways out, they would have to choose the "in-between" method of fiscal policy which, as Hansen puts it, "avoids both the extremes of excessively large expenditures and excessive deficits."[36]

Of course, the choice is limited to the various methods of fiscal policy only if it is believed that business investment and consumers' expenditures cannot be made to increase and thus to take care of a deficiency of effective demand, and if it is believed that unemployment can really be cured by an expansion of effective demand.

Desirable Public Spending

With the exception of Anderson, who calls for "drastic economies in the postwar period" and insists that "proposals for expanding federal expenditures after the war must be fought all along the line" (pp. 51–52), the contributors all advocate a scope of federal expenditures much larger than that before the war.

"It seems difficult," says Williams, "to picture a typical postwar year without considerable expenditure for public works," undertaken not for the sake of employment but as "socially desirable and necessary expenditure (not necessarily financed by deficits), the kind of spending that the community needs to do collectively" (p. 375).

Clark asks whether many of the assets which the government gets by "spending for the sake of making jobs" are not in fact "well worth having"; indeed, "perhaps government does not spend as much as would be warranted in terms of the value of the end-products it creates" (p. 79).

Ellis, who in general is opposed to the idea of public spending to make jobs (except in the postwar transition period), prefers consumption subsidies, such as a guaranteed "national minimum," to public works expenditures (p. 135). But he does recognize that public works may be eminently "desirable." "The direction of public investment should be governed by long-run productivity. For example, to cure a chronic surplus capacity in certain agricultural staples, public works should partly take the form of projects favoring diversified agriculture — experiment stations, schools, etc." (p. 136). "If public works are oriented toward long-run productivity, eventually even to long-run

---

36. *American Economic Review*, Vol. 35, No. 3, June 1945, p. 387.

profitability, toward restoring competition in monopolized fields, and toward fields not well covered by private competition, and if they are timed to operate in a direction opposed to the business cycle, they will strengthen — not jeopardize — the system of private competitive enterprise" (p. 137).

Slichter holds that most public spending in the past was done "in ways which did not permanently increase employment opportunities in private industry." Nevertheless, if more attention is given to the quality instead of merely the "quantity of government spending," the government might devote more of its spending "to projects which increase private investment opportunities," such as TVA, roads, airfields, irrigation projects and scientific research (pp. 311–12).

Hansen is convinced that "wisely chosen" public investment projects "can open up new private investment not otherwise available." He mentions regional resource development, urban redevelopment, and transportation as "best adapted to this purpose" (p. 225). The projects may be self-liquidating, but "nonliquidating projects may be equally valuable. A project should be judged by its over-all productivity for the economy as a whole, and not necessarily in terms of its direct earnings." And we must consider its "effect in opening outlets for the people's savings," not only the direct outlets through the public development project itself, "but even more the induced new private investment outlets which these basic public projects release" (p. 226).

Drawbacks of Public Spending

Clark is afraid that reliance on public works beyond those undertaken for stabilizing cyclical fluctuations might further unbalance "an economy that is already heavily unbalanced in the direction of public works and durable goods in general, as against current consumption" (p. 89). Another of the dangers of using public works as a "remedy for inadequate spending" (p. 89), as Clark puts it, is that the projects may include not merely "things worth doing" but also things in the "leaf-raking" category. Government may be forced into such projects in order to avoid the opposite danger, that its spending goes "into fields where it would compete with private business investment" and "deter so much private investment that it would displace more capital outlays than it made" (pp. 89–90). Significant in this respect is not merely the actual competitiveness of the public undertaking but also the psychological reaction which businessmen seem to have to subsidized government enterprises. "If numerous industries feel that the government may start competing with them in some uncertain future, private capital outlays are pretty sure to be retarded. This is no small part of the dilemma of very heavy public investment" (p. 90).

Williams believes that "the desire to avoid spending merely for spending's sake seems now to be general." In his opinion, it has always been "one of the most difficult questions about public works . . . to assemble enough worthy projects." We shall probably learn to "do a better job in this regard than ever previously," but "the more public spending our program requires, the more we shall need to scrutinize the objects of expenditure" (p. 362).

For much the same reasons Ellis states that the "general presumption" is against public works and in favor of encouraged or even subsidized consumption. "This presumption arises from two maxims of a liberal economic policy: (a) to permit to the individual a free choice of expenditures . . .; and (b) to leave to private enterprise as large a segment of production as possible" (p. 134).

Slichter says that public "deficit spending is less effective than most private investment in raising the national income," and attributes this in part to "the poor quality" of public spending (p. 314). Moreover, public spending "for spending's sake" is likely "to encourage men to look to the government for aid and support rather than to rely upon themselves." And besides the danger of "discouraging enterprise" through actual or expected tax increase Slichter stresses "the danger of the corruption of political life associated with large public expenditures" (p. 319).

A particular difficulty arises in connection with public spending on construction: its effects upon labor cost in the construction industry. Slichter mentions that "to stabilize the construction industry" through public works "might keep wages up in the face of a long-run drop in the demand for construction. Under these circumstances the attempt to stabilize the industry would prevent needed long-term adjustments in the price structure" (p. 312 n). Clark, likewise, points out that "public works to maintain output and employment in the construction industry" may influence "the price-wage structure in precisely the wrong way," especially because government often pays more than private contractors and purchasers. Through such stabilization policies the government might unwittingly "hamstring any private efforts at stabilization" of investment (pp. 105–06).

Long-Run Deficit Financing

Public spending financed by chronic deficits is opposed by five of the six contributors — quite in contrast to their attitude toward occasional or anticyclical deficit spending.

Williams is convinced "that large public expenditure, and especially large deficits, will gradually transform our economic system into some kind of public economy" (p. 360). He is willing to face "large deficits if necessary" during the transition period, but if afterwards "the private economy cannot sustain itself without large deficits" he sees little hope for the maintenance of the "free private enterprise system" (p. 355).

Ellis takes the same view. He finds that deficit spending might be indispensable in the transition period. The "advocate of a liberal economy may hope for basic reforms which will eventually reduce the need for public spending" but "he cannot intelligently counsel economy and caution" for the postwar transition period (p. 137). The long run is a different matter. Ellis "would expect continued resort to deficit financing to carry us along to a fascist or socialist state" (p. 138).

Slichter does not believe that deficit financing will be needed during the postwar transition period. And for the long run he regards it not only as ineffective but positively harmful. "Structural unemployment is not sensitive to the volume of spending," and "lack-of-enterprise unemployment is sensitive to changes in the volume of spending up to a certain point, but beyond this point increases in spending have more effect upon prices than upon employment" (pp. 306–07). Thus, "increases in spending may have a very limited effect upon the number of jobs" (p. 307). Deficit spending is "an attack upon results rather than upon causes"; it "does not remove the impediments to private spending; in fact it may underwrite their retention" (p. 311). Slichter uses actual American experience of recent years to illustrate the relative ineffectiveness of deficit spending in reducing unemployment. He compares the inordinately large increases in government expenditures with the relatively slow and modest increases in employment which were accomplished (p. 313).

The possible harmful effects of large deficits, according to Slichter, are the following: (a) "if financed directly out of current savings, they raise interest rates and limit employment"; (b) "if financed by credit expansion, they raise prices," and thus constitute a hidden and uncontrollable form of taxation; and (c) "by creating expectations of tax increases, they limit the amount of 'purely private' employment" (p. 314). In effect, "the more 'mature' and stagnant the economy, the greater is the danger that deficits will make stagnation worse by causing government expenses to grow faster than revenues and thus limiting the increase in purely private employment" (p. 316).

Anderson is very curt on this subject. He deals with the effects of a chronically unbalanced budget in one sentence only: "If we are reckless about expenditures we shall have chronic deficits, with an undermining of the credit of the government and with currency disorders" (p. 52). In his unbending opposition Anderson seems to reject deficit spending even as a palliative.

Clark accepts long-run deficit spending "as a last resort." "But it should not be a last resort in the sense that we are satisfied to let the matter rest there. If it is necessary, it is because of an unbalance between spending and saving; and it does not cure that unbalance, but may make it worse, unless skillfully handled. It is a palliative, and the need of using it should be a sign of the need of finding something more like a cure" (p. 92).

"It is not a 'palliative'," contends Hansen (p. 207), the only one of the six contributors who urges continuous application of a fiscal program to secure full employment in an economy faced with long-run underemployment.[37] In Hansen's opinion, deficit spending (or, alternatively, tax-financed government expenditures in much larger magnitudes) may be absolutely necessary, "not only to iron out fluctuations, but also to promote rising productivity and higher living standards" (p. 207). And "an ever growing, expanding economy is both a goal in itself and a necessary condition for the achievement of full employment" (p. 226).

The Problem of the Rising Debt

Continuous use of fiscal policy to secure full employment may imply a continuous rise of the public debt. Hansen is fully aware of this, but

---

37. That Hansen is the only advocate of this policy among the contributors should not mislead readers into believing that he represents only a small minority among economists. As a matter of fact, Hansen's ideas on this subject enjoy the widest following.

he is not disconcerted. He points out that an ever increasing public debt need not involve an ever increasing tax burden. "A secular increase in the public debt would lead to difficulties only if the fixed charges on the debt should rise at a faster rate than the national income." If the national income increases "at some minimum constant percentage rate" and if "the debt each year increases by a certain fraction of the total income," the tax rate necessary to meet the interest charges on the debt "will not continue to rise, but will approach a definite limit" (p. 215). "With a moderate and reasonable volume of borrowing, this limit represents a quite manageable tax burden" (p. 217).

Hansen wants to make sure he is not misunderstood; he does not mean to say "that the management of a large public debt is a matter of no concern. No country with a large public debt can hope to achieve economic stability without competent and responsible management by the fiscal and monetary authorities" (p. 217). The inference is clear: competent management can cope with the problems of a continuously rising public debt.

Williams, on the other hand, takes a pessimistic view. If deficits are to be used "not only to compensate for depression, with offsetting surpluses during booms . . . but also to compensate for the long-run contractive tendencies" the ensuing "debt charges would be a growing fraction of national income, and in the process the system of private capitalism would disappear" (pp. 346–47).

Ellis has the same fear. "The increase of the public debt is dangerous to private enterprise from several angles. For one thing, it adds to the amount of fixed income and thus concentrates risk upon fewer incomes, indeed increasingly upon the entrepreneurs or active capitalistic class." Even if the service of a large debt "would represent a relatively small fraction of national income," the question which according to Ellis must appropriately be raised is: "how large is the service of the debt in relation to incomes on venture capital alone?" (p. 138). The "risk of fluctuating national income is the more concentrated upon venture capital income the larger the proportion of fixed capital income to total income." Thus, "an increase of the fixed public debt charges from one per cent to only four per cent of the national income may spell a substantial increase of the concentration of risks upon venture capital, upon which we rely as the mainspring of the economy" (p. 139).

Ellis mentions still other dangers in a large public debt: that monetary management, especially the control of inflation, becomes difficult; that "the debt entails a heavy social cost, despite its being 'owed to ourselves'," because of the burden of taxes upon economic motivation and through several forms of waste and costs connected with taxation; and that a large and increasing *"rentier* class" has "political drawbacks" (p. 139).

After the detailed justification for his rejection of the policy of long-run deficit financing, Slichter hardly needs to add separate reasons for his warnings against a rising public debt. But he does point out that the actual or anticipated tax increases which are bound up with increases in the debt are harmful for "private employment" (p. 314). He not merely opposes further increases in the debt but urges a program of debt repayment. He recommends budget surpluses gradually to repay the debt. This would "help create the expectation of a declining tax burden," which in turn "would be an important stimulus to enterprise — increasing the demand for labor and helping to maintain high employment" (p. 332).

Clark, asking himself whether "our habit of worrying" about a mounting public debt "rests on a mere superstition," finds "that there is more than a superstition there." He mentions two difficulties. "If the government lays taxes to pay the interest, when taxes are already very heavy, the added taxes may become a factor limiting investment and production." And "even aside from tax burdens, the interest overhead would distort the distribution of the country's income in the wrong direction" (p. 91).

Anticyclical Deficit Spending

While they so vigorously resist chronic deficits and an ever increasing public debt, five of the six contributors unequivocally support the use of compensatory deficit spending during the depression phase of the business cycle — public deficit spending to offset temporary private spending deficits. But four of the contributors imply that these deficit periods will be short and will always be followed by periods of private surplus spending and of public budget surpluses devoted to the repayment of the accumulated debt.

Clark states that government spending for public works "without simultaneously taking an equal amount of money out of private pockets by taxes" is "clearly an appropriate thing to do in case of a cyclical decline that centers in private capital outlays" (p. 89). A "regular policy of intermittent increased spending in slack times is logical as a measure to stabilize economic fluctuations" (pp. 121–22).

Williams accepts fiscal policy as an "instrument for business cycle stability." "A policy of cyclically unbalanced budget combined with tax reductions in depression and tax increases during booms could probably accomplish much to stabilize national income" (p. 380).

Slichter is somewhat skeptical about the effect of temporary tax reductions (p. 328) and has also some serious doubts as to the psychological effects of a budget deficit during depression. Deliberate creation of a greater deficit "might be regarded as evidence of financial irresponsibility" and, because of the uncertainties created among businessmen, "accelerate the depression, and retard recovery" (p. 329). But on balance, Slichter favors deficit spending during depression. He thinks deficit financing "superior" to some of his otherwise recommended incentive methods "as a device for limiting cyclical unemployment," that is, as a "convenient offset to the drop in private spending" (p. 319).

Ellis discusses the possibilities of tax reductions and mentions that a "drastic reduction of all tax revenue" would be appropriate "if unemployment is severe. This procedure on the revenue side would follow the pattern of 'compensatory' fiscal policy, which requires a parallel increase of 'spending' on the other side of the budget" (p. 138).

Needless to say, Hansen is an unqualified advocate of the "compensatory fiscal program," with public investment playing the "balancing role." "To this end the government must make sure that public investment expands when private investment is declining" (p. 207). In addition, a reduction of the basic income tax rate during depression should "stimulate private spending" and "reinforce the effect of increased public expenditures" (p. 208).

"Depression Deficits" in Practice

Only Anderson seems to reject the use of budget deficits for cyclical depressions. And only Hansen accepts the use of budget deficits for chronic stagnations. For these two the problems of the practical application of their ideas may be easier than for Clark, Ellis, Slichter and

Williams, who may find that they have not the criteria needed for carrying out the policy which they favor. Directions such as "You should never use it" and "You may always use it to fight unemployment"[38] do not require the discriminating diagnosis of cyclical depression as against chronic stagnation. To make such a diagnosis presents a problem soluble for the past, with hindsight, but hardly for the present, without the gift of foresight.

To take a concrete example rather than a constructed model: what would have been the diagnosis of the situation in the United States late in 1936 and early 1937? Was it "depression" or was it "prosperity"? We knew then that matters had much improved since 1933 but were still pretty sad, with about six million unemployed (or even eight million, according to another count). We knew that this was worse than in any depression before 1931, but better than in any year since 1931; we did *not* know then that 1937 was to be an upper turning point and that things would be much worse in the years to follow. How many economic diagnosticians knew at the time where we stood?[39]

Looking backward, we know that 1936–1937 was the peak of the cycle. Would those who advocate anticyclical deficits but oppose chronic deficits have demanded budget surpluses from 1934 or 1935 on to repay the debt contracted in the early thirties? Of course, there are those who would say that bigger and bolder deficits in the beginning phases of the depression would have prevented things from running down so badly and continuing as miserably as they did. And if larger loan expenditures in those years had put the economic situation into good shape, the suggestion of budget surpluses and debt repayment would not have looked so ironically out of place in the middle of the thirties. But can one be sure that larger depression deficits would have worked? Slichter points to the huge amounts of spending it took to reduce unemployment after 1940 (p. 313). In the light of his discussion — can one be certain that fiscal policy would have succeeded in combating the supposedly cyclical unemployment of the early thirties?

38. Neither Anderson nor Hansen formulate their directions that bluntly. Anderson, for example, merely says that overstrained finance will not permit us to use deficit spending after the war if we are to avoid currency disorders.

39. It happens that this writer read a paper, early in 1937, in which he expressed the same doubts concerning business cycle diagnosis. See *Can We Control the Boom?*, University of Minnesota Press, Minneapolis, 1937, p. 11.

It is by no means impossible that we may again experience "prosperity" with six million unemployed. The question is whether a fiscal policy which intends to be compensatory only with respect to cyclical fluctuations, but not with respect to chronic stagnation, will insist on budget surpluses and debt repayment in the face of unemployment of that size. It is doubtful that such insistence would be politically feasible. Even among economists probably few would want to recognize a state of unemployment of the described dimensions as "prosperity" — although to deny such recognition might be equivalent to giving up the concept of the business cycle and, along with it, the notions of anti-cyclical deficit spending and balancing the budget over the period which used to be called a "cycle."

TRADE UNIONS AND FULL EMPLOYMENT

The problem of the repercussions of liberal public spending upon wage policies is one of the most serious of all postwar problems. Public spending for the purpose of creating jobs is apt to be a dismal failure if the cost of labor is stepped up along with the demand for labor. For those who assume that wage rates will rise only if effective demand continues to rise after full employment has been attained, the problem does not exist. But those who fear that trade unions will press for higher wages long before full employment is reached, have great apprehensions. Depending on their basic philosophies, they (a) forswear all public spending for the sake of jobs; (b) call for permanent governmental wage controls; or (c) hope that the trade unions will practice restraint in wage rate bargaining.

Make-Work Public Spending and the Unions' Reactions

Would union wage policy be more restrained in a privately financed than in a publicly financed expansion? Many answer this question affirmatively, especially if the "full employment policy" of the government should take the form of a commitment or a guarantee. Slichter, for example, holds that a governmental guarantee of employment, "even if in terms of opportunities rather than [actual] jobs," would necessitate governmental wage control, because employment opportunities "depend on the wage structure, upon the policies of trade unions, and upon the results of collective bargaining. Wages may rise so fast in response to increases in the demand for labor that little increase in employment would occur" (p. 308).

Clark refers to the same problem when he states: "Commonly prices and wages stop rising at the crest of a wave of prosperity, when expansion ceases and many employers find that they are paying about as much as they can afford. But would they stop if continued high demand were virtually guaranteed, including a guarantee against shrinkage due to increased costs and prices?" (p. 117).

Wage Increases in Wartime and Peacetime Expansion

There is no doubt that "in normal times . . . wages and prices tend to rise while economic activity is on the way up from depression to prosperity — that is, while there are still idle workers and idle plant capacity." Clark, who makes this statement, adds to it that the record of the American "defense drive and war effort of 1940–1942" gives the suggestion "that a deliberately stimulated expansion may be expected to bring on inflation considerably before full employment is reached" (p. 115). Yet, noting the differences between war mobilization and peacetime expansion, he concludes: "Weighing the pros and cons, it appears that a publicly supported full-employment program would bid up wages and prices probably as much as they rise in a normal business revival and possibly more, but not to the extent that they rose in 1940–1942. This rise might be mitigated by shrewd and businesslike negotiation on the part of government, in administering its own spending; but opinions will differ as to how successful government is likely to be in this direction" (p. 116).

Even this conclusion may seem somewhat optimistic inasmuch as it is based on experiences with "normal business revivals," without taking account of the increase in bargaining strength of the trade unions since the last "normal business revival" — which apparently must have been back in the twenties. Since organized labor acquired its present strength, there have been only two periods of revival: the one which reached its climax in 1937, the other which started in 1940 with the defense and war mobilization. In the former period the wage policies were so aggressive that — according to Anderson (p. 25) and Williams (pp. 369, 372) — they were among the chief causes of a collapse at a time when between six and eight million persons were still unemployed. The latter brought such energetic pressures for higher wages that governmental wage controls had to be introduced to avoid progressive inflation.

During the war, the pressures for higher wage rates were perhaps stronger on the part of employers — bidding up the wages in competing for scarce man power — than they were on the part of unions. The presence of strong national labor organizations probably contributed to the effectiveness of the government's attempts to stabilize wages and to resist wartime inflation. The unions' cooperation in the anti-inflation program, however, was based on an appeal to patriotism. Can we expect a similar performance when it can no longer be regarded as a contribution to the war effort?

Restraint or Self-Restraint of Trade Unions

All the contributors recognize the problem of aggressive wage policies, but their reactions are very different. Anderson, who rejects all public spending for the purpose of job-making, believes that the modification of the labor legislation of the New Deal would reduce the monopoly power of trade unions sufficiently to secure wage structures compatible with full employment. Williams confines himself to the statement that wage rates should rise with the growth of productivity and that a faster rise would cause trouble (p. 369).

Hansen speaks of "the real serious threat of postwar inflation" caused by a "chaotic wage development, destructive of price and general economic stability." He emphasizes that "the upward adjustment [of wage rates] must be limited to the requirements of economic and price stability," that "this is in the interest of the entire wage-earning group, no less than for society as a whole," and that "we must have an enlightened policy against wage inflation" (p. 260). What sort of policy, Hansen does not say, but he gives the impression that he means to direct his remarks to the leaders of organized labor.

Ellis looks to "an improvement in the personnel and outlook of union leaders" as one of the chief safeguards against monopolistic wage increases, but he also mentions that the government should "prosecute outright restraint of trade by unions" and that "universal compulsory federal arbitration" might become necessary (p. 186). His main hope, however, is for "responsible union leadership" (p. 185).

It is significant that some British radical advocates of fiscal policy for full employment, realizing that its repercussions upon trade-union policies may have disastrous consequences, conclude that the present system of wage bargaining by trade unions and employers in individual industries "should be replaced by a system of wage determination on a national basis."[40]

Slichter comes to similar conclusions (even though he does not advocate fiscal policy as the method for attaining higher levels of employment but rather expects private investment to secure satisfactory employment). He remarks with regret that on wage questions each union "is left free to run its own affairs with little or no interference" from the national federations (p. 321). "The federations of labor . . . should have the responsibility of protecting the total volume of employment opportunities from being narrowed by the policies or actions of any given union. The federations of unions have an interest in a well-balanced wage structure, in contrast with the interests of certain strong unions which may push the wages of their members too high for the good of labor as a whole" (p. 320).

Clark counts on "something approaching economic statesmanship" to avoid serious wage inflation. "The probability would seem to be that if a really high level of employment were maintained — if unemployment were approximately stabilized at a 'float' averaging not more than three to four million — there would be a tendency to a gradual progressive rise in prices of the sort that is pushed up by increased money costs. If various powerful groups were to act as if the government's program were a Christmas tree or a grab bag, the inflationary tendency could go far enough to do harm. If the groups follow a statesmanlike policy, the tendency might be kept within harmless limits. Whatever happens, much will depend on whether these powerful groups develop a sense of responsibility in the exercise of their power, and something approaching economic statesmanship" (p. 116).

40. M. Joseph and N. Kaldor, *Economic Reconstruction after the War* (Handbooks published for the Association for Education in Citizenship by the English Universities Press, Ltd.). The statement reads as follows:

"There is a great danger, therefore, that with the present system of sectional wage-bargaining, in a state of full employment a tug of war will ensue between the workers of different industries for larger slices of the national cake, in the course of which wages and prices will continually rise. This senseless chase between wages and prices leaves no one ultimately better off, but must, sooner or later, shake the confidence in the currency and endanger the stability of the whole system.

"A policy of full employment will require, therefore, that the present system of wage-bargaining by trade unions and employers' federations in *individual industries* should be replaced by a system of wage determination on a national basis."

The discussion of the wage structure may be regarded as one phase of the problem of monopolistic pricing. The power of trade unions to bargain for higher wages at a time when unemployed labor is available, is monopoly power. Thus, Ellis speaks of the effects of wage increases which "could come about only from militant exaction by labor monopoly," and he states that in a competitive market economy the "principle of clearing the market must occupy a central place in the national wage policy" (p. 184). Clark, likewise, speaks of "wage rates of a monopolistic character" as obstacles to full employment (p. 103).

While some of the contributors make it quite explicit that they regard the wage problem as one of monopolistic pricing, others do not say a word about it. This difference in emphasis possibly reflects the importance which the authors seem to ascribe to the monopoly question in general.

Monopoly and the Cost-Price Structure

Williams does not say anything about monopoly and the competitive price mechanism. He does speak of the importance of "price-cost relationships" and of making the economy "more responsive and adaptable" (p. 363) ; but he does not state whether monopolistic practices are responsible for distorted price-cost relationships and whether restraints of competition are responsible for the fact that the economy is not sufficiently responsive and adaptable. It may well be that this is Williams' view; but he does not say it, and he gives no indication of the ways by which increased responsiveness and adaptability of the economy might be achieved.

Hansen devotes one footnote to the discussion of monopoly. It reads: "Many economists have rightly been concerned about the apparent growth of monopoly in our economy. Monopoly operates to raise prices and profits. It therefore restricts the volume of consumption expenditures on the one side, and on the other, increases the volume of savings. Moreover, by restricting output it tends to reduce the volume of investment. Thus, all around, the savings-investment problem is intensified" (p. 218).

Beyond this footnote, there is a passage in which Hansen recognizes "that fiscal policy is not enough" and "that restrictive practices constitute a serious menace to full-employment opportunities." But he points out that fiscal policy will not, as many believe, "prevent us from correcting distortions and unbalance in the cost-price structure"; that, on the contrary, it will help to correct them, because restrictive practices "can be attacked and removed far more successfully in an environment of expansion than in one of contraction" (p. 208).

Whether this is true with respect to monopolistic wage bargaining is not so certain. The nature of union wage policies to be expected in an environment of expansion has thrown serious doubt upon it. In any event, the problem does not seem to rate prominence in Hansen's essay.

Slichter also does not give much space to the monopoly issue, but it does figure more prominently in his reasoning. In his discussion of how the government might increase employment, "removing specific obstacles to the expansion of production" is the first item; and the obstacles he lists include monopolistic restrictions (p. 309). In his analysis of the causes of unemployment, the first type, which Slichter calls "structural unemployment" or "market imperfection unemployment," is attributed to five different factors, two of which are results of monopoly: "distortions in the price structure" and "distortions in the wage structure" (p. 306). Incidentally, he does not consider wage structure distortions tractable in an unregimented society. "Removal of wage distortion unemployment is beyond the control of the government unless it is willing to formulate and enforce a national wage policy" (p. 309).

Free Markets and Governmental Restraints

Anderson, who as much as any of the participants emphasizes the significance of "the automatic workings of free markets," holds that the restraints which keep the price system from functioning are "wholly due to bad governmental policy." He thinks "that the disappearance of an adequately free market is a very recent matter" and is not due to any developments in industry itself (p. 29).

In his opinion, the removal of direct interferences by the government would suffice to restore a system of "functional" prices. "We must have flexible wage scales," he says, "as part of a flexible economy in order that we may make rapidly the readjustments needed in a rapidly changing world" (p. 25). But he apparently believes that if government stops "manipulating" the labor market, as "under the Wagner Act, and under the wage and hours legislation" (p. 36), the needed flexibility of wage scales would be restored. Anderson does state that corporate consolidation movements "are harmful and should be prevented, but they are not inherent in the nature of industry itself" (p. 31). Anderson does not regard the much discussed restraints through industrial monopolies as real impediments of a flexible economy in the absence of governmental market restraints.

On the question of the necessary degree of competition and flexibility, Anderson states: "If perfect competition and full freedom of prices in all industries and activities were necessary for the essential functioning of the market-mechanism, the case would be hopeless and would always have been hopeless. But the mechanism can and does work adequately, despite many rigidities, if only new ones are not continually being created" (p. 32).

Workable Competition

This statement by Anderson resembles the notion of "workable competition," which Clark has once presented and to which he again alludes in the following passage: "Competition should be maintained wherever it can be made to work in a reasonably effective and healthy way. The fact that in every particular case it is either mixed with monopolistic elements or otherwise imperfect, does not condemn it. Imperfect competition is the only kind possible; and some grades of 'monopolistic competition' probably come nearer to the economist's ideal of 'perfect competition' than 'pure' and unmitigated competition does" (p. 122).

Clark regards "complete competitive flexibility" as not attainable. A "thoroughgoing competitive system" could not be established "even if the government were to succeed to perfection in its attempts to combat monopoly in the areas of business and industry where it does combat it. There are too many areas in which competition has been deliberately dethroned, with public aid or approval." He lists wages, freight rates, electric power rates and the prices of some agricultural raw materials as being "determined in noncompetitive fashion," and holds that this leaves only little room "within which the prices of manufactured products can be competitively flexible." And he concludes: "When anyone recommends general competitive price flexibility as the correct economic policy, it is fair to expect him to offer at least a glimmering as to how this is to be brought about" (pp. 102–03).

Restoration of Competition

Whether or not Ellis' essay offers this "glimmering," or perhaps a full illumination of the methods by which the American economic system can be made effectively competitive, cannot here be decided. "Reliance upon a competitive price system" (p. 126) and insistence that "economic governance must for the most part consist in the impersonal mechanism of competition and competitive prices" (p. 198), are opening and concluding declarations of his essay. The combination of fiscal and monetary policies "with a balanced program against monopoly restriction" constitutes its "central theme" (p. 190). His antimonopoly program is an arsenal of liberalism.

Ellis' hope that artificial supports of the economy, such as fiscal policy and direct controls, both so dangerous for a democratic society, can be dispensed with in a few years, is based upon the assumption that we immediately begin "to withdraw the bases of monopoly in all fields" (p. 136). He attributes to monopoly "a large measure — perhaps much the largest share — of unemployment and idle funds" (p. 177). And he rejects the widespread belief that monopoly in industry is inevitable owing to a supposed technological superiority of large-scale production. He quotes, with obvious approval (p. 179), a conclusion of Clair Wilcox in a careful analysis of *Competition and Monopoly in American Industry:*[41] "In nearly every case in which monopoly persists, it will be found that artificial factors are involved." Ellis assumes that the removal of these "artificial" factors, including the manifold "contributions of government to monopoly" (p. 181), would go far in restoring a workable competitive economy.

The removal of governmental activities which favor monopoly and restrain competition is, however, a highly problematic undertaking. These government policies may be, as Ellis says, "relatively simple in their theoretical character" in comparison with other aspects of the monopoly problem, "but politically they are frequently the most formidable because they often indicate the capitulation of democratic government to special economic interests" (p. 181). Whether political and economic education will succeed in improving democratic government and in immunizing it against powerful lobbies is an open ques-

41. By Clair Wilcox, Monograph No. 21, Temporary National Economic Committee, p. 315.

tion. Ellis does not try to map an educational or political campaign. He confines himself to brief statements of the strongest "bases of monopoly" and of "policies to combat monopolistic restriction of output," and to "the main outlines of a programmatic attack upon monopoly restriction which will require a decade (or two or three) to be really effective" (pp. 190–91).

Monopolistic Price Inflexibility and Output Restrictions

On first glance it may seem that Ellis' confidence in the survival of, or return to, a state of effective competition contradicts Clark's statement that a "thoroughgoing competitive system" cannot become reality. On closer inspection the contradiction disappears. Like Clark, Ellis does not "aim at some theoretically 'perfect' state of competition" or at "complete price flexibility" (p. 177). He, too, regards it as misleading to attempt an "onslaught against the 'inflexibility' of monopoly prices." For "it is not the inflexibility of monopoly prices but monopoly restriction of output which is at issue" (p. 190).

A similar idea is expressed by Clark when he states: "In the case of monopolistic and semimonopolistic situations the height to which the price or wage rises above a competitive level may within ordinary limits be less important than the restrictive tactics which are used to maintain and protect the monopolistic position" (p. 103). Restrictions of production or of jobs "may directly interfere with mobility of resources and with full employment" (p. 104).

The emphasis upon direct restrictions does not imply that the height to which prices or wages rise is not important. "It is clear," says Clark, "that particular prices or particular wage rates of a monopolistic character may be so high as to be obstacles to full employment" (p. 103). But Clark's approach to the problem of excessive prices and excessive wages is not the traditional one which concentrates on removal of monopolistic restraints and combinations. Although he still feels that "a lively sense of the potentialities of competition" is probably the best "incentive to low-price policy," he relies to a large extent on a sense of "responsibility" on the part of business and labor groups (p. 110). "If monopolistic units persist in following a restrictive and exploitive policy, it may be necessary to attack them formally. But such cases should be exceptional." Instead of having our economic relations "settled for us by governmental coercion, we must learn to settle them among ourselves. This means getting together, each group accepting responsibility for doing its part to make a workable whole" (p. 125).

Forces of Competition Versus Sense of Responsibility

This approach, perhaps, is more consistent than that of Ellis, who relies on the unshackling of the forces of competition as far as business is concerned, but on the sense of responsibility when it comes to labor. Yet inconsistency may well be justified if it is agreed that competition can still be restored in business while in the labor market it is gone forever. It may be the most expedient solution to try hard for effective competition wherever it may be attained and, for the rest, hope for the development and exercise of an enlightened sense of responsibility.

Liberalism has consistently fought the concentration of economic power and the emergence of groups which can wield monopoly power through associative action. Now it seems to many observers that this battle is lost — not merely in the field of labor but throughout the economic system. And those who give up the hope of retaining or restoring competition must either call for direct control and coercion by the government or take to preaching and praying that — in the words of Clark — the "powerful groups develop a sense of responsibility in the exercise of their power" (p. 116).

Clark apparently believes that much *might* be done but little *will* be done to check the monopolistic powers in the field of business. Consequently, he uses the "do your part" approach also with respect to powerful business groups, trying to convince them of the merits and benefits of low-price and low-profit policies.[42] "Granted a general acceptance of the idea that the most crucial product of industry after the war will be jobs" and "that the cost-price structure can be a favoring condition or a hindrance," Clark feels "that the responsibility for making it a favoring factor lies on all concerned." And "associative action on a really broad base seems the most promising approach" (p. 125).

Reliance on "associative action" on a broad base need not imply that the area of group action should be enlarged. What Clark hopes for is not increased power of economic interest groups but more responsible use of the power which they already have.

---

42. Another forceful presentation of the advantages of voluntary low-price policy is contained in Edwin G. Nourse's *Price-Making in a Democracy,* The Brookings Institution, Washington, 1944.

Questions regarding the rate of interest, in particular regarding its variations or its stability, may not be among the most vital problems of the postwar economy, but they are certainly among the perplexing ones. Changes in the interest rate bear on several important economic relationships.

The Sphere of Influence of the Interest Rate

The scope of the interest problem can be judged from the fact that a change in interest rates may affect (a) the volume of investment; (b) the volume of saving; (c) the value of assets of the banking system and the earnings of the banks; (d) the holdings of securities by banks and other financial institutions; (e) the holding or liquidation of securities by individuals and nonfinancial corporations; (f) the cost of servicing the public debt and, therefore, the size and balance of the budget, and the need for taxes. Every single one of these items may play a role in the determination of the current flow of money and income, and may be a retarding or energizing factor, contributing to the expansion, contraction or stabilization of the national income.

Some of the contributors make only casual remarks on the problem of the rate of interest, and even those who deal with it more extensively refer only to one or another of its relationships. A systematic comparative analysis of the different views on the problem must, therefore, be incomplete.

Interest Rates and Investment

Generations of economists have been brought up on the theory that changes in the rates of interest can influence the volume of investment. In recent years, however, it has become fashionable to deny the effect of interest rates on investment.

Hansen makes the statement that "both theoretical analysis and practical case studies indicate that the volume of real investment made by business is but little affected by the interest rate" (p. 255). In other places in his essay, however, he implicitly refutes this thesis. For example, he approvingly quotes[43] that "high borrowing costs would hamper new investment in plant, equipment, and housing [and thus] would

43. From the *Annual Report of the Bank of Canada* of February 10, 1944.

restrict the expansion of employment"; or he finds that an "increase in the rate of interest hits the vital industries" (p. 251); or again he reminds us "how difficult it has been [during the depression] to reduce the rate adequately in highly important areas such as housing and on loans in rural and small communities" and deplores "the deterrent effect which a high rate has on recovery" (p. 252).

The apparent incongruity of the two points of view can perhaps be explained as an unintended overstatement of the "little effect" theory. Hansen probably refers to the different degree of sensitiveness in up-hill and down-hill movements: private investment can easily be discouraged by an increase in interest rates, but not so readily stimulated by a reduction of interest. It is for precisely this reason that Hansen dislikes the use of deliberate variations of the interest rate as an instrument of business cycle control: it works too quickly as a check and too slowly as a stimulus to investment.[44]

A potent reason why business investment has become less sensitive to changes in interest rates is seen by Hansen in the fact that "internal sources of financing are increasingly important and the volume of new financing in the capital market is relatively small" (p. 255). Slichter expresses the same thought when, after remarking that a "rise in interest rates would limit investment," he adds the qualification: "In so far as investments were financed by plowed-back profits, however, the higher interest rates would have little effect" (p. 327 n).

Self-financing out of undistributed profits does unquestionably reduce the effects of changes in interest rates upon investment by corporations. But this applies probably more to a regime of relatively low interest rates than to one of high rates. If interest rates rose to 8 or 10 per cent, business executives would not fail to compare the yield of high-grade loans and securities with the potential rate of return from investment in construction and plant expansion, and they might decide

44. Many practical case studies of the sort which Hansen mentions in support of the "little effect" theory were incorrectly devised. The ways in which the questions were framed predetermined the "findings." The business executives were asked whether interest-rate calculations, especially interest-rate reductions, were among the factors which motivated them in their investment decisions. In order to judge the significance of the interest rate for investment decisions, the executives should have been asked not merely whether they had the interest rate in mind when they made their decisions but also whether they would have undertaken the investments at a 10 per cent, 8 per cent, 6 per cent rate of interest, etc. Only in exceptional instances would an actual investment be "marginal" exactly at the current rate of interest.

against using their funds for real investment. When interest rates are between, say, 2 and 4 per cent, investment financed out of undistributed profits is probably not very sensitive to rate variations within that range.

Clark thinks that the interest rate is of only minor significance for investment "in a dynamic industry," where "the allowance for obsolescence alone dwarfs the element of interest" (p. 111). "A low rate of interest can be a material stimulus to investment in some important areas where maintenance and depreciation are low, risks are moderate and interest is a really substantial part of the cost incurred on account of an investment of capital. This is pre-eminently true of hydroelectric installations and is broadly true of housing. But in the general field of industry and trade, low interest rates cannot accomplish as much as many economic theorists give them credit for" (pp. 110–11).

Interest Rates and Saving

Clark points out that the effects of interest rates upon the average propensity to save may be significant. He states: "Low interest rates are usually thought of as stimuli to investment, but they might have as much effect in reducing long-run net savings, if they became low enough to drive the ordinary middle-class saver into buying annuities instead of holding his principal intact and spending only the income" (p. 96).[45]

45. This effect of lower interest rates is peculiar in that it operates upon the individual saver in a discontinuous fashion (well expressed by the word "driving" him into buying annuities). Assume that one of the motives is to secure for himself a certain income from capital. As long as he buys bonds and plans for his old age to consume only the income but to leave the savings intact for his heirs, every reduction in the rate of interest, reducing the future income from a given capital, may induce the saver to save more so that he may reach the desired size of future income. As the interest rates fall still lower, there may come a point where he feels that he cannot afford any longer to buy future income in this expensive way — and he will be driven into a different form of saving: buying annuities instead of bonds. In order to secure the planned old-age "income" from annuities, much less saving is required and the saver may step up his current consumption — at the expense of his heirs, who will no longer get the benefit from his thrift. But once the change-over from bond buying to annuity buying is accomplished, the effect of further reductions in the interest rate is again in the opposite direction: every reduction means that higher premiums, and therefore higher savings, become necessary for the purchase of fixed amounts of annuities.

From these considerations we may conclude: both the savers who plan for fixed incomes from capital and the savers who plan for fixed annuities must save more as the interest rates are reduced; but savers who, under the impact of lowered interest rates, switch from the one plan to the other, can drastically reduce their rate of saving. Taking all middle-class savers together, Clark may be correct in assuming that the reduction in saving owing to the

Slichter deals with the influence of interest rates upon saving and consumption when he discusses the use of higher rates as a device for checking an inflationary boom. If it is to serve in this capacity, an increase in interest rates should increase saving and reduce consumption. But, according to Slichter, "a rise in interest rates does not appear to be effective in limiting consumption when employment and pay rolls are increasing because when people take a more and more optimistic view of the future, their propensity to consume rises" (p. 327 n).

On the other hand, Slichter does ascribe to the interest rate some influence upon saving and consumption, for he recommends, as one of the safeguards against an inflation during the conversion period, an issue of Victory bonds "paying more than present war savings bonds," which "might cause some people to increase their savings by a small amount" (pp. 279–80).

Interest Rates and the Banking System

An increase in interest rates is equivalent to a fall in the prices of bonds carrying stipulated interest payments. The longer the maturity of the bonds the greater the percentage fall in their market prices when current interest rates go up. Bondholders, thus, suffer a depreciation of their assets and these "losses" may be serious matters, particularly for banks.

Hansen mentions that the use of "interest rate adjustments" to control the business cycle is now widely "regarded as inadmissible" because of the effects which "a substantial fall in bond values" would have on the economy (pp. 250–51). He urges that "the value of long-term government bonds should be stabilized with a minimum of fluctuations" (p. 254), and he seems to concur in the view that "the vast holdings of government bonds by financial institutions, business, and the public generally preclude the use of this [interest policy as a] monetary weapon" (pp. 250–51).

Williams finds that "the banks have pursued a prudent policy regarding the maturities of their security holdings" and, because of the relatively short maturities, are not very vulnerable to a rise in interest rates. Such a rise, nevertheless, may still "find the banks very sensitive" and might "precipitate a wave of government security selling by

---

switch into annuities will outweigh the increase in saving owing to the higher premiums for fixed annuities.

banks." But more important, in the opinion of Williams, is the fact that "the public and the Treasury, as well as the banks, develop a strong vested interest in stability of rates." In view of this development, although "there might be some room for monetary control through variations in the shorter rates of interest," Williams sees "no prospect of revival of a general monetary control in the postwar period" (p. 383).

Ellis does not agree with this. He believes that the use of monetary controls to check inflation may be indispensable, especially if direct controls of spending and prices are prematurely abandoned. Mere restrictions of loans may not suffice to stem inflation; "the ultimate, and indeed the only, recourse is an advance of interest rates and a consequent depreciation of government securities not redeemable on demand." He realizes that the decline in bond prices "would have to be held to moderate proportions in order to prevent a panicky wave of selling on the part of banks and other holders of 'governments' " (pp. 143–44). But "the fact that the English and Canadian authorities seem to have committed themselves" to a policy of stable bond prices at the present low interest rates "does not necessitate a similar course in the United States. Swings in business activity have always been more violent here and the controls must consequently be more severe" (p. 145).

Anderson is still more insistent on this point. Flexible interest rates appear to him a necessary part of a flexible price system. He cites the Federal Reserve banks' rediscount rates of 6 and 7 per cent during the crisis of 1920–1921 as an adjustment which facilitated the quick recovery in the immediately following years (p. 27). At present, the crucial question is whether or not we wish to prevent a postwar inflation: "The existing low interest rates are made possible only by the substitution of bank credit for investors' savings. If bank expansion were to stop today, interest rates would forthwith rise. If, on the other hand, bank expansion is not stopped, we shall have a tremendous inflation. And then we shall see an immense rise of interest rates, the inevitable accompaniment of a great inflation. The choice is not between continuing low interest rates and not continuing. The choice is rather between a moderate and manageable reversal of policy in the near future, and an involuntary submission to very high interest rates at a later date" (p. 49).

Anderson urges that private savers, "attracted by higher yields on government bonds, would make a market for very many of the government securities now held by the banks." They "would pay for them by checking against deposit accounts, canceling a great deal of the inflated deposits, and once more easing the money market situation by reducing the reserve requirements of the banks" (p. 50). The increased interest rates "would involve dangers to the capital structures of those banks now too heavily loaded with long-term government securities." For the protection of the banks Anderson submits a proposal designed to reduce their losses (p. 51).[46]

Interest Rates and the Budget

Hansen favors maintenance of an average interest rate of 2 per cent on government bonds. In his opinion, "a rational management of the public debt and of monetary policy should make a 2 per cent average interest rate on government bonds a reasonable expectation" (p. 216). A higher rate would be undesirable "in terms of the burden of fixed charges on the public debt," apart from other reasons (p. 255). And he declares: "What the desirable level of interest rates may be a decade or so hence, I do not pretend to know, but for the years ahead, I think we would do well to stabilize around present levels" (p. 254).

Williams asks how much the services of the banks "in holding the public debt should cost the Treasury. Interest will be one of the chief items in the postwar budget, amounting perhaps to a fourth or more of federal expenditures. There have been already a number of proposals for reducing the interest on the part of the debt held by banks. My own view," he adds, "is that the amount of interest that could be saved by any reasonable proposal would not be great, and that steps taken in this direction could arouse fears in the rest of the community about the goodness of the government's promises to pay" (p. 384).

Williams emphasizes the desirability — "for the future of the banking system, as well as for stability and growth of the economy" — to "get more and more of the debt" from the portfolios of the banks into

46. Paul A. Samuelson, in a recent article, questions the reasons for concern over the damage which interest rate increases are supposed to do to bondholding banks. He shows that neither the banking system as a whole nor a typical single bank taken by itself is "hurt by an increase in the whole complex of interest rates"; in fact, they are "left better off by such a change." In spite of this, Samuelson argues against higher interest rates. See "The Effect of Interest Rate Increases on the Banking System," *American Economic Review*, Vol. 35, No. 1, March 1945, pp. 16 ff.

private hands (p. 384). He does not say, however, whether this can be achieved at the present low interest rates, in the stability of which "the public and the Treasury, as well as the banks" have developed "a strong vested interest" (p. 383).

Anderson is convinced that private purchasers of the bonds now held by the banks can be attracted only at higher interest rates. "The rates of 2 per cent on ten-year bonds, and 2.5 per cent on twenty-year bonds are simply too low to attract investors" (p. 48). "The notion that we can permanently hold the debt service on the public debt to a 2 per cent rate, that we can permanently service $300 billion of public debt with $6 billion of interest, is fantastic. We had best face the facts now" (p. 51).

The facts, as Anderson sees them, are that an attempt to maintain the present low rates spells inflation. "With respect to the interest burden on the government debt," he says "that this problem becomes progressively worse if we delay it. We can now fund the government debt at moderate rates of interest. . . . If, however, we wait for inflation to come, interest rates will rise rapidly and the Secretary of the Treasury will sweat blood as Treasury bills and certificates fall due, as people cash in their war savings bonds, and as he has to borrow money on the rapidly rising money market — or else print, which would not help the inflation" (p. 51).

Anderson's view of the danger of a postwar inflation is extreme. None of the other contributors is nearly as alarmed. Some of them hold that inflationary and deflationary developments are equally probable, depending on circumstances, and others see deflation as the more likely outcome.

POSTWAR INFLATION OR DEFLATION

None of the contributors attempts to "predict" a postwar inflation or depression. They analyze the factors which may have a bearing upon the question of whether the amounts of money which will be seeking to buy goods and services may be more or less than the amounts of goods and services which will be seeking buyers at the present level of prices. The conclusions cannot be very definite. Too much depends on imponderables. In weighing the probabilities, data known at present may be less significant than assumptions about future mass behavior and future government action.

Moreover, the authors may have different time periods in mind when they weigh the comparative strength of inflationary and deflationary influences. Some may think of the immediate postwar period — reconversion — others of a later period — the "catching-up period." For different phases of the "postwar transition period" the conclusions may well be different.

Inflationary Influences

Anderson can point to the fact that in the past the use of "bank credit as a substitute for taxes" to finance war expenditures "has been the typical breeder" of inflation (p. 45). In this war, "as a result of the government's borrowing at low interest from the banks," demand deposits have expanded from $28 billion in June 1939 to $87.5 billion in December 1944. Money in circulation has expanded between June 1939 and April 1945 from $7 billion to $26 billion. "Obviously, there are the very gravest danger signals here" (pp. 45–46). There are now immense volumes of "idle money in circulation" and "idle deposits in the banks. If these grew active, we should have an inflation that would blow us sky high" (p. 50). In addition to idle money and deposits, people have also large amounts of war savings bonds, which they may cash in at any time and which "are in effect demand deposits" (p. 48).

Slichter looks at the "accumulated needs for goods and services," the "accumulated purchasing power" and the "willingness to spend freely," and analyzes each of these factors (pp. 270–74). He goes into questions such as the needs for "civilian attire," "urgent repair and maintenance work," the needs for automobiles, household equipment, dwelling houses. He estimates the needs of industry, railroads, etc., for restoring inventories, for deferred replacements and maintenance, and for reconversion. He takes into account people's attitudes about spending — caution or impatience — and businessmen's accumulated "new ideas and plans." After comparing factors such as these with factors tending toward deflation, Slichter concludes that "inflationary influences will be far stronger during conversion than deflationary influences" (p. 277).

Ellis inquires into four factors which, "compatible with sustained economic activity, might play a part in preventing a general rise of prices: the growth of production for civilian use, surpluses in the federal budget, the repayment of business and private debt, and continued large holdings of cash relative to income." Ellis believes that rapid conversion would be helpful but still "impotent against strong inflationary pressure"; that "there is virtually no prospect of budget surpluses in the immediate postwar years"; and that private debt reduction in substantial amounts would not be probable. Thus, the outcome "will depend largely on the attitude of the public toward spending. Will individuals and business firms be disposed to hold their money, bank deposits, and government securities, or will they proceed to sell securities and spend money? If they should choose the latter course, an enormous volume of purchasing power could be set loose" (pp. 141–42). Even so, Ellis regards deflationary influences as stronger and wants us to be "prepared for the eventual appearance of inadequate demand. There is only a chance that inflationary pressure may develop before that juncture." This chance is real enough so that we "cannot afford to ignore the possibility" (pp. 140–41) and Ellis prescribes measures to be applied for controlling the inflation if it should come.

Williams, surveying the relevant factors, mentions the federal debt, the large part of it which the banks have acquired, the "huge growth" of total deposits and currency, and the probable "further large increase in the banks' government security holdings and hence in the money supply after the war" (p. 382). But "the quantity of money, by itself, has a permissive rather than a positive effect on prices and production" (p. 383). The actual development "depends (apart from further budgetary deficits) on whether the public will want to liquidate securities to buy consumer goods and to what extent business will liquidate securities, and also borrow from the banks, to finance reconversion and capital expansion." An inflationary rise of prices "could occur in the interval of reconversion while civilian goods are still scarce." The balance of forces, however, seems to Williams to lie on the side of deflation. He is "much more impressed by the longer-run deflationary possibilities" (pp. 382–83).

Clark recognizes that "for some things, like automobiles and housing, the demand will exceed the supply for some time," and that there may be a world food shortage. "If demand in general exceeds supply while civilian production is still getting under way, that would tend to inflation." But he adds that "this would be the lesser evil, as tending to avoid a cumulative depression. There is perhaps more likelihood that the chief discrepancies will turn toward deflation temporarily" (p. 86). Nevertheless, to the extent that increases in wage rates, demanded by the unions to offset reduced hours and loss of overtime pay, "might necessitate price increases, raising the cost of living, they would be fictitious and might start an inflationary spiral" (p. 85).

Hansen mentions two factors as relevant: "inflationary potentialities" arising out of a "postwar restocking boom," and "wage inflation" (p. 256). "The real serious threat of postwar inflation is a chaotic wage development" (p. 260). Other inflationary potentialities, such as the cashing of large volumes of savings bonds, he regards as questionable. He believes that, under full employment, people "are likely to add to their nest egg of savings" and that "only in the event of a prolonged depression is any large net unloading of savings funds in prospect" (p. 250). Thus, he does not share the fear of many that increasing commodity prices, actual or anticipated, might invite large-scale liquidation of bonds and spending of the proceeds.

Deflationary Influences

Hansen is apparently more concerned that consumers' spending may be inadequate and wage rates may not be raised sufficiently. "If wage rates are not adjusted upward," the total pay roll would be "substantially reduced" and prices would fall, presenting "serious deflationary dangers" (p. 258).

Slichter enumerates the same deflationary influences. "Fear of unemployment will cause millions of employed persons to spend their money with caution. In addition, the withdrawal of people from the labor market, the reduction in working hours, and the movement of people from high-paying to low-paying jobs will cause pay rolls to drop more than the supply of goods. This will be a deflationary influence, especially because the drop in pay rolls will reduce the demand for farm products." But, unlike Hansen, he regards the "fears of large and prolonged conversion and deflation unemployment" as "ill founded" and considers the inflationary tendencies to be the stronger ones (p. 268).

It must be noted, however, that Slichter estimates "conversion unemployment," plus normal "seasonal" and other types of "frictional" unemployment, to average 4.5 million persons, "during the first year after the war with Japan" (p. 269). An average of 4.5 million may easily mean six million unemployed during several months; after the overemployment of the war years, this high figure may shock the nation into such gloom that "the danger of deflation unemployment," arising on top of the "conversion unemployment," may not appear to be as "greatly exaggerated" (p. 269) as Slichter thinks.

Apprehensions like these also concern Clark. He agrees that the "heavy transitional unemployment" will not be "as serious as it looks in the statistics," partly because it will be only temporary and "partly because the unemployed will be better financed than ever before. Nevertheless, consumers' incomes will shrink heavily, and the results may be cumulative if revival is too long delayed, making the job of revival that much harder" (pp. 85–86). A possible "exposure to a mood of cynical disillusionment if early steps are bungled and early expectations of speedy readjustment deferred or disappointed" may add to the danger of "a cumulative depression or a depression psychology" (pp. 86–87). More dangerous than the "first reconversion recession" might be a second recession, which is "a real threat and more serious than the first because it will lack the handy ladder of 'backlogs' to climb out on" (p. 88).

Williams sees serious "deflationary possibilities arising out of the abundance of raw materials and man power and the great drop in war expenditures" (p. 383). Williams gives more weight to these deflationary possibilities than to any inflationary tendencies.

Ellis pictures a possible sequence of events as follows: "a short 'shock' depression in the reconversion period, recovery induced by backlogs of demand, and finally the playing-out of deferred demand, and depression" (p. 140). He too thinks that the deflationary influences will be the stronger ones.

Anderson does not mention the word "deflation." He speaks instead of a reduction of demand, calling for an "adjustment." When the government drops out of the market as the best customer, "there must be a great readjustment of prices and of wages." But he believes that "if we are flexible and if the markets are free, we can make our adjustment rapidly." If, on the other hand, the adjustment is resisted — by governmental pressures, trade-union resistance, and public spending — "we shall turn it into a severe depression and we shall ultimately make worse unemployment" (p. 14). If we cling "obstinately to existing wage rates" and if "a policy of high doles or WPA for the unemployed is adopted, we can make this unemployment chronic." Anderson adds sarcastically: "A country can have very heavy chronic unemployment if it is willing to pay for it" (p. 22).

Thus, Anderson, who is the most vocal on the danger of inflation, affirms also more strongly than any of the others the probability of severe postwar depression. There is no inherent inconsistency in such a position; the same influences which may cause depression may also prevent recovery and invite measures which result in inflation.

INTERNATIONAL RELATIONS

International trade and finance, promotion of freer movements of goods, and establishment of institutions facilitating movements of capital between nations, are, for most people, means to serve various ends — increased productivity, a larger national income, a higher level of employment, enhanced stability, more secure peace, etc. Williams, for example, favors "the development of international trade through the freer flow of goods and capital on the same ground" as he has "argued for the revitalizing of the private enterprise system here at home. They are the logical counterparts of each other" (p. 85).

A Means As Well As an End

For at least one of the contributors, internationalism is both a method and an end. Ellis introduces himself as an "internationalist," "favoring the abandonment of all efforts directed toward the insulation of national economies, except limiting immigration, sometimes defensible on both sociological and economic grounds" (p. 126). Internationalism, to Ellis, is a "basic objective," not merely a means for various ends. (But he makes a great concession to other objectives when he approves limitations on migration.) With internationalism as a basic objective, its realization would rate some sacrifices of other ends if it should interfere with them. Fortunately it does not. Ellis also finds it a means for attaining important economic objectives.

To "open up international trade and finance to expansion" is among the measures which Ellis prescribes for "immediate action" in order to achieve "a satisfactory level of economic activity after the war" (p. 136). He also believes freer international trade is a means to more stable prosperity: "Though conceivably achievable without a parallel development of international trade, prosperity in the United States alone would be an unstable state of affairs" (p. 155). But "aside from cyclical depressions, the secular development of the foreign trade of the United States may well spell the difference between success and failure for our domestic policies." With this Ellis refers to "the successful disposition of our flow of savings," which would be "facilitated by really substantial foreign investments" (p. 156).

There are several other phases of our economic life in which, according to Ellis, freer international trade would be helpful: it would solve certain problems of gold accumulation and bank reserves (p. 146); it would help in the elimination of restrictive practices of domestic and international monopolies which may stand in the way of domestic expansion; it would remove one of the continual sources of international conflict (p. 155).

Domestic Prosperity and International Trade

The interdependence between domestic prosperity and foreign trade is hardly doubted by anybody, although it is often stressed that foreign trade depends on American prosperity more than American prosperity on foreign trade.

Ellis states for the transition period that "American employment will depend in small measure upon the state of international trade, but international trade will in large measure depend upon American employment" (p. 154). For the long run, however, he claims an increasing importance of international trade for full employment in the United States (p. 156).

Williams affirms that "economic stability in the leading countries, and particularly in the United States, is a necessary condition of world stability. Economic stability in this country will have to depend primarily upon the domestic policies pursued" (p. 337). While the solution of "our own problem of employment must be predominantly domestic," Williams proposes that "the greatest contribution we can make toward international economic stability will be to solve our problem domestically and to maintain a high, stable, and growing level of production, income, and employment" (p. 389).

In the same vein, Clark holds that "to be rich" is "our duty to the rest of the world, in order that we may first help the rest of the world to their feet and afterward buy their goods, in order that we may send them ours (which they will need) without taint of charity." Thus, "for us to be rich is the greatest service we can render them" (p. 78).

Hansen, likewise, stresses that the maintenance of full employment in the United States "is important not only for ourselves but for the entire world" (p. 204). For "we cannot effectively cooperate with other countries in monetary, trade, and world development programs unless we do a good job of managing our own economy. Upon this depends, in no small measure, world security and world peace. Never was it more true that 'charity begins at home'. Never was it more true that 'we help others by helping ourselves'. Prosperity and full employment in the United States are basic prerequisites to the successful functioning of international political and economic institutions. This is true because high prosperity in the United States means a good market in this country for the products of the entire world" (p. 205).

Anderson also holds that our own policies may be of greatest importance to world developments. But the policies which he has in mind are not the ones which, for example, Hansen regards as important. "Our greatest duty to ourselves and to the world," says Anderson, "in the matter of currency and finance is to balance our own budget and to make our own gold dollar unshakably strong" (p. 57). He also proposes to make the United States a better market for the products of the world, but not through "generation of artificial 'purchasing power' in either the foreign or domestic fields" (p. 55), but just by opening our markets for foreign goods through radical reductions of our tariffs.

Tariff Reductions

Anderson places the adoption of liberal trade policies "second only to the objective of a great world peace." He considers it desirable "that our government should cooperate politically with other governments in bringing this [opening of the markets] about, but if no other government on earth should join us in lowering tariffs, in freeing exchanges, in abolishing quotas, we should still perform our greatest service to our own people and to the outside world *in doing it alone*." Then "our markets would be open, foreign nations all over would bring us what they had to sell and would take our goods in exchange" (p. 56).

Tariff reduction by the United States would also contribute to the solution of the international monetary and financial problems, according to Anderson. For, "the knowledge that the American market for manufactured goods is open to Europe would give Europe credit. American banks would then be justified in giving the stronger European industries credits for raw materials and for a certain amount of vitally needed machinery, having in mind that the raw materials could be worked up and returned here promptly in cleaning up the credits." Anderson emphasizes that "the present is an admirable time for us to lower our tariffs drastically, apart from any reciprocity, particularly on manufactured goods," because "low tariffs could . . . hardly complicate the domestic readjustment problem for any American manufacturing industry" (p. 56).

A harmonious variation of this theme appears in Ellis' part. "A unique opportunity will be provided for an extensive lowering of our tariff barriers, since the war has completely changed the nature of our foreign trade, and since in addition our domestic production has been extensively converted from ordinary purposes. When industry reconverts to peacetime production, the emphasis should be placed on products in which this country has a competitive advantage and does not require the protection of high tariffs or the assistance of export subsidies. Such a shift in production could be accomplished with virtually the same effort as a return to prewar productive patterns. A wholesale lowering of tariffs under these conditions would be relatively 'painless', and the result would be a greatly expanded volume of trade and employment" (p. 157).

Ellis sees great advantages in combining the two methods of creating a greater demand for foreign products (a) through maintaining high incomes in this country and (b) through lowering our tariffs. If we mitigate the "shortage of dollars" in international markets merely through the first method, without a reduction of American tariffs, "our prosperity would be less apt to be communicated to foreign countries through our import demands; and by the same token, our prosperity would be less apt to be maintained" (p. 160). American loans to foreign countries will be highly necessary, but "unless our tariffs are reduced" and permit "the development of larger imports and eventually an import balance by the United States" the loans cannot be repaid. Ellis hopes that the members of Congress, in weighing the advantages of a tariff reduction program, will at last "take a long-range view of American self-interest" (p. 161).

Williams, likewise, favors "the development of international trade through the freer flow of goods and capital" and "emphasizes the volume of trade as a whole, and the cost-reducing effects that can be achieved through a better utilization of the world's resources" (p. 388).[47] If we maintain a high level of income in this country, "we would need large amounts of foreign goods and could most readily afford to take the lead in reducing barriers to the international flow of goods and capital" (p. 389).

Hansen does not fail to mention the desirability of tariff reductions, but he makes it clear that he considers the reduction of trade barriers not as a substitute for fiscal and other financial policies but rather as complementary. He does not advocate a policy of tariff reductions as a means for attaining a high income level, because such a policy will not be adopted under any but prosperous conditions. "It is not easy to reduce tariff restrictions on trade when industries competing with foreign imports are confronted with a seriously depressed domestic market" (p. 208). According to Hansen, commercial policy should include international arrangements for the reduction of trade barriers and the removal of discriminatory trade practices. It should be promoted simultaneously with programs of domestic fiscal, and international monetary and financial policy. "We should advance on all fronts as rapidly as possible. Each program reinforces and sustains the others" (p. 265).

Exchange Stability

The desirability of stable foreign exchange rates is not questioned by any of the contributors who discuss this subject. But the methods which they advocate to this end differ widely.

Anderson adheres to the gold standard method. "When several different countries are all on the gold standard, there is no problem of keeping exchange rates fixed among them. The ordinary machinery of the foreign exchange market will make the clearances." And "when countries have sound moneys, moreover, adequately buttressed by

---

47. Williams does not favor an export surplus as a means for getting "leverage for our own employment at the expense of the outside world" (p. 388). This is a perfectly sound view. But, of course, not all types of export surplus give leverage for employment at the expense of the outside world. Where the export surplus is the effect, rather than the cause, of loans to foreign countries which do not impair, or not greatly impair, domestic investment, it may give leverage to employment in the exporting as well as in the importing country. For illustrations see my book on *International Trade and the National Income Multiplier*, Blakiston, Philadelphia, 1943, pp. 165–74, 214–18.

sound fiscal policies, there is no danger of capricious outward capital movements breaking their exchanges" (p. 59). Anderson rejects international institutions which attempt to stabilize the exchanges without impelling "the finance ministers . . . to pull up and reform their finances and their currencies." He rejects credits which are "not to be accompanied by demands for financial and currency reforms and . . . by demands for firm money markets to protect currency reserves." He favors "the restrictive qualities of the gold standard, which restrains the overexpansion of credit" (pp. 60–61).

Hansen agrees that the gold standard has these qualities and, precisely for this reason, he prefers other methods of maintaining exchange stability, methods which will help a country "to reach an international balance without forcing upon that country a policy of deflation. It is obvious that any country can easily reach a balance in its international accounts by undertaking a rigorous deflation of income and employment to a point where imports are sharply curtailed. But such action does not promote world prosperity and world trade" (p. 262). The proposed International Monetary Fund will help "countries over temporary difficulties in their balance of payment position" and thereby give them "time for making necessary adjustments." Moreover, this "system of stable exchange rates" will include "machinery for orderly adjustment of rates when necessary, thereby preventing disorderly, competitive exchange depreciation" (p. 261).

Williams, as he explains in a footnote, has "had reservations about the Monetary Fund. Some of these have been technical in character." But the largest issue which he raised was whether the solution of the problem should be sought through the establishment of "a general international monetary organization" covering the currencies of all or nearly all nations, or through a more modest system including, at least in the beginning, only the so-called key-currencies, that is, the currencies which are "the chief means of international payment." In any event, he holds, the crucial point in the question "whether we shall be able to restore multilateral trade and a system of reasonably free and stable exchanges lies in finding a solution of England's special problems" (pp. 389–90 n).

Ellis describes England's special problems as follows: having "lost half of her overseas investments" and having "contracted an unfunded debt in the form of blocked sterling balances," will she be able to "export sufficiently to command food and other necessaries from abroad and at the same time amortize her debts" (p. 161)? Ellis discusses briefly the dangers of "freely fluctuating exchange rates" and of attempts at unilateral regulation of the exchanges, usually leading to "bilateral clearing arrangements, which are inevitably discriminatory and restrictive in nature." In his opinion, which tallies with that of Hansen, "the only solution is international supervision over exchange rates, as provided by the International Monetary Fund, to secure an equilibrium adjustment of currency values." The system would rule out "continuous," or even "frequent," revisions of exchange rates, but would permit *"occasional* revision . . . to correct maladjustments." Other features of the plan which Ellis mentions approvingly are the "short-term loans by the Fund to bridge over balance-of-payments difficulties" and "recommendations by the Fund, to countries with balance-of-payments problems, as to appropriate domestic measures to avoid repetition of the exchange-rate revision" (pp. 158–59).

Recommendations, consultation and cooperation are contrasted with credit terms, coercion and competition. Hansen and Anderson characterize in these terms the basic philosophies which underlie their favored methods of achieving international monetary stability. Hansen says: "We shall not make progress through coercive controls. No self-respecting country would join such an arrangement. We shall make progress only through consultation and mutual cooperation in the interest of all-around stability and expansion of world trade" (p. 262). Anderson says: "We do not wish international cooperation in monetary matters except in emergencies. We wish competition, with the central money market of each country obliged to protect its own position, and pulled up when it overexpands credit through the loss of funds to other money markets which are not overexpanding" (p. 55). Anderson would gladly submit to the coercive controls of the gold standard — to "The Tyranny of Gold" — because it is an impersonal control: "Gold is not capricious . . . gold has no intuitions, and gold has very little imagination" (p. 60).

This conflict of issues cannot be resolved. But it seems that the conflict is academic because, in the world of today, we do not have a choice between the "automatic" international gold standard, on the one hand, and the "managed" system of the International Monetary Fund, on the other. All information from England indicates that the real choice today is between managed multilateralism and managed bilateralism. Even faithful believers in the gold standard will have to switch their votes to the "lesser evil" when they recognize that their favorite candidate has no real chance.

Foreign Loans

All the contributors who deal with problems of international finance recognize the desirability of a flow of capital funds from the United States to countries in need of loans.

Anderson mentions that credits to European industries would "facilitate the export of American raw materials and machinery to Europe, giving us markets which we should otherwise lack in the readjustment period" (p. 56). He also states that it may be desirable to have a governmental institution "designed to share risks and responsibility with American investment bankers or with foreign governments, or with investment bankers in other parts of the world." But he wants "to make sure that the loans are carefully considered from the business point of view" (p. 58). He recognizes England's special need for credits: "We want to help England. We must help England" (p. 61). Nevertheless, concerning all foreign lending, Anderson believes that smaller amounts than are usually regarded as necessary will suffice; that loans should be granted only on conditions of financial reforms, and that the plan for the International Bank for Reconstruction and Development should not be accepted.

According to Williams, the "demands for [American] goods to assist in reconstruction" will be large and "it seems very desirable, in our own interest, to define reconstruction broadly and even generously, as meaning, for example, that the capacity of foreign countries to produce and export should be restored as rapidly as possible and with as much emphasis as is prudently feasible upon external aid" (p. 385). And there will be also "demands from the young and from the less developed older countries for capital goods to assist in development of their resources" (p. 386). Much of these demands "will have to be financed by foreign investment, and the capital will have to come primarily from the United States." Since "foreign investment of private capital will involve some kind of insurance" and since "it is equitable that all countries should share in the risk," Williams endorses the plan of the International Bank. He hopes that "through the collective action of borrowers and lenders" it will develop "standards and procedures of sound investment" (p. 387).

Hansen affirms that "the International Bank for Reconstruction and Development can greatly aid in the process of promoting fundamental international equilibrium." The Bank will "enable productive development projects to be undertaken in countries that could not borrow on reasonable terms without the aid of the Bank. The Bank in the typical case will insure and guarantee bonds issued in the ordinary private capital markets" (p. 263). Hansen hopes that this international underwriting institution will promote "a high sense of international responsibility and international good will. Americans looking for outlets for their savings will find here a high-grade gilt-edge security. American exporters will benefit through the enlarged exports of equipment and machinery to the borrowing countries. And finally the American taxpayer . . . is relieved in that other countries undertake two thirds of the risk involved. How any arrangement could be more to our national interest is difficult to see" (p. 264).

Ellis holds that, during the next few years, "the successful disposition of our flow of savings would be facilitated by really substantial foreign investments" (p. 156). "There are indeed overwhelmingly forceful arguments for a large outflow of capital from the United States on the supposition of productive investment: it will help to maintain employment both at home and abroad, and it will contribute to foreign long-run productivity and our long-run real income" (p. 161). In view of the great desirability of "extensive foreign loans," the case for the international investment bank is strong: while "separate efforts by countries individually can go far toward the objective," collaboration, according to Ellis, "increases both the possible extent and the consistency of operations" (p. 169).

III. ECONOMIC POLICIES

A CATALOGUE OF RECOMMENDATIONS

An economist's policy recommendations follow from his choice of objectives and his analysis of economic problems, as conclusions in syllogisms follow from major and minor premises. The preceding exposition of "Economic Objectives" and "Economic Problems" makes it unnecessary to enter into a lengthy discussion of "Economic Policies." Indeed, it was not always possible in selecting the most poignant sentences for quotations in the section on "Economic Problems" to separate the discussion of problems from policy recommendations. It may be desirable, nevertheless, to present here, in catalogue form, an inventory of the policy recommendations contained in the six essays.

In a synoptic catalogue, qualifications and reservations which the authors may have added to their recommendations must be omitted. References to the pages where recommendations can be found, in either explicit or implicit formulation, may take the place of greater accuracy in this catalogue. The recommendations are formulated here in blunt and curt imperative sentences. They are grouped in the following more or less customary fields of public policy:

> Fiscal Policy
> Taxation
> Credit Policy
> Price Control and Rationing
> Antimonopoly Policy
> Wage Policy
> Social Security and Life Insurance
> Housing
> Research and Patent System
> Commercial Policy
> International Finance

No claim is made for completeness of the listing, either as to fields of policy or to the individual recommendations by the six authors. The catalogue covers only public policy; business policies and the policies of organized interest groups are not included. Incidental recommendations which do not fall into any of the listed fields of policy are deliberately omitted. If an author is not listed as endorsing a certain recommendation, this need not mean that he does not favor it. He may have chosen not to discuss the particular subject or the particular phase of the subject. For example, two of the six contributors do not discuss problems of international economics; and even in fields which are covered in all six essays not all six authors have gone into sufficient detail to show themselves as advocates or opponents of a particular recommendation. In several instances, an author who is known to have publicly endorsed a particular policy is not included among its advocates in our catalogue if he does not repeat his endorsement in this volume.

FISCAL POLICY

Federal Budget

Avoid all deficit spending:
Anderson (pp. 14, 52)

Permit anticyclical deficit spending:
Clark (pp. 89, 121–22) ; Ellis (p. 138) ; Hansen (pp. 207, 208, 239) ; Slichter (pp. 317, 319, 332) ; Williams (pp. 346, 359, 380)

Permit deficits during postwar transition:
Clark (p. 88) ; Ellis (pp. 137, 140) ; Hansen (p. 225) ; Williams (p. 355)

Resist long-run deficits:
Anderson (p. 52) ; Clark (p. 92) ; Ellis (p. 138) ; Slichter (pp. 311, 317) ; Williams (pp. 347, 355)

Submit to long-run deficits:
Clark (p. 92, as a "last resort") ; Williams (p. 354, only "modest")

Permit long-run deficits:
Hansen (pp. 215, 217, 225)

Create budget surplus for debt repayment:
Anderson (p. 52) ; Slichter (pp. 297, 317, 332)

Create budget surplus to fight inflation:
Ellis (p. 141) ; Hansen (pp. 238, 256) ; Slichter (pp. 325, 333)

Public Works

Avoid expansion of federal expenditures:
Anderson (p. 52)

Plan projects well in advance:
Clark (p. 88) ; Ellis (p. 136) ; Hansen (pp. 213, 214) ; Slichter (p. 319)

Confine them to socially desirable and necessary projects:
Clark (p. 90) ; Ellis (p. 137) ; Slichter (p. 311) ; Williams (pp. 362, 375)

Should be timed to offset depression:
Clark (pp. 88, 90) ; Ellis (p. 137) ; Hansen (pp. 208, 214, 236, 239) ; Slichter (p. 290)

Choose projects which develop private investment outlets:
Hansen (pp. 211, 225, 226) ; Slichter (p. 312)

Avoid projects which compete with private investment:
Clark (pp. 89, 90, 94) ; Ellis (pp. 134, 137)

Avoid raising or maintaining construction cost:
Clark (pp. 105–06) ; Slichter (p. 312)

Plan public housing construction projects:
Hansen (p. 236) ; Williams (p. 368)

Plan regional resource development programs:
Hansen (p. 236)

Consumption Subsidies and Relief Expenditures

Provide for consumption subsidies to low-income groups:
  Clark (p. 96) ; Ellis (p. 135)

Pay liberal unemployment benefits:
  Clark (p. 86) ; Ellis (p. 135) ; Hansen (p. 218) ; Slichter (pp. 275–76, 327)

Public Debt Management

Try to get more of the debt into private hands:
  Anderson (p. 50) ; Ellis (p. 140) ; Slichter (pp. 279, 297) ; Williams (p. 384)

Fund the debt at higher interest rates:
  Anderson (p. 49)

Issue Victory bonds at higher interest rates:
  Slichter (p. 279)

Repay debt gradually:
  Anderson (p. 52) ; Slichter (pp. 298, 332)

Repay debt when inflation threatens:
  Ellis (p. 141) ; Hansen (pp. 208, 238, 256) ; Slichter (p. 333)

Keep interest rates and bond prices stable:
  Hansen (pp. 252, 254, 255)

Government Guarantee for Full Employment

Assume responsibility for full employment:
  Hansen (p. 206)

Assume responsibility but avoid guarantee:
  Clark (p. 117) ; Ellis (pp. 132, 137, 169) ; Slichter (pp. 304, 308)

Assume neither responsibility nor guarantee:
  Anderson (p. 15)

TAXATION

Personal Income Tax

Reduce it:
  Anderson (pp. 53–54) ; Clark (pp. 91, 96) ; Ellis (p. 138) ; Hansen (p. 243) ; Slichter (pp. 274, 294, 296) ; Williams (pp. 377, 379)

Reduce it especially in lower brackets:
  Hansen (p. 244) ; Williams (pp. 377, 379)

Reduce it especially in upper brackets:
  Anderson (p. 53)

Permit retention of profits by closely held corporations:
  Anderson (p. 52)

Reduce it for incomes from business and dividends:
  Slichter (pp. 295, 318, 319)

Allow abatements on invested income:
  Ellis (p. 175) ; Hansen (p. 242) ; Slichter (p. 295)

Introduce flexible tax rates:
Hansen (pp. 208, 214) ; Slichter (p. 328) ; Williams (p. 380)
Permit averaging incomes over years:
Ellis (p. 172) ; Hansen (p. 241) ; Slichter (p. 295) ; Williams (p. 379)
Eliminate tax-exempt securities:
Clark (p. 91) ; Ellis (pp. 171, 176)

Capital Gains Tax
Reduce it:
Anderson (p. 53)
Permit deduction of capital losses from income up to certain limit:
Slichter (pp. 279, 295)

Estate Tax
Reduce it:
Anderson (p. 53)
Increase it:
Ellis (pp. 127, 134)

Corporate Income Tax
Abolish double taxation of distributed earnings:
Anderson (p. 52) ; Clark (p. 109) ; Ellis (pp. 138, 148, 174) ; Hansen (pp. 243, 244) ; Williams (pp. 377, 379)
Reduce the corporate income tax:
Anderson (p. 52) ; Clark (p. 109) ; Ellis (pp. 174, 175) ; Hansen (pp. 241, 244) ; Slichter (pp. 274, 295) ; Williams (pp. 374, 377, 379)
Permit averaging incomes over years:
Ellis (p. 172) ; Williams (p. 379)
Increase period of loss carry-back:
Ellis (p. 172) ; Hansen (pp. 241, 244) ; Williams (p. 379)
Increase period of loss carry-forward:
Ellis (p. 172) ; Hansen (pp. 241, 244) ; Slichter (pp. 279, 295) ; Williams (p. 379)
Permit quick write-offs of investment:
Ellis (p. 172) ; Slichter (p. 326)
Allow abatements on invested profits:
Ellis (p. 175) ; Hansen (p. 242)
Allow abatements for stable replacement:
Slichter (p. 330)
Reimburse for part of loss when carry-back impossible:
Hansen (pp. 242, 244)

Excess-Profits Tax
Repeal it:
Anderson (p. 52) ; Ellis (pp. 138, 173) ; Hansen (pp. 240, 244) ; Slichter (p. 294) ; Williams (pp. 374, 379)

Repeal it when war orders are cut back severely:
Anderson (p. 52)
Repeal it only after reconversion:
Ellis (p. 173) ; Hansen (pp. 239, 240) ; Slichter (p. 294)
Raise exemptions immediately:
Slichter (p. 294)
Retain excess-profits tax for commercial banks:
Hansen (p. 255)

Excise Taxes

Abolish some, reduce others:
Ellis (p. 138) ; Hansen (pp. 240, 244) ; Slichter (p. 296) ; Williams (pp. 374, 377, 379)

Pay Roll Taxes (Social Security Contributions)

Vary them with state of employment:
Hansen (p. 214)
Raise them:
Slichter (p. 297)

CREDIT POLICY

Interest Rate Policy

Stabilize interest rates and bond prices:
Hansen (p. 254)
Increase bank credit to secure stable prices and low interest rates:
Hansen (p. 225)
Raise interest rates when inflation threatens:
Anderson (p. 49) ; Ellis (pp. 144, 145)
Do not use interest rate increases for controlling booms:
Hansen (pp. 252, 255)

Bank Reserves and Capital

Regulate reserve requirements of commercial banks:
Ellis (p. 144) ; Hansen (p. 254) ; Slichter (p. 290)
Introduce "ceiling reserve" requirement:
Ellis (pp. 144, 147)
Increase minimum reserve requirements:
Ellis (p. 152)
Switch Treasury deposits between member banks and reserve banks:
Ellis (p. 147)
Raise capital-asset ratio of commercial banks:
Ellis (pp. 148, 151)

Selective Credit Control

Prevent bank from holding too many long-term bonds:
Hansen (p. 254)

Retain excess-profits tax for commercial banks:
  Hansen (p. 255)
Control security loans through margin requirements:
  Ellis (pp. 142, 146) ; Hansen (p. 253) ; Williams (p. 383)
Retain control of consumers' credit:
  Ellis (pp. 142, 146) ; Hansen (p. 253) ; Slichter (p. 290) ; Williams
  (p. 384)
Control real-estate loans:
  Ellis (p. 143) ; Hansen (p. 253) ; Williams (p. 384)

Deposit and Loan Insurance

Extend deposit insurance and introduce loan insurance:
  Ellis (p. 152)

Securities Exchange Control

Require no registration statement and only brief prospectus for new issues:
  Anderson (p. 39)
Permit certain now prohibited insider transactions:
  Anderson (p. 41)
Facilitate action by specialists and floor traders:
  Anderson (p. 42)
Reduce reporting requirements:
  Anderson (p. 42)
Facilitate raising of industrial equity capital from personal investors:
  Clark (p. 109)

PRICE CONTROL AND RATIONING

Duration of Controls

Abolish most controls immediately:
  Anderson (p. 49)
Retain price controls for a few years:
  Ellis (p. 141) ; Hansen (p. 256) ; Slichter (pp. 277, 280, 289)
Retain material and rationing controls for a few years:
  Ellis (p. 141) ; Hansen (p. 256)
Establish peacetime Office of Price Research:
  Hansen (p. 260)

Adjustments of Controls

Permit price increases as labor costs rise:
  Slichter (p. 277)

ANTIMONOPOLY POLICY

Encouragement to New Enterprise

Reform patent laws to facilitate competition:
  Ellis (pp. 189, 191, 192, 194) ; Hansen (p. 227)

Reform tax system to remove handicaps on new firms:
Ellis (pp. 172, 176, 192) ; Hansen (pp. 242, 244) ; Slichter (p. 295)
Refuse sales of surplus property to monopolies:
Ellis (p. 192)
Provide government participation in industrial research:
Ellis (pp. 189, 191, 193) ; Hansen (p. 227)

Removal of Public Support of Monopoly

Reduce protective tariffs:
Anderson (p. 56) ; Ellis (pp. 157, 188, 191, 194) ; Hansen (p. 265) ;
Williams (p. 389)
Remove interstate trade barriers:
Ellis (pp. 191, 194)
Repeal price maintenance laws:
Ellis (pp. 191, 194)

Antitrust Action

Provide greater budgets to antitrust agencies:
Ellis (p. 194)
Codify the law of unfair competition:
Ellis (p. 194)
Enact a federal incorporation statute:
Ellis (p. 194)
Prevent monopolistic corporate consolidations:
Anderson (p. 31) ; Ellis (p. 191)
Extend liability for restraint to management of firms:
Ellis (p. 195)
Extend antitrust laws to labor monopolies:
Ellis (pp. 182, 186)

Government Regulation and Operation

Establish yardstick plants:
Ellis (p. 195)
Provide for regulation or nationalization of monopolies:
Ellis (p. 195)
Provide for government competition with monopolistic industries:
Clark (p. 90) ; Ellis (pp. 136, 195)

WAGE POLICY

Postwar Adjustments

Raise wage rates after the war:
Hansen (pp. 256, 258, 259) ; Slichter (pp. 286, 290)
Maintain wage rates after the war:
Williams (p. 369)

Let wage rates react to reduced demand after the war:
Anderson (p. 22)
Reduce wage rates in specific cases:
Ellis (pp. 174, 182) ; Hansen (p. 258)
Raise wage rates as business taxes are lowered:
Hansen (p. 259)

Long-run Adjustments

Raise wage rates as productivity of labor grows:
Anderson (p. 21) ; Clark (p. 118) ; Ellis (p. 183) ; Hansen (pp. 256, 257) ; Williams (pp. 369, 371)
Avoid wage increases beyond increases in productivity:
Anderson (pp. 20, 25) ; Clark (pp. 114, 116, 121) ; Ellis (pp. 182, 184) ; Hansen (pp. 256, 257) ; Slichter (p. 291) ; Williams (pp. 369, 373)
Maintain wage rates at level once reached:
Williams (p. 369)
Avoid general wage deflation:
Clark (pp. 99, 101) ; Ellis (pp. 184, 185) ; Hansen (pp. 258, 260)
Avoid general wage inflation:
Clark (p. 116) ; Hansen (pp. 256, 257, 260) ; Slichter (p. 320)
Avoid monopolistic wage increases:
Clark (pp. 103, 106, 110, 112, 113, 117) ; Ellis (pp. 182, 183, 184) ; Slichter (pp. 306, 320)

Labor Laws and Institutions

Avoid restrictive union practices:
Anderson (p. 17) ; Clark (pp. 103–04, 121) ; Ellis (pp. 135, 182, 183, 185, 186, 192)
Prosecute restraint of trade by unions:
Ellis (pp. 182, 186)
Use minimum wage laws to get greater consumption:
Hansen (p. 218)
Encourage labor organizations to pursue national wage policy:
Clark (p. 110) ; Slichter (p. 320)
Introduce compulsory wage arbitration:
Ellis (p. 186)
Plead for moderation of union leaders:
Clark (pp. 110, 116, 120, 124–25) ; Ellis (pp. 185, 186) ; Hansen (p. 260) ; Slichter (pp. 320, 321)

SOCIAL SECURITY AND LIFE INSURANCE

Social Security Program

Extend the social security program to support consumption:
Clark (p. 86) ; Ellis (p. 135) ; Hansen (pp. 218, 244) ; Slichter (pp. 275, 327)

Vary social security contributions with state of employment:
Hansen (p. 214)
Raise unemployment benefits to 25 per cent of pay roll loss:
Slichter (p. 276)
Increase length of period of unemployment benefits:
Slichter (p. 276)
Introduce "national minimum":
Ellis (pp. 134, 135)
Cover transportation costs of displaced workers:
Ellis (p. 136)
Avoid reserve accumulation of social security system:
Clark (p. 97)

Life Insurance

Permit companies to make loans and direct investments:
Ellis (p. 149)
Have companies undertake investment research on larger scale:
Slichter (p. 323)
Confine new policies to straight life insurance:
Ellis (pp. 149, 150)
Let government offer annuities without reserve accumulation:
Clark (p. 96)

HOUSING

Public Housing Programs

Include public housing projects as outlets for capital:
Hansen (pp. 232, 236) ; Williams (p. 368)
Plan public housing construction chiefly for depression:
Hansen (p. 236)

Private Housing Programs

Reduce construction cost to permit low-cost housing:
Williams (p. 368)
Avert rising construction cost:
Slichter (pp. 299, 312)
Subsidize private housing programs:
Hansen (p. 235) ; Williams (p. 368)
Grant cheap loans for private residential building:
Hansen (p. 236)
Remove obsolete building ordinances restricting construction:
Slichter (pp. 309, 321)

Slum Clearance Programs

Include slum clearance projects as outlets for capital:
Ellis (p. 133) ; Hansen (pp. 232, 236)

Avoid policy of slum abandonment:
Hansen (p. 230)
Provide federal aid for cities buying up the slums:
Hansen (p. 232)
Provide housing subsidies for low-income families:
Hansen (p. 235)
Provide rehousing for people displaced by slum clearance:
Hansen (p. 236)

RESEARCH AND PATENT SYSTEM

Government-Sponsored Research

Subsidize scientific research:
Ellis (pp. 189, 193) ; Hansen (p. 227) ; Slichter (p. 311)
Provide government participation in industrial research:
Ellis (p. 191) ; Hansen (p. 227)
Coordinate research by government agencies:
Hansen (p. 227)

Patent System

Prohibit restrictive licensing:
Ellis (pp. 192, 194)
Provide for compulsory licensing of all patents:
Ellis (pp. 189, 192, 194) ; Hansen (p. 227)
Offer government-owned patents for general licensing:
Hansen (p. 227)
Provide for forfeiture of patents used in illegal restraint of trade:
Ellis (p. 194)

COMMERCIAL POLICY

Volume of International Trade

Expand trade volume:
Anderson (p. 56) ; Ellis (p. 136) ; Hansen (p. 265) ; Williams (p. 389)

Tariffs

Reduce American tariffs:
Anderson (p. 56) ; Ellis (pp. 146, 157, 160, 161, 188, 191, 194) ; Hansen (p. 265) ; Williams (p. 389)
Reduce American tariffs immediately and drastically:
Anderson (p. 56) ; Ellis (p. 157)

International Cartels and Commodity Agreements

Eliminate restrictive trade practices (cartels) :
Anderson (p. 55) ; Ellis (pp. 155, 188–89) ; Hansen (pp. 264, 265)
Avoid international commodity agreements:
Ellis (p. 188)

INTERNATIONAL FINANCE

Stability of Exchange Rates

Avoid fluctuations of exchange rates:
Anderson (p. 60) ; Ellis (pp. 158, 159) ; Hansen (p. 261) ; Williams (p. 389 n)

Restore international gold standard:
Anderson (pp. 59, 60)

Establish International Monetary Fund:
Ellis (pp. 159–60, 169) ; Hansen (p. 261)

Begin stabilization with key-currencies:
Williams (p. 389 n)

Capital Movements

Grant loans to foreign countries:
Anderson (pp. 56, 57, 58) ; Ellis (pp. 156, 161, 169) ; Hansen (p. 264) ; Williams (p. 387)

Establish International Bank for Reconstruction and Development:
Ellis (p. 169) ; Hansen (p. 263) ; Williams (p. 387)

INDEX